THE DOUBLE DEALERS

Books by Alexander Klein:

THE DOUBLE DEALERS

THE COUNTERFEIT TRAITOR

GRAND DECEPTION

THE EMPIRE CITY

COURAGE IS THE KEY

THE
DOUBLE DEALERS

ADVENTURES IN GRAND DECEPTION

Collected and Edited by

ALEXANDER KLEIN

J. B. LIPPINCOTT COMPANY
Philadelphia & New York

ACKNOWLEDGMENTS

Grateful appreciation is expressed herewith to all authors, publishers, periodicals and agents who courteously granted permission to include copyrighted material:

THE FABULOUS BOOM OF BAYANO by W. A. Swanberg. Copyright 1952 by Fawcett Publications, Inc. Reprinted by permission of the author. First published in *True, The Man's Magazine*.

THE MURDERING SLEEPERS by Alan Hynd. Copyright 1955 by Fawcett Publications, Inc. Reprinted by permission of the author. First published in *True, The Man's Magazine*.

SOME SHOTS THAT FOUND THEIR MARKS from *The Compleat Practical Joker* by H. Allen Smith. Copyright 1953 by H. Allen Smith. Reprinted by permission of Doubleday and Company, Inc.

A MASTER CON MAN REVEALS SOME TRICKS from *The Autobiography of Yellow Kid Weil* by Joseph "Yellow Kid" Weil, with W. T. Brannon. Copyright 1948 by Ziff-Davis Publishing Company, Inc. Reprinted by permission of the authors. A TALK WITH THE YELLOW KID by Saul Bellow. Copyright 1956 by The Reporter Magazine Company. Reprinted by permission of the author, Russell & Volkening, Inc. and *The Reporter*.

THE MERRY ANTICS OF IZZY AND MOE by Herbert Asbury. Copyright 1946 by The American Mercury Magazine, Inc. Reprinted by permission of the author.

THE MASTER MAKER OF THE QUEER by Archie McFedries. Copyright 1952 by Fawcett Publications, Inc. Reprinted by permission of the author. First published in *True, The Man's Magazine*.

MADISON AVENUE VS. NAZI INTELLIGENCE by Donald Q. Coster, with Frederic Sondern, Jr. Copyright as "But We Expected You At Dakar," 1946, by The American Legion, Inc. Reprinted by permission of the authors and *American Legion Magazine*.

CONFESSIONS OF A MASTER JEWEL THIEF by Robert Wallace. Copyright 1956 by Time, Inc. Reprinted by permission of the author and of *Life*.

THE LEGAL SHENANIGANS OF HOWE AND HUMMEL from *Howe & Hummell* by Richard H. Rovere. Copyright 1947 by Richard H. Rovere. Parts of this material appeared originally in *The New Yorker*. Used by permission of the publishers, Farrar, Straus and Cudahy, Inc.

THE GOLDEN HUSSY by Charles Lanius. Copyright 1957 by Popular Publications, Inc. Reprinted by permission of Paul R. Reynolds & Son, New York City. First published in *Argosy*.

4

5

6

CONTENTS

7

8

9

PREFACE

Several years ago when I edited the anthology, *Grand Deception,* one of the reviewers took me to task for having written "a serious and unnecessarily erudite introduction to a book of "pure entertainment." This time, although I can't vouch for the "pure" part, I herewith freely admit that my main purpose in compiling this second collection of true adventures in deception was to provide entertainment.

As in the first volume, the deceptions vary widely in motivation, sphere of action, locale and time. Twentieth century and Civil War espionage agents, male and female, rub shoulders with a seventeenth-century highwayman, a Renaissance lover and an atomic physics professor of unique brilliance. Others who share the pages of this book include: master con men and women, and equally skilled hoaxers in the arts, science, literature, journalism and medicine; counterfeiters, detectives and legal lights; the Scots-American medium whose hunting ground, both spiritualistic and matrimonial, was the European aristocracy, and the principals in an extraordinary twenty-year triangle which played itself out within the confines of an ordinary house, and this, mind you, decades before the terms "exurbanite" and "Peyton Place" had been added to the language.

In making final selections my basic criterion was the dramatic or amusing, ingenious or fantastic nature of the hoax, fraud, ruse or imposture. The stories have been arranged neither chronologically nor by categories, but simply for contrast and variety and, in some instances, comparison. No doubt each reader will find the order which best suits his own interests and tastes.

Actually, *The Double Dealers* owes its existence to several factors. Back in 1954 while culling material for the first volume of deceptions, I found myself with more than twice as many stories as I could use. Then, when the book appeared, a number of reviewers, otherwise very kind, chided me for having left out their favorite deceptions. Readers, too, wrote calling my attention to certain accounts omitted from *Grand Deception* and suggesting I include them in a sequel. Also, having become hoax-conscious myself, I began to note in periodicals many new stories of deceptions. So when the publishers asked me to edit a sequel I readily succumbed, confidently expecting to put the book together without leaving my study. It didn't prove that simple, however. One trail led to another and I soon was engaged in far more research than I had bargained for—which led to the discovery of quite a few additional deceptions my previous reading had failed to flush out.

Inevitably, therefore, many masters of deception are not included in this volume, either; it would take a bookcase-full to give all of them their due. One genius, Mantacinnie by name, I cannot leave entirely unacknowledged, although I have space here only for a brief summary of his exploits:

Mantacinnie arrived one day by hired carriage in a certain town in Northern Italy, put up at the best hostlery and announced that he had developed the extraordinary power of bringing back to life all who had died within the past two decades. The local citizenry were somewhat skeptical. But Mantacinnie, imperturbable, visited the cemetery, then had the names of those scheduled for revival listed on several improvised bulletin boards about town, which categorically declared that seven days hence at noon precisely he would raise all these from their graves. Should he, himself, have died, from any cause, by that date, he too would come to life along with the others.

When the deadline drew near, various people—as Mantacinnie had confidently expected—sought him out and each offered him a generous number of gold coins in return for a slight favor: that he be so kind as to permit a certain deceased person to remain undisturbedly resting in peace on resurrection day. Mantacinnie's visitors, naturally, were re-married widows and widowers, heirs, tradesmen who did not relish the prospect of competitors returning to life to plague them as of old, and the like. Many of these avowed their disbelief in Mantacinnie's claimed power, but added that they would be willing to pay a small sum as insurance. In such instances Mantacinnie's smiling suggestion that if they were skeptical they had best save themselves needless expense led to a quick and considerable increase in the "insurance premium" offered. Thus, in a few days' time, Mantacinnie—being a gentle, amenable chap—granted a great many favors and garnered a tidy little fortune, as well as the return favors of a number of the more desirable young ladies of the town.

But the best was yet to come. On the eve of the appointed day, the mayor and the entire town council called on Mantacinnie and beseeched him not to raise *any* dead in the town. Such rescusitations, they explained, would raise hob with everything: their predecessors in office might challenge their right to hold their present positions; in some instances—a man of the world such as Mantacinnie would surely understand—other painful embarrassments would follow; indeed, confusion, chaos, even civil war might break out. The mayor then suggested that, instead, Mantacinnie accept a substantial "honorarium" which he and his colleagues had raised; and he all but thrust a large bag of gold coins into Mantacinnie's arms.

Mantacinnie replied that he was not a hard man; he was quite willing to oblige. But, he pointed out, if he failed to fulfill his announced intentions people would, understandably, doubt his ability to raise the dead. He sympathized with their plight but, no, he would have to decline their well-meant offer. Unless—there was one possible solution to their dilemma. If the mayor and town council were to prepare and sign an official document testifying that they had witnessed him raise the dead, perhaps that would be satisfactory all around.

Some councillors demurred at this, hinting broadly that Mantacinnie was probably just bluffing to begin with. But, spurred by the man's cool imperviousness, the officials decided to take no chances. They paid and they signed.

A man of his word, Mantacinnie left town that very night. And, with the official document authenticating his resurrectionary abilities, he proceeded to reap a continuing harvest of gold coins—and ladies' favors—in other towns . . . in return for his consistent self-control in *not* exercising his power to raise the dead.

Eventually, however, someone (either bold or angry or miserly or impoverished) instead of paying took the risk of stabbing Mantacinnie in the back. Presumably rusty from lack of practice, Mantacinnie failed to fulfill his promise to return to life and remained peacefully thereafter among the deceased whose slumber he had for so many years been threatening to disturb.

One final point: I want to affirm for the record that, although I cannot deny having become, in the late John McNulty's words, "a connoisseur of the spurious," my connoisseurship does not extend to the active practice of "grand deceptions." In fact, the only deception of any note in which I can remember being involved occurred some twelve or more years ago.

One evening that winter I was commiserating with a talented actress in her early twenties, who as yet could boast of no Broadway credits. She

13

complained that the only uncast part she knew of in an immediately up-coming play was that of a thirteen-year-old neurotic. But the next day an idea hit me. I had just written and co-produced a movie short in which a teen-age girl played a small part. My co-producer and I had our actress friend squeeze into the clothes this youngster had worn in the film. With the aid of an improvised strait-jacket device to flatten out her much too developed bosom, she made it. However, even with lipstick removed and all her talents bent toward simulating an eager child actress, the effect was not really convincing.

Then I suggested that she try the opposite approach: play a youngster attempting to appear sophisticated beyond her years. So on went too much lipstick, rouge, eye-shadow and mascara. And she put on shoes with ultra-high heels on which she teetered with quite genuine un-familiarity. And to all this her childish figure and over-bright awkward-ness pathetically gave the lie.

Despite our fears that our hoax might misfire, that those casting the play might accept her as the age her make-up seemed to be striving for (rather than the "nearly fourteen" she would declare), or that they might at one glance consider her unsuited for the part and not even let her read, we decided to gamble on the director's acuteness and penchant for "directing." We won. When she got in to see the director, he at once ordered her with brusque kindness to kick off her high-heeled shoes, wash and wipe her face and "be your age, kid." She followed orders to the letter, read for the part and got it.

Her "guardian" had to sign the contract, of course. And for many weeks thereafter she continued to play the child-role, not only on-stage (to good notices) but off-stage as well—so long as she was on the theater's premises or with any of the cast. She'd sneak off between the acts to a remote corner backstage to get a few puffs on a cigarette. Milk would be brought in for her instead of coffee. And when I called on her backstage it was in the role of an uncle. She insisted that all this off-stage deception was necessary because if the producers found her out they might fire her from sheer pique. But I suspect she simply enjoyed garnering this continual, special proof of her ability as an actress. The hoax was successful right down the line, and my actress friend went on to better and more important adult roles in succeeding seasons.

As for me, I guess as a double dealer I was just a flash in the pan. I quit hoaxing then and there, and my adventures in grand deception have been only vicarious ever since.

14

THE DOUBLE DEALERS

THE FABULOUS BOOM OF BAYANO

by W. A. Swanberg

After dipping his big toe cautiously into the risky waters of stock manipulation for several profitable years, a Chicago broker named Leo Koretz decided in 1916 to dive in headfirst—a decision that was to make a splash heard around the world.

He began in a quiet way by telling a few friends casually that he had bought into 5,000,000 acres of timberland on the Bayano River in Panama. Fortunes were being made right and left in the banana republics at the time, but Koretz did not claim to be in on something good. Indeed, he admitted that his Bayano flyer was an outright gamble, the sort of thing he would never, never advise a client to stake his money on.

"I just got bored dealing in safe, solid stocks," he explained. "This is wildcat stuff. It might come through, sure, but there's a bigger chance that I've poured my money down the drain."

An undersized, nearsighted man of 36 who invariably tilted his cigar at such an upward angle that it almost collided with his horn-rimmed glasses, Koretz made up for his physical unimpressiveness by exuding a personal magnetism that was well-nigh hypnotic. In fact, there were some who later swore he *had* hypnotized them. He had a handclasp and warm smile that made men—and women—feel that he loved them. In his nine years as a broker he had steered clients away from what he described as questionable stocks, always paid dividends right on the line, and had grown quite prosperous in the process. He had hundreds of friends, many of whom liked to stop in at his modest office at 22 West Monroe Street, some to buy, some merely to listen to Leo talk. He was famous for his endless collection of off-color stories which he told with gestures and facial contortions fit to split his listeners' sides.

Naturally, his friends were interested in his Panama plunge, and they inquired about it now and then. Being probably the most skillful propagandist of the pre-Goebbels era, with a full appreciation of the value of a slow and steady buildup, he would grin and say he hadn't lost his

17

shirt as yet. He let the Panama idea take root and grow for some eight months before he was ready to begin the harvest.

In the spring of 1917, Koretz boarded an eastbound train after letting it be known that he was going to Panama to inspect his holdings there. He was gone for six weeks. No one in Chicago—least of all his wife—suspected that he never got any farther away than New York. Always a frequent visitor there, he had long before installed a night-club hat-check girl in an apartment on 44th Street convenient to Grand Central Station so that he would not be lonely in the metropolis. On this trip he spent most of his time hitting the high spots with his play-for-pay companion, and when he finally got back to Chicago, he looked as tired as if he had been trekking for days through the wilds of Panama.

Despite his weariness, he wore an air of smug gratification that did not go unnoticed. When his friends inquired about his Bayano River venture he merely shrugged and replied noncommittally that it was very satisfactory. Without saying so, he gave the distinct impression that he did not want to talk about Bayano.

"He acted as though he were sitting on a huge secret," one of his cronies said later, "and we began to get curious."

This curiosity swelled when Koretz, formerly a fairly conservative man with a dollar, began to act like a maharaja on the loose. He doubled the size of his offices and called in an interior decorator who threw away the cuspidors, laid ankle-deep rugs and finished the place in rose and taupe. He lunched with a companion one day, then took him into the Rolls-Royce showrooms on Michigan Boulevard and in less than ten minutes selected a maroon brougham for which he paid spot cash in thousand- and hundred-dollar bills. He employed a chauffeur in a plum-colored uniform to drive it. He moved his family out of their comfortable Rogers Park apartment and into a twenty-one room showplace fronting on Lake Michigan in suburban Evanston.

All this was so clearly beyond the means of a twenty-thousand-dollar-a-year broker that it caused eyes to widen. Koretz's friends put their heads together, noting that this hog-wild opulence had started soon after his return from Panama. Their curiosity, whetted by his air of close-mouthed mystery, generated a head of steam beyond human endurance. Something had to crack, and it wasn't Koretz. That summer an attorney named Francis Matthews, who had known the broker intimately for fifteen years, walked into the Monroe Steet office and gave him a dressing down.

"Everybody knows you've struck it rich in Panama, Leo," he wound up reproachfully. "Why try to hide it?"

Koretz got up, paced the floor, and for some seconds seemed torn between affection and duty. He finally broke down and admitted that his Panama gamble had hit the jack pot.

"It's mahogany, Frank," he said. "The stuff grows down there like hay, and you have no idea what prices it brings. It's a gold mine! The natives are paid the equivalent of thirty-two cents a day. Already I've got six hundred of them shipping timber out by the boatload. Sure, I've been keeping it under my hat. Hell, man, I'm in the securities business, and if my clients got wind of this, they'd all expect a nice chunk of stock!"

He showed Matthews a cablegram from one A. Espinoza, who he said was his Panama resident manager. It read: OUR SHIPMENTS OF PRIME MAHOGANY LIMITED ONLY BY INADEQUATE MANPOWER AND EQUIPMENT. CAPITAL INVESTED IN BAYANO WILL GIVE TEN TO ONE RETURN BY MOST CONSERVATIVE ESTIMATE.

Matthews, now a little goggle-eyed, seized on that word "capital." If Leo needed investors to help him swing this deal, he said hastily, he, for one, would be ready to aid with a little spare cash.

Koretz slapped him warmly on the back. "You'll be the first one in the door, Frank! So far I'm handling it myself, but this thing is growing all the time. Later on I may be able to deal a few of my closest friends in on it. Until then, don't breathe a word about it!"

Koretz gave the same business to other acquaintances, some of them notorious gossips, then let nature take its course. The news got around fast. Lots of Chicagoans who were only dimly aware that mahogany came from trees were perfectly willing to make money on it. An avalanche of callers engulfed the Monroe Street office.

The broker seemed surprised and annoyed that the secret had leaked out. He told everybody testily that his Bayano project was "only a small thing" and that in any case he was not yet ready to float a stock issue. That "small thing" yarn didn't fool men who had heard the inside story and had seen Leo grow rich on Bayano timber, but he was adamant. His callers went away bitterly disappointed. They were convinced that Koretz had a nice juicy melon he was cutting only for the benefit of a few favored intimates. His flat refusal to take their money created waves of excited rumor and caused the demand for his stock, if and when available, to reach a pitch of downright fever.

It got to a point where Koretz either had to sell stock or make enemies. Being a peace-loving soul who hated any sort of tension or hard feelings, he finally gave in and let some of his closest friends invest anywhere from $10,000 to $50,000 in Bayano Timber Syndicate stock at $1,000 a share. News of this got around. The feelings of other acquaintances were so bruised by this favoritism that he was forced to let them buy stock in order to placate them. By December, he was so hounded by people thrusting money at him that he felt need of an office far enough removed from the Loop to give him some privacy.

He took a suite of rooms at the swank Drake Hotel, letting it be known that his new hide-out was only for the elect. He kept the door locked, so that those who were admitted felt the same glow of pride they were later to experience when gaining entry to an exclusive speak-easy. On the wall was a vast framed photograph showing natives loading timber aboard a freighter, while his ten-foot mahogany desk bore a brass plate engraved with the words:

Made From the First Log Cut
At Bayano, January 23, 1917

Some of the heavier stockholders were presented with round mahogany paper weights stamped with the word Bayano in gilt letters. These gimcracks were turned out at 7 cents apiece for Koretz from wood scraps by a Grand Rapids furniture manufacturer.

Despite all his efforts to discourage buyers, Koretz had sold upward of a half-million dollars' worth of stock by the middle of 1918. He showered Tiffany jewelry on his brunette wife, Mae—gave her everything she asked for except his own presence at the fireside. This was seldom possible, considering his frequent trips, his preoccupation with Bayano business and with a couple of fascinating female friends in Chicago. For two years he had maintained a cozy kitchenette apartment on the South Side for a young woman who thought his name was Alfred Bronson and that he was an Indianapolis merchant. Being something of a share-the-wealther, he now moved her into more sumptuous diggings on Drexel Boulevard. Since he liked to have different women available to suit his varying moods, he also established an understanding with the agreeable secretary of a business friend and installed her in a near North Side apartment convenient both to the Drake and to his Loop offices. When he tired of these two, there were a couple more who were glad to come at a telephone call, or he could always grab a train for New York, where he spent about one week in four.

He regarded these New York trips as a vital part of his program, though most of his time there was devoted to burlesque shows, night clubs and his 44th Street sweetie. He engaged a costly suite at the smart St. Regis Hotel by the year, and occasionally would send himself telegrams at his Chicago address purporting to be from officials of furniture and railroad companies who begged him to set aside a large proportion of his mahogany output for their use, at premium prices. Invariably, when he returned to Chicago there would be a new swarm of eager pleaders for Bayano stock. Now and then, very confidentially, he would show them these New York telegrams and admit with becoming modesty, "We can't come close to meeting the demand!"

Bayano Timber, at the end of the first six months, paid a 5-percent dividend, but most of the stockholders not only left their dividends in to collect further gravy, but also bought more shares. They weren't blind. They could see what Bayano was doing for Koretz, and there was no reason why it should not do the same for them.

Leo now owned two Rolls-Royces and a Pierce-Arrow, had a regiment of house servants, and had acquired a 60-foot yacht complete with crew. But he was still the same old big-hearted Leo. A glutton for caviar, frogs' legs, champagne and anything else that came high, he was fond of taking his friends to the snootiest places, shooting the works on them and picking up the tab, saying airily, "This is on me, folks." Being a two-fisted drinker who got little sleep and spent a large part of his time painting the town, there were times when he simply had to get away from it all and rest his jangled nerves. He selected Hot Springs, Arkansas, as a good spot for the rest cure, having visited there occasionally while he was pushing some pre-Bayano Arkansas land mortgages. He now began to appear regularly at one of that city's flossiest hotels under the name of Herman Bowen.

To Koretz, however, even a rest cure was unthinkable without a woman in the offing. This problem was solved when he spotted the curvy manicurist in the hotel barber shop. He let her pick her own apartment, arranged to take care of her charge accounts and other expenses, and told her he liked green negligees.

While his home establishment in Evanston cost him plenty, it is probable that his far-flung romantic commitments in Chicago, New York and Hot Springs took an even larger chunk of the Bayano winnings, for these ladies all had a weakness for mink and other luxuries. By 1920, the demand for Bayano Timber stock was definitely leveling off, while a graph of Koretz's expenses would have shown a steady upward incline. Koretz saw that a shot in the arm was necessary. He was ready for Phase Two of his program.

The opening gun of Phase Two was fired at Henry A. Klein, an old friend who had grown rich in the wholesale liquor business and had invested heavily in Bayano Timber. Klein walked into the Drake Hotel suite one day to find Koretz simply glowing with good humor. He greeted Klein jovially, poured him a drink and seemed so button-bursting with enthusiasm that Klein naturally asked him what was cooking.

Koretz put his hand on Klein's shoulder and gazed at him earnestly. "Henry," he said, "that Bayano region is a veritable Garden of Eden. Bananas, now—they grow there in such profusion that tons of them just rot on the ground because nobody takes the trouble to get them to market. We're going to let 'em rot. My experts tell me that with a modest investment, coffee, sugar and cocoa could be grown there in such quantities that they would make fortunes. We're not going to bother with that—yet."

Klein was impressed. "But why not exploit those crops?" he wanted to know.

By way of reply, Koretz handed him a cablegram date-lined Panama City, which read:

FOUR MORE GUSHERS STRUCK AT BAYANO. OUR GEOLOGISTS PREDICT 400,000 BBL DAILY MINIMUM. WE CANNOT HANDLE THE FLOW. PLEASE RUSH AR-RANGEMENTS FOR MORE MEN, TANK CARS, PIPELINE AND EQUIPMENT AS PER LETTER APRIL 8.   —A. ESPINOZA

Klein's eyes popped. "Oil!" he gasped.

"Oil," Koretz nodded, handing him a cigar. "We've been working on this thing for a year, but I've kept it quiet—didn't want to raise false hopes. Now it's obvious that the payoff on Bayano mahogany, rich as it is, is peanuts compared with what the oil will bring."

In a voice that was suddenly hoarse, Klein expressed a willingness to contribute financially so that Espinoza would not be deprived of the men and materials he so desperately needed to bring the gushers under control. Koretz thanked him warmly.

"Maybe I can let you in later," he said. "Right now it's not so much a question of capital as it is of getting basic equipment down there. To-night I'm leaving for New York to arrange for the lease of a dozen tankers and the purchase of other equipment."

Koretz let a few other friends in on the secret before he hopped on a train bound for Hot Springs, not New York. He reasoned that a period of absence would make the pot boil more merrily, and he was right. On the next day, dozens of well-heeled Chicagoans called at both of his of-fices and were distressed at being unable to make out checks for stock in Bayano Oil. As always, Koretz forbade his employes to sell stock, reserving this responsibility for himself.

22

The timber magnate spent a pleasant week at Hot Springs, resting and getting some returns on his investment in the blonde manicurist. His sole attention to business during his stay was to dispatch the following telegram to himself in Chicago:

DESPITE ATTRACTIVENESS OF OTHER OFFERS, I URGENTLY REQUEST YOU MAKE NO COMMITMENT ON BAYANO OIL UNTIL YOU HAVE HEARD MINE.

He signed this missive with his Hot Springs alias, Herman Bowen, and a few days later returned to Chicago. As he entered his Monroe Street office, he saw several sharp-eyed lads scuttle away like rabbits. They were office boys posted there by their employers who wanted to be informed the moment Koretz put in an appearance. Koretz walked in, looked at his mail, and informed his secretary, Josephine Schroeder, that he was going home and was not to be bothered that day.

Miss Schroeder dutifully relayed this information to the hordes of callers who soon swamped the place. They felt that the exploitation of Bayano Oil was a matter too urgent to wait, and Koretz, in one of his rare visits at his own home, had to take the receiver off the telephone.

On the next day, as dazed accountants later computed it, Koretz did $180,000 business in Bayano Oil Syndicate stock, even though he shut up shop early and dropped in on his Drexel Boulevard lady. He began by admitting only a select group of seventeen friends, all of them able to invest $5,000 or more, and adopting a sorry-old-man policy toward the scores of others who begged to be taken into the circle.

The seventeen, among them Klein and an insurance broker named Charles Cohn, were properly grateful. They threw a party at the Drake at which Koretz, the guest of honor, was toasted with champagne and hailed as "the man who's going to make a monkey out of Rockefeller." Koretz took this opportunity to display the telegram from Hot Springs. He made a modest little speech in which he admitted that luck had played a large part in the oil strike but stressed that from now on it would take hard-headed business acumen to exploit it. That, he said glowingly, was why he had chosen these seventeen men as charter stockholders in his oil syndicate—because they were all conservative, forward-looking business men, more interested in the proper development of natural resources than in any pecuniary gain. When he spoke in public, Koretz diffused a high-voltage sincerity and charm that made his listeners want to cheer. As one of them later admitted, "It was like a religion with us, following that man and doing exactly as he said."

Koretz turned down scores of pleaders, always with visible regret. "I just wish I could let you in," he would say sorrowfully. A couple of foxy

23

stockholders succumbed to the pressure and did a flourishing black-market business in Bayano Oil shares for which they had paid the face value of $1,000, selling them to outsiders at $2,000 or more. The jealousy and anguish of those outside the circle made life so unbearable for Koretz that at length he capitulated and, as he put it, began to "broaden the base of ownership" in the company. He let more and more buyers in, most of them gladly paying at least double the face value.

Perhaps his most dramatic coup was in the summer of 1922, when he took a boatload of investors and hopefuls for a cruise on Lake Michigan in his yacht. The craft was five miles out of Evanston, and the guests working on their fourth highball, when a speedboat overtook them. A messenger came aboard with a telegram for Mr. Koretz. Koretz tore it open, read it, and smiled.

"Well, well," he said. "Now Standard Oil wants to buy us out."

He passed the yellow slip around. No doubt about it—it was a flat offer of $25,000,000 from Standard Oil for a controlling interest in the Bayano Oil Syndicate. A hush came over the group.

"You going to sell, Leo?" one of the guests whispered.

"Not today," Koretz grinned. "Standard Oil can run their own little party. We'll run ours. How about another drink?" And he tossed the telegram grandly into Lake Michigan while his friends roared their approval. It was perfectly obvious to them that if Standard or some other large oil company gained control, their dividends would not be up to the generous Koretz rate.

Little scenes like this never failed to make old investors toss more money into the kitty, and bring in new ones. Naturally, Koretz's relatives felt there was no reason why they should be left out in the cold when he was minting money for comparative strangers. His elderly mother bought into Bayano for $50,000, while one of his brothers invested $140,000. Koretz had not really wanted to take money from his family. But he did not know how he could refuse them without arousing their suspicions. Even his thirty-five-dollar-a-week secretary, the pretty Miss Schroeder, caught the fever. One day she brought in $3,000 in hard-won savings and asked him to invest it for her.

He patted her back in a fatherly way. "The investment business is a rough game, dearie," he said. "You keep your money." But she was so visibly hurt that he gave in and took the $3,000.

Now at the peak of his career, Koretz was known variously as the "wonder boy" of the financial district, the "oil king," the "new Rockefeller." He felt flush enough to lease a ten-room penthouse apartment on New York's East 55th Street at $16,000 a year under the name of Leland Kurtz—a place he kept strictly for pleasure and at which he entertained a new circle of friends who knew him only as Mr. Kurtz, a rich Milwaukee industrialist. He also developed a liking for Colorado Springs, and took to visiting the western resort every month or so, putting up at the best hotel under the name of Leonard Kinder. He never took his wife along on these jaunts, since they were supposed to be purely for business. To ward off ennui while at Colorado Springs, he took a trim cottage for a Chicago bachelor girl who was a little overpowering as a steady diet but was charming a few days a month. Considering the frantic pace at which he lived and loved, it was no wonder that by 1922 Leo Koretz began to feel vague pains and suffer periods of listlessness that sometimes lasted several days.

But when he shook off his torpor he was still ablaze with the old fire. He had to be. His expenses were enormous, and the rush of new money into Bayano Oil eventually tapered off. To meet this challenge, he formed still a third organization, the Bayano Trust Company, to exploit the hitherto wasted resources of the region—bananas, cocoa, sugar and coffee. He upped his dividend payments to 5 percent quarterly and finally to 5 percent monthly—a rate of return that had economists gasping.

Koretz also started to cast about for a big name, a Chicagoan of such prestige that his entry into the Bayano group would immediately attract more investors. The man he selected was Judge Harry M. Fisher of the Cook County Court, a widely known jurist and civic leader. That turned out to be the biggest mistake Leo Koretz ever made.

Early in 1923, he invited Fisher over to his house, where he gave him the full treatment and spoke indignantly about a man of Fisher's ability having to struggle along on a $12,000-a-year judge's salary.

"That's barely enough to maintain an automobile," he said. "Judge, I need a legal adviser to handle my negotiations with the oil companies, and I want the best. I'll pay you a $50,000 annual salary and give you outright a large block of stock—say about $250,000 worth—if you'll take over the Bayano legal work for me."

Judge Fisher was attracted by this generous offer, but he was also a remarkably astute man who believed in looking before leaping. He told Koretz he would think it over. He began quietly buttonholing Bayano investors and asking them about the Panama enterprises. He was impressed by the reverent way in which the stockholders spoke about Koretz, but another thing impressed him too. That was the fact that none of the men who had invested large sums in Bayano—even Henry Klein, who had sunk $263,000 in the scheme—had ever gone to Panama to give their company a personal look-see. This omission struck Fisher as being downright unbusinesslike. The next time he saw Koretz, the judge admitted interest in his offer but said he could not accept the legal chaperoning of Bayano until a representative group of stockholders had visited Panama and made an on-the-spot examination.

Koretz nodded. "It's just what I've been thinking about, Judge," he said. "You and I and a bunch of the boys will go down there in October."

Fisher noticed, however, that thereafter Koretz seemed to cool toward him and no longer urged him to join the colors. Indeed, Fisher's proposition made him about as attractive as leprosy to the promoter, who immediately tried to shake the judge. But the damage had already been done. Judge Fisher's conversations with stockholders had awakened a few sleeping intellects. Henry Klein, Charles Cohn and several others agreed that it would be a swell idea to send a group down to Panama to see the wells, forests and fruits that were producing all those beautiful dividends.

But by late summer of 1923, troubles were piling high around the boy wonder. For one thing, one of his Chicago lady friends proved such a nuisance that he had to dislodge her by sending her on a cruise around the world, inferring that he might meet her in Paris. For another, he learned that he had diabetes, started to take Insulin—then newly discovered—and among other things was warned to shun liquor. This was a body blow to Koretz, who hated nonalcoholic liquids of any kind.

But worst of all was this talk of sending a deputation to Panama. Koretz knew better than to discourage the idea openly. He was loud in his praise of the plan and confined himself to stalling it off as long as he could without arousing suspicion. He could see the handwriting on the wall, however, and he prepared for the debacle in his customary grand style.

A committee of six stockholders—Klein, E. B. Kitzinger, Harold A. Boysen, E. J. Mayer, M. E. Smith and S. M. Zinner—was elected to make the trip. On November 28, personally escorted by Koretz, they pulled out of Chicago with the enthusiastic shouts of other investors ringing in their ears. "It seemed to all of us," Klein later related, "more like a pleasure trip than anything else. Leo even paid our railroad fares."

Leo did more than that. He showed the six a high old time in New York, took them to a musical comedy and wound up with a lavish dinner in a private room at the old Waldorf, complete with illegal champagne. The centerpiece on the table was an interesting papier-mâché creation—a scale model, Koretz said, of a section of the Bayano country, bristling with oil derricks and showing men, mules and machines laboring to get the riches out to civilization. In a brief but punchy speech, the new Rockefeller expressed his regret at being too pressed by business to accompany the group all the way to Panama. He was glad, he said, that he had six men of such caliber to go down there, size up the entire vast Bayano enterprises, and possibly make recommendations which would result in more efficient operation and a greater return on investments.

On December 1, the six committeemen were feeling just fine as they walked up the gangplank of the Panama-bound *Santa Luisa* with Koretz jovially waving good-by.

He then went into conference with his 44th Street ladylove, appearing next at New York's Ansonia Hotel on December 5 to have dinner with a Mr. Marcy Schoener. Schoener had recently resigned from a lucrative wholesaling job to be general manager of the New York office of the Bayano Trust Company, a project designed to spread the gospel and sell stock in Gotham. Schoener was naturally tickled at his good fortune in falling into such a gold mine, and he talked enthusiastically about the new offices which were being refurbished in the Straus building and were scheduled to open January 8. The fact that Koretz would bother to discuss the future of Bayano with Schoener even as the *Santa Luisa* was making port in Panama is just another indication that he had started so many wheels rolling in so many different directions that he could not stop them.

Schoener pulled out his checkbook and wanted to invest $20,000 then and there, but Koretz shook his head.

"Maybe later on, when you've got the lay of the land," he said, "I'll let you have some stock. You know, Marcy, I'm glad to have you running things for me here. I've been hitting the ball too hard—I'm all fagged out. I'm going to take a rest, a real honest-to-God rest. I'm just going to drop out of sight and let Bayano get along without me for awhile."

That same day, the *Santa Luisa* docked at Balboa. Koretz had told the six emissaries that they would be met by his personal representative, A. Espinoza, who was also president of the Panama Trust Company. Espinoza, he said, would conduct them on a complete six-day tour of all the Bayano lands and enterprises.

Mr. Espinoza unaccountably was missing. They put up at a hotel in

Ancon and sought to locate Espinoza through the Panama Trust Company. They were informed there was no such company. Koretz had also told them of his cable address, "Koretz Panama," so they consulted the cable company. They were told there was no such cable address.

The six were getting pretty fed up with Panamanian inefficiency when they finally ran into an American named C. L. Peck who had done a lot of timber prospecting in Panama and knew the country like a book. They showed Peck a blueprint Koretz had given them, which indicated the Bayano River property. Peck's jaw almost hit his chest as he scrutinized the map.

"Hell's fire!" he exploded. "That's undeveloped government land, and it ain't worth a damn. Nothing but swamps, snakes, alligators and wild Kuna Indians who'd as soon send an arrow through you as not. Fellows—I'm afraid you've been took!"

That was when the Bayano stockholders' committee, looking dazed, headed for the cable office and began to burn the wires.

In Chicago, State's Attorney Robert Crowe took over. It was quickly established that Leo Koretz owned no land on the Bayano River, no timber rights, no wells, no bananas. Amid the wails of investors, detectives and accountants swooped down on the Monroe Street and Drake Hotel offices. They found a large stock of liquor and many green-edged Bayano stock certificates, but no money. Koretz's staff, they discovered, were merely clerical helpers who had no idea anything unethical was going on. Even Miss Schroeder, who herself had lost money in the hoax, was utterly appalled to learn she had been working for the swindler of the century.

It became abundantly clear that the fancy dividends Koretz had paid were merely small fractions of the suckers' original investment. The probe also showed that previous to the Bayano binge, Koretz had done a rushing business in fraudulent Arkansas land mortgages and had been swindling his best friends for at least twelve years.

In New York, Marcy Schoener suddenly found himself without a job, and could only comfort himself with the thought that Koretz had refused his $20,000. In Evanston, Mrs. Koretz was prostrated by the exposure. She knew nothing about her husband's business affairs, she sobbed, and she had no idea where he was now.

State's Attorney Crowe's investigators strenuously tried to find some trace of Koretz, and also of the millions he had swindled, but had no luck at either. The new Rockfeller had cleaned out his bank accounts and safe-deposit boxes before leaving. Apparently the last person to see him before he dropped into a void was Schoener in New York.

28

Among Koretz's effects, however, was found a stack of passion-packed letters from many different women, some addressed to Koretz but others to Alfred Bronson, Herman Bowen, Leonard Kinder, et al.

If there was woe among the investors, there was an equal chagrin among Koretz's women, who either had to find another angel or be tossed out on the street. Detectives interviewed them all, suspecting that the promoter might be hiding under the bed, but had no such luck. None of the women would admit to having any idea where he was, though they all missed him sorely.

In the midst of this turmoil, on December 29, 175 holders of worthless Bayano stock received New Year's greeting cards bearing this cheery bit of doggerel:

> *If I could be transported*
> *This moment to your door,*
> *I'd bring smiles by the dozen*
> *And good wishes by the score.*

They were signed "Leo Koretz," unquestionably in the financial wizard's own flowing hand, and had been mailed in Chicago on December 27. The cops were sure he was not in Chicago and believed that some local friend—probably a woman—had done the mailing for him. The feelings of the stockholders can better be imagined than described.

With angry victims breathing down their necks, the investigators kept a sharp eye on Koretz's mail. On January 12 he received a code cable from Calcutta that got them all excited. It read:

HAVE NOT RECEIVED REMITTANCE FOR NOVEMBER OR DECEMBER. PLEASE SEND
MONEY IMMEDIATELY.   —WATSON

Watson, the sleuths agreed, might very well be an accomplice who had fled to India with part of the boodle. They were quickly disabused of this notion when a Chicago *Tribune* reporter in Calcutta sniffed around and identified Watson as the lady Koretz had sent on an all-expenses-paid world cruise. The newsman pumped her, figuring he had the scoop of the century, but she was terrified at the notoriety suddenly engulfing her. All she would say was that Mr. Koretz had very kindly been footing her bills. She was now flat broke, and friends had to bail her out so that she could take a slow freighter home.

Knowing that Koretz was a diabetic who took daily doses of Insulin, detectives sought to trace him through a check on doctors who employed the drug. This was long before the day when a diabetic could punch his own arm. Insulin at that time was rare, almost priceless, and administered only by a few ultra-progressive physicians. The Insulin trail led to Montreal where Koretz, under another name, had spent ten days taking treatments at a sanitarium, but from that point he dropped out of sight.

As time went on, one of Crowe's detectives made it a point to drop in on Koretz's former lights-o'-love occasionally, on the theory that they might remember something, or might get a letter from him. In November, 1924, he talked with the hot number in Hot Springs, who had gone back to manicuring again and didn't like it. She told him that Koretz had once expressed a liking for Halifax, Nova Scotia, and said he would like to live there when he retired. Halifax authorities were asked whether a man resembling Koretz, possibly inclined to throw his money and weight around, had appeared in that area.

As it happened, one had.

In March, one Lou Keyte had shown up in Halifax, banked a cool $240,000, and bought an estate called Pinehurst, near Caledonia, fifty miles west of Halifax. Pinehurst was famous for having the most fireplaces of any house in the province—sixteen—and was set on 180 acres that overlooked Christopher Lake. The place was considered downright baronial in those parts, but it didn't suit the demanding Mr. Keyte. He spent $50,000 remodeling it and installing a tennis court and small golf course. Keyte did everything in the same grandiloquent style—bought a yellow Rolls-Royce and two other cars, a library of classics bound in morocco, a speedy motor yacht, four saddle horses, and laid out $8,700 for liquor to stock the cellar. Despite those sixteen fireplaces, Keyte got chilly at night, so he had a Halifax tailor make him four suits of silk pajamas lined with rabbit fur, at $150 a throw.

Keyte said he was a New York writer and literary critic drawn to Nova Scotia by its healthful climate and freedom from distracting influences that might interfere with his writing. Oddly, he seemed to go out of his way to cultivate distracting influences. He invited the socially elite of the province out to Pinehurst for an endless succession of noisy and unliterary parties which usually wound up with the grounds littered with empty bottles and stupefied guests.

Keyte especially liked to play host to famous people. When Edna Preston, the New York actress, appeared in person at a Halifax theater, he threw a glittering party for her at the city's best hotel. Zane Grey, the author, visited Nova Scotia on a fishing trip, so Keyte had him out to Pinehurst to discuss literature over a bottle of Five-Star. Grey was startled when a brunette lovely, clad only in an appetizing negligee,

strolled into the room, but Keyte waved her away noncha
secretary," he explained. "Whenever I get an idea, I fire it at

Grey's impression was that Keyte's literary education (
Horatio Alger and Oliver Optic, and he seriously doubte
young woman was intended for shorthand and typing. So d
father, who went to the sheriff, accused Keyte of "bewi
daughter and charged that he was keeping her for immoral
secretarial purposes. A deputy went to Pinehurst and rescu
but it was apparent that bewitching came easy for a man v
supply of loose cash. Her place was soon taken by a divorcé
fornia and the attractive daughter of a Halifax merchant.

For a man who had been around only seven months, and
tranquillity, Keyte had indeed made a loud splash. A ladies'
group in Caledonia had complained repeatedly about hi
and dissolute" parties. He had even managed to get arreste
ing four times. He always tipped the arresting officer libera
his fine with great good humor. The local law didn't know
think of Lou Keyte, who seemed like a prince of a fellov
hadn't caused so much trouble.

Keyte generally answered the description of Koretz ex
wore a luxurious brown beard. The Chicago Sherlocks liste
details with interest that turned to excitement when they w
Keyte was a diabetic and had hired a physician to stay at P
administer Insulin.

Assistant State's Attorneys John Sbarbaro and William
headed for Halifax with a brace of detectives, reaching ther
23. They drove to Pinehurst only to be told that the master
fax on "business"—a word that with Keyte generally meant

It was no task finding Keyte in the provincial capital. All
do was look for his block-long yellow Rolls-Royce, which t
front of one of the better hotels. Keyte visited this hosteli
was believed to be paying the bills of a lady who lived on th
The officers barged in and found the bearded Mr. Keyte ｜
by the woman, who was sitting on his lap. He leaped to hi
lently that she was all but thrown to the floor.

"What the hell is the meaning of this?" he demanded.

"We want you back in Chicago, Koretz," Sbarbaro told h

The oil king cooled off immediately. He lifted his hands
of defeat. "I knew it had to come sometime," he said. "\
make any trouble."

Returned to Chicago, the deflated swindler seemed hurt that his wife and family had disowned him. He made some vague claims that he had fled to Canada in order to recoup his fortune and pay back every penny he owed, but nevertheless he pleaded guilty to charges of larceny, embezzlement and operation of a confidence game. On December 5, 1924 —exactly a year after his disappearance—he was given a one-to-ten year sentence at Joliet Prison.

The wife of one of the Bayano victims, who was a spectator in the courtroom, let out an angry screech at this comparatively light punishment. "Why, he ought to get a death sentence!" she shrilled.

Koretz turned to her. "That's exactly what it is, lady," he said. "I won't live a year behind bars."

Somehow, he managed to lay hands on a three-pound box of chocolates—poison to an advanced diabetic—and he ate them at one sitting. On January 9, hardly more than a month after he entered Joliet, he died in the prison hospital at the age of 45, leaving an estate of exactly $43.76. His widow and a handful of relatives were his only mourners at burial services spoken by Rabbi Felix Levy, who himself had sunk $7,000 in the great Bayano bubble.

Accountants were still having nightmares trying to unravel his frenzied finances and salvage something from the wreckage. From his assets in Canada, New York and Chicago they were able to realize only $342,000 to be prorated to the investors. The figures told them that Koretz had swindled something over $2,000,000, but the figures lied outrageously. Many of his victims were Chicago bigwigs who preferred to take their beating in silence rather than be exposed as suckers. One bank president admitted confidentially to McSwiggin that he had sunk more than $100,000 in Bayano, but he wasn't saying a word about it officially.

"If I did," he said, "the bank directors would fire me and I'd be ruined professionally. The queer thing is, I suspect that two of the directors themselves invested in the Bayano enterprises. "

Three weeks after Koretz's burial, one of his former investors went to the police and demanded that the body be exhumed.

"I have it on good authority that Koretz has been seen in Halifax since his supposed death," he said. "The man who died wasn't Koretz. Through some flim-flam or bribery—you know how clever he was—he managed to get away and have another body substituted for his own."

Dr. W. R. Fletcher, the Joliet prison physician, had the answer for that. To make sure that the ex-oil king did not pull a fast one even in death,

the doctor had the body fingerprinted before burial. Fingerprints, unlike figures, do not lie. There was no doubt that Koretz was dead. About the only person he couldn't swindle was the Grim Reaper.

THE MURDERING SLEEPERS

by Alan Hynd

The January morning was raw and gray when Pinkerton Detective James McParland, sporting a week's growth of beard and clutching a beat-up suitcase, hopped out of a side-door Pullman in the coal-mining town of Pottsville, Pennsylvania. A short, wiry fellow of 29 with a pugnacious face and bright red hair, McParland walked along Centre Street, looking for a lodging house, aware that suspicious glances followed him. Strangers were not welcome in the Pennsylvania coal regions in 1875, and detectives particularly were not wanted. Already seven of them had been murdered by the notorious Sleepers—the tribute-exacting band of goons and killers who controlled the miners.

Under the name of James McKenna, McParland took a room on Centre Street, then visited the bar of the Sheridan House. The proprietor, Patrick Dormer, a hulking mass of meanness with a square, pockmarked face, was tending bar. From intelligence the Pinkertons had gleaned before he had been assigned to ferret out the murderers, McParland suspected the man behind the bar was up to his bull neck in guilty knowledge.

Measuring the detective with his shoe-button eyes, Dormer shoved a bottle toward him, then directed a loaded glance through an open door leading into a back room. Presently several rough-looking characters, who had been playing cards in the back room, drifted up to the bar to size up the newcomer.

McParland, who happened to be a teetotaler, downed several shots of rot gut, went to the toilet, stuck his finger down his throat and got rid of the stuff. When he returned to the bar, he downed several more shots and repeated the performance, unpleasant as it was.

Soon McParland was pretending to be drunk—a vital part of his act

33

because a teetotaler in the coal regions was automatically open to suspicion. Slapping a crisp $10 bill on the bar, the detective paid for his drinks and walked out.

For several days, McParland appeared at the bar of the Sheridan House every few hours and ate his meals at the free-lunch counter. He and Dormer hardly exchanged a word. When he wasn't at Dormer's place, McParland seldom moved out of his room. Several times, while he was down the street at the bar, his room was searched.

Late one afternoon at the bar McParland glanced out the window, uttered an oath and ducked out a rear door. In walked two hard-faced men wearing derbies and chewing on dead cigars—Pinkerton detectives dressed for the act.

"Ever seen this man?" asked one of the Pinks, shoving a fake police flier at Dormer.

It was a picture of the fellow who had just fled. James McKenna, according to the circular, was wanted in Buffalo for murder and for counterfeiting the cleverest $10 bills in the history of bogus currency. He had, it seemed, fatally shot two Buffalo detectives who had attempted to arrest him; there was $1,000 on his head.

Dormer, a man who knew how to keep silent in several languages, studied the picture, then handed it back to the Pink. "Nope. Never laid eyes on 'im."

"Well," said the Pink. "Mind if I tack one of these things up on the wall there?"

Dormer didn't mind.

A couple of hours later, McParland sneaked back into Dormer's. Spotting the poster, he blew up, ripped it from the wall, then turned and glared at Dormer. "You're not for turnin' me in, I hope!"

"Maybe not," said Dormer. "What's it worth?"

"Plenty," said McParland. "Wait. I'll be back."

The detective returned with a stack of one hundred $10 bills—genuine United States currency. "Here," he said to Dormer, handing over the bills. "This ought to square things."

Dormer carefully scrutinized the money, counted it and stuffed it in his pocket. "I won't say a word."

"There's somethin' I ought to tell you," said McParland. "Them bills ain't real. They're counterfeit. They bring me fifty cents on the dollar."

"What!"

"Dormer, you can cut my throat if anybody spots a single one of those bills. And there's plenty more where they come from."

34

Dormer went out and dropped several of the bills around town. When a teller in the local bank changed five of the notes for smaller currency, Dormer felt he was in clover.

Detective McParland had cleared his first hurdle in the long road that lay ahead. But that road, he well knew, was still dangerous. For several years now, the great anthracite coal fields of Pennsylvania—in Schuylkill, Luzerne, Columbia, Northumberland and Carbon Counties —had been the playground of an infamous secret fraternal and labor organization known as The Sleepers. Originally, The Sleepers had been organized when work in the mines was slack and there were two men for every job. But gradually control of The Sleepers had been taken over by toughs; they instituted a system of kick-backs whereby men they placed in jobs forked over anywhere from a tenth to half of their pay. These shadowy Sleeper leaders were the early-day union gangsters, forerunners of the mobsters who now operate on the New York waterfront.

The Sleeper big shots were all Irishmen, long since excommunicated from the Catholic Church. Most of the tribute payers were Irishmen, too. When times were slack, the Polish, the German, the Norwegian and the Russian miners lived on credit or sustained themselves by their hatred of the Hibernians.

Mine policemen, mine superintendents and unemployed workers who spoke out against The Sleepers were either shot, stabbed, strangled, mutilated or clubbed to death and thrown down mine shafts. Mines were dynamited. Sleeper sympathizers were infiltrated into police departments, sheriffs' offices, grand-jury rooms and judicial benches. Law-enforcement was practically nonexistent.

The mine owners hired private detectives to snare the men behind this reign of murder and destruction. In the three years before McParland appeared in the coal regions, seven detectives had been murdered. Finally the mine owners engaged Pinkerton's National Detective Agency, which assigned Jim McParland to spearhead the attack.

One night late in February, after McParland had been in Pottsville for almost two months, an enormous man with a bushy black beard and a hawklike red nose lumbered into Dormer's back room. In the next half hour the knot of goons who hung out in the back room drifted out into the night. Finally the bearded man came out and took a place at the bar beside McParland. McParland knew the other was studying him.

"I hear there's a thousand dollars on your head," the man said.

35

McParland turned to face the bearded one. "What the hell are you talkin' about!"

"Your face is on Pinkerton posters in every town in the coal regions." As McParland feigned alarm, Dormer cut in. "Don't be afraid, Jim. This here's King Jack Kehoe."

Kehoe laughed and shook hands with McParland.

Jack Kehoe—McParland and the Pinkertons suspected—was the kingpin of The Sleepers. He operated a hotel—the Shenandoah House—in Girardsville, a dozen miles northwest of Pottsville. If what the Pinkertons had heard about Kehoe was half true, King Jack, as the man was called because of his size, was one of the most vicious men in the history of premeditated homicide.

Kehoe invited McParland into the deserted back room, and began to question him thoroughly about his past. The detective, prepared for just such an emergency, had every detail of a fictitious past ready and waiting.

Kehoe asked him if he had any of his counterfeits on him. The detective produced a genuine ten spot. "This thing looks as real as a real bill," said Kehoe, in admiration. "You're a very clever fellow, McKenna."

Every so often Kehoe would go peer out a window that looked onto the black hills in the distance. Once, he stiffened perceptibly and seemed to look with increased intensity toward the hills. McParland arose and looked over Kehoe's shoulder. In the distance, the detective could see flashes of light, as if somebody had built a bonfire and was signaling by waving a blanket in front of the flames.

"Do you see what I see?" Kehoe asked, without turning.

"Those signals?"

"Uh-huh."

That's all Kehoe said about the signals. Changing the subject, he said to the detective, "I could use somebody like you—somebody real smart."

"What for?"

Kehoe wanted to plant him as a workman in a mine just outside of Pottsville. McParland was to worm into the secrets of the Coal and Iron Police, an organization employed by the mine owners to protect their property.

"Keep your ears open and your eyes on them Coal and Iron cops," Kehoe said, "and find out exactly what the sonsabitches are up to." McParland was all for it.

Toward dawn, when he was still in the back room with King Jack, the goons returned.

36

"Did you see the signals all right?" one of them asked Kehoe.

"Yeah. Did you have any trouble?"

The goons had had no trouble.

Next day the body of a mine superintendent who had fired a drunken Sleeper and refused to re-hire him was found in the hills where the signals had come from.

McParland went back to his room and got to work writing a lengthy report to the Pinkertons. He used a pencil, lest the scratching of a pen be overheard in the hallway.

Taking no chances that The Sleepers might have a spy planted in the local post office to examine outgoing mail, McParland wrote every report to a mythical sister, care of general delivery, Philadelphia. A woman Pinkerton operative, posing as the sister, picked up the reports. Each message had to be extracted from chatty, innocuous sentences, a word or a letter at a time, by means of a previously determined complicated code which the detective carried in his head.

When he was planted in the mine by King Jack Kehoe, the Coal and Iron Police—who disliked anybody sponsored by The Sleepers—saw to it that he was assigned to a dangerous job. On his third day at work the little Irishman got his right hand caught in a crusher.

McParland contracted blood-poisoning. The detective's arm began to swell as the poison slowly crept up toward his shoulder. There were no miracle drugs in those days.

Taken to a hospital, McParland lay moaning in a ward. A doctor sat down at his bedside at dusk the second day. "McKenna," said the sawbones, "you'd better give us the name of your nearest relative."

"What for?"

"Because I don't expect you to pull through."

McParland had a wife and three small kids in New York State. "I ain't got no relatives," he told the doctor. "Not a living soul."

When the doctor left, McParland, who was a very devout man, began to pray. He asked his Maker to save his life. "Not for my sake," he whispered, "but so I can get back on the job and save some lives."

McParland was in excruciating pain for about an hour. Then he fell into a deep sleep and the sweat began to pour from him.

In the morning he awakened to find the redness and the swelling in his arm greatly diminished and the pain completely gone. Three days later, he was well enough to leave the hospital with his arm in a sling. The doctor who had told him he was dying just scratched his head and said, "I just don't understand it."

Hanging around Patrick Dormer's saloon, McParland would see King

37

Jack Kehoe going into the back room and then he would see the goons leaving. When the goons came back, saying little or nothing, they were smiling like evil Cheshire cats. Later, McParland would hear that somebody had been shot or slugged to death or had dropped from sight.

The little Pinkerton detective had now been in the coal regions for four months. It was early May and spring was in the air. But there was only gloom in the Irish heart of James McParland. Decoded, one of his messages to the Pinkertons ran:

I am sick and tired. I seem to make no progress, and the terrible and long continued state of excitement in the country around here will one day end in something more fearful than has yet appeared. I hear of preparations for bloodshed in all directions. The sun looks crimson to me and the air is tainted with the smell of blood. We must do something to stop the whirlwind that bids fair to destroy everything.

It was now that he suggested to the Pinkertons that they infiltrate another operative into the coal regions. If he learned sufficiently in advance of a plotted assassination, he could slip the word to this second operative and have *him* take steps to thwart the plot.

The Pinkertons took a top official of the Coal and Iron Police into their confidence and planted an operative named Linden into the Coal and Iron protective corps at the Pottsville collieries. Linden—Capt. Robert J. Linden—was a big, middle-aged man of military manner and bearing, with fierce black eyebrows and moustache. When he went to work in the Pottsville mine, he took a boardinghouse room in the block next to where McParland roomed.

One night, shortly after Captain Linden arrived in town, the talk was less guarded than usual between King Jack Kehoe and the goons in the back room at Dormer's. A man named James, a watchman in a Pottsville mine, was to be bumped off and tossed down an abandoned shaft because he had been shooting off his mouth about The Sleepers. The assassination was set for the following night.

When Dormer's closed for the night, McParland sneaked along Centre Street, and made his way to Captain Linden's room. After tipping Linden to the murder plot, McParland sneaked back to his own room.

The next night, around 10 o'clock, the goons set out from the back room at Dormer's, leaving McParland and Kehoe alone. In a little while, Kehoe began to look out the window, toward the hills.

"Any sign of the fire signal yet?" McParland kept asking.

"No, damn it," Kehoe kept answering.

At dawn, Kehoe had still not seen the signal. He was about to leave the back room when the goons returned. Their victim, they reported, had been fired from his job the previous day and had vanished.

The following week, King Jack appeared in the back room with news. He had located James, the watchman, working at a mine near Shenandoah. The second plot for the same assassination called for James to get it the following night. Once more, McParland tipped off Captain Linden. And once more, Linden passed the word along and James got fired and vanished from view before the killers arrived.

Meantime, McParland had been continuing to slip his "counterfeit" ten-spots to Pat Dormer, and Dormer had taken quite a liking to the detective. One night, shortly after the second unsuccessful plot against the life of the watchman, Dormer greeted McParland with an apprehensive look.

"Jim, my boy," he said, "I'm afraid you're in trouble. Bad trouble, too, Jim."

McParland feigned alarm. "Those Pinkerton detectives been around lookin' for me again!"

"No, it's worse than that. You know that watchman King Jack tried to get twice?"

"Yes. What about him?"

"King Jack thinks you tipped him off."

"King Jack's crazy if he thinks such a thing!"

Dormer leaned over the bar and reduced his voice to a half whisper. "*I* believe you, Jim. But you'll have an awful time provin' it to King Jack now."

"Whadda you mean *now?*"

"You didn't know that watchman was back in these parts, did you, Jim? They got him two hours ago."

McParland went back to his room to think things over. He was in a bad spot in two ways. His own life was now in jeopardy. So was the entire investigation into the murdering Sleepers. King Jack Kehoe wasn't around Pottsville; he had gone back to Girardville.

Next night, the little man calling himself Jim McKenna stormed into the bar of Kehoe's Shenandoah House in Girardville. King Jack and four goons were sitting around a table in the rear. McParland was wearing a brass knuckle under the bandage of his right hand.

With fire in his eyes and whisky on his breath, Jim McKenna staggered toward King Jack's table. "So ye think Jim McKenna's a traitor, de ya!" he screamed at the goons. "Well, did ye ever see a traitor who could punch like *this?*"

39

With his left hand McParland dragged one of the goons to his feet, and let him have it on the chin with the brass-knuckle hand.

The goon went down as the three other plug-uglies were rising. McParland, lightning fast, tackled them one at a time, brass-knuckled and kneed them, and down they went.

The first man, rubbing his chin, arose. McParland swung again and hit him so hard that he broke the man's jaw. Two of the three others were out cold, but one of them staggered to his feet. McParland drove the brass knuckle straight into the man's nose and smashed it.

McParland reached for a bottle of whisky on King Jack's table and took several heroic drags. He sat down beside King Jack and, looking The Sleeper big-shot right in the eye, jerked a thumb toward the four men on the floor. "*That's* what I do to men who call me a traitor."

Kehoe was impressed. "It was all a mistake, Jim," he said. "Me thinkin' you betrayed us. Why, no man who fights like that could be a traitor."

King Jack put McParland up at the Hibernian House.

In the middle of the night, the detective heard somebody at his door. It was a girl in bare feet and nightgown. "Let me in," she whispered. "It's not what you think."

"Well, what *is* it?" said McParland.

"Your life is in danger." The girl revealed she had overheard King Jack and several of his henchmen working out a test for McParland. They were going to tell him in advance of a killing. If it went off without a hitch, McKenna was to be sworn into The Sleepers. But if anything went wrong, McKenna was to be shot.

"Why are you telling me this?" McParland asked the girl.

"Because I'm not all bad," she said. "Maybe I'm no good in one way but I can't just hear about men goin' to be murdered and do nothing about it."

Next day Kehoe told McParland every detail of a murder scheduled for that night. Another watchman—a man who had been outspoken against The Sleepers—was to be killed in front of his home when he returned from work about midnight. McParland had twelve hours to tip off the watchman.

He was in a spot to try the conscience of any decent man. He couldn't save the watchman. If he did, his own life would be done for. Not that his own life was so precious; the problem was to save the lives of uncounted men—the men who would die if the detective did not bring these killers to book.

40

As the hour of the watchman's execution approached, McParland felt more and more like a man who was deliberately putting another man to death. At 11 o'clock that night, he was sitting in the bar of the Shenandoah House with King Jack Kehoe when the assassins left. He was still sitting there shortly after midnight when the assassins came back, mission accomplished.

King Jack Kehoe took McParland to an upstairs room. There, while several of his henchmen looked on, he swore the detective into The Sleepers. After the swearing in, McParland said he thought he'd go to bed. When he got to his room, he was heartsick. He got down on his knees and began to pray. The man who had come to the coal regions to avenge murder was asking Divine forgiveness for murder.

McParland's association with The Sleepers was bound to take a turn for the better, and it did a short time later when he discovered that Kehoe was a sucker for ghost stories. As a boy in Ireland, McParland had heard plenty of ghost stories at his mother's knee, and he was quite a story-teller himself. When things were fairly quiet on the Sleeper front, King Jack used to invite McParland up to his private quarters on the second floor of the Shenandoah House and have the sleuth tell him ghost stories.

One night, after he had listened to several stories, King Jack went to a cabinet and produced a small tin box. Opening it, he took out some papers and began to sweat and curse as he labored over them. King Jack was no whiz at paper work.

McParland said, "I think I could be of help to ye if ye'd let me take a lot of that work off yer shoulders. King Jack's too important a man to be burdened by details."

The big Sleeper swelled with pride. "By God, Jim, you're right!" he said. "Here. I'll show you what's to be done."

It was as simple as that. As is often the case in an artfully worked-up detective job, the groundwork is the big thing and the pay-off is practically anti-climactic.

As King Jack revealed the contents of the strongbox to McParland, the Pinkerton sleuth knew that he had hit the jackpot. Here were the names and addresses not only of members of The Sleepers in Schuylkill County and the amounts of their pay they were kicking in to Kehoe but, even more important, the identities of Sleeper sympathizers in key spots in the county's law-enforcement setup. Several cops in Schuylkill County towns and villages were marked down as friendly to The Sleepers, as was a county judge and more than fifty members of the petit jury.

Such information, McParland knew at a glance, was invaluable to the investigation. The only fly in the ointment was that McParland couldn't make notes with King Jack sitting there looking at him. So he carried as much of the information as possible in his head. Later, in his room, working by candlelight, he labored until daylight, reducing to code for the Pinkertons all the names he could remember.

McParland kept telling Kehoe ghost stories, flattering him and helping him with the paper work. And he got several good looks at the contents of that strongbox. Within a month he had apprised the Pinkertons of the identity of every Sleeper and Sleeper sympathizer in Schuylkill County.

McParland was determined to get the kind of murder evidence he could take into court. All he needed was to sit in on a death plot while it was hatched and executed.

Now came a disheartening delay. Kehoe announced that he was going to run for public office—for the office of high constable of Schuylkill County. All murders would be off until after the election.

"You're a wonderful talker, Jim," King Jack said to McParland. "I want you to go around the county makin' speeches tellin' the voters what a wonderful man I am."

It is doubtful if a detective on a murder investigation was ever in a more unique spot. Yet McParland had to accept the task, or run the risk of arousing Kehoe's suspicion. So he set out on a tour of Schuylkill County, making campaign speeches everywhere—in barrooms, on street corners, at the mines. "Elect King Jack Kehoe high constable," he would shout, "if ye know what's good fer ye!"

On election day The Sleepers voted early and often. King Jack Kehoe, murderer, was elected high constable of Schuylkill County.

Kehoe was sworn in as high constable in the spring of 1876—fifteen months after Jim McParland had hopped out of that side-door Pullman to begin his probe into The Sleepers. Now time was of the essence. With The Sleeper big shot occupying the office of high constable, law-enforcement in the county would cease altogether.

McParland, eager to wrap up the case, suddenly realized he was a very sick man. He had been so preoccupied by his work for fifteen months that he had scarcely given a second thought to his health.

It wasn't until the summer of 1876, after he had been in the coal regions for a year and a half, that McParland found himself nearing the end of the trail. By now he was practically a walking corpse. But he was engaged in vital work—serving as a contact man between High Con-

42

stable Kehoe and Sleeper leaders. No murders were yet scheduled, but plots were cooking.

On a breathless night in late July, McParland was at the bar of The Sheridan House in Pottsville, chinning with his old friend, Patrick Dormer, the proprietor. Dormer, talking freely because of the detective's standing with The Sleepers, mentioned an important killing coming up. A policeman named Benjamin Yost in Tamaqua fifteen miles from Pottsville, was to get it. Yost had displeased High Constable Kehoe.

McParland said he knew about it, as indeed he did. He had left Kehoe earlier in the day to go to Pottsville, because the plot called for the assassins to check into The Sheridan House after their work was done.

At 2 in the morning, as the countryside was being lashed by a thunderstorm, the three killers walked into the bar. Wringing wet, they asked Dormer for drinks. McParland, sitting in the back room, summoned the three men. They had never seen McParland and he had never seen them, but they relaxed when he identified himself.

"How did everything go?" McParland asked the leader of the trio— a smallish, wizened man named Hugh McGehan.

McGehan smiled at his companions—younger toughs, Jim Boyle and Jim Roarity. "Tell King Jack we made out fine." McGehan reached into his pocket and handed McParland a gun. "See," he said, "it's empty."

"Are you the only one who emptied his gun into Officer Yost?" McParland asked McGehan, fishing for the kind of evidence he could swear to in court.

"No," answered McGehan, "we all did."

"Let me see your guns," said McParland. "I've got to tell King Jack that I looked at your guns and found them empty."

He got a look at the other two guns, and handed back all three weapons. "That'll be all, men."

McParland went up to his room. An hour before dawn, when everything was quiet, he sneaked out of the hostelry and walked around to the rooming house where Captain Linden was waiting for him. McParland briefed Linden on everything.

Later that morning, Linden, whose movements were not subject to close Sleeper scrutiny, left for Philadelphia to report to the Pinkertons. There, for more than a week, strategy was mapped. With the intelligence McParland had previously relayed after examining King Jack Kehoe's strongbox, the Pinkertons knew just where to strike—not only in Schuylkill County, but in the four other counties where The Sleepers were entrenched.

The great Allan Pinkerton, Scottish-born founder of the organization

43

bearing his name, assumed command. A total of 138 patrolmen and detectives of the New York and Philadelphia police departments were, by special arrangement with the governor of Pennsylvania, secretly sworn in as special cops with jurisdiction in the five murderous counties in the coal region. These special police hit the coal region in a sudden, secret raid that netted 300 Sleepers.

Acting on basic data supplied by McParland, Pinkerton and the visiting officers pounded these Sleepers with questions. They worked in relays, around the clock, giving The Sleepers no sleep.

It was the old story, new in every criminal case. Somebody talked to save his own hide. Then others began to talk. One of the most voluble was Patrick Dormer, the man who had been persuaded with genuine bills that he thought were fakes.

Honest juries gave The Sleepers honest hearings before honest judges. King Jack Kehoe, the three goons who murdered Patrolman Yost, and seventeen other killers walked to the gallows; forty-nine other Sleepers went to prison. Jim McParland left the coal regions, rejoined his wife and kids, and regained his health. He lived to tell his grandchildren of his two years in the valley of death.

SOME SHOTS THAT FOUND THEIR MARKS

by H. Allen Smith

LOVE THAT SECRETARY

A letter came from a man in the Middle West who had been reading some of my books. He insulted me at the outset by saying he knew I wouldn't even read his letter. My secretary would read it, but I wouldn't. The remainder of his impertinence was addressed to my secretary and, as he warmed to his task, he expressed the hope that she was young and redheaded and beautiful.

I have no secretary and have never had one. But I invented one now. I wrote to this worm. I pretended I was my secretary. I told him he must have possessed psychic powers, for I was truly young and redheaded and people thought I was not bad to look at. I said he certainly sounded in his letter like a real interesting fellow. The kind of masculine man I (the redheaded secretary) was just dying to meet. Maybe he would be coming to New York someday. If he ever did, please let me know—I'd ask the boss to let me off work for a day *and a night* and meet him in New York and we'd have dinner and go places and *do things.* I signed the letter "Eunice Wagstaff." And mailed it.

Two days later Western Union phoned my house and asked if we had a Eunice Wagstaff around the place. Fortunately I remembered the letter and took the message. My letter had had more than its desired effect. The telegram to Eunice Wagstaff said: "Leaving for New York and you tonight. Meet me tomorrow Hotel B——."

I debated with myself about stopping him. Then I decided that he had it coming. Haven't heard another peep out of him to this day.

THE PIECE OF STRING

The most celebrated of all British practical jokers was William Horace De Vere Cole. He was a citizen of substance and had a large house in a fashionable section of London. One day he was hanging some paintings in his home when he ran out of twine. He put on his hat and walked to the nearest stringmonger's shop and bought a ball of twine. On his way home he saw an elegant Englishman, a stranger, approaching. The man was so stiffish, so splendidly dressed, that Cole could not pass him up. Quickly he whipped out his ball of twine and stepped up to the gentleman.

"I say," he spoke with some show of deference, "I'm in a bit of a spot. We're engaged in surveying this area in order that we may realign the kerb, and my assistant has somehow vanished. I wonder if I could prevail upon your time for just a few moments."

"To be sure," said the stranger, ever the proper Englishman.

"If," said Cole, "you'd be so kind as to hold the end of this string. Just stand where you are, and keep a tight hold on it, and we'll be finished in a few moments. It's really quite important."

The splendid gentleman took hold of the end of the string and Cole began backing away from him, unwinding the ball. He continued all the way to the corner, turned the corner and disappeared. He proceeded, still unwinding the ball, until he was halfway up the block, at which point the string gave out. He stood for a moment, not knowing quite what he should do now. He had about decided to tie the string to a doorknob when Providence sent him a second gentleman, fully as elegant and polished as the first. Cole stopped him. Would the good sir be

45

so kind as to assist him in an engineering project? Certainly! Cole handed him the end of the string and asked that he simply stand firm and hold it. Then Cole disappeared through an alleyway, hastened to the shop for another ball of twine, and returned to his home to resume hanging pictures. Cole never knew how long those two men stood holding the string.

THE TELEPHONE

It has been said that the man who contributed most to the practical joke was Alexander Graham Bell and this joke involves Bell's invention. At the time Fred Hawthorn pulled it, the telephones in Skylark were almost all of the stand-up receiver-on-the-hook variety.

One Sunday around noontime Fred telephoned the homes of six of his friends. He is, to be sure, an excellent mimic, so he disguised his voice and said he was from the engineering department of the telephone company.

"I'm calling," he said, "to warn you that some time this afternoon we are going to clean out the telephone lines. We would advise you to cover your telephone—tie a sheet over it, or put a pillowcase over it, or even a large paper bag, because we're going to *blow* out the lines, and if you don't have your instrument covered, there'll be dirt and grease all over the house."

Having made his six calls, Fred waited an hour or so, and then started a tour of the affected households—just casually dropping in of a Sunday afternoon. In every case he found the telephone covered. Not only that—the folks were staying in the same room with it, keeping their distance, but watching it closely, waiting for the hiss or roar or whatever would come when the lines were blown out. Most of them had had phone calls during the afternoon, but they had forborne answering, save in the case of Dr. Gerrity. When his phone rang he took the pillowcase off of it, picked up the receiver and without asking who was calling, roared into the mouthpiece:

"Good-God-don't-call-this-number-don't-you-know-the-phone-company's-blowing-out-the-lines-this-afternoon!"

With which he slammed up the receiver and quickly replaced the pillowcase.

SOTHERN VS. THE GENERAL VS. EVERYBODY

[E. A. Sothern, a celebrated actor of his day, perpetrated one of his most effective cumulative hoaxes in a Philadelphia hotel.] He was having breakfast in the dining room when he noticed an irascible old gentleman who was muttering and complaining about the service. Questioning the headwaiter, Sothern found out the man was a General, a bachelor, a permanent resident of the hotel and a permanent grouch.

Forgetting the General for the moment, Sothern took some letters from his pocket and, running through them, happened on one that was a prop letter—a letter which was used in the course of a play. It began:

"Young man, I know thy secret—thou lovest above thy station; if thou hast wit, courage, and discretion, I can secure to thee the realization of thy most sanguine hopes."

Sothern glanced over at the crotchety old General, then called a waiter and instructed him to leave the room, then return and hand the letter to the man. When the letter was given to him, the General adjusted his spectacles and began reading it, half aloud. He read it over several times, growing more bewildered with each reading, and then summoned the headwaiter and demanded to see the servant who had brought him the letter. That worthy couldn't be found, and now the General began to storm and rant. Soon he was kicking the furniture and threatening to punch the idiot who had sent him the insane note.

Meanwhile three ladies joined Sothern at his table and, noticing the General's behavior, asked about him. "Please keep very quiet and don't attract his attention," Sothern warned the ladies. "He's an escaped lunatic, a murderer. The keepers are just outside the door, waiting to seize him, and that letter was sent in as a decoy." The ladies became alarmed and left the table, hurrying through a door at the other end of the room.

Now a waiter captain, witnessing the hurried departure of the ladies, came up to Sothern and asked if they had been dissatisfied with their breakfasts. Sothern told him that the youngest lady in the group was actually the General's daughter, that she had written the letter to him, that she was a dangerous maniac at times and that he, Sothern, had asked the young woman's friends to get her out of the room before she flew into a homicidal fit.

Was this enough? Not for E. A. Sothern. He finished his breakfast and went to the desk in the lobby, where he approached the clerk and asked whether the headwaiter was quite sound in his mind. He told the clerk that the headwaiter quite clearly hated the General. "If I were you," he said to the clerk, "I would test it by going up to the headwaiter suddenly and asking, 'Don't you think you will get yourself into trouble about that letter of the General's?'"

The clerk went at once to the headwaiter and asked the question. The

47

headwaiter began stammering excitedly, completely confused and frightened by the way things were going. The clerk had his back to Sothern, who now began making signs to the headwaiter that he'd better get out of the way, that the clerk was armed with a knife and might become violent at any moment.

At this point the angry General came stomping out of the dining room, headed for the desk, and the entire ground floor of the hotel was in a hubbub—each person thought that all other persons were hopelessly mad, and on the verge of homicidal assault. Sothern quickly paid his bill, grabbed up his bag, and departed.

VAN GOGH'S EAR

Back in 1935, in New York, the first American showing of Van Gogh was held at the Museum of Modern Art. There was much publicity about Van Gogh in the New York newspapers, but the emphasis was on the lurid character of the artist's life, especially on the fact that he had cut off his own ear. When crowds began flocking to the exhibit, Hugh [Troy] argued with his friends that most of the customers were sensation-mongers rather than art lovers. He decided to test the question. Using chipped beef, he modeled a grisly and withered ear and mounted it in a blue velvet shadow box carrying a neatly lettered inscription:

THIS IS THE EAR WHICH VINCENT VAN GOGH CUT OFF AND SENT TO HIS MISTRESS, A FRENCH PROSTITUTE, DEC. 24, 1888.

Hugh took the little box to the museum and surreptitiously placed it on a table in a room where the Van Gogh pictures were hung. Then he stood back and watched. The chipped beef ear immediately stole the show—the customers ganged up around it, chattering about it, fascinated by it, ignoring the paintings all around them.

COMMAND PERFORMANCE

Pomposity in all its varied forms irritated Hugh. One summer Sunday a very rich and famous lady held a benefit "carnival" on her estate at Sands Point, Long Island. Assorted entertainers and artists were "commanded" to appear and contribute their services, and among them was Hugh Troy. On his arrival at the big house, he was escorted into the presence of the great lady. "I am giving two minutes to each of you people," she said imperiously. "You are to paint a picture for the auction. Now your two minutes are up. Kindly leave."

The affair was strictly by invitation, and the only people invited were the cream of the social register crowd. Hugh went out and found the supply of art materials. Then he retired to a quiet spot on the premises to paint. He didn't paint a picture—he painted signs. When he had them finished he carried them out the long driveway to the big stone gate which stood beside the busy highway. He placed the signs all around the entrance to the estate, then hitched a ride back to Manhattan. The signs said:

PICNIC PARTIES WELCOME
BASKET PARTIES INVITED
FREE MERRY-GO-ROUND FOR THE CHILDREN
LEMONADE FOR ALL

THE FLYPAPER REPORTS

Hugh Troy went into the Army in World War II and during those exciting years I often caught myself wondering about him and what he might be doing in the way of confounding the brass. Now I know some of it. He took officers' training and in time was sent to a Southern camp which was largely devoted to giving fledgling officers actual experience in leadership. Almost at once he found himself in rebellion against the enormous amount of paperwork he was required to do. Reports, reports, reports, and more reports. He was required to fill out reports on the most trivial details of camp operation, and these reports, great bundles and bales of them, went in to the Pentagon. He thought it was pretty ridiculous and he wanted to protest, but of course he couldn't go to someone and say, "This is pretty ridiculous." He just sat back and waited for inspiration to strike. It struck. In his company's mess hall he had noticed the flypaper ribbons. They were suspended from the ceiling on either side of the hall—ten on one side of the room, ten on the other.

Hugh devised a special report blank and had it mimeographed. It was in re the number of flies trapped during each twenty-four hour period on the twenty flypaper ribbons. The report included a sketch plan of the mess hall, showing the location of each flypaper ribbon in relation to entrances, tables, lights, windows, kitchen and piano. And each flypaper ribbon was identified by code number. Hugh filled out his first flypaper report, making it as complicated as he was able, showing that during the twenty-four hour period covered by the report, Flypaper

Ribbon X-5 trapped and retained 49 flies. Ribbon Y-2 did even better—63 flies. And so on. He slipped this report in with the day's accumulation and off it went to Washington. Every day thereafter he sent in his fly-paper report. He never did find out exactly what happened in the Pentagon. But he does know that his innovation had quite far-reaching results. About a week after he had sent in his first report, two of his fellow officers called on him.

"You been catching any hell from Washington," they wanted to know, "about some kind of goofy flypaper reports?"

"Why, no," said Hugh. "I don't quite get what you mean."

"It's about a daily report on flypaper ribbons in the mess halls," said one of the officers. "We've been getting directives out of the Pentagon, raising hell with us, wanting to know where our flypaper reports are, why we haven't been sending them in. Do you know anything about flypaper reports?"

"Certainly," said Hugh. "I send mine in every day."

They protested that nobody had told *them* about any flypaper reports, and Hugh showed them the mimeographed blank. They took copies, so they could have some made up for themselves, and they passed the word along to all the other officers and from that day forward every bundle of reports that went in to Washington from the camp included a census of dead flies on the flypaper ribbons. Hugh thinks it's entirely possible that the Pentagon also raised hell with officers at other posts, and set them to work on flypaper reports, and that in the end the daily flypaper report became standard procedure in the Army of the United States.

THE FOLKLORE OF CHAMORRO

Captain Hugh Troy went to the South Pacific with the 21st Bomber Command, 20th Air Force, Major General Curtis LeMay commanding. In the midst of a bombing war General LeMay received word that a government folklorist was arriving on the island for the purpose of gathering native tales, and that he should be accorded full co-operation. General LeMay, somewhat impatient at such doings, thought immediately of Captain Troy and Captain Troy was told to cope with the folklorist and get rid of him as quickly as possible. Captain Troy occupied a tent with three other Intelligence officers and they were brought into Operation Folklore.

Hugh was acquainted with a small native boy named Emmanuel.

Both the boy's parents had been killed by the Japs and he lived with his old grandfather. Emmanuel had learned English in the American school and, of course, also talked Chamorro. He was a bright boy and he would do anything on earth for Hershey bars and comic books. Captain Troy struck a deal with him.

The folklorist arrived and stated his needs to Captain Troy. Among other things he said that he undertood the chief currency in the islands was whisky—that a man with a supply of whisky could get anything he wanted. Accordingly, he had brought along a half case of good whisky and he would be willing to pay at the rate of one bottle for every authentic folk tale Captain Troy could get for him. Captain Troy licked his lips and then spoke of the boy Emmanuel. He said that Emmanuel knew all the important folk tales of the islands, but that the boy spoke nothing but the native tongue. The folklorist said that could be handled—he had with him a technical sergeant who understood the language.

So Captain Troy set up the procedure. The Jap bombers came over each night and during that period there was nothing for the four Intelligence officers to do but lie in their cots and wait for two or three hours till the raid was over. They began calling this period the "Mother Goose Hour." For it was then that, under Captain Troy's able direction, they invented the Chamorro folk tales. Captain Troy, with considerable experience in the production of books for children back home, had a wide knowledge of Mother Goose, Aesop's fables, Andersen, the Grimm Brothers, Uncle Remus, Winnie the Pooh, and so on. He drew on all of these sources in constructing fables and fairy tales for Saipan. Once they had polished up a good folk tale, Captain Troy would meet secretly with little Emmanuel, and drill it into him in English. Then the folklorist, the sergeant-interpreter, and Captain Troy would call upon Emmanuel and his grandfather. The boy played his part beautifully and got five chocolate bars and five comic books for each performance. He would sit at the feet of his grandfather and address his story, in his native tongue, to the old man. The sergeant sat near by, taking it all down, and the scholar from Washington stood with Captain Troy, drinking it all in, unutterably thrilled at the way things were progressing. The boy would finish telling his story, his old grandfather would make a vague sort of guttural sound, and a date would be made for another performance the next day.

Back in camp the sergeant would begin translating at once, and the folklorist was in ecstasies—these tales were absolutely fabulous! They

51

would open up a whole new field of inquiry, for there seemed to be definite European and even some American influences in them. One day Captain Troy asked the sergeant what it was the old grandfather grunted out at the end of each of Emmanuel's stories. The grave-faced sergeant said it was rather difficult to translate literally but that what the old man was saying was, "Horse manure." Apparently the sergeant didn't tell the folklorist.

The thing went on until Captain Troy and his tentmates had all the whisky, and Emmanuel was loaded with chocolate bars and comic books, and then the folklorist flew away, to return jubilantly to Washington with the most magnificent yield of his entire career. If he ever found out the truth, Captain Troy doesn't know it. Nor does he feel much like asking.

"THE CROWN PRINCE" VS. HOLLYWOOD

In 1947 the Crown Prince of Saudi Arabia, His Royal Highness Emir Saud, spent a month touring the United States. Accompanied by a retinue of guards and servitors, robed and hooded and wearing jeweled daggers, the Crown Prince spent several days in Hollywood and the newspapers made a lot of fuss over him. From the time of Douglas Fairbanks on the glittering folks of the movie capital have always gone hog-wild over any kind of royalty.

Jim Moran schemed his scheme. First he studied the manners and habits of Arabian royalty, and informed himself on protocol, and dietary laws. He examined photographs of the royal party and drew up his requirements in the way of costumes, which he got from one of the big wardrobe companies. He enlisted the services of three actors, two to be his servants and one to be his traveling companion. He was fortunate in getting an actor who could actually speak the Crown Prince's language to serve as the companion.

Jim checked the itinerary of the real prince and found out that the royal party was to leave town on a certain evening—he didn't want to run the chance of getting crossed up with Emir Saud himself. On that evening Jim and his three companions got themselves into their robes and whiskers, and had their faces stained. A reporter and a photographer from the Associated Press were called in and briefed on every move that was to be made. And Jim got together his jewels—a double handful of dime store gems plus one magnificent amethyst, which cost him thirty dollars and which might have passed for a diamond worth more than a Metro musical.

Meanwhile a phone call had been made to the management of Ciro's. The Crown Prince and party desired to dine at the restaurant that evening. The Prince required a certain table and its location was specified. The management of Ciro's gave every assurance that the table would be held—that everything possible would be done to make the Prince's visit a memorable one.

That evening a huge limousine pulled up at Ciro's and out of it first came the two servants. Arms folded, they marched in, surveyed the scene, checking details, conferring with the management. Then, everything seeming to be in order, the Prince and his companion entered and walked swiftly to their table. The Prince and companion sat down at the table; the two servants stood behind them.

Ciro's that night was loaded with important customers, mainly from the film colony, and most of them just simply abandoned their manners and stared. Jerry Wald and his orchestra were on the bandstand and whenever they were playing, the dancers, important people of Hollywood, gravitated toward the Prince's table, shoving and almost gouging to get up close and stare. The Prince and his men ignored them.

During a lull in the proceedings the Prince spoke sharply to one of the servants, who bowed low and then walked to the bandstand. In a thick accent he told Jerry Wald that His Royal Highness would enjoy hearing *Begin the Beguine.* No sooner said than done. The orchestra played the number and when it was over, the Crown Prince nodded his appreciation. Then from his belt he took a goatskin pouch and opened it and spread the jewels out on the table, poking through them, looking for a particular one. He settled on a stone (the thirty-dollar amethyst) that looked like a whopping diamond. He handed it to the servant, muttering something, and the servant went again to the bandstand and presented the gem to Mr. Wald. A loud buzzing of conversation passed through the room—everyone had witnessed every detail of the drama. Five or ten minutes later the Associated Press reporter ducked into the men's room, and the attendant there said to him:

"Lawd a mercy! That Mista Wald won't never have to lead no dance bands no more long as he lives. That King out there give him a diamon' big as a hen's aig! That Mista Wald's fixed for life!"

At last the Crown Prince decided it was time to leave. He clapped his hands together. One of the servants adjusted his robes. He and his companions stood up. The dance floor was clear, so the royal party started across it, toward the entrance. All eyes in the place were on them. Suddenly there was a rattling clatter—the goatskin pouch had fallen open and all those jewels had spilled out on the glistening floor. The royal party paused, and the servants started to bend down and pick up the jewels. But His Royal Highness barked a command, waved his hand imperiously, and the four Arabians continued toward the door, leaving the jewels. They had bounced and scattered in all directions and now, almost instantly, Ciro's turned into a mad scramble. Down on the floor went some of the greatest names in Hollywood, both male and female. Chairs and tables were knocked over and some of the waiters joined in the scramble.

The Crown Prince and his people didn't even turn around to look. They marched out of the place, got into their limousine, and departed allegro. Mission accomplished.

"DR. TRUMAN" IN ACTION

In 1947 President Truman was preparing for his trip to South America. He was to be accompanied by correspondents for the wire services, including Tony Vaccaro of the Associated Press. Mr. Vaccaro was first notified that he wouldn't have to take yellow fever shots if he didn't want to. He didn't want to. Mr. Vaccaro had a lively horror of the hypodermic needle and everyone knew it. Then quite suddenly the order was changed and Mr. Vaccaro was escorted, almost by force, to the White House clinic. "I don't believe in shots!" he protested loudly, but the doctor told him to lower his trousers and lie down on a couch, facing the wall—the President himself had decided that everyone on the trip had to take the shots.

Mr. Vaccaro was lying there, facing the wall, hull exposed, when he heard the door open. Footsteps across the room. Cold metal against his hide. Then a voice, "This won't hurt you a bit, Tony." He recognized the voice and turned and found the President of the United States bending over him. In the President's hands was a huge hypodermic device ordinarily used by veterinarians, its cylinder loaded with a red fluid. Mr. Vaccaro took one look at this weapon and started to shriek; then he saw the big grin on Mr. Truman's face, and sighed with relief as he realized it was all a joke. He did manage to say, "Mr. President, I don't ordinarily greet the President of the United States from this position."

54

A MASTER CON MAN REVEALS SOME TRICKS

by Joseph "Yellow Kid" Weil, with W. T. Brannon

Joseph "Yellow Kid" Weil, probably the most famous American confidence man of the twentieth century, reformed late in life. After his release from jail in the 1940's, Weil wrote his memoirs, detailing the methods by which he had relieved an untold number of victims of an estimated eight million dollars. Weil operated hundreds of schemes. Once he tried to go straight and took a job selling a Catholic encyclopedia. But the Weil touch crept in. Calling himself Daniel O'Connell, he told a priest in Flint, Michigan, that the Holy Father, Pius X, had expressed the wish that at least two thousand copies be placed in homes in Flint. The priest bought the first set in town. On the strength of the priest's order, Weil, in three days, sold eighty sets, on which his commission totalled $1,600. But the priest discovered the imposture and withdrew his order. Thereupon, Weil returned to his first love, selling fake or nearly worthless mining and oil stock to big businessmen, including bankers. In this portion from his autobiography, Weil makes it crystal clear why seeing is not always the best reason for believing.

My stock story was basically the same for more than twenty years. However, each victim was different, and the situations varied. Strangely enough, the victims themselves made suggestions that helped me to improve the scheme.

For example, Bobby Sims, heir to a soap fortune in Cincinnati, called my attention to an article in *McClure's,* then one of the nation's leading monthlies. The article, titled "$100,000 A Year," was written by Edward Mott Woolley and was the success story of a mining engineer named Pope Yateman who had taken over an almost worthless mine in Chile and made it pay, though he had been compelled to pipe water for more than a hundred miles. I bought as many copies of that magazine as I could find and fetched them to Chicago. At the first opportunity I took them to Jack Jones, operator of the Dill Pickle Club.

Jones was noted principally for his operation of the Dill Pickle, and only a few knew of his real activities. These were carried on in the daytime when the club was closed. Jones had a well-equipped printing and bookbinding plant in the same building.

Jones employed linotype operators, printers, binders, and one engraver. Their specialty was first editions of famous books. The engraver, whom I knew only as Hymie, was an old-time hand-engraver who could copy anything from fifteenth century bookplates to Uncle Sam's currency. He had a secret process for giving the books the appearance of age. Jones put the volumes, with their yellowed pages, into circulation through underworld channels. For books that had cost him about a dollar to produce he received twenty-five dollars.

In his spare time at night, while Jones was busy at the Dill Pickle Club, Hymie turned his talent to engravings of United States currency. He turned out some pretty good counterfeits. He also agreed to do all my printing and engraving. He made fake letterheads, stock certificates, letters of credit, calling cards, and any other documents I needed.

Now he made a cut that showed me as the famous mining engineer, copied the rest of the article, printed the requisite pages and rebound the magazines. Even an expert would not have known the magazine wasn't exactly as it had been published. These magazines were destined to play a big part in my future activities. Who could resist the advice of the $100,000-a-year mining wizard who had taken copper from a worthless mine in Chile?

I was never so crude as to call anybody's attention to the magazine. As soon as I had picked out the victim, I sent on a couple of men with a copy of the faked magazine. These men called at the town's public library and asked for the file of *McClure's*. They removed the issue containing the Pope Yateman story and substituted the one containing my faked photograph.

Later on I started my negotiations with the victim in the role of Pope Yateman. After some preliminary talks I would mention that I had other matters to attend to and left the victim in the hands of Deacon Buckminster, who had been introduced as my secretary, Mr. Kimball.

"Did you read the article about Mr. Yateman in *McClure's?*" Buck would ask in a casual manner.

"Why, no, I don't believe I did," the victim usually replied. "Do you have a copy of it?"

56

"No, I don't," Buck would say. "But I'm sure you can find it in the public library if you're interested."

Naturally the victim was interested. As soon as he had read this success story and had seen my picture in a magazine on file in the library of his own town he had no doubts at all about my identity. More important, he had new respect for my business acumen. As soon as we had made certain he had read the magazine, my stooges called again at the public library and used their sleight-of-hand to remove the faked magazine and return the original. You can imagine the victim's amazement, after being swindled, to go to the library and look up that article only to find that the picture did not resemble me at all!

A variation of this scheme I used later when Franz von Papen became German ambassador to the United States. I purchased 200 copies of a Sunday issue of the Washington *Post*. They were turned over to Hymie with an article I had written, a photograph of von Papen, and photographs of Buckminster and myself. Hymie had to duplicate the first and last sheets of the main news section in order to get the article in. Prominently displayed was the picture of von Papen, flanked on one side by Buckminster and on the other by me. The article told of the two plenipotentiaries who had accompanied von Papen to America. Their mission was to purchase industrial and mining property for German capitalists and for the German government.

I always carried a copy of this paper in my bag. If I had a victim in tow, I would manage, while removing something from the handbag, to let the paper fall out. The victim would see the spread and would be properly impressed.

"May I have a copy of that?" he would ask.

"I'm sorry," I would reply, "but this is the only copy I have with me. But I shall be happy to send you a copy as soon as I get back to Washington."

The reason for this procedure was that I made it a rule never to let any documentary evidence get out of my hands. Though I displayed thousands of fake letters, documents, stock certificates, etc., to prospective victims, I was always careful to recover them. . . .

As the years passed and we gained experience in the stock swindle other props were added. These included fake letters from J. P. Morgan, Walter C. Teagle, and numerous other big figures in the financial world.

I bought a supply of postage stamps of various foreign countries. By writing letters of inquiry to hotels or firms in large cities all over the world I had a sample not only of their stationery but a specimen post-mark as well. I had postmarking outfits made for all the larger cities of the world. They had loose dates that could be changed at will.

Props played a big part in my success in selling fake stocks. We usually heard of a brokerage house that was moving or going out of business and rented the quarters completely furnished. With the furnishings all in, all we had to do was hire a few girls to look busy. Generally they were students from a business college who needed typing practice so they copied names from the telephone directories.

One of the most impressive layouts I ever used was in Muncie, Indiana. I learned that the Merchants National Bank had moved to new quarters. I rented the old building, which was complete with all the necessary furnishings and fixtures for a banking venture.

For a week before I was ready to take my victim in, I had my stooges call at the new Merchants Bank. Each time they went in they secretly carried away a small quantity of deposit slips, counter checks, savings withdrawal slips, and other forms used by the bank. In that manner we acquired an ample supply to spread over our counters.

I bought as many money bags as I could find, but couldn't get enough. So I had the name of the bank stenciled on fifty salt bags. The money bags, together with large stacks of boodle and some genuine silver, were stacked in the cages of our paying and receiving "tellers."

When I brought the victim in and asked to see the president of the bank we were told we would have to wait. We waited an hour during which the place bustled with activity. People would come in to patronize the bank. Most of these were girls from the local bawdy houses, interspersed with denizens of the underworld—gamblers, thugs, touts. There was a steady stream, and the bank appeared to be thriving. Occasionally a uniformed messenger came in with a money bag. These messengers were streetcar conductors off duty. They wore their regular uniforms but left the badges off their caps. The victim never suspected a thing. Fully convinced that he was in a big active bank, he relied on the president's reference, went into the stock deal with me and ultimately lost $50,000.

I have used banks many times to convince victims of the soundness of my schemes.

Leach and Company was a large brokerage house in Youngstown, Ohio. It had a national reputation. Near by was a bank, one of the largest in Ohio. One day I went in and asked to see the president. I was shown into his private office, a spacious room with a high, paneled ceiling and expensive mahogany furnishings. I told the president I had come to Youngstown to purchase one of the steel mills. (I rather favored the Youngstown Sheet and Tube Company.) I asked his advice, and he said he thought it couldn't go wrong.

"I hope you'll remember this bank when your deal has been completed," he smiled.

"I certainly shall. By the way," I said, "do you happen to have a spare office here in the bank where I might carry on our negotiations? Any room not in use will do."

"I have an excellent place," he replied. "My own office. Any time you want to hold a conference, bring your people in here. I'll get out and you can have complete privacy."

"That is very kind of you," I said. "I'll probably take advantage of your offer within the next two or three days."

Two days later, when I had brought my victim to Youngstown, I called the bank president and asked for the use of his office at 10 A.M. He assured me that it would be available and unoccupied.

I told my victim that we were going to see Mr. Leach, the owner of Leach and Company, who was also interested in buying the stock. When we entered the big office of Leach and Company, I addressed a man in shirt sleeves who stood near one of the counters. (He was my stooge, planted there for the purpose.)

"Can you tell me where we'll find Mr. Leach?" I inquired.

"See that big bank across the street? Well, that's where he spends most of his time. He's the president of that bank."

We went across the street and entered the bank. Near the door a well-dressed man without hat or topcoat walked idly about. He was another stooge.

"Do you have a Mr. Leach here?" I asked.

"We certainly do," the stooge replied. "That's his office over there." He pointed across the room to the door marked PRESIDENT. "There's Mr. Leach now, going towards his office."

The man walking across the floor was our Jimmy Head. He was well dressed and had a dignified bearing. We hurried across the room and caught up with him just as he reached the office door.

"Mr. Leach," I said, "I'm Dr. Weed—Dr. Walter H. Weed. I've come to talk to you about some mining stock I believe you're interested in."

"Ah, yes, Dr. Weed. I've heard a great deal about you. Won't you step into my office where we can talk in private?"

He opened the door and we went in. I led the way, followed by the

59

victim. The room was unoccupied. Jimmy Head had never before seen the inside of this office. But he sat down at the broad desk of the bank president as though he had grown up in these surroundings. We began to discuss the stock deal and remained in the office for about half an hour. Nobody bothered us. By the time we were ready to go, the victim was firmly convinced he was dealing with the biggest banker in Youngstown. Head shook hands with us and saw us to the door. He, too, left as soon as we were out of sight.

A TALK WITH THE YELLOW KID

by Saul Bellow

"I have always affected a pearl stickpin upon my neckwear," says Yellow Kid Weil. The Kid, who is now in his eighties, is an elegant and old-fashioned gentleman; he likes round phrases and leisurely speech. One of the greatest confidence men of his day, he has publicly forsworn crime and announced his retirement. A daughter of his in Florida urges him to pass his remaining years with her, but he prefers Chicago. He will tell you that he knows of no better place, and he has lived in many places. Chicago is his city.

As we stood talking in the lobby of the Sun-Times Building not long ago, a young photographer came running up to the famous criminal, threw an arm about his narrow old shoulders, and said affectionately, "Hi' ya, Kid. Kid, how's it goin'?" At such moments his bearded old face is lit with a smile of deepest pleasure, and looks of modesty and of slyness also steal over it. Bartenders, waitresses, reporters know him. The vanishing race of old intellectuals in the neighborhood of Bughouse Square respects him. Real-estate men, lawyers, even judges and bankers will sometimes greet him. Why should he live elsewhere? He was born in Chicago, his career began there.

It was Bathhouse John Coughlin, Chicago's primitive alderman and illustrious boss, who named him the Yellow Kid. Bathhouse had started out in life as a masseur in the old Brevoort Hotel. When he attained great power he was not too proud to talk to a young fellow like Joe Weil, as the Kid was then known. Weil came often to Coughlin's saloon. An early comic strip called "Hogan's Alley and the Yellow Kid" was then appearing in the New York *Journal,* to which Coughlin subscribed. Weil followed it passionately and Bathhouse John saved the papers for him. "Why, you're the Kid himself," Coughlin said one day, and so Weil acquired the name.

The Kid is now very frail, and it becomes him. His beard very much resembles the one that the late Senator James Hamilton Lewis, a great dandy, used to wear. It is short, parted in the middle, and combed into two rounded portions, white and stiff. Underneath, the Kid's chin is visible, an old man's chin. You think you have met with a happy old quack, a small-time charlatan who likes to reminisce about the wickedness of his past, until you become aware of the thin, forceful, sharp mouth under the trembling hairs of old age. It is the mouth of a masterful man.

He must once have been very imposing. Now there is a sort of fallen nattiness about him. His shoes are beautifully shined, though not in the best of condition. His suit is made of a bold material; it has gone too often to the cleaner, but it is in excellent press. His shirt must belong to the days of his prosperity, for his neck has shrunk and the collar fits loosely. It has a green pattern of squares within squares. Tie and pocket handkerchief are of a matching green. His little face is clear and animated. Long practice in insincerity gives him an advantage; it is not always easy to know when he is being straightforward.

By his swindles he made millions of dollars, but he lost as many fortunes as he made, and he lost them always in legitimate enterprises. It is one of his favorite ironies and he often returns to it. His wife was forever urging him to go straight. He loved her, he still speaks touchingly of her, and for her sake he wanted to reform. It never worked. There was a curse on any honest business that he tried, whether it was giving pianos away as a coffee premium or leasing the Hagenbeck-Wallace circus. The voice of fate seemed to warn him to stay crooked, and he did not ignore it.

The years have not softened his heart toward the victims of his confidence schemes. Of course he was a crook, but the "marks" whom he and his associates trimmed were not honest men. "I have never cheated any honest men," he says, "only rascals. They may have been respectable but they were never any good." And this is how he sums the matter up: "They wanted something for nothing. I gave them nothing for something." He says it clearly and sternly; he is not a pitying man. To be sure, he wants to justify his crimes, but quite apart from this he believes that honest men do not exist. He presents himself as a Diogenes whose lifelong daylight quest for absolute honesty has ended in disappointment. Actually, he never expected to find it.

He is a thinker, the Kid is, and a reader. His favorite authors seem to be Nietzsche and Herbert Spencer. Spencer has always been the favorite of autodidactic Midwestern philosophers, that vanishing species. During the 1920's the Kid belonged to a Bohemian discussion group on the Near North Side called the Dill Pickle Club. Its brainy and colorful eccentrics, poets, painters, and cranks have long been dispersed by adverse winds. Once Chicago promised to become a second London, but it was not to be; bowling alleys and bars increased, bookshops did not. New York and Hollywood took away the artists. Death did the rest. Herbert Spencer also was destined for the dustbin.

But the Kid is still faithful to him; he spends his evenings at his books—so at least he says—meditating upon the laws of society, the sanctioned and the unsanctioned, power and weakness, justice and history. I do not think the Kid loves the weak, and he dislikes many of the strong, especially politicians and bankers. Against bankers he has a strong prejudice. "They are almost always shady," he says. "Their activities are usually only just within the law."

The twilight borderlands of legality attract the Kid's subtle mind. Not long ago he was picked up in the lobby of the Bismarck Hotel on suspicion. He had merely been chatting with one of the guests, he told me, but the manager was worried and phoned the confidence squad. The Kid is used to these small injustices and they do not offend him or disturb his tranquillity. In court he listened attentively to the case preceding his own, that of a bookie.

"Why should this man be fined and punished?" said the Kid when his turn came at the bar. "Why should he be punished for betting when betting is permitted within the confines of the track itself?" The judge, to hear the Kid tell it, was very uneasy. He answered that the state derived revenues from the track. "I would gladly pay revenues to the state," the Kid said, "if I could rent a building within which confidence games would be legal. Suppose the state were to license me. Then confidence men operating outside my building could be arrested and imprisoned. Inside the door licensed operatives would be safe. It makes the same kind of sense, Your Honor." According to the Kid, the judge could make no cogent reply.

Perhaps the Kid's antagonism toward bankers rests on an undivulged belief that he would have made a more impressive banker than any of them. In his swindles, he often enough pretended to be one. . . .

At one time the Kid was actually the legitimate officer of a bank, the American State Bank on South LaSalle Street in Chicago. He and Big John Worthington, a confidence man who closely resembled J. Pierpont Morgan, together paid some seventy thousand dollars and obtained controlling interest. The Kid became a vice-president. He started a racket in phony letters of credit by which he made about three hundred thousand dollars. He was not caught. . . .

Sometimes the Kid posed as a doctor, sometimes as a mining engineer or as a financial representative of the Central Powers, a professor or a geologist. He put magazines and books into circulation from which original photographs were removed and pictures of himself inserted. All his life long he sold nonexistent property, concessions he did not own, and air-spun schemes to greedy men.

The Kid's activities landed him in jail now and then—he has served time in Atlanta and Leavenworth—but he says, and not unbelievably, that he did not have many dull days. His total gains are estimated by "the police and the daily press" at about eight millions. Most of this money he lost on his bad investments or squandered in high living. He loved wild parties, show girls, champagne suppers, European trips. He had his clothes made in Bond Street or Jermyn Street. This English wardrobe is still good; real quality doesn't go out of fashion. But almost everything else is gone.

"Before I reached the years of maturity," the Kid said, "I fell in love with a young woman of the most extraordinary pulchritude. I brought her home one night to dinner. My mother," he said with a bluster of his whiskers and looking gravely at me with the thin diffused blue of his eyes, "was renowned for her perfection in the culinary art. We had a splendid meal and later my mother said to me, 'Joseph, that is a most beautiful young woman. She is so lovely that she cannot be meant for you. She must have been meant for some millionaire.' From that moment I determined that I too would be a millionaire. And I was." The sexual incentive to be rich, the Kid told me, was always very powerful with him.

"I was of a very fragile constitution, unfit for the heavier sort of manual labor. I knew I could not toil like other men. How was I to live? My power lay in words. In words I became a commander. Moreover, I could not lead a tame life of monotony. I needed excitement, variety, danger, intellectual stimulus.

"I was a psychologist," he went on. "My domain was the human

63

mind. A Chinese scholar with whom I once studied told me, 'People always see themselves in you.' With this understanding I entered the lives of my dupes. The man who lives by an idea enjoys great superiority over those who live by none. To make money is not an idea; that doesn't count. I mean a real idea. It was very simple. My purpose was invisible. When they looked at me they saw themselves. I only showed them their own purpose."

There are no longer such operators, says the great confidence man, perhaps jealous of his eminence. Where are they to come from? The great mass of mankind breeds obedient types. They express their protests in acts of violence, not ingeniously. Moreover, your natural or talented confidence man is attracted to politics. Why be a criminal, a fugitive, when you can get society to give you the key to the vaults where the greatest boodle lies? The United States government, according to the Kid, runs the greatest giveaway program in history.

The Kid at one time tried to form a little independent republic upon a small island made of fill, somewhere in Lake Michigan. His object was to make himself eligible under the foreign-aid program.

A public figure, something of a famous man, a dandy and a philosopher, the Kid says that he now frequently does good works. But the confidence squad still keeps an eye on him. Not so long ago he was walking down the street with a certain Monsignor, he tells me. They were discussing a fund drive in the parish. Presently the con squad drew alongside and one of the detectives said, "What you up to, Kid?"

"I'm just helping out the Monsignor here. It's on the level."

The Monsignor assured him that this was true.

The detective turned on him. "Why, you so-and-so," he said. "Aren't you ashamed to be wearin' the cloth for a swindle?"

The thought so enraged him that he took them both to headquarters.

The Kid laughed quietly and long over this morifying error; wrinkled, bearded, wry, and delighted, he looked at this moment like one of the devil's party.

"They refuse to believe I have reformed," he said. The psychology of a policeman, according to the Kid, is strict, narrow, and primitive. It denies that character is capable of change.

So much for the police, in their ancient office of criminal supervision. But what about the criminals? The Kid did not think much of criminal intelligence either. And what does the underworld think of confidence men? I asked. Gangsters and thieves greatly dislike them, he said. They never trust them and in some cases they take a peculiar and moral view of the confidence swindler. He is too mental a type for them.

"The attitude of the baser sort of criminal toward me is very interesting," he said. "They have always either shunned me or behaved with extreme coldness to me. I never will forget a discussion I once had with a second-story man about our respective relations to our victims. He thought me guilty of the highest immorality. Worst of all, in his eyes, was the fact that I openly showed myself to people in the light of day. 'Why,' he said to me with an indescribable demeanor, 'you go right up to them. *They see your face!*' This seemed to him the worst of all deceits. Such is their scheme of ethics," said the Kid. "In their view you should sneak up on people and burglarize them, but to look them in the eyes, gain their confidence, that is impure."

We parted on noisy Wacker Drive, near the Clark Street Bridge. No longer listening to the Kid, I heard the voice of the city. Chicago keeps changing and amazes its old-timers. The streetcars, for instance, are different. You no longer see the hard, wicked-looking, red, cumbrous, cowlike, trampling giant streetcars. The new ones are green and whir by like mayflies. Glittering and making soft electrical sounds, one passed the Kid as he walked toward the Loop. Spruce and firm-footed, with his beard and wind-curled hat, he looked, beside the car, like the living figure of tradition in the city.

THE MERRY ANTICS OF IZZY AND MOE

by Herbert Asbury

Prohibition went into effect throughout the United States on January 16, 1920, and the country settled back with an air of "Well, *that's* settled." There had been a liquor problem. But a Law had been passed. Naturally, there was no longer a liquor problem. . . .

The Anti-Saloon League estimated that prohibition could be enforced for less than $5,000,000 a year, so eager were the people to enter the shining gates of the dry Utopia. Congress appropriated a little more than that amount, enough to set up an enforcement organization and to provide about 1,500 prohibition agents. These noble snoopers, paid an average of about $2,000 a year and hence immune to temptation, were supposed to keep 125,000,000 people from manufacturing or drinking anything stronger than near-beer. They didn't, but two of them made a spectacular try.

In a $14-a-month flat on Ridge Street, in New York's lower East Side, lived a bulbous little man named Isadore Einstein, whom everyone called Izzy. He had been a salesman, both inside and on the road, but was now a minor clerk at Station K of the New York Post Office. It required very shrewd management to feed, house, and clothe his family—his wife and four children and his father—on the meager salary of a postal employee. He was looking for something better, and decided that he had found it when he read in his newspaper about the government's plans to pay enforcement agents up to $2,500 a year.

But James Shevlin, Chief Enforcement Agent for the Southern District of New York, was not enthusiastic about Izzy. "I must say, Mr. Einstein," he said, "you don't look much like a detective." And that was the truth. Probably no one ever looked less like a detective than Izzy Einstein. He was forty years old, almost bald, five feet and five inches tall, and weighed 225 pounds. Most of this poundage was around his middle, so that when he walked his noble paunch, gently wobbling, moved majestically ahead like the breast of an overfed pouter pigeon.

But Izzy was accomplished. Besides English and Yiddish, he spoke German, Polish, and Hungarian fluently, and could make headway, though haltingly, in French, Italian, and Russian. He had even picked up a few words and phrases of Chinese. Moreover, Izzy had a knack of getting along with people and inspiring confidence. No one, looking at his round, jolly face and twinkling black eyes, could believe that he was a government snooper. Down on the lower East Side in New York he was the neighborhood cutup; whenever he dropped into the corner cigar stores and the coffeehouses his witticisms and high spirits never failed to draw an appreciative crowd.

"I guess Mr. Shevlin never saw a type like me," Izzy said afterward. "Maybe I fascinated him or something. Anyhow, I sold him on the idea that this prohibition business needed a new type of people that couldn't be spotted so easy."

Whatever the reason, Izzy got the job.

"But I must warn you," said Shevlin, "that hunting down liquor sellers isn't exactly a safe line of work. Some law violator might get mad and try to crack a bottle over your head."

"Bottles," said Izzy, "I can dodge."

Izzy's first assignment was to clean up a place in Brooklyn which the enforcement authorities shrewdly suspected housed a speakeasy, since drunken men had been seen staggering from the building, and the air for half a block around was redolent with the fumes of beer and whiskey. Several agents had snooped and slunk around the house; one had watched all one afternoon from a roof across the street, and another had hidden for hours in an adjoining doorway, obtaining an accurate count of the number of men who entered and left. But none had been able to get inside. Izzy knew nothing of sleuthing procedures; he simply walked up to the joint and knocked on the door. A peephole was opened, and a hoarse voice demanded to know who was there.

"Izzy Einstein," said Izzy. "I want a drink."

"Oh, yeah? Who sent you here, bud? What's your business?"

"My boss sent me," Izzy explained. "I'm a prohibition agent. I just got appointed."

The door swung open and the doorman slapped Izzy jovially on the back.

"Ho! ho!" he cried. "Come right in, bud. That's the best gag I've heard yet."

Izzy stepped into a room where half a dozen men were drinking at a small, makeshift bar.

"Hey, boss!" the doorman yelled. "Here's a prohibition agent wants a drink! You got a badge, too, bud?"

"Sure I have," said Izzy, and produced it.

"Well, I'll be damned," said the man behind the bar. "Looks just like the real thing."

He poured a slug of whiskey, and Izzy downed it. That was a mistake, for when the time came to make the pinch Izzy had no evidence. He tried to grab the bottle but the bartender ran out the back door with it.

"I learned right there," said Izzy, "that a slug of hooch in an agent's belly might feel good, but it ain't evidence."

So when he went home that night he rigged up an evidence-collector. He put a small funnel in the upper left-hand pocket of his vest, and connected it, by means of a rubber tube, with a flat bottle concealed in the lining of the garment. Thereafter, when a drink was served to him, Izzy took a small sip, then poured the remainder into the funnel while the bartender was making change. The bottle wouldn't hold much, but there was always enough for analysis and to offer in evidence. "I'd have died if it hadn't been for that little funnel and the bottle," said Izzy. "And most of the stuff I got in those places was terrible."

Izzy used his original device of giving his real name, with some variation, more than twenty times during the next five years. It was successful even after he became so well known, and so greatly feared, that his picture hung behind the bar in many speakeasies, that all might see and be warned. Occasionally Izzy would prance into a gin-mill with his badge pinned to his lapel, in plain sight, and shout jovially, "How about a drink for a hard-working prohibition agent?" Seeing the round little man trying so hard to be funny, everyone in the place would rush forward to hand him something alcoholic, and Izzy would arrest them and close the joint.

Once he went into a gin-mill where three huge portraits of himself, framed in what he described as "black, creepy crape," ornamented the back bar. He asked for a drink, and the bartender refused to serve it.

"I don't know you," he said.

"Why," said Izzy, laughing. "I'm Izzy Epstein, the famous prohibition detective."

"Get the name right, bud," growled the bartender. "The bum's name is Einstein."

"Epstein," said Izzy. "Don't I know my own name?"

"Maybe you do, but the low-life you're trying to act like is named Einstein. E-i-n-s-t-e-i-n."

"Brother," said Izzy, "I ain't never wrong about a name. It's Epstein."

"Einstein!" roared the bartender.

"Epstein!" shouted Izzy.

"You're nuts!" yelled the bartender, furiously. "I'll bet you anything you want it's Einstein!"

"Okay," said Izzy. "I'll bet you the drinks."

The bartender called his other customers, and after much argument and pointing to Izzy's pictures, they agreed that the name was Einstein. So Izzy—or rather the government—had to buy nine drinks, and the bartender served them, and shortly after went to jail.

After Izzy had been an enforcement agent for a few weeks, he began to miss his old friend Moe Smith, with whom he had spent many pleasant evenings in the East Side coffeehouses. Like Izzy, Moe was a natural comedian, and, also like Izzy, he was corpulent. He tipped the scales at about 235 pounds, but he was a couple of inches taller than Izzy and didn't look quite so roly-poly. Moe had been a cigar salesman, and manager of a small fight club at Orchard and Grand Streets, New York City, and had invested his savings in a little cigar store, where he was doing well. Izzy persuaded him to put a relative in charge of the store, and to apply for a job as enforcement agent.

68

As soon as Moe was sworn in as an agent, he and Izzy teamed up together, and most of the time thereafter worked as a pair. Their first assignment took them to Rockaway Beach, near New York, where they confiscated a still and arrested the operator. This man apparently took a great liking to Izzy, for after he got out of jail he made several trips to New York especially to urge Izzy to go on a fishing trip with him.

"I'll take you three miles out to sea," he said. "You'll have quite a time."

But Izzy firmly declined the invitation. "Sure he'll take me out to sea," he said, "but will he bring me back? He could leave me with the fishes."

In those early days of the noble experiment everything that happened in connection with prohibition was news, and some of New York's best reporters covered enforcement headquarters. Casting about for a way to enliven their stories and provide exercise for their imaginations, they seized upon the exploits of Izzy and Moe. The two fat and indefatigable agents supplied human-interest material by the yard; moreover, they were extraordinarily co-operative. They frequently scheduled their raids to suit the convenience of the reporters and the newspaper photographers, and soon learned that there was more room in the papers on Monday morning than on any other day of the week. One Sunday, accompanied by a swarm of eager reporters, they established a record by making seventy-one raids in a little more than twelve hours. . . .

Hundreds of stories, a great many of them truthful, were written about Izzy and Moe and their grotesque adventures, and they probably made the front pages oftener than any other personages of their time except the President and the Prince of Wales. . . .

What the newspapers enjoyed most about Izzy and Moe was their ingenuity. Once they went after a speakeasy where half a dozen dry agents had tried without success to buy a drink. The bartender positively wouldn't sell to anyone he didn't know. So on a cold winter night Izzy stood in front of the gin-mill, in his shirt sleeves, until he was red and shivering and his teeth were chattering. Then Moe half-carried him into the speakeasy, shouting excitedly:

"Give this man a drink! He's just been bitten by a frost!"

The kindhearted bartender, startled by Moe's excitement and upset by Izzy's miserable appearance, rushed forward with a bottle of whiskey. Moe promptly snatched the bottle and put him under arrest.

One of Izzy's most brilliant ideas was always to carry something on his raids, the nature of the burden depending upon the character of the neighborhood and of a particular speakeasy's clientele. When he wanted to get into a place frequented by musicians, for example, he carried a violin or a trombone, and if, as sometimes happened, he was asked to play the instrument, he could do it. He usually played "How Dry I Am." On the East Side and in the poorer sections of the Bronx, if the weather permitted, Izzy went around in his shirt sleeves carrying a pitcher of milk, the very pattern of an honest man on his way home from the grocery. Once in Brooklyn he was admitted to half a dozen gin-mills because he was lugging a big pail of dill pickles. "A fat man with pickles!" said Izzy. "Who'd ever think a fat man with pickles was an agent?"

"When Izzy operated on the beaches around New York he always carried a fishing rod or a bathing suit; he had great success one day at Sheepshead Bay with a string of fish slung over his shoulder. The doorman of the Assembly, a café in Brooklyn which catered to judges and lawyers, let him in without question because he wore a frock coat and carried a huge tome bound in sheepskin. Once inside, Izzy opened his book and adjusted a pair of horn-rimmed spectacles and, with lips moving and brow furrowed, marched with stately tread across the room and barged into the bar. Without lifting his eyes from the book, he called sonorously for "a beverage, please," and the fascinated bartender poured a slug of whiskey before he realized what he was doing. When Izzy and Moe visited Reisenweber's, a famous and expensive resort on Broadway, they carried two lovely blondes and wore "full-dress tuxedos," with rings on their fingers, sweet-smelling pomade on their hair, and huge imitation-pearl studs in their shirt fronts. The headwaiter asked them for references when they ordered liquor, and Izzy searched his pockets and pulled out the first card he found. It happened to be the card of a rabbi, with which Izzy planned to ensnare a sacramental-wine store. But the headwaiter, a man of scant perception, bowed deferentially and sold them a bottle of whiskey. "He deserved to be arrested," said Izzy, indignantly. "Imagine! A rabbi with a blonde and no beard!"

Up in Van Cortlandt Park, in New York City, near the public playing fields, was a soft-drink establishment which was suspected of being one of the retail outlets of a big rum ring. Many complaints were made to enforcement headquarters that customers had become tipsy after a few shots of the soda water sold in the place; one woman wrote that by mistake her milk shake had been filled with gin. Bad gin, too, she added. The job of getting the evidence was given to Izzy. It proved a difficult task, for the owner of the joint would sell liquor to no one he didn't know personally. So on a Saturday afternoon in November Izzy assembled a group of half a dozen dry agents, clad them in football uniforms, and smeared their arms and faces with fresh dirt. Then Izzy tucked a football under his arm, hung a helmet over his ears, and led them whooping and rah-rahing into the suspected speakeasy, where they shouted that they had just won the last game of the season and wanted to break training in a big way. The speakeasy owner, pleased at such a rush of business, sold each agent a pint of whiskey. "Have fun, boys," he said. "The same to you," said Izzy, handing him a summons.

Flushed with this striking success, which showed that at heart he was a college boy, Izzy went to Ithaca, N.Y., to investigate a complaint by officials of Cornell University that some soda fountains near the campus were not confining their sales to pop. Izzy disguised himself as an undergraduate by putting on a little cap and a pair of white linen knickers, not so little, and for several days strolled about the campus. He hummed snatches of Cornell songs which he had learned, and played safe by addressing everyone with a mustache as "Professor," and everyone with a beard as "Dean." Having located the soda fountains which sold liquor, he dashed into them one by one, establishing himself as a student by shouting, "Sizzle Boom! Sizzle Boom! Rah! Rah! Rah!" The speakeasy boys thought he was a comedian, which indeed he was, and they gladly sold him all the booze he wanted, after which he went from place to place distributing "diplomas," or summonses.

From Cornell, and without the blessing of the student body, Izzy rushed into Harlem to investigate a complaint about a grocery store. . . . Izzy disguised himself as a Negro, with his face blackened by burnt cork and a rich Southern accent rolling off his tongue. He visited the store and awaited his turn in a long line of impatient customers. He found that to buy a half-pint of whiskey (four dollars) a customer asked for a can of beans. If he wanted gin (two dollars) he asked for tomatoes. Izzy bought both beans and tomatoes and came back next day with a warrant and a truck. Besides the groceryman, he hauled away four hundred bottles of gin, some empty cans, a canning machine, three barrels of whiskey, and a barrel of pickles which contained one hundred small bottles of gin. . . .

The trail of illegal liquor led Izzy and Moe into some mighty queer places, but they followed wherever it led, and were always ready with the appropriate disguise. Dressed as a longshoreman, Izzy captured an Italian who used his cash register as a cellarette; its drawers were filled with little bottles of booze. In the guise of a mendicant, Izzy pawned an old pair of pants for two dollars in Brooklyn, and snooping about the pawnshops a bit found ten thousand dollars' worth of good liquor wrapped in clothing that had been left as pledges. He got into the Half Past Nine Club, on Eighth Avenue, as a prosperous poultry salesman, playing tipsy and carrying a sample, and found a large stock of liquor in a stuffed grizzly bear. . . .

For more than five years the whole country laughed at the antics of Izzy and Moe, with the exception of the ardent drys, who thought the boys were wonderful, and the bootleggers and speakeasy proprietors, who thought they were crazy and feared them mightily. And their fear was justified, for in their comparatively brief career Izzy and Moe confiscated 5,000,000 bottles of booze, worth $15,000,000, besides thousands of gallons in kegs and barrels and hundreds of stills and breweries. They smashed an enormous quantity of saloon fixtures and equipment, and made 4,392 arrests, of which more than 95 per cent resulted in convictions. No other two agents even approached this record. . . .

Izzy and Moe made many spectacular raids in Chicago, Detroit, and other cities ruled by the gangsters and the beer barons, but they never encountered Al Capone, Johnny Torrio, Frankie Yale, or any of the other great hoodlums who were the real beneficiaries of the Eighteenth Amendment. If they had, there is little doubt that they would have taken the triggermen in their stride, for neither Izzy nor Moe lacked courage. Izzy didn't approve of guns, and never carried one. Moe lugged a revolver around occasionally, but in five years fired it only twice. Once he shot out a lock that had resisted his efforts, and another time he shot a hole in a keg of whiskey. Izzy said later that guns were pulled on him only twice. The first time was on Dock Street, in Yonkers, N. Y., where he had spent a pleasant and profitable evening with raids on five speakeasies. To make it an even half dozen, he stepped into a sixth place that looked suspicious, bought a slug of whiskey for sixty cents, and poured it into the funnel in his vest pocket. While he was arresting the bartender, the owner of the joint came into the bar from another part of the house.

"He pulled an automatic from behind the bar," wrote Izzy. "She clicked but the trigger jammed. It was aimed right at my heart. I didn't like that. I grabbed his arm and he and I had a fierce fight all over the bar, till finally I got the pistol. I don't mind telling you I was afraid, particularly when I found the gun was loaded."

On another occasion an angry bartender shoved a revolver against

72

Izzy's stomach. But Izzy didn't bat an eye; he calmly shoved the gun aside.

"Put that up, son," he said, soothingly. "Murdering me won't help your family."

Fortunately, the bartender had a family, and Izzy's warning brought to his mind a vision of his fatherless children weeping at the knee of their widowed mother, who was also weeping. He stopped to think. While he was thinking, Moe knocked him cold. . . .

During the summer of 1925 the almost continual stories about Izzy and Moe in the newspapers got on the nerves of high prohibition enforcement officials in Washington, few of whom ever got mentioned in the papers at all. National headquarters announced that any agent whose name appeared in print in connection with his work would be suspended, and perhaps otherwise punished, on the ground that publicity brought discredit to the service. At the same time a high official called Izzy to Washington and spoke to him rather severely. "You get your name in the newspaper all the time, and in the headlines, too," he complained, "whereas mine is hardly ever mentioned. I must ask you to remember that you are merely a subordinate, not the whole show." For a while Izzy really tried to keep away from the reporters and out of the papers, but both he and Moe had become public personages, and it was impossible to keep the newspapermen from writing about them. When they refused to tell what they had done, the reporters invented stories about them, so a stream of angry denials and protests continued to come from Washington.

Finally, on November 13, 1925, it was announced that Izzy and Moe had turned in their gold badges and were no longer prohibition agents. Izzy's story was that he had been told he was to be transferred to Chicago. He had lived in New York since he was fifteen years old, and had no intention of ever living anywhere else, so he refused to go, and "thereby fired myself." Government officials, however, said that Izzy and Moe had been dismissed "for the good of the service." . . .

Both Izzy and Moe went into the insurance business, and did well. They dropped out of the public eye, and remained out except for an occasional Sunday feature story, and a brief flurry of publicity in 1928, when Izzy went to Europe and returned with some entertaining accounts of his adventures.

THE MASTER MAKER OF THE QUEER

by Archie Mcfedries

There were, in the closing years of the nineteenth century, just three criminals who, operating in both the United States and Europe, were clever enough to induce continual headaches among the high brass of Pinkerton's National Detective Agency, Scotland Yard and the French Sureté. One, Max Shinburn, was the king of the bank burglars. A second, old Adam Worth, became the elder statesman of the international criminal realm, a sort of underworld Bernard Baruch who, from Olympian heights, advised other criminals and dreamed up master capers. The third, a German by the name of Charles Becker, alias the Dutchman, was a counterfeiter—by all odds the greatest counterfeiter in history.

Becker did his own engraving, personally printed his stuff, and set up fake brokerage houses for slipping it into legitimate commerce. In a quarter of a century of operations here and abroad he manufactured and dumped millions of dollars in phony currency and securities in various cities in this country and in England, France, Italy and Germany.

Even the United States Secret Service, which in its long and impressive history has seldom been thrown for a loss by even the best of counterfeiters, was never able to catch up with Becker. The story is told about a Secret Service operative comparing a Becker $10 bill, known to be a counterfeit because of its serial number, with a genuine one, and disconsolately remarking, "No wonder we can't catch up with who's making this stuff. Why, it's better than ours!"

Perfectionist that he was, the Dutchman frequently destroyed large batches of his work, representing months of arduous toil, because the stuff, while satisfactory to everybody else, including his victims, wasn't, for some real or imaginary reason, satisfactory to him. Once, in England, he put a match to almost £50,000 in Bank of England currency because, when he crumpled it, it made an infinitesimally different sound

74

than that made when he crumpled a genuine note. Another time, in San Francisco, Becker destroyed a small fortune in United States $10 gold-backs because, his acute olfactory sense told him, they *smelled* different than Uncle Sam's product.

Realizing that a man under suspicion would have two strikes against him if he couldn't establish a practically uninterrupted record of gainful employment, Becker was always engaged by day in some legitimate enterprise. He was, by turn, a stockbroker in London and a saloonkeeper in Brooklyn. He was, in fact, a pillar of the community in Brooklyn. A flesh-and-blood Jekyll-Hyde, he went to a Lutheran church on Sundays where, ironically enough, he took up the collection, and at night, when somebody else tended bar for him, descended to a private chamber in the cellar and worked far into the early hours at his counterfeiting.

Becker was a man of Spartan habits. He neither smoked nor drank, ate sparingly, and was a marathon walker. Despite the fact that he made important money, both legitimately and illegitimately, he was a frugal man. He had hordes of money—money that ran well into the millions of dollars—hidden away in places that only he knew about.

Although springing from middle-class people in Wurttemberg, in central Germany, and receiving only a meager formal education, Charles Becker had a genuine thirst for knowledge and became a truly cultivated man. Educating himself, he was able to read and speak, in addition to German and English, French, Spanish and Italian. He was a devotee of classical literature, music and art. He attended concerts and the opera in whatever city he happened to be. He knew his way through the corridors of the great art museums of Europe, and the Metropolitan in New York, as well as he knew his way through the streets of Brooklyn. His great love, though, was the Louvre in Paris. From time to time, when manufacturing money and French government securities in Paris, the Dutchman spent much of his daylight time in the Louvre.

The Dutchman was born in 1846, the only son of a Wurttemberg butcher who, because of the frail health of his wife and only daughter (who was younger than Charles), and resultant doctors' and hospital bills, had, all his adult life, been fighting a delaying action with the wolf at the door. Among Becker's earliest memories, he was one day to tell the Pinkertons, were those of his old man tearing his hair as he sat under an oil lamp at the kitchen table of a night, trying to think up ways and means of keeping out of sight of his creditors. The elder Becker's financial plight inculcated in the boy what was to be a lifelong fear of insolvency.

75

Becker as a boy was a gifted artist. At the age of eight, he was drawing pictures of his parents and sketching street scenes in his native Wurttemberg. But he was more than an artist; he was equipped with what amounted to photographic sight. He could look at a face or an object, study it for a minute or so, and then reproduce it on paper without so much as glancing at it a second time. When he was only ten, Charles was so good at briefly studying a signature and then reproducing it that people from all over Wurttemberg asked him to reproduce their signatures and then stood around in open-mouthed admiration at the feat.

Charles was taken out of school at the age of twelve so that he could support the family. His father's butcher business was going from bad to worse and so was the health of his mother and sister, to both of whom he was devoted. Charles, because of his artistic bent, become apprenticed to an engraver—the only one in town.

At the age of fourteen Charles knew more about engraving than his boss did and, on all counts, turned out work superior to that of his employer. But, in the custom of the day, the employer continued to pay him coolie wages.

As the years passed, Becker began to feel like a horse galloping on a treadmill. When he reached the age of twenty, he was still an apprentice to the engraver. Since there wasn't another engraving establishment in Wurttemberg, Becker was stuck. There didn't seem to be any promising employment in any other line in town and going to another city to get employment in the engraving line was out of the question for living expenses away from home would eat up all his pay.

Charles was twenty when he fell in love. The girl, Clara Bechtel, was a shopkeeper's daughter—a soundly constructed little blonde with a beautiful and guileless face and the instincts of a bitch.

What with working for coolie wages, and having to throw his earnings into the family pot, young Becker was in a genuine fix. It was now that he found himself in company with that great legion of men who have done foolish things for a woman. He went to a jewelry store in a neighboring town, palmed himself off as somebody he wasn't, selected an engagement ring, and paid the jeweler with a check to which he affixed the signature of one of Wurttemberg's leading citizens.

Clara Bechtel was very happy with the ring, and Charles was very happy at securing the franchise to Clara, but the police were far from enthusiastic about the rubber check. They soon caught up with Charles. Clara Bechtel lost the ring and took the franchise away from Becker.

76

But, since Becker's old man was such an upright citizen, and since Charles' mother and sister were in such poor health, some prominent Wurttemberg citizens talked the jeweler into dropping his charges. Thus young Becker escaped prison. But he couldn't get a job of any kind, in his home town or anywhere else in Germany. It wasn't that he didn't try. He bummed his way throughout the country, seeking employment of any kind. But always he was asked to supply a dossier on his past—something he was in no position to do.

Then, within the space of four months, he suffered a triple blow. His mother died. Then his sister died. Then his father popped off with a heart attack. Two doctors ascribed the deaths of Becker's mother and sister as at least partially due to the disgrace brought on the family by Charles and the death of the father wholly due to grief over the loss of his wife and his daughter. The way Becker was one day to rationalize the whole thing was that had he had enough of his own money to buy an engagement ring for Clara Bechtel, the deaths of his mother, sister and father would not have come about when they did.

When his father was laid away, in a grave alongside those of his wife and his daughter, Charles went to the gravesides one night and made a vow. He vowed that money, the thing that had brought about disgrace and triple tragedy, would, for the remainder of his days, be his sole motivating force. He would, by any means at his command, accumulate money and plenty of it. Thus it was that in the year of 1867, when Charles Becker was twenty-one, he bummed his way westward to France and shipped as a stoker on a passenger steamer to New York.

Becker's first work for pay in the New York underworld came as a result of a contact with an old-time house burglar named Jenkins. Jenkins was in the market for a look-out. Jenkins, who was impressed by Becker's obvious smartness, and by his looks, hired him on the spot. Becker, at twenty-one, was a compact, alert-looking fellow—sober-looking, shrewd and utterly mirthless.

One dark night Becker loitered in the shadows on Fifth Avenue while Jenkins jimmied his way into a Fifth Avenue mansion. He had no sooner climbed in the window and closed it behind him than a cop swung around the corner. Becker, spotting the cop, stood there in the shadows, hardly daring to breathe. Then he heard a crash from within the mansion. Jenkins had knocked over a piece of furniture.

Becker saw the cop stop and stiffen at the sound of the noise. The bluecoat was certain to go in and investigate. Becker's problem was to get the cop out of there, so that Jenkins could get out of the mansion

77

before the occupants, awakened by the crash, discovered him. Becker materialized from the shadows, panting as if from a hard run, and yelled to the cop, "Officer, please come quick! A man is being robbed around the corner." When he got around the corner with the cop, Charles looked around, scratched his head and said, "They must have taken the man *with* them."

"They? Was there two robbers?"

"Oh, no sir. *Three.*"

The cop and Becker split up, to look for some trace of the robbers. A couple of hours later, Becker tied up with Jenkins in a thieves' lair down near the Hudson River waterfront. "Boy," said Jenkins, "you've got a great future ahead of you."

Becker traveled up and down the Atlantic seaboard with Jenkins for three years, acting as a look-out. If he saw a cop beginning to act in a suspicious manner in front of the place where Jenkins was plying his trade, Becker would yell at the top of his voice, "Help! Help, police!" The yell from a half block away served two purposes. It drew the flat-foot from the house where Jenkins was and it served notice to Jenkins to get to hell out of there. Becker, who could out-run anything carrying a nightstick, would keep yelling, "Help! Police!" as he ran further and further away from where Jenkins was, drawing the cop along with him but eventually leaving him puffing far behind.

Never deviating from his ambition to pile up a fortune, Becker was spending all his spare time preparing for the future. Like a fellow fresh out of college, looking around for what seemed to offer the best on the long haul, Becker devoted part of his spare time to boning up on under-world scuttlebutt, and the rest of it reading—reading practically every kind of nonfiction he could lay hands on, from philosophy through biography and history to comparative religion.

Becker decided to make counterfeiting his life work. There were two basic reasons for this decision. Engraving was the most important adjunct of the counterfeiting art and he was a superb engraver. The counterfeiting field was, unlike several other professions outside the law, uncrowded. This was because it demanded infinitely more skill (and of a highly specialized nature) than the average criminal could easily acquire.

Becker shuddered when he studied some of the queer that the boys were shoving. The art work was amateurish, the paper was terrible, the green ink on bills of low denomination was bluish and the gold ink on the classy stuff was sometimes practically pink.

78

It was a tenet of Becker's philosophy that haste makes waste. He wanted to prepare himself thoroughly before entering his life's work. While he knew how to engrave bills, he knew nothing about inks, dyes and bleaches. So he hunted around until he got a job in a New York chemical plant.

Stealing materials from the plant, in quantities so small that they were never missed, he set up a little laboratory in a furnished room he was occupying down near the waterfront. His first project was to acquire paper on which to print his counterfeits. Becker decided that Uncle Sam was putting out the best paper possible for his purposes, so he decided to use it. After considerable experimentation, Becker was able to bleach a $1 bill white without destroying the paper. Very few men have been able to do this in the long history of bogus money.

Now that he had a method of getting paper, Becker engraved a copy of a $10 bill. Then he went out and bought a small printing press. The first sample bill didn't quite satisfy the Dutchman. Neither did the second. Nor the third, the tenth, nor the hundredth. Becker, burning each bill after he had detected something wrong with it, worked for more than a year before he found one that satisfied him. The result was that he came up with the kind of bill that prompted the Secret Service operative to remark that Becker's stuff was better than the genuine.

Becker, bold as brass, went into a bank with the first piece of queer that satisfied him. He slapped it on the counter of a paying teller's cage and asked the man to break it up into ones for him. The teller, from force of habit, began to make a cursory examination of the bill. "What's the matter?" asked Becker. "Do you think it's *counterfeit?*" "Oh, not at all, sir," said the teller. "I guess I just do this to all bills. Now how did you say you wanted your change—in ones?"

Still holding his job in the chemical plant, Becker began to roll out ten spots on his little home press. From the beginning, he was a man who believed first in quality, then quantity. He made only a few bills each week, averaging about ten. He usually passed the money in banks, asking that it be converted into bills of smaller denomination. . . . He knew that if he could get away with passing Uncle Sam's queer on banks he could, in the future, get away with practically anything, anywhere, in the counterfeiting line. . . .

Somehow or other, the word got around the New York underworld that Charles Becker had perfected a fine $10 bill. It was his erstwhile employer, Jenkins, who tipped him off. "Charlie," Jenkins said, "you've

79

got to cut a lot of people in on what you're up to or they'll squeal on you."

Becker was outraged. The big boys had wanted no part of him when he had hit the country, a greenhorn, trying to get a toehold. Now that he had something, five years after, they wanted in on it. "I don't know who told you to tell me this," he told Jenkins. "But you can take them an answer from me. You can tell them to go to hell."

Knowing that the big boys were a vengeful crew, likely to rat on him, Becker took his counterfeiting equipment over to the New Jersey meadows one night and buried it. What he had learned about bleaching and inking could be utilized in Europe as well as in America. Anyway, he would one day come back to America, under more auspicious conditions, dig up his equipment, and take up where he had been forced to leave off.

Accomplices now began to populate Becker's realm of thought. He had decided that in the long haul he would have to be more than a lone wolf if he wanted to clean up important money. The time was certain to come, he knew, when some of his stuff would be recognized. That being so, there would be a chance that he would be recognized, too. Thus he would have to insulate himself from possible danger.

When thinking of accomplices, Becker instinctively thought of a young fellow named Little Joseph Elliott—of the diminutive stature and the baby face. Little Joe, according to the best available information on the fellow, came from an aristocratic family in upper New York State. Society life had palled on him and he had come down to New York. The excitement of the underworld had appealed to him and he had caught on doing odd jobs for the big boys when the big boys were in need of a guileless countenance. At night, Little Joe traveled with the upper-crust set attending parties and squiring debutantes around.

Elliott had one failing. He was a kleptomaniac. He just couldn't control his impulse to steal things. "I understand," Becker said to Little Joe, "that you empty ladies' pocketbooks when you go to big parties."

Elliott just looked at Becker and nodded.

"Aren't you afraid you'll get caught?"

"Nobody ever suspects me," said Elliott. "I take only small things that I can stuff in my socks and my shoes. Then I leave my empty wallet in the bedroom where I've gone through the pocketbooks and go downstairs and start to dance. Then I stop and scream that I've been robbed. That's all there is to it."

Becker outlined for Elliott his plans for the future—the setting up of fake brokerage houses in Europe. "You could be the messenger boy,"

80

he explained to Elliott. "You look young enough." Elliott was all for it; there would be some fine stuff to lift in Europe.

Needing two other men besides Little Joe Elliott for what he had in mind for Europe, Becker began negotiations with a nondescript, thirty-ish character named Joe Chapman, who had worked in a Chicago bank before taking home some of the inventory and getting a jolt in Joliet for it, and a middle-aged Russian jack-of-all-crimes named Carlo Sisco-vitch—a tall brooding man who had a passion for playing the violin.

There were several conferences in the back rooms of waterfront saloons at which Becker, the youthful executive, talked over his plot for the future with Elliott, Chapman and Siscovitch. There was never the slightest question among the other three that Becker was boss. It was Siscovitch, an eager man, who asked Becker when he planned to take off for Europe. Becker told the man not to think so hastily. There was groundwork to be laid in the U.S.A. before the departure for Europe. It was Becker's thought to arrive in Europe with cash, and plenty of it, so that he wouldn't have to begin operations with a speed not commensurate with safety.

Becker said he thought he would need about $100,000. Why so much, the boys wanted to know. Now Becker uncorked something that had never been thought of in the underworld up to that time—an employer-employe relationship that would no doubt meet with the approval of present-day labor leaders. Becker was going to put the boys on a salary, whether they worked or not. He was, in short, going to give them security.

Now Little Joe Elliott brought up the question of where, when and how Becker intended to get the hundred grand to take off with. "We'll rob a bank," Becker said quietly.

Becker instructed Elliott, Chapman and Siscovitch to start growing beards and to stand by. Then he got a leave of absence from his job in the chemical plant on the grounds of ill health. Thorough fellow that he was, he showed his employers a forged doctor's certificate. Starting to cultivate a crop of spinach himself, he took off for Philadelphia. Not finding what he wanted in Philly, he dropped down to Baltimore.

In Baltimore Becker found exactly what he was looking for—an empty building on South Street that was flush up against the back of the Third National Bank. The back of the building was of red brick. Dropping into the bank to get change for one of his counterfeit $10, Becker saw that the rear of the bank was of yellow brick. The strong box's vault, Becker noticed, was in the rear of the jug.

In those days vaults were not impregnable as they virtually are today.

It was Becker's guess that the rear of the Third National's vault comprised nothing more than the rear of the bank building's brick wall.

By the time Becker returned to New York, the beards of his three employes were sprouting in fine fashion. And so was his own. Studying the three, Becker decided that Siscovitch, a black-haired man, should be the man to go to Baltimore and rent the empty building. "But before you go," he told the Russian, "I'll bleach your hair and beard blond."

Arriving in Baltimore, Siscovitch, under the double cover of a beard and a bleach, went into the offices of John S. Gittings, a private banker who owned the empty building, and palmed himself off as a representative of Stabler & Company, a big Milwaukee grain and feed outfit. "We are going to open a Baltimore branch," the Russian told the banker, "and we think that empty building next to the Third National Bank would be ideal for our purposes."

Siscovitch, following Becker's instructions, started to haggle about the price of the rent. That was sound psychology; anyone up to anything would hardly be constrained to nurse nickels. The Russian and the banker struck a compromise, papers were signed for a six-month lease, with an option for a three-year renewal if business warranted.

Next week the boys moved in, all of them hiding behind crops of dyed spinach. The place soon took on the atmosphere of a branch of Stabler & Company, with big sacks of grain and bottles of samples on the desks of the four crooks, and the boys busy at their desk shuffling papers or darting in and out, obviously in quest of business.

Becker began to run into the bank almost daily to get a bill changed, the while making careful mental measurements of the inside and outside of the jug in its relation to the ground floor of the phony quarters.

Next Becker went out, bought a huge map of the United States, placed it over the spot in the wall that corresponded to the rear of the vault and stuck colored pins in the map to represent activity at Stabler & Company up and down the Atlantic seaboard. He estimated that it would take two nights to get through to the bank's vault—one night to remove the red bricks from the Stabler wall, and one night to remove the yellow bricks that comprised the rear of the bank's vault. The plot was to remove the Stabler bricks on a Friday night, keep the hole in the wall covered with the map all day Saturday, and then, on Saturday night go through to the bank, get whatever was there, and get out of town.

First, though, there was a cop to be cultivated—the cop who had the night beat on South Street. This particular cop, Becker discovered, was a nosy character. It would be necessary to condition the cop to the fact that the representatives of the grain company often had to work nights. "Golly," Becker would say, as he left the false front about midnight, "but I'm tired. Work. Work. Work. Nothing but work."

There would come the happy night, Becker knew, when he would be leaving the South Street front with a bag stuffed with money. So he started leaving the place with a bag stuffed with grain. One night his suitcase came open and some of the grain spilled on the pavement just as the cop was approaching. The cop helped Becker put most of the grain back into the bag and Becker gave him a couple of cigars.

Like most well-organized plots, the actual break-through into the bank was practically anticlimactic. Becker, accompanied by his little helpers, was back in New York, with $416,000 in cash, before the Third National Bank of Baltimore opened for business on the Monday morning. Everybody shaved off his beard, Siscovitch dying his hair back to its natural color, and Becker, wouldn't you know it, reported back to work at the chemical plant.

Little Joe Elliott, Chapman and Siscovitch were champing at the bit, hot to get off to Europe. But Becker, putting them on his payroll at $1,000 a month each, with a promise of a raise within a year, instructed caution. The New York police and the Pinkertons would be watching the passengers on all outgoing transatlantic liners for at least a year. And Siscovitch and Chapman, both of whom were known to the cops and the Pinkertons, might find it embarrassing to have to explain why they were leaving the country.

The Dutchman was twenty-seven years old when, in company with Little Joe Elliott, he landed in London. Becker, posing as a young business executive, bought a handsome three-story brick house on Leamington Road. Little Joe, assuming the role of an idle playboy, went to a hotel. Siscovitch and Chapman came over separately. The plot was that whenever a meeting was necessary all four men were to get together at the Blue Anchor Inn, a thieves' lair down by the East India docks.

First thing Becker did was to set himself up in a modest brokerage office in London's financial district. Becker hired a couple of male clerks and, with the clerks, started to hustle around for business—bond, brokerage or financial business of any kind, so long as it was strictly legitimate. In a matter of months, the fellow was making expenses. Not only that, but the future in legitimate enterprise looked most promising.

But the Dutchman's real work went on at night in a special room on the third floor of the house on Leamington Road—the work of counterfeiting. He assigned Little Joe, Chapman and Siscovitch to pick up, bit by bit so as not to arouse suspicion, everything he would need to make money—dyes, bleaches, inks, acids and engraving and printing equipment. Becker employed two maids and both were instructed never to try to tamper with the padlock he kept on the door of his secret room.

Becker decided that his first production would be a £5 English note, then the equivalent of $25 in American money. Bleaching the paper of authentic £1 notes was simple for the Dutchman. But Becker had to labor by night for more than nine months before he created an engraving that satisfied him. And when he got the right engraving, he wasn't satisfied with the ink.

Elliott, Chapman and Siscovitch, who had meantime been raised to the equivalent of $2,000 a month each, should have been happy, but they weren't. Idleness palled on them and Becker began to fear that Chapman and the Russian might take on jobs for somebody else and run the risk of getting caught.

When Becker finally produced a £5 note that satisfied him, he took it to a bank. He told a teller that he had acquired the note from a man he was suspicious of and wanted to know if the note was counterfeit. The teller examined it, pronounced it genuine, and told Becker he had nothing to worry about.

But Becker, the painstaking Teuton, was still not satisfied. He went to, of all places, Scotland Yard with the bill. There he told the same story he had told at the bank. He walked out of the Yard with the bill in his pocket and the assurance that it was genuine.

Now Becker was really ready to roll. He set Siscovitch and Chapman up in a second brokerage office several blocks from his own. His own brokerage establishment had by now caught on sufficiently for him to send some business elsewhere. Thus whenever anybody came in to sell, rather than to buy, securities, the Dutchman sent them around to the Siscovitch-Chapman outlet.

Siscovitch and Chapman were now going under assumed names, the better to insulate themselves from, for example, William A. Pinkerton, a snoopy man who seemed constantly to be either arriving in or departing from London. The boys were calling their front Williamson and Larkin, Ltd. And Little Joe, wearing a handsome purple-and-gold uniform, was the messenger boy for the Siscovitch-Chapman front, dashing through London's streets on his bicycle at such a fast clip that he created an entrancing purple-and-gold blur.

84

The whole setup quickly shook down into a cozy one for the Dutchman. The good securities that were bought with the bad money at the phony brokerage house were turned over to Becker's legitimate front and sold there for genuine money. Then Becker stuffed the genuine money in safety deposit drops under assumed names.

Since Becker was such a meticulous counterfeiting craftsman, loath to so much as entertain the idea of letting anyone assist him in order to step up production, he eventually faced a problem. The phony front of Williamson and Larkin, Ltd., was unloading the Dutchman's spurious £25 notes in return for genuine securities faster than Becker could turn the stuff out. A man with superb physical stamina, Becker sometimes worked at his counterfeiting right through the night, snatching only a couple of hours of shut-eye before checking in at his legitimate investment front. But even that was not enough to meet the demand for his phony £25-ers. So he decided to bring out two new issues—£100 notes and £500's.

It was a whole year before Becker produced the two new issues to his satisfaction. He made his usual test before beginning to put the stuff out in quantity. He went to a bank with samples and the samples were pronounced genuine.

Within a year, by 1876, when Becker was thirty, his counterfeits were clearing through the fake brokerage house run by Chapman and Siscovitch on an average of £5,000 a month. His legitimate brokerage house had achieved sufficient success for him to meet operating expenses with enough left over to speculate in the market. Thus he began to clean up as an honest speculator. Everything considered, the Dutchman was salting away an average of half a million dollars a year.

The Dutchman now had a staff of four in his legitimate investment business and he began to take off more and more time, the better to travel on the Continent. He was on familiar terms with the head waiters in the best restaurants and hotels in the French capital and, although always a spare eater, he was now a knowledgeable and fastidious one. Although having little taste for society as such, Becker joined a couple of clubs. Occasionally he threw a party at his Leamington Road home.

Women, like everything else, always came second to money with Becker. When the mood was on him, he would have a lady in for the night. But, all things considered, he probably got more kick out of turning out those fake notes than he did out of the ladies.

It was now, as he was well into his fourth year of operations in Europe, that the Dutchman decided to open branch offices in Paris—one legitimate, one illegitimate. Opening a branch of his legitimate firm of Charles Becker, Investments, on Rue Scribe and hiring some French help was simple. Becker was able to speak French.

Setting up a phony front through which to funnel counterfeit stuff took a bit of doing. He had to scout around for a manager of the false front. Becker looked up George Wilkes, bogus English nobleman and confidence man de luxe, and outlined the fine points of what he hoped would be a long and profitable association. He informed Wilkes that there would be no cut of the swag, only a salary. Wilkes blinked. He had never heard of anything of the kind. In his long career as a confidence man he had always been declared in for a juicy slice of the take.

No matter. This time it would be different. "You've been arrested several times and in jail three or four times," Becker pointed out. Correct. "Well, you'll be running no risk with me. My counterfeits are so perfect that they are never detected until it is too late to trace their origin."

How much, Wilkes wanted to know, would Becker pay him? A salary of £1,000 a month until things in Paris got rolling, then twice that amount. It would take anywhere from nine months to a year. "And I'll be on salary all that time—and doing nothing for it?" asked Wilkes. Becker nodded and looked hard at Wilkes. "My friend," said Wilkes, looking for all the world as if he had just located a pigeon, "it's a bargain."

In Paris, Becker bought a handsome residence within walking distance of the Louvre. He worked by day in his legitimate brokerage office and at night at his counterfeiting work in a secret room in the new house. The French money wasn't as hard to duplicate as the English stuff, because it wasn't so meticulously made. So Becker, somewhat to his own surprise, was rolling off the first high-denomination franc bills within ninety days.

Wilkes, calling himself Sir George Wilkins, was soon ensconced in a lush office near the Paris Bourse as the president of Wilkins, Ltd., Investments. Sir George, with his devastating charm, soon drummed up quite a bit of trade by contacts he made while sitting at the more fashionable sidewalk cafés or in the tonier restaurants inhaling Scotch and sodas. Since he was in a position to offer comparatively high prices for depressed, though sound securities, he was, within a matter of months, being offered so much stuff that Becker couldn't turn out counterfeit money fast enough to absorb it all.

Becker now decided to begin the manufacture of counterfeit securities.

His first production was a French government bond. He gave it to Wilkes with instructions to take it to a bank, say that he questioned its authenticity, and ask that it be scrutinized. Sir George returned to Becker beaming. "They said," he reported, "the bloody thing couldn't have been more genuine." So the French government bonds, as well as the French franc notes, began to come off the Becker press as fast as the Dutchman could roll them out.

Becker himself was an extremely busy young man by now. Having two operations—one legitimate, one illegitimate—running in each of two cities, he was constantly shuttling back and forth between Paris and London. When in London, he met Chapman, Siscovitch and Little Joe Elliott only at the Blue Anchor Inn, never contacting them anywhere else.

By the time Charles Becker had been in Europe five years, he was really in high gear. He was one day to estimate for William A. Pinkerton that by the year 1878, when he was only thirty-two, he had more than three million dollars. But, Becker, having amassed a big pile, had a craving for a still bigger one.

He went to Italy, and opened legitimate and illegitimate branches of his business in Rome. He hired local talent, both honest and dishonest, in his offices. Then he went to Berlin and duplicated the process. By the time he was thirty-five he was flitting about Europe like a phantom, first in London, now in Paris, now in Rome, now in Berlin. By this time the international exchanges were flooded with bogus currency and bogus securities. International balances were thrown out of kilter and nobody could understand why.

Becker was in the Louvre one day, snappily turned out in morning coat, striped pants, spats, cane and gray hat viewing a picture when a curious thing happened—one of those singular incidents that would seem to stretch the long arm of coincidence all out of shape but which nonetheless must be accepted as truth because there it is, down in black and white, in the Pinkerton archives. Becker heard a girl and a man talking to each other directly behind him. Although almost fifteen years had passed since he had last heard the girl's voice, Becker recognized it almost instantly. It was the voice of Clara Bechtel, the girl who had disenfranchised him when he had fallen into disgrace as a result of passing a bad check to purchase her engagement ring.

Becker, while not brooding over Clara Bechtel, had always kept the girl in his but-don't-forget mental file. He had always held her indirectly responsible for the deaths of his father, mother and sister. There would come, he had always hoped, a day when he would somehow meet up with Clara Bechtel again and even the score.

He turned around. The girl was Clara Bechtel, all right, older, but prettier and more exciting, if anything, than when he had known her. The gentleman with her was about sixty—expensively dressed, pot-bellied, and nasty-looking. . . .

"Why Charles!" Clara said. "How wonderful to see you again!" Now she introduced Becker to her husband, a Mr. Benedict. Benedict didn't seem to relish the introduction and made short work of the encounter with Becker by hustling his wife off to another room in the Louvre.

Becker followed Mr. and Mrs. Benedict and noticed Clara glancing back over her shoulder whenever she could without her husband knowing it. A couple of minutes later, Clara excused herself fom her husband and went into a ladies' room. When she came out and rejoined Benedict, she dropped a little ball of paper to the floor and left the room with her husband.

On the street he read what Clara had written to him—a note that he was to keep in his possession to the end of his days and which he was one day to show to William A. Pinkerton:

> Please forgive me for not sticking by you years ago. I was young and did not know what I was doing. I am desperately unhappy. Will you please meet me in the lobby of the Hotel Grand tomorrow afternoon at three. "He" won't be around.

When he met Clara, he took her for a carriage ride. She repeated, over and over again, what she had said in the note. Would Charles forgive her for her youthful mistake of almost fifteen years before?

"Your husband seems to be a very jealous man," he said. "What would he do if he ever found out you were unfaithful?"

Benedict would divorce Clara. He had told her as much several times.

"But he seems to be rich," said Becker. "Isn't it worth your while to stay with him?"

"But you are rich, too, Charles," she said. "That is obvious."

Becker allowed that he was making out all right.

Becker and Clara presently had an intrigue going. The plot was that Clara was to divorce Benedict and marry Becker. Becker, one day, dropped a note to Benedict. The signed "A Friend," advised Benedict that his wife had a lover. Benedict could confirm the awful truth if he crashed into a certain room in a certain Left Bank hotel at a certain hour on a certain day.

88

On the day in question, there were Becker and Clara, in their birthday suits. Presently there came a rapping on the door. "Who's there?" shouted Becker.

"Open up! Open up!" came a voice from the other side of the door. Before Becker could answer, the knob in the door turned and in walked Benedict. Becker had purposely left the door unlocked. Benedict tried to knock Becker down. But he was no match for the virile Dutchman. He was a match, though, for his wife. "I never want to lay eyes on you to the longest day I live," he told Clara. Then he walked out of the room.

"Don't worry," Becker assured Clara. "We'll get married when he divorces you. Let's meet at Napoleon's Tomb tomorrow at three."

Becker got into his clothes, kissed Clara, and left the room while she was still getting dressed. He was never to lay eyes on her for the rest of his life. He had, after almost fifteen years, evened an old score.

One day, in 1885, when Becker had been in Europe for twelve years, he met Wilkes in the back room of a restaurant on the Left Bank in Paris, only to find Sir George in a high state of excitement. "Billy Pinkerton stopped in to see me today," Wilkes told Becker. "You know what that means, don't you?"

Next day the Paris newspapers carried stories to the effect that some French government securities had been found to be counterfeit. It seemed that the French government, annoyed by inexplicable discrepancies in its fiscal accounts over a period of years, had put the Sureté on the job. The Sureté had established that there were more issues of certain securities on the market than had been printed.

The announcement that certain French money and securities were tainted with counterfeits created a panic. Speculators didn't know whether the securities they held were fake or genuine. Security prices on the Paris Bourse took an awful tumble. Word of the Paris debacle spread throughout the financial capitals of Europe.

"George," Becker said to Wilkes when they met, "you must close up and disappear. I'm afraid of Pinkerton." Wilkes agreed that Becker's concern was sound.

"What about money?" asked Wilkes.

Becker handed the con man an envelope. Wilkes counted out the equivalent of $50,000—two years' salary in advance. Becker and Wilkes would, Becker assured Sir George, tie up somewhere at a later and more propitious time. Wilkes had just one question to ask. Was this money Becker was giving him genuine or counterfeit? "Genuine, of course," said Becker.

Becker, seeing the handwriting on the wall, dropped back to London to warn Little Joe Elliott, Chapman and Siscovitch of what was up.

Becker gave the trio a bundle of good money and told them to duck down to the Blue Anchor and stand by for further developments. Then he set about trimming his sails, preparing for the storm. He hopped over to Rome, closed up his fake front there and then went to Berlin and did the same thing.

Becker had the equivalent of three million dollars in English bank notes tucked away in safety deposit boxes throughout London. He decided to get the money out of the country. But how to get it out?

Becker decided to consult Adam Worth, who had the setup to resolve his problem. Worth said he would get the money out of the safety deposit boxes and have it transferred to New York for Becker but the price for his services would come high. "How high?" asked Becker. "One fourth of what I handle," said Worth.

Becker began to scream that he was being swindled. Worth told him to take it or leave it. Becker had no choice but to take it. At least he could rest assured of a square shake. Worth was the soul of integrity, except when dealing with honest men. Becker knew that he would have his three million dollars, less Worth's handling charges, waiting for him in New York whenever he got there—if it took ten years.

Charles Becker was forty years old when, in company with Little Joe Elliott, he arrived back in the United States in 1886. First thing he did was to go into the underworld, establish contact with a representative of Worth's, collect the two and a quarter million waiting for him and, under an alias, stick it away in several safety-deposit boxes.

Looking around for a place to settle down, and a business to get into, Becker gravitated to Brooklyn. There, on Fulton Street, he saw a fine four-story brick building with a ground floor that could be converted into a saloon. He bought the place and within six months had opened up the saloon, which was known simply as "Becker's."

Becker's was a superior watering hole, with a handsome mahogany bar, art work on the mirror behind the rows of bottles back of the bar, sawdust on the floor, a substantial free lunch at the far end of the bar, and a ladies' entrance in the rear of the joint. Becker tended bar himself, from opening time in the morning until closing time early the following morning in order to save the expense of an extra bartender.

Within a year, Becker's caught on, but good. On a Saturday night the customers were three deep at the mahogany. The tables-for-ladies section was just as popular as the bar itself. Becker always kept a steam-

90

ing boiler of pork, sauerkraut and potatoes, which cost a dime a plate, and he did the serving himself.

Only one thing was taboo in Becker's: drunkenness. A lush was shown to the door before he ever got off the ground; if he displayed reluctance to depart Becker walked around from behind the bar and personally heaved the man right into the street. This appealed to other patrons, especially the ladies and to the cop on the beat.

Becker was never again to equal the exploits of deception he had carried out abroad. For some inexplicable reason, he now married a plain, unsophisticated old maid whose family patronized his restaurant. With millions at his disposal, Becker avoided criminal activities for a while. Later he carried out several schemes quite unworthy of his talents. Once he was arrested and turned state's evidence in return for immunity. The famous detective, Billy Pinkerton, now took to hanging around Becker's bar. This apparently challenged Becker into further action. He dug up the counterfeiting equipment he had buried in New Jersey many years ago and began turning out fine $10 bills. Sporting a goatee and calling himself Baron von Brickel, Becker went to San Francisco and established the same type of false brokerage operation he had run in Europe. Then one day he took somebody's bona-fide check for $64, and raised it to $20,000 and cashed it. In due time, Becker, who throughout his career never faced a counterfeiting charge, was convicted of check-raising. In 1906 he died in San Quentin at the age of sixty.

MADISON AVENUE vs. NAZI INTELLIGENCE

by Donald Q. Coster, with Frederic Sondern, Jr.

One night late in October, 1942, the formidable German U-boat packs in the South Atlantic received an order to speed to a rendezvous off Dakar. The packs slid quickly to their positions, and soon over a hundred Nazi submarines had taken station in a tight semicircle around Africa's western tip. Ashore, Vichy French troops manned for action the powerful coastal defenses which two years before had repelled the

British-Free French assault led by General de Gaulle. The American invasion across the Atlantic was steaming into an ambush which might well cripple it. At least, that is what the German High Command thought.

On the night of November 7th, however, German radio stations suddenly interrupted their programs for a news flash. *"Achtung! Achtung! A large enemy army is on the northern coast of Africa. . . ."* Our invasion forces had surprised the Germans by landing at points some 2000 miles from where they were expected. The Dakar Cover Plan, one of the most effective ruses of the war, had been successful.

A most important link in the chain of deception was forged by Donald Coster, a soft-spoken young New Yorker who had been an advertising agency executive in private life. Coster was by no means the usual carefully trained, hard boiled agent of international skulduggery. Yet he beat the Germans at their own game with the misleading combination of common sense and naive disregard for the traditional rules of international intrigue.

Coster had entered the conflict early in 1940, driving an ambulance of the American Field Service for the French Army. He was captured, spent several unpleasant weeks in German hands, was released, and came home to join the Navy. His knowledge of French pushed him into the Office of Naval Intelligence in Washington. When Colonel William Donovan established the Office of the Coordinator of Information—later to become the office of Strategic Services, Coster was transferred to the new agency. But let Don tell his own story.

* * *

One Sunday morning I was called into Colonel Donovan's office. "You are going to Casablanca," said the Colonel. "It's the most important place in the world at the moment."

I blinked.

"French Africa will be invaded one of these days," he continued, "by either the Germans or ourselves. You are to help prepare for either eventuality. We must know the German plans."

"Yes, sir," I gulped.

"A German Armistice Commission is in Casablanca, enforcing the terms the Nazis imposed on the French in 1940. You might try to make them believe that, if and when we invade, we will come in through Dakar. I'll leave the method of doing that up to you."

I swallowed hard as the full significance of the Colonel's casually spoken words sank in.

"And you'd better stop by at London, Lisbon and Gibraltar to pick up what information you can from British Intelligence. That's all."

I felt like Little Red Riding Hood about to enter a whole forest of wolves—at midnight. Gestapo gunmen, superspies and ingenious Nazi methods of assassination chased each other past my mind's eye.

A few days later I found myself a "vice-consul" in the pay of the State Department. Donovan used this cover to cloak his agents operating in officially neutral Vichy-French territory.

In Washington I was rushed through a quick course of instruction in the code I was to use, and very little else. The elaborate spy school, which later trained our agents in everything from safecracking to the tricky technique of contacting another agent on a street corner in hostile country with minimum risk of detection, had not yet been set up. I didn't even know how to pry open a desk drawer. I was acutely conscious of my inexperience as I flew to London.

Then the first of Coster's Curious Coincidences took place. An English girl whom I met through friends somehow picked up a hint that I was going to North Africa. She begged me to try to find and help a very dear friend of hers—an Austrian named Freddy—who had been in the French Foreign Legion and was now probably in a Vichyite concentration camp near Casablanca. I was one very embarrassed spy. No one was supposed to know where I was going. But I promised half-heartedly that I would try to find the Austrian.

In London, Lisbon and Gibraltar I met the "heavy brass" of the British intelligence services. They were smooth, formidable-looking men who had a calm self-assurance which made me feel uncomfortably inadequate. I was pretty quiet when the grownups talked. They told me about General Theodor Auer, chief of the German Armistice Commission—evidently a sinister opponent. His counterintelligence system was well organized and ruthless.

The Englishmen shook their heads dubiously over my chances of convincing the *Herr General* of anything important that wasn't true; he knew all the tricks. And I should be careful, they warned, of my health. The Germans had a way of handling troublesome people: they were lured into back alleys and knifed. Just before my plane took off from Gibraltar, one hard-faced Englishman patted me on the shoulder: "Good luck, old man. We'll be thinking of you." I thought I detected a rather funereal tone in his voice.

In Casablanca only a few of our top diplomats knew what Colonel Donovan's men were doing. The regular consular staff was continually irritated by their young and inexplicable assistants, who had little interest in regular consular duties and had a most unconsular way of talking to dock foremen, fishermen and other odd characters. We also had a hard time concealing from some of our inquisitive colleagues the radio transmitters with which we sent reports.

With a *Croix de Guerre* in my buttonhole, and my command of French, I found it easy to make friends and dig up information. A number of trustworthy anti-Vichy people helped in checking the reliability of our sources. The owner of a fishing fleet drew a chart for me of the practicable sea approaches to the Moroccan coast. A French architect, who had escaped from forced labor in Germany, arranged to follow me to church two Sundays and in the cover of a pew hand me drawings of the newest German flak towers—towers he had been compelled to help build. All this was valuable information, but I was getting no closer to General Auer.

Then, one evening, Coster's second Curious Coincidence occurred. Another "vice-consul" and I were sitting in a disreputable water-front café, where we listened for information on ship movements. Two young men passed our table. "Walter," called out my companion. The newcomer stopped. "Meet a friend of mine—Donald Coster. He's in the Consulate too." The young men sat down. They were Austrians, they said, who had been in France when the Germans invaded. They had joined the Foreign Legion, been interned in a Vichy concentration camp, and had managed to escape to Casablanca. "When suddenly, one day"— Walter was telling the story—"who should I see on the street but Teddy Auer, the General who runs the German Armistice Commission. I knew him in Paris before the war.

"Well," Walter concluded blithely, "we made a deal with him. We supply him with information, and he keeps us out of jail. We're both violently anti-Nazi, of course, and we want the Germans' hides."

My mind started turning over—fast. Either Walter and his companion had been set on my trail by Auer, and this was a trap; or it was a heaven-sent opportunity. I was still thinking, hard, when the Austrian whose name I had missed turned to me. "So you arrived recently from London," he sighed. "I have a most wonderful girl there. If only I could get back . . ." I had pulled out my wallet to pay the check. Suddenly the Austrian almost jumped across the table at me. "It's her handwriting!" he yelled, pointing at an envelope in the wallet. It was a letter I had received from the London girl, and the handwriting was large and distinctive. This, of course, was Freddy, the man she had asked me to find.

94

A definite scheme evolved in my mind that night. I would be a stupid loudmouthed playboy, and in my frequent cups feed the Austrians accurate but unimportant information which they would pass on to Auer. I had read about that in books, and I didn't think it had a prayer of succeeding. But I couldn't think of anything else.

A few days later it developed that Auer not only believed the Austrians when they reported their new acquisition but opened a bottle of champagne.

"*Ja*. All fools, these Americans," said the General. "Make them drunk, and they talk."

Auer's first demands for information were not difficult. The General was apparently trying out his new source of information for its precision in small things.

Then, one day, the two were unusually concerned when I met them. The *herr General* had been very excited the night before. "You Austrian pigs," he had shouted. "You don't know this American at all. You have been stealing my money." Freddy and Walter assured him that they did know the American very well, and could prove it. "Then prove it, and soon, or I'll teach you what it means to cheat a German general."

I saw my plan tottering. Auer was suspicious. He would turn his counterintelligence people loose on us, and our whole espionage operation—which had gone along with surprising lack of interference from the Germans—would be jeopardized. Then suddenly the light dawned. Why, tell the General that if he wants to see what good friends we are, he should come to that black-market restaurant overlooking the sea tomorrow night and watch us having dinner together.

"I'll put on a show that will convince him," I added.

The color shot back into the Austrians' faces. "And the General will pay for the dinner," said Walter gravely.

I shall never forget that night. All of us equally jittery, we were just starting on our black-market steaks when the gaunt, blond unofficial ruler of French North Africa, flanked by the key members of the German Armistice Commission, stalked in and took places nearby. I kept feeling the General's stare right on the back of my neck.

And then I got pretty fried. I banged on the table, told some indiscreet stories about the State Department, shouted for more wine, argued with the waiter, kept clapping Walter and Freddy on the back, leveled an occasional belligerent glance at the Germans and mentally held my breath.

Gradually the Austrians began to relax. "Very good," Walter murmured. "The *Herr General* is pleased. I know the signs. He is relaxing. He is impressed."

95

To clinch it, we parked our car outside the German Consulate afterward, and sang raucously.

The next day Freddy presented the General with a bill of several thousand francs for our dinner. Auer beamed with pleasure as he handed over the money, with a substantial bonus. *"Sehr gut, mein Junge,"* he laughed. "Now you find out *important* things for me about the Americans from that fool."

I could hardly believe my good luck. The General now began to invite the Austrians to all his lavish parties. They heard much conversation on subjects that interested us deeply. German chemists were working on mass production of a new gas. The High Command had given up the idea of invading French Africa through Spain. Every night we sent out such bits of information by radio and pouch.

I hinted to Freddy and Walter periodically that an American invasion was being set up. By July, Auer was obviously worried, and ordered the Austrians to devote themselves entirely to finding out when and where the Americans would strike.

"Tell Auer," I said, "that the invasion plan is definitely settled. We will be landing at Dakar late this autumn." Then I spent a sleepless night. Would Auer fall for it? Had Freddy and Walter been planted by Auer to play the game on me that I wanted to play on him? If I had guessed wrong, I would be responsible for the loss of many Allied lives.

Next morning the Austrians were jubilant. *Herr General* had shouted with delight, "We'll catch the American swine! They'll walk into a beautiful trap. This news must go at once to the High Command!"

He had pushed buttons and shouted for aides. And a long message had gone off to Wiesbaden. Then champagne had been broken out and innumerable toasts drunk, to Hitler, to the glory of German arms, to Auer's "stanch Austrian friends," and even to "the stupid American." Freddy and Walter had been rewarded with a large sum of money.

My contribution to the Dakar Cover Plan was complete. It was, of course, supported by other feints and intentional "leakages" of information, all designed to cast further suspicion toward Dakar.

A few months later I had the thrill of my life. I landed on D Day on the beach at Oran—1900 miles from Dakar. *Operation Torch* overwhelmed French North Africa with few shots fired, not a single ship of our huge armada sunk en route. Proceeding to Tafaroui airfield, where 600 prisoners were taken, I was instructed to contact the Vichyite commanding officer. His face got very red when I approached him. He pointed an accusing finger at me.

96

"Why are you Americans here?" he exploded. "We were expecting you at Dakar!"

CONFESSIONS OF A MASTER JEWEL THIEF

by Robert Wallace

Nineteen years in the clink, followed by a spell of good, clean living, can raise hob with a man's reputation. The great Arthur Barry, for example, recently got off parole at the age of 59 and is now free for the first time to talk about some of the details of his astonishing career. But public memory is a fickle thing and doubtless there are people who no longer recall who Arthur Barry is and what he does, or did.

Arthur Barry was an incomparable second-story man; even the phrase, in the age of the ranch house, must be explained to the children. Second-story men are not often in the news today, but there was a time when they were aristocrats among thieves and when Barry himself was a king. There are elderly detectives still active today who regard him as the greatest jewel thief who ever lived. In the 1920s Barry collected a pile of loot valued somewhere between $5 and $10 million. He rarely robbed anyone who was not in the Social Register, his manners were impeccable and his working uniform was often a tuxedo. He seldom carried a gun or a knife, never indulged in violence and almost invariably left a favorable impression upon his victims, whom he called clients. In his prime he looked much like Ronald Colman; wealthy matrons, awakening at night to find him puttering about their bedrooms, often failed to scream.

Today Arthur Barry is a $50-a-week counterman in the Montrose roadside restaurant in Worcester, Mass., his birthplace. He has held the job since his release from prison in 1949, has established himself as a reputable and popular citizen and recoils at the very thought of shinnying up a porch column. Most of the customers who drop in at the Montrose for a sandwich have no idea they are being served by one of the archthieves of all time. They give him 15¢ tips. This is agreeable to Barry, who would as soon forget all about his earlier life. But, like many retired and reformed thieves, he occasionally feels the tickling little feet of morals creeping on him.

97

Sometimes, although he is childless, he is concerned about the problem of wayward youth, which he somehow feels is wayward in a way that he was not. Upon his recent release from parole, he agreed therefore to discuss some of his old business affairs, provided that he might make a personal observation at the end.

In some ways his stories may set the minds of a few people at rest. There are individuals in Greenwich, Conn., for example, who have been tormenting themselves for 30 years with the question of how any thief could have managed to get into the home of the late Percy Rockefeller, which was guarded by two ferocious, wide-awake watchdogs, steal $20,000 worth of jewels and escape undetected. "The crime is unsolved," Barry says, "and naturally I deny all knowledge of it. But," he continues with a dead-pan expression, "I can tell you what I told the police chief confidentially when he asked me how I *thought* it might have been done."

Arthur Barry did not become a bigtime thief until after World War I and thus the first 23 years of his life were relatively uneventful. Born in Worcester in 1896, he was the ninth of 12 children of immigrant Irish parents. He remembers his parents as being firm but fair in their treatment of him and his brothers and sisters, all of whom turned out well. Barry's father was a brewer whose union wages were low but adequate. It was a fine and close-knit family, of just the sort that social theorists point to today, saying, "If we had more good old-fashioned American families like this, we would have fewer crooks on our hands."

Barry attributes his downfall in the main to simple physiological mischance; he matured too early and was full-grown at 13. The companions he sought out were of his own size but considerably older, and in his efforts to ingratiate himself with his elders he presently found himself running errands for some sinful people. One of these was a "peteman," in the language of the trade, a master safecracker named Lowell Jack, who was then in semiretirement and made his living by manufacturing special tools and nitroglycerin. Lowell Jack had no difficulty making the nitrogylcerin: he simply heated dynamite and water in a bucket on the kitchen stove and bottled the essence. But he needed a good delivery boy who would not drop the stuff in a public place and damage a number of bystanders. He employed young Barry, at $4 or $5 per delivery, and sent him on trains to other New England cities. Barry did just as he was told and soon became a trusted member of the small-time Worcester underworld. As he rode from city to city, a quiet, manly youngster of 14 in knickers, with his bottle of nitroglycerin in a cotton-filled suitcase between his knees, he was the perfect picture of the noble lad of whom people say, "If we only had more fine boys like this one."

Barry committed his first burglary at 15, a small job that netted him less than $100 but a thoughtful and deft one all the same. His victims were a middle-aged couple who ran a dry goods store and brought the day's receipts home with them each evening, there being no night depositories at the Worcester banks in those days. For several days before the robbery, while the couple was at work, Barry entered their house through an unlocked window and prowled about, looking for the place where, if he were a middle-aged man who ran a dry good store, he would hide the money. Eventually he found it, an empty desk drawer that seemed to have the smell of cash lingering in it. On the night of the burglary he entered the house through the same unlocked window, tiptoed directly to the drawer, removed the money and tiptoed out.

"No, I was not frightened," he says. "If they had awakened, the advantage would have been all mine. I was wide awake, they were groggy. I knew what was behind every door as well as they did. I could have been halfway down the block before they got organized." Careful preparation and a fine grasp of the probabilities were Barry's greatest business assets. They made violence unnecessary.

Barry committed a number of other minor burglaries during his formative years, then interrupted his career to serve in the Army in World War I. He was wounded in action and recommended for a Silver Star, but went AWOL before he could get it. After the war he settled in New York. It had never seriously occurred to him to follow any honest profession; his problem was merely to decide what sort of thief he would be. Safecracking and bank robbery did not appeal to him, and ordinary burglary and holdups struck him as unprofitable and somehow disreputable. Although he had only a high school education, Barry was a polished individual, a good conversationalist and something of a dandy. There was only one specialty that seemed appropriate for him: jewel theft.

Jewel theft was attractive because of the ease with which, in the 1920s in New York, a thief could dispose of his loot. "Why," Barry says, "there were fences in those days who could have got rid of the Statue of Liberty. Sometimes they had to send the big, recognizable jewels to Amsterdam to have them recut, but not often. I do remember that they once sent over a big emerald of mine, the size of a walnut, and some thief in Amsterdam stole it. But usually they were very reliable." At that time it was also possible for fences, many of whom operated as "private detective agencies," to deal directly with insurance companies. "They'd go to the company, say they had accidentally found the jewels in a hollow tree, and sell them to the company for 10% or 20% of the insured value. This was better than a total loss for the company."

Having decided what to steal, Barry had only to decide whom to steal it from. "I noticed that a lot of wealthy women who came into New York shopping used to wind up their afternoons at the casino up in Central Park. So I'd go up there myself to look them over. When I spotted a woman who had plenty of diamonds on her, I'd follow her out to her limousine and take the license number. Then all I had to do was to go to the nearest phone, call up the police traffic bureau and say, 'This is Patrolman Schultz, badge number 465786. I've got an accident up here, and I need the name and address of Cadillac sedan, New York plate number XYZ-123.' The traffic bureau never took the time to check on Patrolman Schultz. They'd simply give me the name and address."

Barry also selected his victims from the society columns, paying particular attention to announcements of wedding and engagement parties in the estate section on the North Shore of Long Island, his favorite hunting ground. On the afternoon of a party he would drive out to the Island, park his car near the estate in question and change into formal clothes. Then he would crash the party. Lawn parties were particularly easy for him since he had only to climb unnoticed over a wall or through a hedge, pick up a drink and a canapé from a passing waiter and mingle with the guests. Thereafter it was easy for him to get into the house, wander upstairs and make a mental sketch of the floor plan. Often he was able to enter the master bedroom and locate likely hiding places for jewelry, although on such preliminary forays he never stole anything. Sometimes he unlocked a half-dozen windows in strategic spots, hoping that they would remain unlocked for a day or two, and occasionally he cut off the burglar alarm system. If he was discovered wandering about the house, he pretended to be a drunk looking for a place to lie down. No one ever challenged him. His stage presence was faultless, his taste in clothes excellent and his grammar good enough to fool the King of England—which, as a matter of fact, it did, at a time when Edward VIII was Prince of Wales.

Barry encountered the prince on an evening at a speakeasy on 59th Street and made a very favorable impression on him. They had several drinks in the course of two or three hours, during which the prince chatted gaily and perhaps a little too informatively. A few days later, early on the morning of Sept. 9, 1924, a thief entered the home of Mrs.

Joshua Cosden at Sands Point, Long Island and made off with $150,000
worth of jewels, including some which belonged to guests of the Cos-
dens, the prince's cousin, Lord Louis Mountbatten, and his wife. It
was almost as though someone, in the vulgar phrase, had fingered the
job.

The proceeds of a $150,000 robbery could not support Barry in the
style to which he was accustomed for very long. He could sell only the
most valuable jewels and for only a fraction of their worth. His usual
procedure was to break up the compound pieces, such as necklaces, pins
and brooches, at once and throw away the gold and platinum settings
and the smaller stones. The safest depository for these, he decided, was
New York Bay. He was a frequent passenger on ferryboats, a fine-look-
ing gentleman standing by the rail flicking what appeared to be cigaret
ashes into the water. To this day New York Bay mud along the line
between the ferry slips at the Battery and Staten Island has a high as-
say value.

Because his cash realizations were low in relation to the value of what
he stole, Barry was obliged to make numerous business trips to the suburbs. After the Cosden affair he paid a call at the home of a Social Reg-
isterite named John C. Greenleaf of Hewlett Bay Park, Long Island
and took $10,000 worth of jewels. He had also stopped at the residence
of Mr. Harold E. Talbott, who would someday become President Eisenhower's Secretary of the Air Force, and had taken $23,000 worth. Be-
cause he knew that Major Tommy Hitchcock, the polo player, was a
man of substance, Barry visited him as well but got away with jewelry
worth only $900. As he examined it during his getaway, Barry was so
miffed that he threw a lot of it into a brook.

Despite occasional disappointments of this sort, Barry did very well
during the mid-'20s, averaging about half a million dollars in thefts per
year. He extended his territory up into Dutchess County in New York
and in that area in 1926 he performed a feat that aroused real awe in
police circles. Having discovered that the master and mistress of a large
estate kept their jewelry in a 150-pound safe in their bedroom closet,
Barry climbed into the bedroom on a ladder, tiptoed to the closet and
silently hoisted the safe on his shoulder. (Although he stands only 5 feet
8 inches, Barry was and still is a man of astonishing physical strength.)
Without a sound he withdrew the way he had come.

Silence and deftness also characterized the great Hotel Plaza robbery
on Sept. 30, 1925, in which jewelry valued at $750,000 disappeared in
broad daylight from the six-room suite of Mrs. James P. Donahue,
daughter of F. W. Woolworth. Among the objects stolen were a 10-carat

diamond ring worth more than $50,000 and a rope of pearls valued at $450,000. These were taken from a dressing table in Mrs. Donahue's bedroom while she sat in a tub in a bathroom only a few feet away. A maid was in a nearby room and a masseuse in another. No one heard a sound. No arrest was ever made for the theft and the jewels were recovered by an insurance detective not long afterward and returned to the police. "Whoever took those pearls," a police captain remarked at the time, "really knew what he was doing. There were five ropes in the drawer, four imitations and the real one. The imitations were good enough to fool an oyster."

"The easy way to tell a real pearl from an imitation," Barry says with a reflective smile, "is to rub it gently across your teeth. A real pearl produces a somewhat grating, sandpapery sensation, but a fake is smooth and slippery."

The only one of his 150 major thefts for which Barry was prosecuted, convicted and jailed was the stealing of some $100,000 in jewelry from the late Jesse Livermore, the Wall Street operator, whose summer home was in Kings Point, Long Island. It took place early in the morning of May 29, 1927 and was a double-headed operation: the Livermores had some house guests at the time and Barry robbed them too.

During the Livermore burglary, as in many others in which he could not handle all the details by himself, Barry had an accomplice, a strong-arm named "Boston Billy" Monaghan. Barry did the thinking and talking while Monaghan stood ready to take care of anyone who interrupted the proceedings. At 2:30 A.M. on the night of the burglary Barry and Monaghan placed a ladder beneath a second-story window and climbed up. They entered the room occupied by the house guests, Mr. and Mrs. Henry Aronsohn. Almost at once the Aronsohns awakened.

"Good evening," Barry said, speaking in the low and gentle tone he invariably employed. "We have only come to take the jewelry, and not to hurt anyone. Please don't be upset." Then he walked across the room to the bedside table and cut the telephone wires.

"Oh," said Mrs. Aronsohn. "I feel ill. I think I am going to faint."

"Please don't, madam," Barry said. "Would you care for an aspirin?"

"I believe I would," Mrs. Aronsohn said. She got up and went to the medicine cabinet in the bathroom while Barry picked up the jewelry on the dressing table. It was not a large haul, worth perhaps $5,000, and included an object that Barry rarely bothered to steal, a wristwatch. However, both the watch and its band were of platinum; Barry appraised them at $1,500.

"Please don't take my nickel-plated watch," Mr. Aronsohn said. "It was a gift from my mother."

"Ah, well," Barry said, "I had a mother myself. If you cooperate, I may leave it with the Livermores on my way out."

After warning the Aronsohns not to make any outcry or approach the window—with a vague gesture Barry peopled the dark landscape outside with a horde of thugs who were waiting to shoot—Barry and Monaghan went to the Livermores' bedroom.

"It was a good risk," he recalls today. "We would have been in a jam if the Aronsohns had started yelling, but they didn't. In fact, I never found anyone who did. If you spoke quietly and reassured them, they'd relax. Sometimes the newspapers carried stories about clients of mine who claimed they had made trouble for me—'Socialite grapples with intruder in darkened bedroom'—but believe me, nobody ever grappled with me. And another thing: some of my clients were crooks themselves. On the day after a job I'd read stories which listed all kinds of things I hadn't stolen at all. The clients would hide them and get the money from the insurance company. Sure, I was a thief and I'm sorry now, but you'll find a lot of people in the Social Register who are also thieves and aren't one bit sorry."

In the Livermores' bedroom Barry awakened Mrs. Livermore by shining his flashlight in her eyes. "She didn't scream. She just said, 'Who is it?', and then Livermore woke up and I said, 'Good evening, J.L.' This burned him. Only his friends called him J.L. His wife, who was about 20 years younger than he was, called him Pops. 'Don't reach for the telephone, J.L.,' I said. 'The wires are cut. All we want is the jewelry, and we'll be on our way.'"

Barry took about $95,000 worth of gems from the dressing table and bureau, noticing as he searched through the drawers that Mrs. Livermore seemed uncomfortable. She was sitting up in bed, wearing only a nightgown, but was too frightened to reach for her bathrobe. Barry picked it up and put it around her shoulders. "You're a devil," she said as he did so, "a real devil."

"Thank you, madam," Barry replied. "Would you like a cigaret?"

He lighted the cigaret for her, then offered one to Mr. Livermore. "I smoke cigars," Livermore growled. "Take the jewelry and get out of here."

"Please don't take my little pinky ring," Mrs. Livermore said. "Pops gave it to me."

Barry examined the little pinky ring, which he appraised at $15,000. But with a shrug he tossed it back to her.

"Hey, listen!" Monaghan said.

"And please don't take Pops's little pinky ring," Mrs. Livermore said. "I gave it to him."

Barry calculated the value of Pops's little pinky ring at $20,000 but returned it anyway.

"My God," Monaghan said. "Let's quit while we're winning."

"Oh, you're a devil," Mrs. Livermore said again.

As they left, Barry tossed one more item to Mrs. Livermore. "Would you mind giving this nickel-plated platinum watch to Mr. Aronsohn?" he said. "His mother gave it to him. Good night." They made a clean getaway. But within a week Barry was in jail.

It was not a professional blunder that brought about his arrest but, as he supposes today, a woman. Although he was married, Barry was a formidable ladies' man. "That's where all the money went," he explains. "You have no idea how expensive it can be. I was quite fond of several girls in the chorus of *Blossom Time* and I used to take them all out at once. Funny thing, there was a number in that show in which all the girls were crowded onstage, with the ones in the back row standing on ladders. The stage manager once came to me and he said, 'You've got to stop keeping my girls up so late. They're all groggy. I've got a stagehand standing under each ladder to catch them, but someday we'll have a hell of an accident around here.' "

Barry suspects that one of his girls, in a fit of monogamous jealousy, went to the police and told them that he had committed the Livermore burglary. At any rate someone did, and he was arrested by a platoon of cops at the railroad station at Ronkonkoma, Long Island, at 7:30 o'clock on a summer Sunday evening. He was sentenced to 25 years in Auburn Prison.

As he began his sentence Barry was 31 years old and might have been released on parole, if he had behaved well, at the age of 47 or 48. But he did not behave well. On July 28, 1929 he shot his way out of Auburn in one of the boldest, wildest jailbreaks in U. S. prison history.

The break came on a quiet, cloudy Sunday afternoon. According to custom, most of the 1,700 convicts in the 14-acre prison were allowed the freedom of the yard at that time. Some of them, including Barry, could walk up and down in the cell block corridors. At the end of Barry's cell block there was a solid steel door containing a mail slot. Beyond this door was a guard room and beyond that, by a grievous error of prison design, was an arsenal full of guns and ammunition. There were only two guards in the room between cell block and arsenal and one of them had the key to the arsenal in his pocket.

104

To get into the arsenal Barry needed only two pieces of equipment. One was a birthday cake made for him by a convict who worked in the prison bakery. The other was a tennis ball stolen from the recreation yard; it had been punctured and filled with ammonia from the prison laundry.

Carrying the cake in one hand and the tennis ball in the other, Barry tapped with his foot on the steel door at the end of his cell block. One of the guards peered through the mail slot; he could see only Barry's head, shoulders and the cake. Three other convicts, who were to make the escape with Barry, crouched beside the door and were out of the guard's field of vision.

Barry explained that the cake was a present for a convict in another cell block. Would the guard open the door, take the cake and see that it was delivered? The guard agreed, unlocked the door to receive the cake and instead got a faceful of ammonia. He cried out and covered his eyes with his hands. Barry dashed past him, making for the other guard who sat in a chair, his gun across his knees, at the opposite end of the room. The second guard managed to fire two wild shots and was overpowered.

Barry and his three companions quickly opened the arsenal and armed themselves with riot guns. The shots fired by the guard had already aroused other guards nearby and had also been heard by hundreds of convicts in the prison yard. Barry stepped out onto a balcony which jutted off the guard room above the yard. Raising his gun, he fired a shot into the air and shouted, "We're breaking out! If anybody wants to come along, come now!" A wild shout went up from the prisoners, who began to run toward the building.

As the mass of convicts stormed into the building from one side, Barry and his companions dashed out the other, heading toward the main gate. As they ran they fired bursts from their riot guns at the guards who manned the 20-foot stone wall which enclosed the prison. The guards ducked and were able to return only scattered and inaccurate fire. Barry reached the locked gate and dashed into the "balky," a tower which housed a winding staircase leading to the top of the wall. He climbed it so quickly he has no recollection of doing so, emerged on top of the wall and stood for an instant surveying the long drop down to the street. A bullet fired by one of the guards tore into his lower leg, nicking the shinbone but not breaking it. Another bullet smashed into his back, high up, above the lung. He turned and dropped over the wall, still carrying his gun in one hand. As he hit the sidewalk his left foot struck a six-inch stone sill at the base of the wall and he toppled over backward. He got up quickly, feeling a sharp pain in the foot. He had broken two toes.

Outside the prison, Sunday afternoon traffic on State Street, one of the main thoroughfares of Auburn, moved sedately along. Barry stepped out into the street, leveled his gun at the driver of a passing car and forced him to stop. As he got into the back seat of the car, Barry was joined by a second convict named Pawlak, a life-termer, who had followed him over the wall.

There were three people in the car: a young man named Jacob Reese of Auburn, his wife and 4-year-old son. "Drive slowly and you won't get hurt," Barry said. "Just get into the main stream of traffic and keep going. Don't speed and don't try to signal anybody." Reese did as he was told. Inside the prison, meanwhile, rioting broke out and raged for hours, so that the attention of all police within 50 miles was fixed on the prison itself and not on the few men who had managed to escape.

Outside the town Barry and Pawlak forced the Reeses out of their car and headed for Syracuse, 26 miles away. In the suburbs of Syracuse, Barry spotted a house that appeared to be unoccupied. He drove into the empty garage, closed the door to hide the car from the road and then broke into the house.

Inside they found bandages and tape for Barry's wounds and a closet containing a few pieces of men's clothing. There was only one suit, which happened to fit Pawlak. The best outfit Barry could assemble consisted of a cap, a sweater, a pair of knickers and some loud golf socks. "I figured I would last about two minutes in public in that getup," he says, "but what else could I do? I put it on." In order to put on the golf socks, Barry had to remove his shoes, and as soon as he did so he realized his mistake. "My broken toes started to swell like sausage balloons," he says. "Somehow I got my foot into the sock, but the foot would go only part way into the shoe. So I doubled my broken toes up underneath and forced it in. I can still hear the bones grating."

After leaving the house, Barry and Pawlak set out on foot through the suburbs, looking for a second car to steal. Presently they located one in an attached garage beside a large house. For several hours they hid in a culvert beneath a road, watching and waiting until half an hour after the lights had gone out. Then they slipped into the garage. "I got into the car, and Pawlak got behind it to push it. We figured that if we could roll it down a little hill, we wouldn't have to start the motor until we were out of earshot."

Pawlak began to push the car and moved it about five feet, so that the

106

hood and windshield were outdoors. "I was just sitting there, hoping Pawlak wouldn't get tired pushing," Barry says, "when WHAM! a bullet came through the windshield. There was a guy on the second floor of the house aiming a gun at me. 'Stop or I'll shoot!' he says, after he's already shot. The bullet didn't hit me, but it might just as well have. Both my eyes were filled with splinters of broken glass. I was blind."

Pawlak panicked. He dashed out of a door at the rear of the garage, leaving Barry alone in the car. "I never saw him again. A little while later, the police caught him," Barry says. "I sat in the car for a couple of seconds, waiting for the guy to shoot again, not caring whether he hit me or not. Then I figured I had only one chance. So I pried open one of my eyes with my fingers and started the car with the other hand. I could see a little, enough. I drove that car out of the garage and down the driveway, thinking the guy would shoot me dead any second. He fired two or three times, but only hit the car, and suddenly I was out of there safe, driving down the road. Or at least I was safer. I was driving 50 miles an hour without lights, blind in one eye and still holding the other open with my fingers."

Soon the car, its gas tank apparently punctured by bullets, sputtered to a stop. Barry got out and began to limp through backyards in the wet darkness, still heading for the center of town. "I stumbled through flower beds and got mud all over my pretty golf socks, all the way up to my knees. It was about 4 o'clock in the morning, pouring rain, and I was getting weaker all the time. A Chihuahua could have come out of one of those houses and beat me up. Finally I floundered right into a fishpond, about a foot deep. I just stood there in the water and wanted to die.

"But after a while I walked out of the pond and sat on a rock beside it. I thought to myself, you'd better try to get clean, get the mud off yourself. So I took off those shoes and socks and washed the socks in the pond. And then I put the socks back on. Have you ever tried to put on a pair of wet woolen socks, over a pair of broken toes, in the rain, with two bullets through you and your eyes full of broken glass? Let me tell you something. Right then and there was when I finally realized what a damned fool I had been all my life. I was cured. If I lived through that one, I'd never steal anything again."

Somehow Barry survived the night, reached the center of town and had breakfast in a diner. To his surprise his strange costume and his eyes, one swollen shut and the other open a quarter of an inch, did not seem to attract much attention. "I suppose I looked like a crazy drunk, staggering around after an all-night bender, and nobody wanted to get near me. I thought that if I could get on a train and reach Albany, where I had some friends, I might have a chance. So I went to the station and bought a ticket. Then I looked out on the platform. Three state troopers."

In a last burst of ingenuity, Barry approached a newsboy who was walking the platform with an armload of papers. "I'm Mr. Gallagher," he said in a very low voice, handing the boy a quarter. Then, loud enough for the troopers to hear, he said, "Son, do you know that fat man who gets on the train every morning about a half hour after I do?" (Today Barry says, "There's always a fat man who gets on every train every morning at any station. I just hoped that kid would know his name.")

"Sure," the newsboy said. "You must mean Mr. Morell."

"Thaaaat's right," Barry shouted. "Well, you tell Mr. Morell that I'll be at his house tonight for dinner at 6, O.K.?"

"Yes, sir, Mr. Gallagher," the boy said, "I'll tell him."

Barry turned and boarded the train. The troopers ignored him.

In Albany one of Barry's friends gave him new clothes and found a doctor who would treat his wounds. That night, refreshed and alone, he moved on.

For more than three years Barry was a successful fugitive. He made his way south to New York, then to New Jersey, where he settled in a small town not far from Flemington. His wife joined him there. He took the name of a man he had once known, James Toner, and became a salesman of windshield wipers. He committed no more burglaries, kept the peace admirably and attracted no attention. But on the night of Oct. 22, 1932 there came the inevitable pounding on his door.

"Do you know what it was?" he says indignantly. "The Lindbergh kidnaping. The cops and the FBI had been going through every town near Flemington checking the background of every new resident. They weren't even looking for me."

For a time Barry was the prime suspect in the Lindbergh case and in a half-dozen other major crimes that had taken place during his vacation from Auburn. But after examining Barry closely, Dr. J. F. ("Jafsie") Condon, the celebrated middleman in the kidnaping, announced firmly that Barry was not the man to whom he had given the ransom money.

"Police chiefs from all over the place came to question me," Barry says, "including a nice guy from Greenwich, Conn. He figured I must have robbed the Percy Rockefeller house in his town in 1926 and he wanted to know how I did it. Of course I told him I didn't know a thing about it, and he said, 'Now look, Arthur. We're alone in the room. I'm not saying you did it or didn't do it. But let me tell you about it. That house is surrounded by a big stone wall, and between the wall and the house there are two of the toughest watchdogs you ever saw. I went out there with a couple of detectives and we tried to go over the wall, just to see if it was possible, and the dogs damned near killed us. Now if you were going to get into a place like that, what would you do?' "

"I told the chief it was all confidential and hypothetical, and then I said I'd try horsemeat. Throw it over the wall and see what happened.

"And then I said that if the dogs didn't like horsemeat, if they were sophisticated dogs, I'd try steaks. And if this didn't work either, I'd try something else. By this time the chief was hopping up and down in his chair. 'What?' he says. 'WHAT would you try? I've been busting my brains over this for six years.'

"Well, I said, if I were going to commit a dastardly crime like that, I'd go to a kennel and I'd buy a female dog in heat. Then I'd tie a rope around her collar, tie the other end to a tree outside the wall, and I'd lower her over the wall. After about five minutes I'd climb over the wall myself, walk into the house and steal $20,000 worth of jewelry. On the way out, so there wouldn't be any evidence, I'd pull my dog up over the wall after me, and drive back to New York.

"I thought the chief was going to die, but after a while he stopped laughing and said he would send me a box of cigars after I got back to jail. I got them an hour later."

Barry spent the next 17 years in jail, most of them in Attica Prison in New York and five of them in solitary confinement as punishment for his escape. Upon his release in 1949 he went home to Worcester and got a job with a boyhood friend who operates a chain of four restaurants. During the period of his parole, one of his chores involved collecting the receipts from all four restaurants and carrying them unguarded to the bank. "I never thought I would live to see the day," a Worcester policeman recently remarked, "but I have seen it, and there's no doubt of it. He's an honest man." Barry is not only honorably employed but has some active extracurricular interests as well. Recently, with the members having full knowledge of his past, he was elected commander of a local veterans' organization.

"I am not good at drawing morals," Arthur Barry said when asked

109

for the personal observation he said he wanted to make at the end, "and I don't want to bore anyone, but I would like to say this. When I was a young man I had many assets. I was not only intelligent, I was clever. I got along well with people on any level and, if I do say so, I had guts. I could have gone anywhere—to Wall Street, maybe—and made an honest fortune. So when you put down all those burglaries, be sure you put the big one at the top. Not Arthur Barry robbed Jesse Livermore, or Arthur Barry robbed the cousin of the King of England, but just Arthur Barry robbed Arthur Barry."

THE LEGAL SHENANIGANS OF HOWE
AND HUMMEL

by Richard H. Rovere

Although only Howe appears as the on-stage executor of the deceptions reported here, both members of the celebrated firm of Howe and Hummel were probably involved in planning them, as the title above duly credits.

HALF A LIFE *is* BETTER

Once Howe set at liberty a professional arsonist named Owen Reilly by demonstrating to the court that it could not, unless it possessed superhuman wisdom, sentence Reilly to anything, even after Reilly had pleaded guilty to a felony. Reilly, one of a number of young men who supported themselves by setting fire to buildings for people who felt that the insurance on their properties was more to be desired than the uncertain revenues they might bring in the future, had ignited a row of stores on the lower East Side. He was arrested, and he retained Howe to defend him. Howe or some other legal eagle in the office read up on the statutes covering arson and found that by pleading Reilly guilty to attempted arson, rather than letting him stand trial for having committed arson, they could save the firm the bother of a trial and save

Reilly the possible inconvenience of going to prison for the rest of his life. The District Attorney and the judge agreed to accept the lesser plea. When Reilly came up for sentence, Howe rose and solemnly stated that the law provided no penalty for the crime of attempted arson. The court begged enlightenment. The sentence for attempted arson, Howe said, like the sentence for any crime attempted but not actually committed, was half the maximum imposed by the law for the actual commission of the crime. The penalty for arson was life imprisonment, no less. Hence, if the court were to determine a sentence for Reilly, it would have to determine half a life. "Scripture tells us that we knoweth not the day nor the hour of our departure," Howe said. "Can this court sentence the prisoner at the bar to half of his natural life? Will it, then, sentence him to half a minute or to half the days of Methuselah?" The court agreed that the problem was beyond its earthbound wisdom. Reilly walked out, presumably to arm himself with a new supply of matches and tinder, and the legislature revised the arson statutes soon thereafter.

OPEN SEASON FOR MURDER

Once, in 1888, Howe very nearly forced the courts to declare an open season for murder. A cop-killer known as Handsome Harry Carlton had been convicted for the first-degree murder of Patrolman Joseph Brennan. He came up for sentence in December of 1888, the year the legislature abolished hanging as the established mode of execution and substituted electrocution. Howe studied the new edict, known as the Electrical Death Penalty Law, and discovered, to what must have been his ghoulish delight, that its authors had most seriously blundered. They had left an interval of almost seven months in which murder might be committed with impunity. The plan of the Legislature, when it had passed the law early in 1888, was to abolish hanging as of June 4 of that year and to institute electrocution on January 1, 1889; murderers convicted after June 4 were to be kept alive and in prison until the electric chair was ready. That was what it intended, but it was not what it said. The act provided that no one was to be hanged after June 4 and that electrocution was to begin on the first of the following year, but it carelessly went on to say that electrocution "shall apply to all convictions for crimes punishable by death on or after that date." Hence, the state had deprived itself of the legal power to execute anyone who killed with malice aforethought during a period of almost seven months. More than that, since death was the only punishment then provided for first-

III

degree murder, no punishment at all could be prescribed. An act for which no penalty is prescribed by law cannot properly be called a crime. When Handsome Harry, standing at the bar, was asked by the court what he had to say about why judgment of death should not be passed against him, Howe stepped forward and told the court, "He has this to say: He says that Your Honor cannot now pass any sentence of death upon him. He says that the Legislature by its enactment of Chapter 499 of the Laws of 1888, a statute passed, approved, and signed by the Governor . . ." The startled judge agreed that, by the wording of the law, he had no power to sentence Carlton or any other first-degree murderer. The newspapers made the most of the story, and the effect on the community was comparable to that of the Orson Welles' terror fifty years later, when a radio play about an imaginary invasion of the earth by men from another planet was widely mistaken for a news broadcast describing an actual event. The Tombs and every other place of detention in the state had not only the usual accumulation of murderers awaiting execution but also those who had been held over since June for the January unveiling of the hot seat. If Howe was upheld, all their sentences would be voided and the courts might be forced to dismiss all first-degree indictments for murders committed in the state between June 4 and December 31, 1888. Indeed, by extension, anyone who killed with intent in the remaining few weeks of the year could kill with impunity. The whole prospect was so distressing that Inspector Byrnes of the New York Detective Bureau and District Attorney Fellows had to release statements assuring the community that come what might, measures would be taken to insure its safety. They were not necessary. Howe was perfectly right in his reading of the law, but the higher courts took the position that no mere slip in syntax could be allowed to jeopardize human life and that the intent of the Legislature, no matter how awkwardly expressed, had not been to declare a Borgian holiday. Handsome Harry swung in the Tombs courtyard a few days after Christmas. He was the last man to hang there.

THE PITY OF IT ALL

Howe not only played the assigned part of the advocate: he staged whole productions. Any lawyer worth his fee, for example, will wring tears and sympathy from a jury with talk about a defendant's grief-stricken mother, his faithful wife, and his innocent children. Howe did it, too, but the talk was only part of the act. He brought the wife and children right into the courtroom and sat them down on the front bench. He had them perfectly trained to enact cross-bar pantomimes of devotion and trust with the prisoner at the counsel table. If by chance a particular defendant did not have a pretty wife, fond children, or a snowy-haired mother, he was not for that reason deprived of the sympathy they might create on his behalf. Howe would supply them from the firm's large stable of professional spectators. Repulsive and apelike killers often turned up in court with lamblike children and wives of fragile beauty. There are several cases on record in which the bench felt called upon to rebuke Howe for insinuating to the jury that the incarceration or execution of a defendant who, to the best of the court's knowledge, was single and childless when he was arrested would bring tragedy into the lives of so many people seated about the courtroom; and there is one instance of a stern reprimand from a judge who felt that a jury was somehow being imposed upon when, just as Howe reached the family motif in his summation, a young lady on the front bench found it the appropriate moment to bare her breast to the infant in her arms and look tenderly in the direction of the prisoner at the bar.

According to one of the earlier accounts of Howe's career, he discovered the appeal to American juries of mothers and children when he was trying his first murder case in New York. The case, as reported, was quite a spectacular one. It took place in 1863, and the defendant was William Griffin, the first mate on a merchantman that had been commandeered by the Union. Griffin was a Confederate sympathizer and made several efforts to persuade the master of his ship to go South and run the blockade. The master refused. One day he was found dead in his cabin. Griffin asked the owners to make him master, but they declined to do so. A new captain was appointed. Griffin asked him to desert with the ship. He, too, refused, and he, too, died shortly thereafter. By the time the third master was found dead in his cabin, the suspicions of the owners and of the government authorities were aroused. The body of the third dead captain was sent to Boston, where the contents of the stomach were analyzed and found to contain copper sulfide. Griffin was arrested and retained Howe to defend him. There was no question as to his guilt; he offered to plead guilty to manslaughter, but the federal government, which was prosecuting the case, would not accept the plea because of the element of treason in the crime. There were two trials. In the first the jury disagreed because Howe had made a strong case for the guilt of the government's chief witness, the steward of the ship, who had testified that he had seen Griffin rubbing some sub-

113

stance or other on the captain's claret glass. The government's case in the second trial was the same, and Howe offered the same defense. This time, however, the United States Attorney tried to influence the jurors by bringing in the three widows of the three murdered captains. Howe saw the disadvantage at which this put him, but he quickly overcame it. His own wife and his small daughter were in court that day. He built his entire summation around them. "Will you," he asked the jury, "on the sole authority of this disreputable scullion make that woman a widow—that child an orphan?" He said the same thing in different language for over an hour. Griffin was acquitted. "Probably there has never occurred," one thoughtful reporter observed, "a better illustration than this of the ready adaptation of circumstances to meet a sudden emergency."

TEARS AND TERROR

When Howe spoke of mothers and children, he generally cried. He was an automatic weeper. He could cry at will. "He was known as the most accomplished weeper of his day," Samuel Hopkins Adams wrote not long ago. "He could and would cry over any case, no matter how commonplace. His voice would quaver, his jowls would quiver, his great shoulders would shake, and presently authentic tears would well up in his bulbous eyes and dribble over. It was a sickening spectacle, but it often carried a jury to extraordinary conclusions." The dampness in the air must have been oppressive when Howe went to work. "After recess," the *Herald* said in an account of the trial of Annie Walden, the Man-Killing Race-Track Girl, who not long before had embroidered a gentleman's midriff with the contents of a six-shooter, "while Miss Walden, gently encouraged by her attorney, was telling her story in an almost inaudible voice, the third juror cried softly, the sobs of juror nine could have been heard in the corridors, and there was moisture in the eyes of all but one or two of the other jurors. The prisoner's many devoted friends held handkerchiefs to their eyes, and when Lawyer Howe spoke, his voice was full of tears." Miss Walden, too, was acquitted.

The lachrymose stage of a Howe trial was generally the closing one; the tears symbolized only one of several emotional experiences through which Howe led his auditors. He could make a jury laugh and he could frighten it into an acquittal. Once, he used sheer terror to free a killer. This was in the trial of Ella Nelson, another woman who had done in her sweetheart. Howe made his usual defense in such cases—that the man had been trying to commit suicide and that the woman, in wrestling the gun from him, had ended by doing, accidentally, what she had striven to prevent—and he saw that this time it was not going down so well. Francis L. Wellman, one of New York's most successful prosecutors, and a man who often opposed Howe, told the story several times in his books and in his lectures. "Howe," he wrote in one account, "simply frightened the jury into acquitting her. The summations had taken until far into the night, and the atmosphere in the courtroom was dark and eerie. Everyone was tired and nervous. The defendant, dressed all in black and wearing a heavy veil, sat facing the jury with her hands covering her face. Suddenly, as he came toward the end of his summation, Howe, still talking, walked over behind the prisoner and—his voice booming about what I do not know, for his words were obliterated in all our minds by what immediately followed—encircled her with his arms, took hold of each wrist, and flung them outward, at the same time grinding his fingernails into her flesh with a force that must have produced excruciating agony. Ella Nelson screamed as that jury and everyone else in the courtroom had never heard a human being scream before. Words can scarcely tell the effect it produced, but the records can. Howe ended his summation then and there. I was so nervous that I could scarcely muster my thoughts for my own address, and when I was done the jury, still unnerved, staggered from the courtroom, and came back with an acquittal in a few minutes. In the telling of it, there is nothing to suggest why the agonized wail of a defendant should secure her freedom; just as easily, one might suppose, it would signify her guilt. Nonetheless, Howe, the master of jurors, had calculated aright."

"THE LAMB OF GOD"

There was nothing Howe would not do to get his effects. Once he made an entire summation, hours long, on his knees. He could make a jury believe anything. In the Ella Nelson case, pleading accident, he made the jury believe that Miss Nelson's trigger finger had accidentally slipped not once but six times. Perhaps his most spectacular piece of speechmaking was his defense of a man named Edward Unger, who after killing his lodger, a certain Bolles, had thrown Bolles' head into a ferryboat paddle wheel and had, like the Hackensack Mad Monster, sent the rest of the body to Baltimore, that inexplicably popular boneyard. The prosecution based its theory of premeditation on the care with which Unger had disposed of his client's remains. Howe made no attempt to refute this entirely reasonable contention until the very end of his speech. Then, as though seized by a vision, he announced to the jury that Unger had killed Bolles in an uncontrollable fit of passion and had cut him up as a humane and fatherly afterthought. In fact, he said, Unger had not really dismembered Bolles at all. The hand had been his, but the force that guided the hand was the three- or four-year-old daughter, apparently genuine, whom Unger was at that moment dandling on his knee. As Howe developed this story, Unger had had to get rid of Bolles' body in order to spare his child the sight of death. "Yea," Howe said, " 'twas she who really did it, 'twas she, 'twas she. This innocent child, this lamb of God, guided the hand of this miserable wretch into his horrible deed. He knew, yes, even this lowly creature, knew that he could never face his Maker after curdling the soul of this babe with the sight of what her father had done. Could you send a man to his death for what a child hath done, for what a man hath done for the love of child?" The jury could not. Unger got off with manslaughter.

A BEE IN EVERY BONNET

Wellman, in one of his books, recalled a Howe client who came into court with his head swathed in yards of white muslin, as if to suggest an ailment of the mind that required bandaging lest the brains fall out or attract infection. Wellman, as prosecutor, told the jury that he had questioned the defendant before the trial and that the man's head had then been unbandaged and apparently unlacerated. But it did no good. Throughout the whole trial the prisoner simulated a kind of village idiot's tic, "twitching the right corner of the mouth," Wellman said, "and simultaneously blinking the left eye." As soon as this idiot left the court, however, "the defendant's face resumed its normal composure, except for the large grin that covered it as he lightly removed the cloths from about his forehead." Apparently, Howe used bandages on several occasions, for there is a report of a case in 1873 in which the defendant, one William Blakely, came into court with his head tied up, and, when he heard the jury's verdict of not guilty, "leaped from his seat, gave one loud shout of joy, tore the now useless bandage from his head, and speedily disappeared." Wellman told a story of a prisoner whose insanity, according to Howe, was accompanied by muteness, and who, having testified in an improvised sign language, walked over to his lawyer at the happy conclusion of the trial and said, "Silence is golden." The story is too good not to be apocryphal, but it suggests the measure of Howe's inventiveness.

116

Another notable acquittal through simulated lunacy was in the case of Alphonse Stephani, a wealthy young man who had murdered his late father's attorney, one Clinton G. Reynolds, because the attorney was not settling the estate to Stephani's satisfaction. Stephani tended to be rather attractive in his general contours. A graphic description of what Howe's make-up did for him survives in the address to the jury by the Assistant District Attorney who was trying the case. "Instead of the handsome, neatly dressed rich man's son whom we saw before this trial opened," the prosecutor told the jury, "you jurors saw a wild, unkempt creature, a Caliban in ugliness. Stephani's hair, let me tell you, had been untouched by shears or brush for months. He still wears the clothes he had on when arrested, but the fine linen is now in tatters and almost black. His outer garments are greasy and crusted with accumulations of intentionally spilled food. Not a word has he spoken to anyone, he whose speech was once so fine and elegant. With large black eyes as deep and mournful as Edwin Booth's, he has stared gloomily at nothing. Lear was a model of sanity beside him. But now let us look at the facts. There has been some testimony to show that he had fallen off a horse many years ago. . . ." But the prosecutor's facts made poor evidence compared with what the jurors saw. Stephani was not convicted.

"A TRUE HISTORY OF A GREAT CITY'S WILES AND TEMPTATIONS"

Howe and Hummel were never above encouraging new crime as a means of creating future business for themselves. In 1888 they wrote a book which had exactly this for its purpose. The book is, all things considered, a remarkable contribution to the national literature. Its title in full is *In Danger, or Life in New York. A True History of a Great City's Wiles and Temptations,* and it is signed "Howe & Hummel, the Celebrated Criminal Lawyers." Written somewhat in the fashion of the *Police Gazette,* which exposed the lasciviousness and corruption of metropolitan life in such a manner as to make them all but irresistible, *In Danger* professes a high moral purpose. It is prefaced by the pious declaration that it was written out of the authors' conviction that, in the words of a clergyman whose sermons had moved them both, "It had been well for many an honest lad and unsuspecting country girl that they had never turned their steps cityward nor turned them from the simplicity of their country home toward the snares and pitfalls of crime and vice that await the unwary in New York." These words, which

117

are almost the first in the book, are the last to be addressed to the honest and unsuspecting. The rest are for the dishonest and suspecting, and the book is in fact a kind of Real Estate Board brochure apprising out-of-town criminals of the superior facilities offered by New York and of the first-class legal protection available on Centre Street at "what we may be pardoned for designating the best-known criminal law offices in America."

It is possible to imagine a thief of the nineties coming to New York from Boston, say, or Philadelphia, with a copy of *In Danger* to keep up his enthusiasm en route, and, later, having the book propped up before him as he jimmies a safe or practices palming gold watches at home. Whereas the *Police Gazette* was merely titillating, *In Danger* is instructive. First it entices the larcenous with mouth-watering descriptions of the city's "elegant storehouses, crowded with the choicest and most costly goods, great banks whose vaults and safes contain more bullion than could be transported by the largest ships, colossal establishments teeming with diamonds, jewelry, and precious stones gathered from all the known and uncivilized portions of the globe—all this countless wealth, in some cases so insecurely guarded." Then it tells in gratifying detail, how in this wonder city "all the latest developments in science and skill are being successfully pressed into the service of the modern criminal." It describes the workings of a dozen skin games, gives the mathematical formulas for rigging the odds on horses and cards, and explains the methods of the most successful jewel thieves. It offers what is probably the most thorough and technically reliable discourse ever written on "the traveling bag with false, quick-opening sides," "lady thieves' corsets," and "the shoplifter's muff." Workable instructions are given for the home manufacture of all sorts of burglarizing equipment. The book enables any halfway intelligent reader to make a shoplifter's muff by ripping the stuffings out of an ordinary one and inserting a wire frame. "With one of these muffs," the authors say, "shoplifting is so easy as to be successfully practiced by novices." "In no particular," they go on, "can the female shoplifter be distinguished from other members of her sex except perhaps that in most cases she is rather more richly and attractively dressed." It is a fairly safe bet that a shoplifter who had read her Howe & Hummel carefully would be indistinguishable from others of her sex, for she would have been well instructed on the importance of neat and conventional dress in working hours, and she would have had an advanced course in spotting store dicks before they spotted her, looking carefully for them in their concealed perches "on seats suspended from the ceilings and in the folds of heavy draperies." Howe and Hummel leave their readers with a low impression of New York detectives generally, and they bring the gladdening intelligence in regard to the regular force that "instead of surrounding thieves with a network of evidence to convict them, the New York headquarters detectives furnish them with all the facilities for escape known to modern criminal practice." . . .

The folly of retaining any firm other than Howe & Hummel is illustrated by the story of Harry Weiler, who, after employing Howe & Hummel to defend him for the murder of his wife, had a falling out with his lawyers. Howe & Hummel had gotten Weiler a hung jury on the first trial, and were prepared to go on getting disagreements until the District Attorney gave up. Weiler, however, got uppity and hired another lawyer. He was promptly convicted and hanged. The value of good and steady relations with the firm is pointed up by the case of Maria, a girl who worked Boston night boats both as a prostitute and a thief. Maria's work was perilous, and she was frequently caught. However, she never "let her indignation get away with her but kept quiet and employed Counsellor Howe to defend her." Maria was probably a fictitious name, for the implication was that she was still profitably on the job at the time of writing. . . .

THE GOLDEN HUSSY

by Charles Lanius

For brains, beauty and brass, the world has rarely seen the likes of Conning Cassie Chadwick, who parlayed a vivid imagination and a genius for graft into millions of the finest green-paper dollars ever manufactured by a United States mint. As the lusty nineteenth century swooshed pell-mell into the speed-crazy twentieth, green-eyed, auburn-haired Cassie, the lush, passionate daughter of a poor Canadian section hand, was the queen of her profession.

The way she bamboozled a shrewd, reputable but mouthy Cleveland lawyer into believing that she was financially backed by Andrew Carnegie, the fabulously rich and powerful steel master, was sheer genius. As he spread the news, the magic of Carnegie's name hypnotized many

119

of the nation's brainiest businessmen, who shoved large bundles of greenbacks her way as fast as she could spend them. That was very fast indeed, and for a while she managed to blow about a million a year.

But on the bright fall day he invited Cassie to lunch in New York's Holland House the big-shot Cleveland mouthpiece knew only that he was a mighty lucky fellow. Surprised and enormously pleased that chance had brought him together with the stunning wife of Dr. Leroy Chadwick of Cleveland's socially prominent Chadwicks, he savored the delicious moments.

Back in Cleveland he had covetously observed the lovely Mrs. Chadwick, but he was far too cautious and eminently respectable to risk being caught making a pass in their hometown. But New York was different and for three days he had happily squired her about the big city in a kind of giddy seventh heaven. And she had been charmingly responsive.

But calculating Cassie, who had carefully contrived to meet her hometown admirer "accidently" in New York, was a long way ahead of him. Appraising her patsy, she decided that he fitted perfectly into the master plan for the most fantastic coup of her career. The attorney was a garrulous windbag, but had a definite knack for imparting confidential tombstone secrets convincingly. Suddenly she interrupted one of his entertaining anecdotes.

"I'm so sorry," she said with a note of regret in her voice, "but I have an important appointment this afternoon and must leave in a few minutes."

"What a shame!" replied her host, genuinely put out. "Who's the lucky man?"

Cassie laughed gaily. Then she became serious, seemed to hesitate. Then, "Do you happen to know Andrew Carnegie?"

"Well, no, I don't," he replied.

"Come with me then," said Cassie, rising, "and I'll introduce you. I'm on my way to see him now."

"I had no idea you knew Mr. Carnegie that well," said the lawyer, puzzled.

Cassie blushed, lowered her lovely green eyes and turned away. "Neither has any one else," she said. "However, I have known Mr. Carnegie extremely well over many years."

The lawyer hailed a hack and Cassie ordered the driver to take them to the Carnegie mansion at Fifth Avenue and Ninety-first Street. At the mansion, Cassie laid a hand on his arm.

"I think it would be better," she said softly, "if I had a few minutes alone with Mr. Carnegie to prepare him. I think I should explain that you are Cleveland's leading lawyer and that your advice on financial matters could be invaluable at home. You won't mind waiting a few minutes, I know."

"Oh, not at all, not at all."

Cassie hopped down from the cab and tripped through the iron gate and up the path to the door of the mansion. As the door opened, she turned and coquettishly flipped her gloves toward the lawyer and then slipped inside the house as though she owned it. Once inside she told the housemaid she wanted to see the housekeeper.

"I telephoned for an appointment this morning," she said.

The girl showed her into the domestics' parlor and the housekeeper joined her after a few minutes. Cassie explained that she wanted to check on the reliability of Hilda Schmidt, a maid she was thinking of hiring, who had formerly worked at the Carnegie mansion. The housekeeper was surprised.

"Why, I never heard of her."

It was Cassie's turn to show surprise, and the women thoroughly enjoyed themselves for a few minutes discussing the "deception of some people." When the subject was exhausted, Cassie asked if she might write a short note and killed another quarter of an hour scribbling. The women had another chat and all together Cassie remained in the Carnegie mansion about forty-five minutes. Then, carrying a bulging envelope of documents, she hurried apologetically to the waiting lawyer.

"I'm so sorry," she exclaimed, "but Mr. Carnegie is ill today. But he told me that he hopes to meet you another time."

Then as he helped her into the cab her foot slipped and she contrived to spill the envelope of documents. As he stooped to help gather them up it took only a quick glance to see that one was a note made out to Cassandra L. Chadwick and signed by Andrew Carnegie for a cool half-million dollars. There were three other notes for the same amount along with other securities running into some pretty big figures.

As the cab headed downtown Cassie appeared disturbed about the mishap. She sat quietly, but as they neared the hotel she turned and faced him squarely.

"You saw what is in the envelope, didn't you?"

"I must be honest with you," said the lawyer, "and tell you that I did —partly."

121

"I know you are a man of honor," Cassie began hesitantly, "and won't reveal . . ." She stopped short and said, "No, I'm going to tell you the truth, but you must promise never to divulge what I am about to say."

The lawyer promised.

For several years Cassie had steeped herself in details about Carnegie's life. Eagerly lapping up everything ever written about him, she had learned, for example, that because of his strong devotion to his mother he had refused to consider marriage until after her death. She had even been to Skibo Castle, Carnegie's home in Scotland, while on a European holiday with "Dr. Roy," as she called her husband.

Big fat tears came to her eyes as, between convulsive sobs, she poured out a moving tale of an illegitimate birth. Yes, she told the gaping, fascinated lawyer, Carnegie was her father. He had loved her mother, but because of old Mrs. Carnegie they couldn't marry. Then her mother died and she was brought up by foster parents in Canada. But Mr. Carnegie had always provided amply, very amply.

Arriving back at the hotel Cassie dried her eyes, stuffed the envelope in the vault and invited the thunderstruck attorney to her suite. She told him that Mr. Carnegie had advised her to have a trustworthy lawyer, completely without Carnegie connections, draw up an agreement in such a way that the secret would be kept but her interests protected in case something happened to him. She handed him a list, written in "Mr. Carnegie's own handwriting," of securities totaling $10,900,000 which Mr. Carnegie held for her.

"I know very little about legal and financial matters," murmured Cassie, fluttering her long eyelashes, "and I would like you to draw up the agreement. Mr. Carnegie thinks I should deposit the $7,000,000 in securities now in the vault downstairs with a reputable bank at home for safekeeping. Could you advise me about that, too?"

The flabbergasted lawyer did exactly what Cassie figured he would. He recommended Ira Reynolds of the Wade Park Banking Company in Cleveland. Reynolds was a bankers' banker with an unimpeachable reputation for strict integrity. Then, swearing never to breathe a word to a single soul, the lawyer drew up the agreement, hightailed it for Cleveland and had the time of his life confidentially broadcasting the astonishing secret all over the city.

Back in Cleveland, Cassie handed Reynolds a sealed envelope and a list of the securities it was supposed to contain.

"Here are seven million dollars in bonds and other securities," she said. "I leave them with you for safekeeping. But under the peculiar circumstances I want a note from you, a receipt to protect my loved ones in case anything happens to me."

The tightlipped banker thought about that for a moment and reached for his pen. After hearing the lawyer's eyeball account, it never occurred to the honest man to look into the sealed package.

A short time later Cassie wrote him that she had lost her list and requested him to send her a copy. The unsuspecting Reynolds sent the copy by return mail, signing his name at the bottom.

Before long, practically the whole country was whispering that Cleveland's charming Mrs. Chadwick was really the illegitimate daughter of the steel tycoon. The whole country, that is, except the privileged few pussyfooting around the forbidding, unapproachable Carnegie, who at the time had never heard of Mrs. Chadwick. But the tough old man was the least of Cassie Chadwick's worries.

She knew that old Andy, as well as being a philanthropist, was as unforgiving and ruthless as any man who ever lived. She figured rightly that no sane person would have the guts to risk the imperious steel king's vindictiveness by flaunting a bastardy rap in his face. On the other hand, she didn't mind being a bastard so long as she was a rich and beautiful bastard.

The two documents signed by a banker of Reynolds' standing and the juicy gossip about old Andy's illegitimate daughter opened the country's vaults to Cassie. At first she borrowed only modest amounts like $50,000 at a clip, paid the interest promptly and the loans when necessary. She even borrowed $75,000 from Oberlin College in Ohio on her unsecured note. Then, her credit established, she went after the big dough.

The Chadwicks never had it so good, and lived it up in the grand manner. Bankers and loan sharks soon discovered that Cassie seemingly had no business sense at all and an almost utter disregard for financial values. She was always in need of ready cash to cover her expenditures, and willing to pay big interest rates.

Gorgeous Cassie had the morals of an alley cat and the conscience of a starving wolverine, but she was extremely generous. The jewelled tokens she gave away at her lavish parties were often worth small fortunes and Clevelanders vied for invitations.

Traveling like royalty in Europe, she bought fabulous jewelry, including a $90,000 pearl necklace. By simply flourishing a letter from her fellow Clevelander, Senator Mark Hanna, the big boss of the Republican Party, which in effect told customs officials to lay off his friend Mrs. Chadwick, she brought the pretties home duty-free.

With Cassie it was a case of easy come, easy go. From the time she was fifteen and took a farmer boy in her hometown of Eastwood, Ontario, for a diamond ring, she had conned her way through life. Of course, they spent long hours frolicking in neighborhood haystacks, but that was only because she enjoyed the sensation and the husky young farmer happened to be handy.

But delectable blond Cassie wasn't the kind of girl you could keep down on the farm. Deciding to travel at about the same time she heard about a wonderful invention called the bank check, she had some calling cards printed reading "Miss Bigley—Heiress to $15,000." Journeying to Toronto, she showed the hungry merchants her card and proceeded to push a batch of what was probably the crudest rubber that ever bounced.

Her pitch was corny but it worked for four free-wheeling days. Then she felt the heavy hand of the law. As the gates of the hoosegow clanged shut, she managed to convey the impression that what was happening to her shouldn't be happening to a dog. Even the tough old matron felt sorry for her. In court she sat wide-eyed and silent through a parade of witnesses.

"Haven't you an explanation?" asked the judge, who had been giving her a full-blooded masculine onceover. "Don't you wish to make a statement in your own defense?"

"No, sir," replied Cassie contritely.

After a moment's thought the judge went into a whispered consultation with the prosecutor. He tapped his forehead meaningly and the prosecutor promptly petitioned that the prisoner be discharged on grounds of insanity. The judge apparently didn't think she was nutty enough for the looney bin and turned her loose.

Cassie scooted out of Toronto fast. Unrepentant, and pausing in Eastwood only long enough to write her married sister in Cleveland to expect a visitor, she took off to invade the United States. Now twenty, poised and superbly stacked, she attracted boisterous, booming Cleveland's males as honey draws flies.

Cassie was never exactly promiscuously promiscuous. She insisted that her boy friends be well-heeled, and culled them over to find a pigeon. She soon had Dr. Wallace Springsteen, a promising young physician whom she met at a church social, securely on the hook.

The marriage lasted only three days. During the honeymoon a bailiff appeared and attached the furniture to pay for some walloping trousseau bills Cassie had charged to the doctor. He looked at the total and fainted dead away. He came to screaming, so Cassie walked out.

"Such a stuffy man," she told her sister, "and, Mary, I don't believe his papa is nearly as rich as he said."

Springsteen sued for divorce and faded out of her life.

Deciding that travel would mend her broken heart, she didn't let the fact that she was broke deter her in the least. She went downtown, visited three mortgage brokers, and on the way home bought two tickets for a vaudeville matinee the following afternoon. She invited Mary to see the show, but the next day was almost prostrate with a pounding migraine.

"But, darling," said Mary, "I can't go and leave you ill, alone."

"Now, Mary," gushed Cassie, "I insist that you go on and enjoy the show. Why, it makes my head worse to think of wasting the tickets."

Mary toddled off, and when the first mortgage broker arrived at the appointed hour, Cassie's noggin was miraculously clear as a bell. She mortgaged Mary's furniture for $240, and as the other brokers arrived on schedule, completed similar deals. By the time unsuspecting Mary fluttered in babbling about that "wonderful, wonderful show," Cassie had more than $700 in traveling money stashed away.

Off to Buffalo on the morning express, she registered at the best hotel in town. Before nightfall it was well established that the lovely Mrs. Gwendolyn de Rimford was the wife of Otis de Rimford, the rich gold mine operator, presently on his way from China to join her. They planned to build a summer home nearby, believing that the lake air would improve Mrs. de Rimford's delicate health.

Everyone felt a little sorry for the charming, ailing woman, "alone and all," and the respected ladies at the hotel were delighted to introduce her to the town merchants. Being good businessmen, they encouraged her to run up huge bills and even advanced modest sums of cash against the day the mining magnate hove into town and paid for everything. Even the hotel manager let her dip into the till for $1,500.

When she had milked the Buffalo burghers dry, Cassie sent herself a telegram instructing her to meet her husband in Chicago where he was detained on business. Leaving in storage a couple of newly purchased trunks filled with newspapers, she skedaddled to Erie, where Mrs. de Rimford evaporated and Lydia Shoreham, General Tecumseh Sherman's niece, was born.

For several years Cassie made a good living taking the suckers in eastern cities. Although she managed to stay a jump ahead of the law, she tired of the road and went back to Cleveland where she met and married William Scott, a wealthy landowner. In less than a year she went through Scott's bankroll, so she kissed him tenderly and said goodbye.

Cassie next appeared in Toledo as Madame Lydia Devere, the clairvoyant. Her system of penetrating the past, future and present was practically foolproof. By putting a couple of intelligent private eyes on the payroll she soon knew more intimate details about the lives of Toledo's leading citizens than the police department and the sheriff's office combined. And what she learned she sold for plenty.

Almost her first customer was the jealous wife of a rich contractor who suspected her spouse of playing musical chairs with the blond wife of a prominent attorney. But she couldn't catch them at it and the suspense of not knowing for sure was driving her crazy. Madame Devere announced that the fee for the information would be a flat $1,000.

"All right," said the woman, "it's worth it to know the truth. And if what I suspect is true, I'll dismember the stupid, double-crossing so-and-so."

"That is your affair," replied Madame Devere in her best professional manner. "I concentrate best during the full moon. It begins tomorrow. Come back in three days and I'll tell you the truth. Be sure you bring the money."

Within twenty-four hours her efficient hawkshaws had the affair nailed down, complete with dates and times. Madame Devere asked the contractor to call at her house and told him about his wife's visit and what she had learned of the liaison. Her price for silence was $5,000 cash on the barrelhead.

"But that's blackmail," protested the contractor.

"So!" replied Madame Devere sweetly.

The contractor knew he was on the hook and paid up. The same day she summoned his blond girl friend, who donated $800 and a diamond ring to the kitty. The contractor's wife threw in her $1,000 and was greatly relieved to discover that her husband's interest in the lawyer's wife was purely platonic. Madame Devere netted about $7,000 after expenses.

For three years Cassie prospered as Madame Devere, the all-knowing clairvoyant. She was the best-dressed woman in Toledo, owned a fortune in jewels and had a safety-deposit box stuffed with cash. But she hungered for more, and since she was a crook at heart, her larcenous instincts overcame her better judgment.

A lovesick clerk proved her undoing. She had wheedled him into discounting $20,000 worth of notes at the First National Bank of Toledo. It was a straight banking transaction except that the notes turned out to be phony. In exchange for his liberty, the patsy spilled the beans. Charged with forgery, Cassie got nine years in the Ohio State pen at Columbus. She was checked in as Lydia Devere.

Cassie was a model prisoner and charmed the entire institution. She especially captivated a male member of the Board of Pardons who worked so hard in her behalf that in slightly less than three years she was paroled in custody of her sister in Cleveland. Dyeing her hair copper, Cassie carefully kept her nose clean for the next three years until the end of her parole in 1896.

During this period of inactivity she met Dr. Leroy Chadwick, a slender, mustached widower with aesthetic tastes, who was the very essence of respectability in Cleveland. He was also rich, ready and ripe for plucking. Early in 1897 they married in Canada and Cassie moved in as mistress of the huge Chadwick mansion.

Dr. Roy soon discovered that his bride was a whizz at figures. In no time at all she was handling all the family's finances, and the Chadwicks began living on a lavish scale. Dr. Roy had money, all right, but not enough to finance Cassie's extravagances. They caught up with her and she was forced to put the mansion in hock.

As the pressure built up, Cassie was perfecting her biggest swindle of all. Learning that her dupe, the Cleveland attorney, was making a business trip to New York, she put her plan in action by hopping an earlier train. When he arrived, she was comfortably installed in the hotel where he habitually stopped, and the rest was a matter of colossal nerve, timing and knowing exactly how much heat to turn on to keep him goggle-eyed.

Dr. Roy, an easygoing fellow in love with his wife, abhorred money matters and had always let Cassie hold the purse strings. Although frequently dazzled by her free spending, he attributed their new affluence to her extraordinary financial genius.

Whenever she ran short of folding money she looked up a sucker and slipped him a monetary mickey in the form of a "promise to pay at dividend time." She gaffed Banker Herbert Newton, a flint-hearted Bostonian, for $195,000. In Pittsburgh, James Friend, a multi-millionaire manufacturer, shelled out $850,000 and was delighted to do business with her.

Sometimes Cassie didn't even have to ask for loans. Loan sharks came to Cleveland and urged her to accept their money. Charles T. Beckwith,

127

president of the Citizens National Bank of Oberlin, knew a good thing when he saw it. He called on her, and she took $700,000 of his bank's cash.

Cassie rode high on the tiger's back until toward the end of 1904. Dr. Roy was gadding about in Europe and Cassie was on a spending spree in New York when the blow fell. Banker Newton sued to recover his loan and there was a disastrous run on Beckwith's bank. The newspapers screamed that Mrs. Chadwick was into the institution for a total of $1,250,000 and Beckwith keeled over from heart failure.

Newspapers dug up the startling fact that a former convict ran Cleveland society and had taken the country's top financial brains for a ride. Cassie's total depredations were estimated at more than $20,000,000.

Bank runs were reported from almost every city Cassie had ever visited. A couple were ruined and a bank at Elyria, Ohio, staved off a panic only by producing a mortgage on the Chadwick mansion, securing $40,000 Cassie had borrowed. Reynolds, a sharp banker, quickly merged the Wade Park Bank with the Cleveland Trust Company, which announced that it had none of Cassie's paper.

Many of Cassie's victims never came forward at all. Some feared ridicule and others still believed she was Carnegie's illegitimate daughter and that he would eventually pay off everything.

Cassie was extradited to Cleveland and went on trial in March, 1905, with sixteen indictments against her. Carnegie was summoned as a prosecution witness but was never called to the stand. She was found guilty on six counts and sent to the Ohio State Penitentiary for ten years.

The strain of the arduous trial had taken its toll. Now in her midforties, she began to look it. Toward the end of 1907, the confinement got her and she sickened. Then in October, the magnificent swindler who had reveled in opulent splendor, turned her face to the wall and died on a hard prison cot.

KING OF THE SPOOK WORKERS

by William Lindsay Gresham

The year, 1868. The place, London. The town house of a noble lord. A clear, crisp winter evening.

The curtain of our true melodrama rises to reveal a Victorian drawing room, jammed with sofas, massive oak tables, spindly tables of mahogany, armchairs, footstools, bric-a-brac. A mixed gathering, gentlemen in tail coats and white stocks, ladies in the enormous hoop skirts of the era, billowing with petticoats of a stiff material called crinoline. Buzz of excited conversation held in check by a note of reverence and awe.

The doorbell jangles, and then the butler announces, "Mr. Daniel Dunglas Home."

He stands, smiling wanly, upon the threshold. The host hurries forward, takes his arm and presents him to the company. He kisses the ladies' hands with a stateliness already a bit old-fashioned, and when he comes to you and grips your hand between his two cold, moist palms you shudder in spite of yourself. He is a gaunt, cadaverous man, a couple of inches under six feet. His voice is hollow, low-pitched, with a faint trace of a Scottish burr. You are prepared to dislike him at once.

He is about to pass on when he pauses, shades his eyes with his hand and says softly, "Three years ago you had a splendid idea which might have developed into something profitable. But the conditions were not right for its inception. Now . . . you have met a person—a lady, in all likelihood—who will help you to achieve what is nearest to your heart." The china-blue eyes seem to search into your very soul. "Isn't that right?"

A swift review of your past finds just such a situation. You nod, puzzled. Home smiles, giving out warmth like a fireplace on a cold night, and places his hand gently on your shoulder.

"I thought so. Awfully good to have you with us. God bless you."

He passes along. Your hostility has vanished. It is simply impossible to dislike the fellow, in spite of the rumors circulating about him—charlatan, cheap humbug, and hints of "secret vices." Home comes, sees and conquers.

129

After a tray of wine has gone the rounds, the host invites you into a small sitting room. Here he becomes simply one of the group. The king of the evening is Home, the greatest spirit medium who ever lived.

A lively fire is popping on the hearth and Home places a wire screen before it. Then he takes you gently by the hand and says, "Our new friend . . . over there behind the large table."

You squeeze into your place between a long oak table and the wall. A lady is placed on each side of you; between the billowy oceans of taffeta you feel hemmed in and a little trapped. One by one the medium assigns the places. The company of eight are seated along the edge of the table and at each end, leaving the other side empty.

Home draws up his chair.

"I feel that conditions are excellent this evening," he murmurs dreamily. "Excellent. My lord, will you lead us in prayer?"

The old earl, in a muffled and somewhat embarrassed tone, prays, "for open hearts, charity, courage and for greater knowledge of God's will for all present." A chorus of subdued "Amens" follows.

Rap! Rap! Rap! Rap! Rap!

The sounds seem to come from the table on which everyone has placed his hands, palms down, little fingers touching those of his neighbors.

Home sighs, closes his eyes and says softly, "They wish the alphabet. Will you, sir, start to repeat it, letter by letter?"

This means you.

You begin. "A— B— C—"

At L there is a loud rap. You start again, to be stopped at E. Then at S again.

Home speaks, "The message is clear. *Less light.* Is that it?"

Rap! Rap! Rap!

Languidly he rises and blows out the flame of a candelabra on the mantelpiece. This leaves the room illuminated only by the bright flicker of the fire.

More raps, and then the table tilts and gyrates, the hands of the sitters seemingly try to hold it down but to no avail. Home leans back in his chair, his eyes closed. From his lips comes the voice of a child.

"Good evening, everyone. This is Danny Cox. Your lordship . . . please, m'lord . . ."

The old earl leans forward intently. "Yes, my dear boy?"

"Please tell Mama and Papa not to mourn for me so. Tell them not to be sad. There's a little dog here, very much like our Toby at home . . ."

The messages come, the voices change. At last Home sighs and opens his eyes. "Did anything of interest occur?"

The tension broken, the sitters all babble at once. Home rises, stretches his gaunt shoulders. Then he resumes his chair and asks, "May we have the accordion?"

The host quietly gets up and brings it. The medium takes it, a small instrument, in his left hand by the end which has two bass keys. His other hand is seen lying motionless on the table top. As he holds the accordion by one end its bellows quivers and elongates. A faint melody comes from it:

> "Ye banks and braes of bonnie Doon,
> How can ye bloom sae fresh and fair . . ."

You strain your eyes in the gloom to see what is moving the accordion but it seems to be fingered by an invisible hand. The firelight glints from a metal ornament on the case as it continues to play.

Home holds it across the table to the lady on your right. She seizes it by the bass end and again, with no motion of her hand or fingers, it goes on playing softly. Then it is twitched from her grasp, floats and skitters across to the medium and then off and under the table, this time moaning in discord.

Home speaks gently. "Hear the discordant notes? That means that someone here is not in harmony with the others."

This strikes at you, for you have been wondering: *How does he make the thing play without touching the keys?*

Beneath the table the instrument bumps along, coming to rest under the chair of the host.

The girl on your left tenses and whispers, "Something is *moving* under the table cloth."

Home's hands are outstretched before him on the velvet covering. He moans softly. The cloth at his right is pushed up; you can see it dimly against the firelight. Then, sliding over the edge of the table, comes a slender white hand that glows faintly. It feels its way down the table, seems to pick up a pencil and write on a tablet. The pencil drops, a page is torn off and folded and a note is tossed down before you. Later it proves to be a greeting from your grandmother in the spirit world.

The hand now approaches the medium, gently feels its way up his shoulder and caresses his hair. When it passes across his face, you see that the wrist terminates in a faintly luminous cloud. At last it vanishes below the table again.

Home smiles, rises and goes to the fire. He kneels down, removes the screen, stirs among the coals with the poker, picks out a blazing coal between thumb and forefinger and carries it to the host.

Standing above him, the medium asks resonantly, "Have you faith?" The old man frowns.

Home turns away. "I'm afraid not enough, my lord."

A lady stretches out her hand, her eyes, in the firelight, flowing with fanatical devotion to the medium.

Gently he lays the red coal in her palm and asks, "Do you feel anything?"

"It's . . . it's *warm*. Not painfully."

"Faith. Faith. How great is faith," the medium says in a sort of chant. He picks up the coal, now black, and returns it to the grate, takes the shovel and extinguishes the fire somewhat with ashes. The room is now dark, save for the pale oblongs of starlight which are the windows.

His voice comes from the darkness beside the curtains. "I . . . I am rising. They are bearing me up gently . . . gently as a mother lifts her dreaming babe from its cradle. I am rising . . . up . . . up . . ."

The girl beside you now grips your hand tightly. "Look. Look! He is being *floated* across the window."

Sure enough, against the faint gray of the night sky you see the form of the medium, seven or eight feet from the floor, lying horizontally in the air; it floats across the window and then slowly returns.

His voice comes again, faintly. "Now I am descending, gently, gently as a snowflake . . ."

He steps forward out of the darkness to the last glowing embers of the fire, warms his hands, crosses the carpet to the gas jet, turns it on and lights it by pointing to it with his forefinger.

Home, now collapsed in a chair, is deathly white. The host rings and sends for a bottle of porter for their honored guest.

That is what you would have seen, had you lived in London during the 1860s—had you moved in high society, and had you been fortunate enough to be admitted to a séance by the king of the spirit mediums, Daniel Dunglas Home.

Daniel Home played his role on the off-beat from start to finish. His life, or the facts of it, are commonplace and an open book. He lived with the privacy of a goldfish all his days and he died at the age of fifty-three, full of honors and decked out with diamonds—jewels he had been given by the crowned heads of Europe.

He is regarded as the greatest enigma of physical research, the one "medium" who was never exposed and discredited, the medium who never took cash for his séances, the only one whose phenomena remain "inexplicable."

In the 1850s the Western world was on the verge of a religious upheaval. Darwin and his champions had blown a wide breach in the bulwark of "fundamentalism." And the time was ripe for a re-evaluation of creeds and dogmas. The old-fashioned hell-fire preachers, after scaring a portion of every generation into St. Vitus dance or atheism, were being forced to pull in their horns.

The time was over-ripe for an explosion of religious fervor in a different direction. But when it came it came in a totally unpredictable fashion—in a widespread, fanatical belief in messages purported to come from spirits of the dead, transmitted by certain gifted individuals called mediums. Sometimes these messages came from the mouth of the medium, who was in a state of trance. But as often, the signals from the other world were conveyed by means of raps on tables and woodwork. It is significant that the spirits never thought of this means of making themselves known until the invention of the Morse telegraph in 1844.

Born on March 20, 1833, in the hamlet of Currie, Scotland, not far from Edinburgh, Home was christened Daniel Dunglas *Hume*. His father, a workingman given to strong drink, sired numerous children. Little Dan was given to a childless aunt to raise and she emigrated to the States, settling in what is now Norwich, Connecticut, when Dan was nine.

He was sickly from the start and spent much of his childhood in bed, dosed with home remedies for "his chest." He fought tuberculosis all his life. Few men ever had a more dismal start and from so meager an inheritance built so glittering a life.

A pampered invalid child, unable to play with other children, Dan specialized in all of the non-athletic arts, reciting the heart-throb narrative poems of the day, singing sentimental ballads and accompanying himself on the piano. If his early personality disgusted the more robust of his neighbors as saccharine and more than slightly phony, middle-aged women doted on him.

Then, when he was in his teens, came the mania for spirit rappings. On his mother's side—the McNeills—he was descended from Highlanders possessed of the "second sight" and Dan soon began entertaining his aunt and her friends with accounts of angelic visions and heavenly dreams in which he saw his dead relatives living blissfully in the hereafter, imploring the living not to grieve over them. Then Daniel began to produce raps.

A boy who is forced by ill-health to spend much of his time in bed will

133

practice various skills as an outlet for his energies. Some become whittlers, some water colorists. Dan became an adept at producing raps. Relations with his aunt, Mrs. McNeill Cook, became strained the more Dan leaned toward spiritualism. Mrs. Cook, a devout member of the Kirk of Scotland, would have no doings with such impious things.

One morning in 1850—Dan was seventeen—he came into the kitchen where his aunt was preparing breakfast and suddenly a torrent of raps began to resound from the floor, the woodwork and the table itself.

Mrs. Cook blew her cork. Screaming, "So ye've brought the devil into my hoose, hae ye?" She picked up a kitchen chair and shied it at Daniel's head.

He ducked without much difficulty and left the cottage in silent dignity. Mrs. Cook threw his Sunday suit out the window after him.

On leaving his foster mother's home, Daniel retreated to a previously prepared position—the house of some kindly, credulous neighbors who were fascinated by the new fad of spirit rappings.

Dan now claimed that his father was really an illegitimate son of the Earl of Home and he began to spell his name with an "o" although he always pronounced it "whom." This gave him the added glamor of noble birth—even with a bar sinister—which went over big in Connecticut. In the evening, after the supper dishes had been cleared away and the family sat about the dining-room table, hands pressed against its surface, waiting for the spirits, they were not disappointed. The table began to rock and roll.

Much of an acrobatic table's behavior depends on the unconscious pushing and pulling of the sitters, helped out by the medium, of course. Dan discovered the postern gate in the human mind by which it can be entered unobserved—suggestion.

"Look, look—the table is trying to tip up at my end! Don't you feel it? I can't hold it down. . . . Do you feel it dipping under your hands?" His shock of auburn hair bent intently over the polished surface, his long, waxen hands spread before him, his intense, pale face taut, Daniel conjured spirits from the vasty deep. "Wait! Over Miss Cynthia's head . . . a spirit light. A spark . . . no, now it's like a pale green cloud. . . . Don't you see it?"

They saw it. They felt ghostly touches on their shoulders and hair, heard strange whispers (ventriloquism is an ideal art for an invalid boy to master).

The more séances Dan held the more remarkable grew the phenomena. If you place your fingers on a polished table top, press hard and

134

then let one finger slip a fraction of an inch, you will be rewarded by a distinct rap. Similarly, if you brace the heel of your shoe against one of the legs of your chair and slip it the same way you'll get another rap. But that is only the kindergarten stage of the art. Tie a bolt or a small fishing sinker on a black silk thread and let it down a crack in the woodwork or a hole in the wall, and you can produce raps that sound—in a silent house at night—like the blows of a sledge hammer.

Dan decided then and there never to take money for exercising his gifts of mediumship and he stuck to it through thick and thin all his life. And there were some thin times, too. He was intelligent enough to realize that if he took no money there was no legal fraud and he counted on his powers as a charm artist always to have a roof over his head.

Dan mastered the speech of cultured people as he was later to master several European languages. He soaked up elegant manners like a blotter. When he wanted something he subtly let his friends know it and when they got it for him it always seemed to be their idea. His gratitude was explicit, delivered with the intense, burning sincerity of the talented confidence worker.

Going from one family to another, learning his trade of professional mystery man and charmer, Dan made the acquaintance of many of the most prominent spiritualists in the northeastern United States. Finally when the chill of a New York winter laid him low with a serious chest complaint, his doctor, an ardent spiritualist, told the youth that only the climate of Europe could save his life.

In 1855 he sailed for England, his passage paid by a Mr. and Mrs. Jarves of Boston, wealthy cosmopolites, art collectors and spiritualists. He knew not a soul in Europe but he had a little black book of addresses and the first of these was a Mr. Cox, who ran a hotel in London. Mr. Cox was a spiritualist, and Dan and he became lifelong friends. Dan paid no board at the hotel; or rather, he paid in raps, table tipping and "messages."

Dan by this time had discovered another trick of the trade: You can tell a person of the marvels which have happened to other people in your presence and he will soon take some of them and retell them as his own adventures, without realizing that he is decorating the truth. Much of the myth of Home can be explained by this simple manipulation of minds.

One of the most persistent legends about Home, which got a powerful assist from his own memoirs, was that he always performed "in the full light." The hell he did! By "full light" his Victorian chroniclers meant the flicker of a double gas jet sometimes helped out by a brace of candles. And in such a light most of the business went on under the table. Dan—or the spirits, rapping on the table—would call for "less light" and it was logical; only in the dark can you see the luminous forms, faces and hands.

Once in England and safely ensconced at Cox's spiritualist hotel, he found that the *haut monde* of believers were awaiting him with open arms—the Baroness de Ruthyn, the Marchioness of Hastings, Lady Combermere, Sir Charles Isham. He dined out every evening on the strength of what he could make the dining-room table do after dinner. He kept to his original principle of never accepting cash, but he let it be known that he liked beautiful things, such as diamonds, which are a medium's best friend.

Invitations came so thick and fast that Dan could afford to play hard to get. This boosted his stock. It became impossible to have a "sitting" with Mr. Home unless one could secure an introduction into his circle from someone whose social position was unassailable. The penniless Scots laddie was doing all right.

It is no discredit to such men as William Cullen Bryant, famous American poet and editor of the staid New York *Evening Post,* the great English novelist, William Makepeace Thackeray, or later the eminent chemist, Sir William Crookes, that they were mystified by the things they saw happening at Home's séances. They were men of great intelligence but they simply were not trained observers of mediumistic tricks.

Once in a great while there were bitter articles in the press, such as the time Miss Celia Logan, a lady journalist who moved in high circles, saw Home place something quietly on the mantelpiece. The host saw it too and slipped it in his pocket. Afterward it proved to be a vial of olive oil in which bits of phosphorus had been dissolved. During the evening Home had produced glowing spirit hands. Such unfavorable press notices had no effect on Dan's staunch supporters. A lifted eyebrow and a word on the lengths to which some sceptics would go in order to discredit him and the glorious truth of survival which he, by means of his spirit controls, was bringing to the world. This was more than enough.

Since Dan always played it safe, never openly took money, and paid his way with mystery and fascination, his marks never "rumbled" and his "gaffs" never beefed. He gave them nothing to beef about. And while he frequently performed before sceptics, they were always gentlemen, and Dan was the guest of honor of mutual friends. To have grabbed a spirit hand would have been an insult to the host.

There was one time, though, when Dan had a very close shave indeed. This involved Britain's most romantic couple—the poet, Robert Browning, and his wife, Elizabeth Barrett. Elizabeth was an ardent spiritualist, Robert a thunderous sceptic. It was the only subject on which they ever seriously disagreed. At the one séance with Home which the Brownings attended, the medium brought forth a ghostly face resembling, in the dim light, a baby's head; he claimed that it was a son of Robert Browning's who had died in infancy. Here Dan Home's pipe lines of gossip did him dirt. The Brownings had, in truth, lost a baby—Elizabeth had had a miscarriage, but there were no infant deaths in their marriage, and the inference was that Robert had had a son out of wedlock. In a towering rage the poet seized the ghostly face and later claimed that he had found it to be "the rascal's bare foot."

After scoring a tremendous success in Britain, Dan left for the milder climate of Italy and the colony of English and Americans who wintered there.

Then, in Rome, on the tenth of February, 1856, Home's "power" strangely left him. The spirits informed him that it would return in one year to the day but now he was without it. There has been much speculation about this odd circumstance. One explanation has never been advanced and it is this: Dan may have had a genuine religious conversion. In any event, he took instruction and became a Roman Catholic. Then, on returning to Paris, he found himself broke and friendless, except for his confessor, the famous Father Xavier De Ravignan, a Jesuit scholar, to whom Dan had been referred by the Pope. Without his miracles—viewed as black magic by the church—Home was just a "vulgar American."

His fashionable friends faded away; he had no wonders to amuse them now. People who knew him by sight would see him sitting for hours in a church, his pale, haggard face twisted by some inner torment. Then, true to their promise, the spirits returned—to the day.

And with them came a messenger from Louis Napoleon, Emperor of the French, demanding a séance. In vain did Father Ravignan entreat Home to fight against the powers of darkness. Daniel explained that he had no control over the mysterious presences; he was merely the medium through which they manifested themselves to the living. The good father offered to exorcise the demons, but Dan bade him a tearful farewell. Dan could turn on real tears at the drop of a friendship. The Tuileries and all the pomp and glitter of the French court were waiting for him—people who had plenty of spare diamonds. He put on his good suit, took his courage in both hands, and presented himself to the Emperor and his beautiful, stormy Empress Eugenie.

Our only account of what happened that night is from Dan's own memoirs and according to him he did everything but raise a fresh corpse. Whatever happened, Louis Napoleon and Eugenie were duly impressed, and Dan came through with flying colors and more jewelry. Soon he had the nobility in the hollow of his bony hand.

He came back to the United States just long enough to collect his little sister, Christine, and take her back to France. The Empress wanted to have her educated at a convent school at her expense.

Dan's life was brightened at this point by romance. He met a Russian girl of good family, a little seventeen-year-old beauty, and they announced their engagement.

Alexandre Dumas, creator of the Count of Monte Cristo, a jovial, 300-pound mountain of a man who never stopped talking about his own greatness, delighted in Dan Home, who was a magnificent listener. Dumas gleefully agreed to go along to Russia as Dan's best man. The bride, Alexandra de Kroll, was the daughter of General Count de Kroll of the Imperial Russian Army.

Dan was a miracle man in very truth now, for the girl's family—Czar Nicholas had been her godfather—offered no objection to her marriage to a penniless adventurer of humble origin who was obviously in wretched health.

It seemed as though Dan were on Easy Street at last. The following year a son, Grischa, was born to the happy couple. But in those days no one knew that tuberculosis is contagious. Little Sacha began to lose weight. Her eyes grew too large and bright. Soon Daniel was accepting invitations alone while Sacha stayed home and in bed. After four years she died, believing to the end in the genuineness of her husband's psychic gift.

Home was sincerely stricken by her death. Also it was a double tragedy, for a venomous cousin of Sacha's started suit to regain her estate. Dan was broke in England, with a small son to support. Kindly spiritualists offered to care for the child but Dan needed cash. He tried lecturing, giving dramatic readings, acting. Finally he got an advance on his memoirs and this tided him over for a while. A friend of his helped him write the book. At last a group of sympathetic spiritualists founded a Spiritual Athenaeum in London and made Dan its full-time secretary on a small salary and gave him rooms over the office and hall.

But misfortune was lying in wait like a dragon around a bend in the road. This dragon was named Mrs. Jane Lyon. She was seventy-five years old, a widow, and she believed in spirits. She wanted to get in touch with her dead husband, Charles. Charles arrived on schedule, speaking in the trance voice of Dan Home, and expressed his great love for the medium, advising Jane to give Dan some 40,000 pounds in cash and securities. The old woman, much taken with Home, insisted on adopting him as her son and he began to sign himself Daniel Home Lyon. Hurriedly liquidating some of his windfall, he sent a good sum to his aunt in Connecticut to buy a house—he was always coopering his bets and if times got bad enough he now had a place to duck into. Then the axe fell. Dan's spirit controls had overlooked an important precaution. They did not counsel Mrs. Lyon against consulting another medium. The second medium's production of dear Charles warned Mrs. Lyon that Dan was a fraud and to get her money back. She asked Dan for it and he refused. His mission was a sacred one and the money was sorely needed to spread the revelation of immortality. Mrs. Lyon took him to court.

The press held high holiday with "Daniel in the Lyon's den," but at the trial Dan was reserved and polished, all too plausible. He defended himself ably. Mrs. Lyon showed herself to be a lying, coarse, social-climber type who drew scathing comments from the judge. But the court ordered Dan to return the money.

Broke again.

But friends rallied 'round. One of these was the young Lord Adare, later the Earl of Dunraven, an Irish sportsman and big-game hunter. He was a popular youngster and Dan set about fascinating him so deliberately that he was later accused of homosexuality, although there is not the slightest evidence for it. Dan just turned on the charm.

In Adare Dan found a perfect foil. The young viscount was an excellent hypnotic subject. On late visits Dan often slept on the spare bed in Adare's room and a highly suggestible person usually talks in his sleep. At such times a skilled operator can switch the normal sleep into hypnotic sleep and give post-hypnotic suggestions. These can well take the form of hallucinations: "When I tap three times tomorrow night you will see clearly the spirit of Adah Mencken hovering over my head . . ."

Adah Mencken was an American actress, the toast of the fast set in London and Paris. She had recently died, but kept appearing in spirit to Adare after he had gone to bed, praising the talents of Dan Home. A critic said, "I don't know anything about spiritualism, but that part about appearing after the chap had gone to bed—that was Adah to the life."

Into his magic circle Dan now drew the old Earl of Dunraven, Adare's father; a dashing young officer, the Master of Lindsay—later the Earl of Crawford—and his cousin, Captain Charlie Wynne. Eventually Adare published a book on his experiences in spiritualism with D. D. Home, and the miracles recounted therein did much to build Dan's legend.

The greatest marvel in the book is an account of a supposed levitation performed by Home wherein he went into an adjoining room on the third story of the house, threw up a window, and was "levitated" along the wall outside, appearing at the window of the séance room, raising it and stepping through to the floor. There has been more argument pro and con and more fantastic explanations advanced for this "levitation" than for everything else Dan Home ever did, yet on stripping down to the facts, we find an explanation so simple that it is incredible that grown men in their right minds could be taken in by it. Dan had only to go into the next room, make plenty of noise raising the window, then pussyfoot down the hall and back into the séance room, sneak over to the window, slide behind the heavy draperies, raise the sash, slip out, hold on for a moment and then noisily step into the séance room again, claiming to have been levitated out of one room and into the other. For both rooms were pitch dark!

But lest we think too harshly of the three young blades who reported it, let us remember the powerful build-up that an expert like Dan could give to such monkey-shines: the aura of mystery which always clung to him, the blue-eyed innocence of his gaze, the dreamy charm of his personality, the great bulk of legend and the wonders told of him by the fashionable world, the simple religious faith which he exuded, the eloquence of the prayers with which he began a séance, the spiritual timbre of his voice raised in an old hymn—all this was potent stuff when aimed at three hard-drinking young fellows who came from a social milieu in which "cleverness" was distrusted while courage and devotion to duty was the ideal.

The miracles recounted by these three men set the élite world once more at the feet of the Scottish-American wizard.

Although he had been a great favorite at the French court, when the disastrous Franco-Prussian War broke out Dan showed up at the headquarters of the German Army as an accredited correspondent for the San Francisco *Chronicle*. Adare, also a correspondent, had gotten him the job. Always a "quick study," Dan picked up journalese in no time. His dispatches were sentimental "think pieces," flowery "color stories" and rewrites of handouts, full of "usually reliable sources." Between battles, in the billets of the German officers, he made the tables tip and float. And on several occasions, with his pal Adare, he gave a hand with the wounded under fire. Cold courage, after all, was Dan's stock-in-trade.

The ruin of Louis Napoleon by the war reduced the number of Dan's patrons and cut off a source of jewelry and fur coats. He began trying out bolder and bolder effects. He constantly warned his admirers against other mediums who were, he insisted, all frauds. But Dan was an eager listener when their tricks were recounted to him. When he heard of a new wonder-worker who produced some striking piece of spirit business, the same effect often found its way into Dan's séances some time later.

One of the boons to "spook workers" of this period was the invention of the "patent pocket fishing rod." This was a collapsible device of telescoping steel sections which could be carried in a pocket or saddlebag, when it was no larger than a lead pencil, but could be extended to five or six feet. One of these, painted dull black, came in very handy for causing distant chairs to leap and glide, making glowing hands float over the heads of sitters and even brush their cheeks. On one occason Adare spotted it without knowing what he was seeing. He wrote:

". . . going to the window he folded the curtains around him, leaving only his head clear. We all saw a very curious appearance form itself about his head; it looked at first like a lace handkerchief, held out by a stick or support of some sort; soon however, it became more distinct and appeared to be a shadowy human form enveloped in drapery; it was about two feet in length."

On sifting the mass of material about Home's doings one is struck by the similarity of all his séances. After he got his bag of tricks perfected he seldom changed the act.

Dan begins with the raps in the "full light" of candles. Next the table tips, slides and cavorts. Here, I have deduced a piece of equipment which has never before been suggested. So often the large tables of his séances were observed to rise straight up in the air for a foot or more. Now the standard mediumistic dodge for this one is for the medium to wear a heavy leather belt under his vest. There is a hook in the front of it. A confederate is similarly equipped, and at a signal they hook the table from opposite sides and heave it up.

But Dan never had anyone to help him. His sitters were constantly changing. He worked solo. Somehow he must have had a device by which he could raise a heavy table by leverage. A hinged steel bar which could open out at an obtuse angle could be carried under the coat, one arm in the sleeve and one hanging close to the body. Covered with velvet, this would not have been observed and Dan could snake it out and under the table during some of the hymn singing. With it opened out and one end braced under the center post of the table, he could, by stepping on a stirrup attached to the other end, lever up the table, balancing it by the pressure of the sitters' hands against its top.

Believers down the years have often pointed out that whereas other mediums insisted on sitting in a cabinet to work their wonders, Daniel Dunglas Home operated while seated at the table—or near it—in the light. I suspect a dummy hand, probably made of flesh-colored leather. In the dim light of a shaded candle or a dying fire, this dummy could be placed on the table, or hooked on his vest, leaving his real right hand, with a black mitten or glove to conceal it, free to do its work.

Dan's fire-resistant tricks are in the program of many a carnival fire king but I doubt that Dan used their methods; he probably simply had a bit of asbestos cloth with which he handled the live coals and on which he placed them when he conducted his faith trial by setting a coal in the hand of a firm believer. It would work, in a room almost completely dark.

Adare and Lindsay testified that they had several times observed Home's body elongate by at least a foot. But a similar illusion is being presented today by a magician who is billed as "the man who grows." It is clever showmanship and muscle control.

There remains only the levitation, observed by the sitters against the faint light of the window. And here we have an explanation right under the voluminous skirts of the female sitters—that stiff material called crinoline which made their hoop skirts fluff out like haystacks. A life-size silhouette of Dan, cut from black crinoline, could be carried under the coat and at the proper time unrolled, creased down the middle and passed before the window on one end of his telescopic reaching rod.

There were mediums by the score in Europe and America, doing the same stunts. Of them, only Dan Home was never exposed. Of all that shady host of rappers, players of accordions in the dark and producers of glowing faces, only Dan has the distinction of a biographical note in the Encyclopaedia Britannica.

At last romance again smiled upon our Daniel. This time the lady's name was Julia de Gloumeline. She, too, was a Russian of good family, but she was not an impressionable child like poor Sacha. Julia was a sophisticated, cosmopolitan young woman. She fell deeply in love with Home, and the wedding went off without a hitch in October of 1871. Shortly after that, the long litigation with Sacha's relatives was decided in Home's favor. Miracle man? He battled the Russian nobility in a Russian court and won!

This time Dan really had it made. Sacha's estate gave him a comfortable income of his own, and his diamonds were safe from the unsentimental clutches of pawnbrokers. In Julia he had a doting wife, a gracious hostess and a staunch believer in his spiritual powers. After Home's death she wrote a glowing biography of him with love in every line. Dan had pulled off another miracle by keeping a secret from an intelligent wife over the years. Of all his fabulous feats this one seemed to me the greatest.

Dan slowly began to "pack the racket in." He gave fewer and fewer séances; the phenomena grew more and more trivial. He was just not exerting himself. And why should he? He had gotten where he wanted to be after many tortuous ups and down. Finally he withdrew tactfully from his old friends, the "real gone" believers in spiritualism, and developed a new set among the idlers of the fashionable resorts. A celebrity himself, he associated only with other celebrities and socialites. Mark Twain knew him and liked him.

Dan leisurely wrote his third book, "Lights and Shadows of Spiritualism," telling people how to trap fraudulent mediums who used mechanical rappers, reaching rods and luminous gauze.

In his declining years he was a familiar figure at spas and health resorts, his gaunt frame more cadaverous than ever, leaning heavily on his cane, his fingers and shirt-front ablaze with diamonds, rubies and emeralds. Finally, on June 21, 1886, his frayed lungs gave up. He was buried in the Greek Orthodox cemetery of St. Germain-en-Laye at Auteuil.

In his day he had "performed" before such noble sitters as the Emperor and Empress of France, Queen Sophia of the Netherlands, King Maximilian of Bavaria, Czar Alexander II of Russia (a close friend), the King and Queen of Wurtenberg, the Crown Prince of Prussia, the Duchess of Hamilton—the list reads like an Almanach de Gotha. Thousands of séances and never once caught faking.

Wise as a serpent, gentle as a dove was Dan Home, one of the greatest con artists ever to gaze with passionate, utter sincerity into the wondering eyes of a mark. He was probably the highest-paid amateur in the history of show business.

143

THE AWFUL DISCLOSURES OF MARIA MONK

by Allen Churchill

In 1836, New York City was torn by religious controversy. Already, the passions that flamed later into the Know-Nothing agitations were smoldering throughout the country, and, as always, they burned most violently in the metropolis. There, Protestant preachers thundered wildly extravagant charges at the Catholics; and the Society for the Diffusion of Christian Knowledge and others like it, "designed to arrest the progress of Popery," flourished. Pillars of society were active in these organizations—Samuel F. B. Morse, Dr. W. C. Brownlee, and others. But the person who gained most fame from this Pope-baiting was a girl named Maria Monk.

Maria Monk had all the requisites for the notoriety with which New York has always rewarded soiled ladies who distinguish themselves. She was young, demure, and, by the admission of no less an authority than James Gordon Bennett, pretty. She was the mother of a child about whose paternity she was exceedingly vague. And she was, apparently, the author of *The Awful Disclosures of Maria Monk*.

When *The Awful Disclosures* was published in January, 1836, Maria had been in New York about six months. Accompanied by a Canadian clergyman, the Rev. W. K. Hoyt, she had come from Montreal. Hoyt liked to say that he had redeemed Maria from a life of sin while carrying on his work as president of the Canadian Benevolent Association. But in her franker moments, Maria contradicted him flatly. She said that the reverend gentleman had merely been amenable to her solicitations on a Montreal street corner.

According to her book, Maria had spent part of her nineteen years preparing to become a nun in the famous Hôtel Dieu nunnery in Montreal. Her five years as a novice had been comparatively serene, and little space was devoted to them. But, as soon as she became a nun, she was involved, according to her story, in all sorts of horrors. The remotest cellars of the Hôtel Dieu, she declared, were strewn with the bones of nuns who had resisted the advances of amorous priests. The sisters were abused constantly, as well as honored by almost nightly visits from clerical gentry who came from a nearby monastery through subterranean

144

passages. The presence of her own "heavenly cherub" she ascribed to one of these nocturnal amorists, although Hoyt claimed the credit, and the Canadian authorities later presented fairly conclusive proof which placed the responsibility on a Montreal policeman.

The book abounded in grisly episodes. Thus, one of the nuns who had been guilty of some slightly seditious utterances was described as being stretched out on a mattress

> with her face upwards, and then bound with cords so that she could not move. In an instant, another bed (mattress) was thrown upon her. One of the priests, named Bonin, sprang like a fury first upon it with all his force. He was speedily followed by the nuns until there were as many on the bed as could find room, and all did what they could do, not only to smother, but to bruise her. Some stood and jumped upon the poor girl with their feet: and others, in different ways, seemed to seek how they might beat the breath out of her body. After the lapse of fifteen or twenty minutes, Father Bonin and the nuns ceased to trample on her and stepped from the bed. They then began to laugh. . . .

The priests from the nearby monastery were characterized as inhuman monsters by words such as these:

> Being within the walls of that prison house (the Hôtel Dieu), where the cries and pains of the injured innocence of their victims would never reach the outside world, for relief or for redress for their wrongs, without remorse or shame, they would glory, not only in sating their brutal passions, but even in torturing, in the most barbarous manner, the feelings of those under their power.

From these and other incidents, Maria concluded that "speedy death can be no great calamity to those who lead the lives of nuns." And, finally, she offered to go through the Hôtel Dieu "with some impartial ladies and gentlemen, that they may compare my account with the interior parts of the building, and if they do not find my description true, then discard me as an impostor."

For two years, said her story, Maria was a nun. During that time she suffered almost every known torture, the most subtle of which was a diet of garlic and eels. Finally, she managed to escape.

Maria's alleged revelations produced an instantaneous uproar. Almost in no time the book sold 20,000 copies. Temporarily at least, Catholic circles were too stunned to make an effective reply; and, meanwhile, the book was given the stamp of authenticity by the printed approval of the Society for the Diffusion of Christian Knowledge and its figurehead-

145

president, Dr. Brownlee, pastor of the Collegiate Dutch Reformed Church and author of the bulky best-seller *Popery*. The publication of the book was hailed by militant Protestants everywhere as the Catholic debacle. Protestant sermons rang with triumph, Protestant papers ran editorials celebrating the complete rout of the Papists, and Protestants themselves went about feeling smugly at peace with the Lord. This state of affairs lasted almost a month, until newspapers and delegations of outraged citizens began arriving from Montreal.

Dispatches from that city included the affidavits of Maria's mother, a charwoman in the military barracks in Montreal, and of a Dr. Robertson, who described an episode which, he claimed, had caused him acute embarrassment. Two years before, he said, a girl had been brought to his house in Montreal after a half-hearted attempt at drowning herself. In the presence of the crowd that had gathered, she festooned her arms about his neck and addressed him as "Father." At this, the crowd became uncommonly interested and the doctor forthwith hustled the girl into his office. There she told him that her name was Maria Monk and that for four years her mother had kept her chained in a cellar from which she had just escaped. The doctor examined her for marks of ill-treatment, but finding none, turned her out. Less than a year later, he continued, he was visited by three excited citizens who far into the night regaled him with tales of atrocities committed at the Hôtel Dieu. On investigation, he found that Maria was spreading the tales as her experiences.

Mrs. Monk, in her affidavit, laid about her with verbal cudgels that spared no one—her daughter least of all. At the age of seven, she asserted, Maria had rammed a slate pencil through her head. Unfortunately, she had survived, and ever since had told terrific lies. She had held several jobs as a servant, which her prevarications had invariably caused her to lose; and several times she had been arrested. As for her having been a nun, that was nonsense.

Further, Mrs. Monk stated that in August, 1835, the Rev. Mr. Hoyt had come to see her. They had discussed Maria, and Hoyt had astounded her by excusing her daughter's aberrations because of the dreadful experiences she had undergone in the convent. "What convent?" demanded Mrs. Monk, and Hoyt began carefully to explain that Maria had spent seven years in the Hôtel Dieu. Mrs. Monk promptly invited him to leave the house. Twice Hoyt came back; the last time with different tactics and $500. Flourishing the money, he offered it to Mrs. Monk if she would swear that the convent story was true. Once again

146

she ordered him out, and not even the dramatic appearance of her daughter with a small baby in arms moved her.

With these statements to back them up, the Catholics began a fierce defensive battle. In hot language and with a bewildering array of witnesses, both sides thrashed out for months the pros and cons of Maria's story, using not only church journals but every New York newspaper as well. Soon the controversy spread beyond New York to the country at large, and provoked heated discussion everywhere. On several occasions, Maria was questioned by representatives of both camps. Her showing at these examinations was poor; but Protestant public opinion, guided apparently more by her youth and demure prettiness than by anything else, was still hugely in her favor. The *Protestant Vindicator,* newspaper of the Society for the Diffusion of Christian Knowledge, fought most valiantly for her cause by publishing statements signed by prominent citizens affirming their belief in the story. The *Vindicator* found further verification in a mysterious pile of planks that had appeared in the yard of the Hôtel Dieu. In the words of its Canadian correspondent, these planks were "wonderfully and gradually used in progressing some improvements in the building," and the *Vindicator* deduced that evidence of Maria's disclosures was being covered up. It reported as well that sinister figures had been seen lurking about New York, and concluded that they were Papists awaiting an opportunity to abduct Maria.

Maria, during all this clamor, was leading an erratic life. In the fall of 1835, members of the Society for the Diffusion of Christian Knowledge had persuaded the righteous Dr. Brownlee that it was his duty to win Maria away from Hoyt. To Brownlee, Maria was just another black sheep strayed from the fold, but to other members of the Society she represented possible royalties. The reverend doctor subjected Maria to almost daily pleas, exhortations, and threats of hell-fire. The Brownlee side-whiskers finally won the day. Maria moved to his house where she dwelt under the care of his wife. Hoyt complained that she was a "damned jilting jade."

Until the publication of the *Disclosures,* Maria remained quietly in the Brownlee household. But, shortly after, she decamped with John J. L. Slocum, a young clergyman and a protégé of Dr. Brownlee's. For a minister of the gospel, Slocum proved an alert business man. Within a few months, as Maria's "next friend" in legal language, he sued Harpers', publishers of the book, for Maria's share of the royalties, all of which had been palmed by the Society. At the trial of this suit, in August, 1836, the whole story was exposed.

It developed from the evidence that only the foundation of the story was Maria's. Several terms in a reformatory had furnished her with the atmosphere and a few of the details. As a tale of woe, her original story had earned her sympathy and extra fees when she plied her trade in Montreal. Hoyt had written the first draft of the book, and had come to New York to peddle the manuscript. Friends in the Society for the Diffusion of Christian Knowledge saw at once its possibilities, but in order to be sure of a thumping sale decided to make it more sensational. To achieve this end they appointed a Committee of Publication. The Committee gave the Hoyt version to Theodore Dwight, who read Spanish, Italian, French, and German works on the subjects of convents and torture. His finished manuscript had delighted everyone concerned—especially Maria, who offered to elope with him from sheer gratitude.

Dr. Brownlee was profoundly shocked at the exposure of the hoax, and acknowledged that he had been hoodwinked. The Committee of Publication, however, stuck firmly to its guns, declaring that Dwight had merely been the "scribe." The public's faith in Maria, which had begun to evaporate when it became known that she was living with a clergyman without benefit of clergy, now disappeared almost entirely. The New York *Herald* summed up by ordering "ye withering fingers of scorn, unskin yourselves at once." By this time, however, thousands of copies of the book had been sold.

What little faith remained in Maria's story was shattered in October when Col. W. L. Stone returned from Canada. The doughty Colonel, editor of the *Commercial Advertiser* and possessor of a country-wide reputation for probity, had suspected Maria from the first. He had offered to escort her to Montreal and with her face the Canadian authorities. When Maria refused, pleading fear for her life, Colonel Stone went alone. He reported to the *Commerical Advertiser* that he had been conducted through the Hôtel Dieu, had examined everything with "eagle-eyed attention," and had found only kindness and peace. After talking to a nun 105 years old, he had gone to the monastery, where the priests all seemed very, very mild. In the last paragraph, the Colonel worked up enough bitterness over the injustice done these new friends to declare "MARIA MONK IS AN IMPOSTOR, AND HER BOOK AND ALL ITS ESSENTIAL FEATURES ARE CALUMNIES."

Almost a year later on the night of August 15, 1837, Maria wandered into the house of a Dr. Sleigh, a Philadelphia clergyman and friend of Brownlee's. After swearing him to secrecy, she confided that she had been kidnaped by a group of priests and was being held captive in a nearby convent. When asked how she had escaped, she replied vaguely that she had come out to buy some toothache drops, and had to hurry back. Nevertheless, she seemed disposed to stay, and announced that one of her clerical captors had succumbed to her charms and proposed marriage. The fact that her suitor claimed possession of $4000 seemed to influence her greatly in his favor. At last she wandered out, promising to come back in the morning. Dr. Sleigh was much alarmed until someone told him that the abduction was in all probability a publicity stunt for the *Further Disclosures of Maria Monk,* which was soon to be published. He then wrote a pamphlet on the interview.

The *Further Disclosures* sold amazingly well—so well, in fact, that Slocum welcomed Maria back and persuaded her to give him the English rights to both books. Then he departed for London where the volumes were published by the Catholic Truth Society.

If the subject of Maria had not been a tender one with Dr. Brownlee and his fellow clergymen, her end would have been excellent material for their sermons. For twelve years she haunted the dives and grog shops of the Bowery until, on October 11, 1849, only 32 years old but already a haggard woman, she was caught picking the pocket of her current paramour and sent to jail. She died there soon after, and none of the newspapers paid her the compliment of an obituary.

Since 1836, three hundred thousand copies of *The Awful Disclosures of Maria Monk* have been sold. It is still printed, bought, and, in many cases, believed.

DRAFT BOARD NIGHTS

by James Thurber

I was called almost every week, even though I had been exempted from service the first time I went before the medical examiners. Either they were never convinced that it was me or else there was some clerical error in the records which was never cleared up. Anyway, there was usually a letter for me on Monday ordering me to report for examination on the second floor of Memorial Hall on the following Wednesday at

9 P.M. The second time I went up I tried to explain to one of the doctors that I had already been exempted. "You're just a blur to me," I said, taking off my glasses. "You're absolutely nothing to me," he snapped, sharply.

I had to take off all my clothes each time and jog around the hall with a lot of porters and bank presidents' sons and clerks and poets. Our hearts and lungs would be examined and then our feet; and finally our eyes. That always came last. When the eye specialist got around to me, he would always say, "Why, you couldn't get into the service with sight like that!" "I know," I would say. Then a week or two later I would be summoned again and go through the same rigmarole. The ninth or tenth time I was called, I happened to pick up one of several stethoscopes that were lying on the table and suddenly, instead of finding myself in the line of draft men, I found myself in the line of examiners. "Hello, doctor," said one of them, nodding. "Hello," I said. That, of course, was before I took my clothes off; I might have managed it naked, but I doubt it. I was assigned, or rather drifted, to the chest-and-lung section, where I began to examine every other man, thus cutting old Dr. Ridgeway's work in two. "I'm glad to have you here, doctor," he said.

I passed most of the men that came to me, but now and then I would exempt one just to be on the safe side. I began by making each of them hold his breath and then say "mi, mi, mi, mi," until I noticed Ridgeway looking at me curiously. He, I discovered, simply made them say "ah," and sometimes he didn't make them say anything. Once I got hold of a man who, it came out later, had swallowed a watch—to make the doctors believe there was something wrong with him inside (it was a common subterfuge: men swallowed nails, hairpins, inks, etc., in an effort to be let out). Since I didn't know what you were supposed to hear through a stethoscope, the ticking of the watch at first didn't surprise me, but I decided to call Dr. Ridgeway into consultation, because nobody else had ticked. "This man seems to tick," I said to him. He looked at me in surprise but didn't say anything. Then he thumped the man, laid his ear to his chest, and finally tried the stethoscope. "Sound as a dollar," he said. "Listen lower down," I told him. The man indicated his stomach. Ridgeway gave him a haughty, indignant look. "That is for the abdominal men to worry about," he said, and moved off. A few minutes later, Dr. Blythe Ballomy got around to the man and listened, but he didn't blink an eye; his grim expression never changed. "You have swallowed a watch, my man," he said, crisply. The draftee reddened in embarrass-

150

ment and uncertainty. "On *purpose?*" he asked. "That I can't say," the doctor told him, and went on.

I served with the draft board for about four months. Until the summonses ceased, I couldn't leave town and as long as I stayed and appeared promptly for examination, even though I did the examining, I felt that technically, I could not be convicted of evasion. . . .

During my last few trips to the draft board, I went again as a draft prospect, having grown tired of being an examiner. None of the doctors who had been my colleagues for so long recognized me, not even Dr. Ridgeway. When he examined my chest for the last time, I asked him if there hadn't been another doctor helping him. He said there had been. "Did he look anything like me?" I asked. Dr. Ridgeway looked at me. "I don't think so," he said, "he was taller." (I had my shoes off while he was examining me.) "A good pulmonary man," added Ridgeway. "Relative of yours?" I said yes. He sent me to Dr. Quimby, the specialist who had examined my eyes twelve or fifteen times before. He gave me some simple reading tests. "You could never get into the army with eyes like that," he said. "I know," I told him.

Late one morning, shortly after my last examination, I was awakened by the sound of bells ringing and whistles blowing. It grew louder and more insistent and wilder. It was the Armistice.

I STOLE A MILLION

by Robert Page
as told to Barney Nagler and Collie Small

My racket was gypping insurance companies. I got them for a million dollars. Not long ago I stood up in front of a judge in a New York court and traded the million for four-to-eight in Sing Sing, but it took detectives and fraud investigators fifteen years to tumble to my racket. They knew I was working, but they never knew how. I drove them nuts.

It wasn't easy. I had to study broken bones until I was an expert. I could read X rays. I knew insurance law, so I posed as a legitimate insurance adjuster and fooled my best friends. I even posed as a lawyer and fooled judges in their own courtrooms. Not bad for a guy who never got past the fourth grade in school.

I discovered this insurance racket in the Building of the Forty Thieves in downtown New York. This is a building where a lot of lawyers have offices and a lot of guys hang out looking to make a buck. I met Harry S—— in this building and he taught me the pattern.

At first we were chasing ambulances. I would run into him sometimes when he was going out on a case. He was a con man who originated in Jersey somewhere and he looked like more of a judge than anything else. He was older than me. I wasn't twenty-eight yet. I am forty-four now.

All this was businesslike. We used to get tipped off by city hospitals on accidents, but the competition was tough. There were other guys in the same business. We were able to shake some of them down by using phony cops to chase them, but the lawyers started to get into the racket and that ruined it for us.

S—— knew about fraudulent insurance claims and he taught me what he knew. About 1933 we branched into fake-accident claims. A Bowery bum got us started.

One day I was standing on a street corner with S——, and a car making a turn hit a derelict. The car stopped. The bum got up, brushed his pants, and went away. I took the license-plate number of the car and reported a hit-and-run case in order to get the accident on record. I then turned the case over to an attorney who knew what it was all about but didn't want me to explain fully as he figured it was a racket. The attorney agreed to work for a one-third cut of the settlement.

I then called police headquarters and told them, "This is Walsh, Badge Number such-and-such," and the fellow on the other end said, "How do you feel today?" I said, "Okay," and gave him the license number and asked him what the owner's name was. He was very helpful and got me the information. I then called the car owner on the phone, saying I represented the social service at Bellevue Hospital.

I told him we had a bill for medical treatment and asked for the name of his insurance carrier, which he gave me. I ventured on jokingly that the fellow has developed a dread disease due to this accident and that I hoped he carried enough insurance. He admitted he carried a twenty-to-forty-thousand-dollar policy and he volunteered the name of his insurance broker.

A summons was served for $25,000, and a physical examination was arranged at the attorney's office. My partner dressed as the bum for the act and displayed an X ray showing a fracture of the shoulder. I had not known about this X-ray side line before.

Three weeks after the examination my partner and I called an adjuster we knew in this particular company and asked him to see what figure he could put on this particular case, if any. Later in the day he gave us a figure of $4,000.

We waited a little while and then called this adjuster again and told him we needed another $500 to settle the case, which brought the figure up to $4,500. We then told the attorney that we had to bribe the adjuster with $1,000, which we kept. Later we gave the adjuster $200 to keep him happy, and the lawyer, who was working on one-third and thought we really gave the adjuster $1,000, came in for a piece. He never knew we chiseled him and split $3,100.

Now that I had seen the way my partner's pattern worked, I became very much interested. At this time my partner was losing his money on horses and in dice games and was forever borrowing money from me to support his habit. I quit him and went on my own. He has no police record. He was never caught. But he is on the rocks today.

I saw immediately that I would need a file of X rays to build up my pattern of operation. My first step was to go to the Municipal Lodging House, which had bums and derelicts. I spoke to a bum with a cast on his arm and asked him how old the injury was, where the break was, how he got it, and if there was any lawsuit pending. I then took him into my car, saying I was a student from some medical school and was making a study of fresh fractures. If he would comply with my request and have X rays taken at a doctor's office in the Bronx I would give him two bottles of whisky and $5 for himself.

Ten minutes after the X ray was taken the doctor convinced me this bum was telling the truth that it was a fresh injury. I then made a deal with the doctor for a dozen plates with two views of the fracture, and gave him $75 for these X rays.

Later I got X rays of other fractures, but these first X rays were all alike except each plate had different initials and there was no doctor's name on them to trip me up. They usually put a patient's initials on X rays for purposes of identification. One plate had the initials "D.C.L." on it and I used it under such names as David C. Levy, Daniel C. Levine and others. This fooled the insurance investigators, who were always checking to see if a claimant had a previous accident with them.

I now set about getting people to work for me who could pretend they got hurt in the fake accidents as the victim. They were called "floppers" and "divers." A flopper is a person who knows how to fake getting hit by a car making a turn at an intersection. This person dashes out to cross the street as the car comes around the corner at low speed. He puts his hands on the front fender and flips over backward and lays in the street groaning.

It is very hard to get good actors. Some floppers were very good actors, but others would only wince here and there. Floppers could work at any time of day, but not divers. Divers were best at night.

A diver is a person who takes a car going straight down the street, maybe thirty miles an hour. This party stands several feet off the curb and as the car approaches he runs out and sort of crouches while he slams his hand against the door, making a very loud noise. He then falls into the street. The car stops, and from there on the routine is the same as it is with a flopper.

I collected $1,750 on my first case. I found a truck driver who would play ball. He told me the stops on his route and I introduced the party to be injured to the driver. I then selected a street corner that had no drugstore. I did not want them picking him up and carrying him into a drugstore instead of sending him to the hospital, which was very important as I had to have official records when I got ready to make my claim.

Before the "accident" took place it was necessary to set up a fake address for the "injured." I soon found this was the most important link if my case was going to stand up. This job took several days.

If possible I preferred to deal with prostitutes who operated in apartment houses, since they moved around a lot and were hard to keep track of. However, I also knew many other people I could go to who would say the injured lived there if an insurance investigator came around. I would give them $10 or $15 to say this.

I would give the injured a name like Joe Marino and the next day I would go to the superintendent of the building and ask him what apartment Marino lives in. The superintendent would say no, there was no Marino there. I would then say, "Oh, he lives upstairs with John Jones," and the superintendent would give me the number of the apartment that Jones lived in.

A day later my lieutenant would go to the superintendent and ask him again what apartment Marino lived in. The superintendent would still not remember Marino so my lieutenant would say, "He is the fellow that broke his elbow in that big accident. He lives with John Jones." Now the idea was planted in the superintendent's brain, and when the insurance investigator finally got around to checking the address the superintendent would tell him, "Sure, Marino lives here. He's the guy who broke his elbow in that accident. He lives with John Jones upstairs." This would convince the investigator that there really was a Marino and that he really lived there.

Now comes the accident. I picked up the flopper in my car, told him his name and address, and drove around for an hour to make sure I was not being tailed. Finally we got to the street corner I had picked. The truck arrived on schedule and the flopper went into his act. I paid him $10 for this. It was a good performance.

While my flopper was laying in the street groaning, a cop came up and wanted to know what is going on here. I stayed off in the crowd and watched the stage play. The cop called an ambulance, which soon arrived, and after the flopper was taken away the cop made out his report describing the accident. Now the accident was on the police record, which was important.

At the hospital the flopper made out that his elbow was badly injured. The act had to be very good in order for the intern to suggest X rays. However, the flopper then refused to have X rays taken there, saying he wanted his own doctor to take them. The intern then entered the case in the hospital records as a possible fracture. It was important for the intern to diagnose the injury as a possible fracture, since it opened the way for me to use one of my phony X rays later. If the intern diagnosed the injury as contusions or abrasions I would have to drop the case, as contusions and abrasions are not worth the trouble.

One week after this phony accident I turned the case over to an attorney. This attorney was what you call book-smart, but he could not move around very fast and he did not know I was outsmarting him with a fake. All he was interested in was his check. The attorney sent a claim letter to the owner of the truck, which was forwarded to the insurance carrier.

In about ten days the adjuster from the insurance company called up the attorney and asked what the injury was. The attorney said it was a bad injury but that he could not tell him any more as he did not have a complete medical report. He then told the adjuster to arrange a physical examination with the insurance company doctor, but said it could not take place for several weeks since the injured party was not available just then.

It was important now to get a private doctor to put this fake case into his own files. I went to see a doctor who thought I was a legitimate insurance adjuster and told him things looked very bright for him in the future as I was interested in him and would like to see him picking up some extra change as an insurance-company doctor.

I then told him about the case and asked him to make out an index card for his files showing that he had treated the "injured." I told him he had nothing to fear so long as he did not give me anything in writing. All I wanted was for him to say he had seen the patient if the insurance company called and to tell them to call the attorney if they wanted more information. I paid him $50 for this, but before I left his office I lifted some of his letterheads and put them in my pocket.

The next step in this pattern was to make out a medical report on the doctor's stationery. I forged the doctor's signature on this report, which I wrote myself. The report stated: "This patient is under my care for the following injuries sustained on such and such a date: contusions and abrasions of right elbow; fracture of internal condyle of right humerus. X-ray examination reveals fracture of internal condyle. This patient will require further treatment."

I did not use the original flopper to take the insurance-company examination as I did not want to make him feel too important in the setup. I hired a thief instead from the Bronx who had the same type of build as the original flopper, and I gave this bum $15 to take the examination.

Eight weeks after the "accident" the doctor from the insurance company examined the patient. The reason it was eight weeks was that it takes about eight weeks for adhesive-tape markings to go away, and I could not appear in, say three weeks, with this bum who showed no evidence of ever being bandaged.

First, though, I took the bum to the scene where the "accident" happened so he could answer questions. I gave him his age and fixed his date of birth. I told him the name of the doctor who was supposed to have X-rayed him and treated him. I further explained to him when the X ray was taken, when the adhesive strapping was applied, how often he saw the doctor, when the strapping was removed, the amount of bakings and massagings that followed, and the medical fees up to date.

At the examination the insurance doctor just looked at the phony X ray and asked the patient to squeeze his hand to see if there was a loss of restriction. After this quick examination the insurance company settled for $1,750.

In the 15 years I worked this racket I came up against only a few thorough doctors. They were real heavyweights, but I had a system for them, too. When one of my injured was to be examined by a heavyweight

I knew was thorough, I would use an old pickpocket's trick to discourage him. I just gave the "injured" a couple of shots of whisky and all the garlic he could eat and I have yet to see a doctor who could stand the smell when the patient blew in his face. The doctor would get desperate from this man's breath and would give him a fast once-over and tell him to put on his coat and wait in the outer office while he filled out his report. It was easy.

In all, I cashed over a million dollars' worth of insurance-settlement checks but I never kept any records. I never put a cent in the bank, even under an assumed name, as it would have been lost if I died. Sometimes I had as much as $20,000 in my apartment in the Bronx which I paid $60 a month for. I kept the money mostly in $500 bills and concealed them in a book called Ivanhoe, which was in a stack of other books in a closet.

My files were in my head. I had to be thinking all the time as it would have been fatal to backtrack on myself. I had to be careful that a flopper did not take two flops in front of the same cop or be picked up by an ambulance and taken to a particular hospital where he could be recognized as a repeater.

I also had to be careful not to let an insurance company maneuver me into a position where I would have to permit a re-X ray since my client naturally had not been injured in the first place.

I also learned not to let a flopper or a diver take a car with a low license number, as this would indicate that the car belongs to an important individual and I did not wish to become involved in a lot of publicity. Once a flopper picked such a car in front of the Waldorf-Astoria, and when the cop came over to question the driver I heard him say, "Hello, Judge." I became somewhat nervous on hearing that this fellow was a judge so I eased over to the flopper and told him to get going. The flopper then picked himself up and said, "Sorry, I did not watch where I was walking," and we let the case go.

If the company got stubborn and tried to make me agree to a re-X ray, I would immediately go up and see the company adjuster and would represent myself to him as a lawyer. I would give him a little bottle of Chanel No. 5 for his wife and then we would talk about the case. I would tell him I was short of money and was trying to settle the case in a hurry as I was selling my client out by not fighting for a bigger settlement for him and this naturally was to the company's advantage. This worked about 90 per cent of the time. When it did not work and the company still wanted a re-X ray I would drop the case as it would be too risky to argue any more.

I could do more tricks with my X rays than a monkey with a peanut. By this I mean I could easily switch a right shoulder to a left shoulder or a right elbow to a left elbow. As I built up my file of X rays I specialized in shoulders and elbows.

When I had X rays taken of these Bowery bums, I made sure they were taken from an angle where the heart did not show. If it did show, I could not switch rights and lefts. Sometimes I would get a lady bum on the Bowery with a broken shoulder and would have her X-rayed. In cases like this I would make sure that the X-ray angle did not show her breast shadow as I could not pass it off as a man's picture if such a shadow showed.

I never let my floppers see my settlement checks from the insurance companies as this would have made them very angry. They thought I was getting around two or three hundred dollars per accident, which I told them I had to split with doctors, lawyers, insurance adjusters and so forth. I was really getting up to five or six thousand. I had to pay off a few lawyers and what not, but I could chisel them, too.

I kept a stable of six or eight floppers and divers all the time. I dressed the floppers and divers to look like people from the neighborhood the accident was in. In 15 years I never saw a flopper or diver even get bruised. While they were laying in the street putting on the act, it was funny that nobody ever tumbled to the fraud. Even though they were supposed to be hit by a car, their clothes never got torn and their faces were not even dusty.

I usually had at least one woman flopper in my stable. One of the best was Miss X, who I found by chance when I staged a flop at Fifty-seventh Street and Seventh Avenue. (She was not in the picture at this time as she was a pickpocket who specialized in clipping "binger" bags which are women's purses with easy clasps to open.) One of my henchmen was informed by me to break this play up as a crowd was gathering around the woman, who had grabbed hold of Miss X, practically with her hand in this woman's bag.

As quick as a flash my henchman removed a hub cap from my car, which was parked near by, and took out a phony police badge which I had hidden there. My henchman immediately walked into the crowd and flashed the badge at a young rookie cop who was trying to take over, and said to this cop, "I am from headquarters. I have been watching this young lady. I will take over."

My henchman then walked away with Miss X in tow and two blocks away I picked them up in my car. I then told her we were not coppers and she thanked us very much and we went to dinner. From that time on we became very friendly. I could see that we would be a great team so I gave her the proposition and she liked it very much.

Now my problem was to get rid of the lady flopper I already had working for me as she was indulging in drink for quite some time. The mode of operation here was for her to stage an accident in front of the Roxy Theater. When this accident was over I had two men who looked like police officers pick her up and scare the daylights out of her. They let her go and she called me that afternoon and told me she had to quit and gave me the reason and I agreed with her.

Miss X, who I now had a great interest in, took her place. She had a hair-trigger mind and soon became an expert in this field.

Once I experimented with a phony basal skull fracture, but it was necessary to keep this type of patient in a private hospital and pay a doctor to say he was treating the patient, and this proved too expensive.

In this basal I got an accomplice at Bellevue Hospital to make a spinal tap on a stiff in the morgue there. I then pricked my own finger to get some blood which I put in the test tube of fluid to indicate a basal skull fracture.

This was a little too complicated for me, and the guy I had posing in the hospital as the injured party kept raising the ante on me. I did not make too much on this case although I collected $5,500 on the settlement with the insurance company.

Most of the doctors I worked with were innocent and I feel sorry for them now, especially if the D.A. catches up with them. About 75 per cent of the lawyers in with me knew what was going on. However, I always felt safest with adjusters as I knew the value of injuries, could argue liability and discuss loss of earnings and pain and suffering. I always took this particular job on my hands as this was a most important task. . . .

This fake accident racket was a hobby to me as well as a lucrative livelihood and I felt just like a fellow who went to work with a lunch basket and no worries on his mind. My only fear was that I had too many people to work with me as I was involved with several floppers and a number of doctors and lawyers. I then observed about three years ago that someone must have fingered me as strange things began to happen.

I could not figure out what had put them on my trail. I started thinking that maybe I was overworking the elbow and shoulder fracture angle by having my floppers fake too many accidents against a certain bus company in New York.

I was always on the alert and did not trust private phones. If an attorney called me at home with news of a settlement he would use this peculiar code: "Somebody called you today and wants you to call him at Circle 7-1598." The last four figures meant that this was the price we could get if we settled a case that was then pending. The cops took it all down but I doubt if they got any information this way.

(*Detectives agree with Page. Except for one conversation that betrayed Page at the very end, his conversations were gibberish as far as the police were concerned and admittedly led them up one blind alley after another.*)

Although I was making very good money it was necessary for me to live the life of an ordinary fellow as I could not afford to draw attention to myself. People thought I was a public adjuster and adjusters do not make much money. I paid $60 a month for my apartment, and I drove an old 1937 car to be respectable. I also made it a habit to pawn my ring or watch every so often to put on a good front and make people think I was poor.

Several times I looked to go legitimate when I thought things were getting too hot, but I did not find any lucrative openings.

Early in the war I tried selling used cars but this was a bigger racket than the one I was already in. Also, about this time there was a new rule that salesmen for this company I was working for had to be bonded. As this required finger-printing I did not wish to be exposed as a criminal since I had been in a number of reformatories as a kid for stealing and picking pockets and had done time in Atlanta for peddling dope.

I did not get any breaks as a kid as my father was a poor tailor on the East Side, and I quit school after the fourth grade. I escaped twice from reformatories, once by hitting a guard with a shovel who threatened to give me a beating with a bamboo stick.

At one time I met a fellow from the reformatory and he gave me a terrific proposition selling heroin and morphine, but I was arrested and sent to Atlanta. I never knew what a dope fiend was until I got to Atlanta as I always sold to another seller. When I saw what this stuff did to them I hated myself for ever bothering with them. I did not have any trouble for 12 or 13 years. About three years ago, however, as I was doing my shopping in some market in the Bronx, I observed a man with a movie camera taking my picture as I came out. This made me very nervous as I was now certain they knew who I was and what I was doing.

I did not know who this fellow was with the camera but as he hopped back into his automobile I jotted down the license number. That night I had no sleep in me just worrying about this particular incident.

160

The following morning I called police headquarters and gave them a fictitious badge number and supplied them with the plate number of this fellow's car. They gave me his name and I found out that he was a private detective. This annoyed me very much as I had thought he was a regular copper.

Eventually I found out that the people on my trail were from the Association of Casualty and Surety Companies, which investigates fraud for insurance companies. I do not know how they tumbled to my racket.

(*The association first stumbled on Page when he presented a claim against a car owner whose policy had been in effect only 17 days. At the time, the association suspected only simple collusion between the car owner and the "injured," who was one of Page's floppers. Investigators did not realize at first that they had picked up the trail of a master swindler.*

(*A special agent for the association, then established definitely that it was Page who was masterminding the accident racket. Following up a claim presented in the name of Robert C. Levy, the agent went to an auto-parts company where Levy supposedly had been employed. Page had arranged with the owner to say that the non-existent Levy had quit because of an injury, but the association investigator pursued the lead and eventually found that a man named Robert Page sometimes used the name of Robert C. Levy on business cards purporting to show that he was an insurance adjuster.*

(*For several months the association could not tell whether it had a mouse or a lion by the tail. Page was so slippery that he successfully eluded half a dozen agents on his trail, including an ex-spy chaser from the O.S.S. Furthermore, the association was so baffled by Page's antics at times that it questioned its own conclusions. In November, 1945, the association turned the case over to the District Attorney, Frank S. Hogan, whose problem then was to trap Page in a doctor's office with the "victim" of a phony accident.*

(*Lieutenant William Grafenecker, head of the District Attorney's detective squad, assigned detectives Julius Salke and George Doane exclusively to the case. Under Grafenecker's direction, Salke and Doane trailed Page every day from the moment he left his house until he returned to go to bed at night.*

(*This went on for almost three years, but they were never able to catch the wily Page staging an accident.*)

I began to notice that two detectives named Salke and Doane were tailing me. Once I thought I had slipped them for good when I did not see them following me in their car for several days, but then I discovered they were always in the car ahead of me and were tailing me from the front by watching me in their rearview mirror. I had never seen this particular pattern before.

There were times when I would observe Salke and Doane on the Bronx River Parkway and I knew where to duck and how to lose them, and I would see their car go shooting on ahead. I would then go to Brooklyn and lo and behold they were either in front of me or behind me. I learned after my arrest that they knew the pattern of my rounds and if they lost me one place they knew just where to pick me up again. The way they always turned up was uncanny.

(Ironically, Robert Page was caught through a case involving a settlement of only $140, the smallest in his 15 years of operation. He was trapped because he broke his iron-clad rule of never talking business over his home telephone. In this one fatal lapse, Page made an appointment with a doctor for the examination of a flopper he identified as Daniel Cozzi.

(The detectives had at last trapped Page. At the hour of the scheduled appointment they went to the doctor's office, posed as patients in the waiting room and overheard the doctor's and Page's conversation. This was the proof the District Attorney needed.)

I was very surprised when the judge said I was an unregenerate thief as I had tried to go straight several times but did not have good fortune. The judge gave me four-to-eight in Sing Sing. This sentence is more than I anticipated but I am man enough to take it as all my life I lived with the adage that in playing with fire I will get burnt some day.

When I last talked with Page—which, of course, is not his real name—he was out on parole and he told me he was trying to make an honest living. A.K.

THE HUSBAND IMPOSTOR

by Martin Fass

Many a man has coveted his neighbor's wife. Arnold du Tilb did something about it. This daring impostor started off modestly, poaching for rabbits on the royal preserves. When chance made him an inadvertant peeping Tom, he aimed for tastier and more exciting game. He wound up his short but merry career poaching another man's beautiful wife, money and large estate. Du Tilb literally stepped into the husband's breeches.

Like many men of high ambition, du Tilb, the only son of hard-working French peasants was born poor in the tiny village of Sagias. Poverty in the 16th century was really bottom as any respectable historian will gladly tell you. "The nights in Languedoc are long," went a familiar folk saying, "but the peasants are too tired to enjoy them."

As a boy, du Tilb was a talented mimic. He could imitate the mincing walk of a strumpet or roar like an angry bull. He was equipped with an amazing ability to watch someone for a minute and then imitate exactly his facial expressions, his mannerisms and his speech.

He was a master of double-talk and took particular delight in ribbing foreign travelers. Slouched in a corner of the inn at Rieux, du Tilb listened carefully to the melodic pattern of their speech. Then he'd strike up a conversation by improvising a string of gibberish. At first, the strangers were certain the boy spoke their native tongue and strained to understand what he was saying. This was the cue for the innkeeper and the hangers-on to burst out laughing. Usually, the travelers joined in good-naturedly and tossed the boy a few coppers.

When Arnold was 22, his father died, and shortly afterwards, his mother. Alone, du Tilb turned his talent to poaching in the nearby royal forests—a dangerous occupation. To be caught was to be hanged.

He formed a partnership with a wastrel nicknamed "the Mole," a man with small, beady black eyes set close together in a pinched face.

Utilizing his gift for mimicry, du Tilb worked out a simple but effective stratagem. Before setting and clearing their traps, du Tilb posted himself within hearing distance of the gamekeeper's cottage. Crashing through the underbrush, he howled like a wounded stag, to lead the gamekeeper on a wild, fruitless chase. The Mole then cleared the traps in safety.

But setting a few crude traps nightly was hardly the high road to riches. As the demand for contraband game far exceeded the supply, du Tilb worked out a unique mass production scheme he called "fishing for rabbits."

They hung a large fishing net across a narrow defile. Shouting and beating the bushes, they drove scores of frightened rabbits into their trap. The plan was a fantastic success.

Periodically, they scouted the forest to find effective spots for their "fishing net." One night, after a particularly long hike, they came to a lovely pool set in a natural, grassy hollow. The Mole refused to walk another step. Clutching his empty bottle to his bosom, he flopped into a thicket and passed out. Du Tilb stretched out and was soon snoring merrily.

Next morning, the crackling of dry branches on a path that led to the clearing woke du Tilb. All his senses alert, he hardly breathed. What he saw couldn't have shocked him more than the gamekeeper's hounds.

A lovely woman strolled into the hollow. The expensive brocades she wore marked her as a person of means. She looked vaguely familiar, but du Tilb felt that way about every woman he saw. Gaily, she kicked off her shoes and dug her toes into the soft, mossy turf. Then slowly, almost lazily, she unhooked her clothes.

Du Tilb watched in fascinated admiration. Her body was supple; her skin smooth and white as apple blossoms. She unpinned her hair and the blonde tresses fell to her hips.

At the edge of the pool, she knelt and let the water trickle through her fingers. Then she slipped into the clear water and splashed about like a carefree wood nymph.

Du Tilb wondered how she'd react if he stepped out of the thicket and surprised her. He was figuring an opening gambit when a hoarse voice whispered: "Ah now, that Catherine Guerre. What a tasty morsel."

The Mole, wide awake, grinned at him idiotically. Du Tilb decided it was an impossible situation. If he accosted this lovely creature now, the Mole was sure to leer at her over his shoulders. And the Mole was hardly a man to inspire confidence in a woman well brought up. Besides, du Tilb decided, she was probably a woman who preferred slow cultivation. He determined to make it his business to do just that.

When tired of her sport, she climbed onto a rocky ledge and jumped lightly ashore. Singing softly, she danced about until dry. Deftly she arranged her hair and dressed. In a moment, she was gone.

If he had seen her before, du Tilb realized that he'd never truly appreciated her charms. The Mole, a repository of local information, supplied the details du Tilb wanted. The 18-year-old Catherine lived in the nearby village of Artigues. She was married and had a year-old son. Her husband, Martin, according to the Mole, was a scoundrel, always in debt and always quarreling.

Du Tilb, a homespun philosopher, firmly believed that a quarreling husband encourages a straying wife. So for weeks, du Tilb tried meeting Catherine. He even took to attending church services. His continued presence in the little village began to stir up gossip, but by then he was too intent on his pursuit to care.

The Mole, meanwhile, couldn't resist boasting to his drinking companions of the new way "to fish for rabbits." An informer tipped off the gamekeeper. The Mole scooted into hiding nearby. Du Tilb left behind both fishnet and Catherine in his hasty flight.

Wandering across France for the next eight years, he lived by his wits, usually one jump ahead of the local gendarmerie. Then, by chance, he bumped into Martin Guerre who was serving time in the army. Seeing Guerre stirred up du Tilb's vivid memories of Catherine.

In no time flat, du Tilb was treating for drinks, and Guerre was spilling the story of his life. He had left home six years ago after a bitter quarrel with his father-in-law.

"He was a meddler," Guerre complained. "He stuck his nose in all my affairs. I couldn't belch without him asking what I had for dinner."

What was worse, the penurious old man controlled the purse strings and questioned every penny Guerre spent.

"Well, drink up," said du Tilb with cheerful optimism. "The old man can't live forever."

"The cantankerous old goat will outlive us both," Guerre roared. "I'll never go home."

"You'll get fed up with soldiering soon enough," du Tilb said, "and then you'll be glad to go home, old man or no old man."

"Not me," Guerre promised. "Army life isn't bad. The food's good. I have money in my purse. And there are always plenty of women around."

Guerre, du Tilb concluded, was a fool, and he had a natural bent to take advantage of a fool—especially a fool with a beautiful and lonely wife. It was then that du Tilb conceived his grand and daring scheme for impersonating Guerre and presenting himself to Catherine as her husband.

The more he thought about his idea, the more he relished it. He examined Guerre with new interest. There was a superficial resemblance between them. Although Guerre was slimmer and taller, both were swarthy. Both had large, prominent brown eyes. Both were the same age.

To duplicate Guerre's mannerisms and speech patterns was a simple matter, and six years could account for certain changes in a man. But to be accepted by Guerre's wife and close relatives, he would have to acquire an encyclopedic knowledge of Guerre's history and habits—

including the most intimate details. Overcoming his aversion to discipline, du Tilb joined the army.

Soon du Tilb and Guerre were the closest comrades. They got drunk together, caroused together. Guerre, a talkative, self-centered egoist found in his new friend the perfect listener. No detail of Guerre's life was too insignificant, no story too boring. Astutely, du Tilb pumped his man, and Guerre never tired of these flattering attentions.

Guerre withheld nothing. Once Guerre had come home drunk. When Catherine tried to bar him from their room, he forced open the door, ripped off her clothes and took her by force.

Du Tilb collected an amazing and detailed fund of fascinating information about Guerre's marital life. He learned, among other things, that Catherine was ticklish and just where Guerre tickled her. He was told that her pet name was "Chouchou." That she was shy and modest during the day, but a veritable demon of passion in the darkness of their fourposter.

When du Tilb wasn't gleaning information from Guerre, he diligently practiced impersonating him. Inside a year Du Tilb was ready to become Guerre.

One night, he slipped away to leave Guerre talking to himself. Back in Artigues, du Tilb stopped first at the inn. The *patron* stared at him. Du Tilb chided the man for not recognizing him, attempted to borrow some money, was refused, grew angry and at once established himself as the long-lost Martin Guerre.

At Guerre's house, du Tilb took his "wife" in his arms. The lonely woman, overcome by his sudden reappearance, wept with joy and clung to him.

"Yes, yes, my Chouchou," du Tilb whispered in her ear. "We'll make up for the lost years."

Catherine's father hopped about impatiently. Finally, unable to contain himself, he pulled them apart.

"Just because you've come back," he warned, "doesn't mean you can squander my money. I'm not dead yet."

"Old man," du Tilb said, "everyone makes a mistake. You were right, and I was wrong. But from now on, you will find me a changed man."

Guerre's four sisters hugged and kissed their long lost brother. And even Catherine's uncle, a shrewd peasant who reputedly didn't trust his own wife, was taken in by du Tilb's performance.

Du Tilb regaled them with tales of his adventures. Finally, he excused himself. He was tired, had traveled far. He needed sleep. Cather-

166

ine blushed. Everyone laughed uproariously, and after a hundred ribald suggestions, the family, at long last, let the couple retire.

In the splendid isolation of the fourposter, du Tilb finally took possession of Guerre's lovely wife. As Catherine later confided to one of Guerre's sisters, her husband was indeed a changed man—more tender, devoted and an infinitely more skilled lover than he had been before.

Du Tilb and Martin Guerre's wife lived happily together for three years. During this time, two children were added to the family.

Du Tilb might never have been detected. Unfortunately, a busybody traveler tarried too long, drank too much, and gossiped too well. He was chatting with Catherine's uncle when the name Martin Guerre was accidentally mentioned. The stranger declared that 18 months ago he had seen and talked to an invalid of that name in a distant province of France. Guerre hadn't changed seemingly for he hadn't failed to mention that he didn't intend going home while his father-in-law was alive. The stranger added that the Guerre he saw had lost a leg in the battle of St. Quinten.

The uncle was flabbergasted. He questioned the traveler closely, but couldn't shake his story. A skeptic and stubborn troublemaker, the uncle now recalled little circumstances, unnoticed before, that made him suspect du Tilb was an impostor.

For one thing, this Guerre wasn't quarrelsome enough. For another, his manner of speaking and his language, though at times artfully interlarded with patois and unintelligible gibberish, was very different from the real Guerre's speech. A Biscayan, Guerre used a curious mixture of Spanish, French and Gascon, very difficult to imitate.

The uncle decided they had all been duped and wasted no time in disclosing his suspicions to Catherine. His niece threw a catfit. She accused him of being a mean, and vicious man. As for du Tilb, he laughed it all off as a garbled tale told by a drunken busybody.

From that day on, suspicion bred interminable quarrels. The family divided into passionate factions. Soon everyone in the village was drawn into the dispute. No one, however, could convince Catherine that her happiness had been founded on a mistake.

After three months, Catherine broke under the implacable pressure put on her by her uncle, and the jeering taunts of many of the villagers. Her father decided there was only one way to still the malicious gossip of the villagers. They must get legal certification that her husband was genuine. The only way to do that was to bring the case to court.

Du Tilb agreed and was taken into custody, imprisoned by the order of the Criminal Judge of Rieux, and the time of trial fixed. An excited crowd jammed into the court. A statement by the talkative traveler concerning the absent Martin Guerre was read. The judge then ordered the prisoner to speak in his own defense.

"The accusation against me," he began, "is based solely on the statement of a stranger who undoubtedly was drunk and talking nonsense. If gossip becomes law, old women will be queens."

Du Tilb went on to admit freely that he had been a wastrel. But, he insisted the years away from his wife and family had taught him a bitter lesson. What he couldn't understand was why Catherine's uncle was so intent on persecuting him.

"When I came home," said du Tilb, "no one doubted my identity— not my wife, my father-in-law, my sisters. And even my uncle, who now finds truth in the wild drivel of a stranger, even he welcomed me with open arms."

Catherine Guerre, called to testify, cried out, "If this man is not my husband, then I have lost my honor and my reason."

A stream of witnesses testified in his behalf. The four sisters of Martin Guerre, all well known to be women of character, were positive the prisoner was "our dear brother, Martin."

The prosecutor then called 37 witnesses who were well acquainted with Martin Guerre. They swore that the prisoner was not, and could not be, Martin. Some recalled physical differences—Guerre's nose was flatter, he was thinner and taller.

The shoemaker, who had for many years made shoes for Guerre, stated that his foot was size 12; but that the prisoner's was just short of 11.

One neighbor testified that Guerre had been an excellent wrestler and cudgel player, of which the accused was wholly ignorant.

Moreover, ten witnesses who had known or were related to Arnold du Tilb, swore that the prisoner was, and could only be Arnold du Tilb.

The prosecutor summed up, and, the evidence on both sides being closed, the judge gave his verdict: Arnold du Tilb was guilty as charged. He was sentenced to death.

But du Tilb fought back. He appealed to the Parliament of Toulouse, which at that period was a court of justice as well as a registry of royal edicts. The Parliament, Solomon-like, determined to take no further proceedings until some effort was made to locate the alleged real Martin Guerre, the so-called man with the wooden leg.

A wide search was started, and after several months, the wandering husband was found. He was brought to Toulouse secretly. A day was fixed for the final trial. Parliament assembled at an early hour. After the formal charges were read, the prisoner reasserted his innocence and bitterly complained of the hardships and injuries he had suffered.

With the setting complete, the real Martin Guerre walked into court. Shocked though he must have been by Guerre's sudden appearance, du Tilb stared at Guerre as though he were a stranger.

"Who is this man?" du Tilb inquired casually.

Guerre turned livid. Hardly able to contain his anger, he spluttered: "Me? I am Martin Guerre. And you have abused the confidence of a comrade."

With complete self-possession, du Tilb turned to the judge. "This man is either mad or an impostor."

An observer later wrote: "At that moment, Guerre seemed the impostor, and the prisoner a wronged man."

Then came the crucial moment of the trial. Martin Guerre's wife and his four sisters had not yet seen the genuine Guerre. The first of the five to enter the court was the eldest sister of Guerre. The instant she saw her brother, she burst into tears. Taking him in her arms, she begged him to forgive her. The others, coming into court one by one, soon left no doubt as to which man was Martin Guerre.

During this scene, poor Catherine stood trembling at the entrance of the court. One of the four sisters led her to Martin. She fell to her knee and tried to kiss his hands. He pushed her away roughly.

"A wife," he said with contempt, "always has ways of knowing a husband unknown to every other living soul. It is impossible that a woman can have been imposed on if she had not entertained a secret wish to be unfaithful."

"That may be so," said the judge, "but any husband who leaves a beautiful woman to waste her best years alone deserves some punishment. I suggest you be more forgiving."

As for du Tilb, the fact that he had so nobly and generously filled in during Guerre's absence did not help him. He was pronounced guilty of fraud, adultery, sacrilege, rape and theft. He was condemned to make the *amende honorable* in the marketplace of Artigues, attired in a shirt, with bare head and feet, a halter round his neck, and bearing a lighted torch in his hand. There he was to demand pardon of God, the King, the nation, and the family he had so cruelly outraged. It was further ordered that he should be hanged before the dwelling house of Martin Guerre, and after death his body burned to ashes.

Du Tilb continued to maintain his innocence. Then, as the day of execution approached, his firmness deserted him. In an interview with the curé, he confessed his crimes in detail.

As he stood on the scaffold, du Tilb looked at Catherine Guerre. "Forgive me for wronging you. Despite my lies, remember I truly loved you."

Catherine's father wasn't present. The strain of the trial had proven too much even for the durable old man, and he had passed on.

Arnold du Tilb died offering prayers to the Almighty to pardon his sins.

Today, male devotees of the wandering eye would take a more charitable view of du Tilb's fatal conquest. And women, in view of his single-minded devotion, would certainly judge him more kindly. Perhaps some day both male and female aficionados of the game of love might even be moved to erect a monument to this talented scoundrel who literally lost his head over a woman.

THE MYSTERY OF THE MINO TOMB

by *Albert Franz Cochrane*

Do you think that you would make a good amateur detective if occasion ever arose? Most of us do. Very well, then, the question is this: Did, or did not, the Boston Museum of Fine Arts pay one hundred thousand dollars for a masterpiece of Italian Renaissance sculpture or for worthless forgery?

The problem is not just a battle of critics. That stage was passed long ago. As it stands today, it is one of cold deductive reasoning, of cause and effect, of whys and wherefores.

Moreover, it is not just a question of whether or not the Mino Tomb is beautiful. It is magnificent, and so conceded by an unending list of world-renowned scholars who have come to Boston to see the sculpture, and, seeing it, have stayed to dispute its authenticity while agreeing on its beauty.

For some ten years the Museum's own staff of experts endeavored by every means at its command to determine whether the Mino Tomb is a costly fake or a Renaissance masterpiece.

170

The results of their investigation are unparalleled in the annals of art: a confessed "forgery" has been "proved" genuine by scientific means. The evidence on either side is amazing and overwhelming. . . .

In the pronouncement of science, which came after four years of most intensive and painstaking research, the Boston Museum believes that it has found the answer that it has sought—the sculpture is genuine Renaissance.

But scarcely had the Museum spoken its mind than a letter arrived from London addressed to the Director, Mr. George Harold Edgell. It was from Sir Eric Robert Dalrymple Maclagan, the distinguished head of the Victoria and Albert. The Englishman congratulated his American colleague on the findings, but also begged leave to remain in the rank of the doubters. . . .

The cannonading started in 1928 when Alceo Dossena, an obscure Italian sculptor, who was to become the most celebrated forger of his century, hurled a verbal bombshell into a pleasantly tranquil art world. "In the Museum of Fine Arts, Boston, the U.S.A.," he said, "is a marble tomb exhibited as the work of Mino da Fiesole. I made it." But let us go back to the beginning of our story.

In the fall of 1922, Mr. Charles H. Hawes, then associate director of the Boston Museum, sat in the office of the Hofmuseum in Vienna, enjoying a pleasant chat with the head of that institution, Dr. Gustavo Gluck. Among other things, Doctor Gluck spoke of a new and important accession, a magnificently carved memorial tomb of one Maria Catharina da Savelli, from the hand of the fifteenth-century Florentine sculptor, Mino da Fiesole. It had not yet arrived for installation, but Doctor Gluck graciously showed photographs to his colleague. So beautiful was it that the Bostonian could easily admire it beyond the perfunctory praise expected of well-bred visitors.

Months passed, and back in Boston Mr. Hawes, occupied with the manifold duties of his office, ceased to think of the Mino Tomb until, by chance, word came through Miss Alice V. V. Brown, professor of Fine Arts at nearby Wellesley, that the sculpture was again on the market.

Monumental works of the Italian Renaissance are great rarities, and it is no exaggeration to say that the chance to pick up an example in a state of almost perfect preservation might never again present itself. Only one crack ran through the central slab, cutting the marble effigy of the sleeping figure and the sarcophagus on which she rested. And, as so often happens in ancient art, that crack seemed to add the final touch of æsthetic beauty. Age had hall-marked it for its own; the crack whispered softly of passing centuries that had mellowed and stained the Carrara to a rich golden hue. No wonder the Boston Museum, with so rich a prize within grasp, promptly cabled for photographs to a Florentine dealer into whose hands the tomb had now come.

There are several accounts as to why the Mino sculpture was lost to Vienna. The official one is that the museum failed to raise the necessary money. This is plausible enough, for in those years ready cash was scarce among the defeated Central Powers. Another version is that the officials became suspicious after closely examining their purchase. Some years later, when its forgery was openly asserted, Dr. Leo Planiscig, custodian of the former Imperial Museum in Vienna, who is ranked as a world-scholar of Italian Renaissance sculpture, revealed that he had been taken to a cemetery near Florence and "there offered this monument, the existence of which I had not heard of before. It was claimed that it had been found by a monk in an abbey near Siena destroyed by an earthquake in the 18th Century. I investigated, and compared it with a similar sculpture in Florence, which I knew to be genuine. The difference in the lines of the face was obvious. The classic were strong; those of the fake, sweet, sentimental, modern, and identical with those of a fake wooden Madonna claimed to be a Simone Martini which had been offered me in 1921 by a Venetian dealer. Upon return to Vienna I found the monument at the Hofmuseum, but I managed to have it rejected, whereupon it was returned to Italy and later sold to Boston."

Museum ethics, in which the time-honored principle of *caveat emptor* is neatly balanced against scholarly respect for differing judgments, prevented these details from being known to the Boston Museum when it opened negotiations with Signor Volpi, the noted dealer, who maintained as showrooms the famous old Florentine palace, the Casa Davanzati, furnished at all times with masterpieces of Italian art.

The Mino Tomb was viewed by John Briggs Potter, an adviser to the Museum, and a Bostonian of remarkable and independent discernment. His report enthusiastically backed the opinion of Mr. Hawes, and found reflection round the council table of the trustees. And so the marble came to Boston in the spring of 1924, for the tidy but not exorbitant sum of one hundred thousand dollars.

Art corruption in Italy is a three-cornered and rather friendly game of wits between buyer, seller, and the authorities. Playing it for high stakes is half the fun of connoisseurship. Curators and experts strop their wits in daily contact with sharpsters and hone them on no end of clever forgeries—and succumb to surprisingly few of either. The other half of the fun comes from the discovery of a previously unknown work or master, or the "re-discovery" of a lost or forgotten one. Hunting down obscure records, comparing brush and chisel strokes for clues to authorship, building a theory or tearing another's down—these provide the thrills and rewards of art scholarship. If there be anything that connoisseurs enjoy more than artistic achievement it is the challenge of the chase.

There of course is where the Mino Tomb scores double. It is both magnificent and mysterious. Run your fingers over the delicately chiseled face of the lady in marble and you are amazed at its masterful rendering of planes so subtle as to escape the eye, gradations so finely achieved that only the caressing hand of a blind person or an artist could fully comprehend them. Incidentally, Maria Catharina Savelli contributed no little to the attractiveness of the Tomb by dying while yet a young and pretty Roman matron.

The Savelli were one of the four most powerful families inhabiting the Seven Hills. Two of their number became popes, and the Castle Gandolfo, which often appears in to-day's news as the favorite papal residence outside the Vatican, belonged to them in medieval times. No wonder that Maria Catharina, if indeed it be she who sleeps in unchanging marble, is an aristocratic beauty, for she was one of the culminating products of a long line of Romans. About a century after her death, which occurred nearly two decades before Columbus was born, a whole series of tragic events overtook the Savelli, and the family became extinct. With them went any possible record of the Mino Tomb.

Maria had not rested in Boston a year when ugly rumors began to emanate from Paris. Report had it that somewhere in Italy a great master-forger was turning out classical and Renaissance art with the ease of the masters themselves.

Then in the fall of 1928 the storm broke. One Alceo Dossena, an unknown sculptor, had brought suit against the firm of Fasoli & Palesi for $66,000 allegedly due him in back wages on a contract calling for the payment of $100,000 over a period of ten years. He had been employed, said his complaint, to create authentic works of art in the spirit of the various classical periods, cracks, stains, and all. And then, with surprise and indignation, he had learned that they were being sold as genuine antiquities! Moreover, he had learned that they were fetching the fabulous prices of originals, of which but a fraction was passed on to him-

173

self and his workmen. Dossena had for years carried on his activities in a closely guarded studio, unknown to fame. There also he kept the photographic records of his works, and—it is said by some of those who later visited that now famous atelier—kept also a finger, a toe, or other sculptured member broken from the finished carving to help suggest authentic age and to prove indisputable authorship should occasion ever arise.

Boston's lady has a toe missing!

In November, 1928, the transoceanic cables sizzled with Dossena's revelations. Boston, said the report, had been the first major American victim. The forger also claimed representation in the Metropolitan, Cleveland, and Frick museums. Included also were the museums of Munich and Berlin, together with numerous private collections on both continents. The Metropolitan admitted ownership of a Dossena version of an archaic Greek maid (which it had been dubious about and had not placed on exhibition); and the records of the Frick collection now reveal that back in 1924 Miss Helen C. Frick did exchange a sizable lump of the coke fortune for a pair of Dossena marbles attributed to the famed primitive, Simone Martini, a painter who had never before been known to work in sculpture.

Santayana was perhaps the first philosophical writer to evaluate correctly the subtle influence that rarity and price have on æsthetic judgment. It is always difficult to question an object valued at a king's ransom. The huge prices demanded and received for Dossena's works— prices never before equaled in the forgery racket—and the very audacity with which his re-creations were presented as unique examples of rare masters, carried bold assurance of authenticity. Miss Gisela M. A. Richter, the Metropolitan's curator of classical sculpture, has described the sum demanded of her institution for two more Dossenas offered it as staggering.

But the Metropolitan, despite its hope of adding to its collections two highly important Grecian sculptures, did examine the marbles thoroughly, and then packed them back to the dealer. A few months later the Cleveland Museum picked one of them up at the bargain price of $120,000.

Cleveland, in fact, bought two of Dossena's masterpieces. The first was a comparatively inexpensive wooden Madonna attributed to Giovanni Pisano, costing $18,000. As the director phrased it, "while no exact attribution can be made, there is at this moment no known artist to whom it could logically be ascribed if not to Giovanni Pisano. It is

174

by the hand of a master, and if not by Giovanni himself, then by someone worthy to be called his equal." Three years later I was privileged
to view the Madonna in the director's office just before she was deported. The museum, aided by X-ray, had discovered modern nails im-
modestly hiding behind the gilt, and thus had learned to its dismay that
the "master worthy to be called his equal" was Alceo Dossena.

The downfall of Dossena was inevitable but long delayed. For
months before his suit against his employers became public the chain
of evidence was slowly closing about his little workshop on the Ripetta.
It was being welded, link by link, by the late Mr. John Marshall, the
eminent archæologist and European representative of the Metropolitan.
It was he who had purchased for that museum the little Greek girl.
Shortly afterward he had been offered by the same source the temple
fragment later acquired by Cleveland. But this time Marshall was not
satisfied and refused to buy. It was then that its sponsors made the blun-
dering and fatal move of sending it directly to the Metropolitan for con-
sideration. Examination having dashed her high hopes of a rare find,
Miss Richter, in a letter to Marshall, made mention of the incident.
Naturally enough, Marshall then recalled the archaic maiden with the
neck and ankle nicely broken in token of antiquity and fell to wondering if she too could be false.

Marshall went to work on the case with all the care and cunning of
a detective. He spent weeks in discreet questioning. Then in Rome
another piece turned up. Marshall was promptly on the job. Where had
it come from? And where had it been before that? Marshall never lived
to see Dossena. Sudden death intervened. (If this were fiction, a sinister
motif would be read into Marshall's demise on the eve of sensational
disclosure. But his death was from natural causes.)

The search for Dossena was continued and successfully terminated
by Mr. Harold Woodbury Parsons, a Bostonian who acts as European
agent for museums at Cleveland and Kansas City. Journey's End for
the forger came over a café table amply supplied with good wines. Parsons found Dossena at an auspicious moment soon after the artist had
heard from a disgruntled Venetian dealer the enormous prices which
his creations were fetching, while he himself was having difficulty meeting the payroll of his assistants. Dossena talked.

News of Marshall's investigations had already brought Miss Richter
to Rome. It was only after considerable difficulty that she was able to
see Dossena. But when she finally gained admission to the studio, he
proved to be both pleasant and obliging. He showed photographs of

various of his works and others still in the making. He also demonstrated his methods of achieving his remarkable effects of time-staining. Other fortunate visitors to the atelier remember the sculptor as a tall, well-built, but slightly stoop-shouldered man, with graying hair brushed back from a powerful brow. He was keenly interested in archæology and chemistry.

In his preliminary court action against the dealers, Dossena charged that one of the partners had endeavored to do away with him by denouncing him to the authorities as an anti-Fascist plotter. The sculptor produced records to prove that he had indeed been arrested on the charge and sent to prison, but had been able to establish his loyalty. After long delay a date was appointed for hearing evidence in the Dossena suit. The stage was set for a grand show, but the curtain failed to rise. Some say the difference was settled out of court, others that the case was quashed because influential persons were involved.

For some time thereafter Dossena rode a cresting wave of fame, hailed on all sides as a super-genius, a *maestro*, at home in all ages of art. Patrons now flocked to his studio for "re-creations," among them Prince Borghese to commission a portrait of his Princess carved in the manner and dress of the Early Renaissance.

And in but slightly lessened numbers came museum officials with disquieting doubts and photographs. Would the *Maestro*, they begged, kindly recollect if he had or had not executed such-and-such an ancient sculpture now in the possession of their institution? In a letter to the editor of an Italian journal Dossena complained of their importunings. These gentlemen, he said, were supposed to be experts. Why must they bother him with questions?

Meanwhile the Boston Museum played a lone and unenviable role, stoutly maintaining that it had not fallen victim to the Italians. No one from the Boston Museum ever asked Dossena to prove what he had said about the Mino Tomb. No one from the Museum even asked him if he had said it. No one from the Museum ever saw Dossena or tried to see him. And no one from the Museum ever will see him—for Alceo Dossena died of a stroke in Rome early in 1938. Scarcely had he been laid to rest when Boston dragged the Mino Tomb from oblivion and put it on exhibition again beneath spotlights as genuine Renaissance.

What a chain of circumstantial evidence! Does it not suggest that, victimized, the Museum tried to save face, first by denying that it had been defrauded and then by assiduously avoiding the sculptor who might prove it wrong? . . .

176

Even before the Dossena exposé the heavy guns of critical opinion had begun their creeping barrage. First to the attack was Mr. H. Wareham Harding, an authority on old ivories, who came from New York to complain about the meticulous carving of the tomb. Only a forger, he said, afraid to let himself go, would be so careful with the chisel. Then came a venerable and respected dealer from Paris. With a pocket lens he minutely examined the marble, and then pronounced its surface to be doctored with wax. Later examination proved this to be so.

Suspicions continued to multiply, but within the Museum itself was a strongly entrenched determination that the Mino Tomb was to be included as one of the chief glories of the new wing, then nearing completion, and there it would be shown regardless of questioning rumors. The new wing, however, was to be under the jurisdiction of Mr. Edwin J. Hipkiss, curator of decorative arts, and quite naturally he objected to the inclusion of a challenged piece. In a last-minute effort to forestall its display there in the face of gathering storm, the curator interviewed various members of the art committee privately and obtained sufficient votes to have it withdrawn from the show several days prior to the formal opening of the new galleries. Within a fortnight thereafter the Dossena revelations broke over an amazed art world.

The Boston Museum's experts examined the tomb's inscription. Mino da Fiesole, its reputed sculptor, was born in 1431. The tomb bore a date of 1430!

Down into the storage vaults went the lovely Mino, and down after it, for a period of years, flocked the experts, each with a theory.

Not all of their opinions are in quotable form, for many experts when examining a work of art known to be suspect prefer the ambiguity of verbal pronouncement to an unequivocal written and recorded statement. But the appraisal of such a world authority as Eric Maclagan had no hedging. Sir Eric said the tomb wasn't genuine—and he hasn't changed his opinion. The type of lettering in the inscription is later than Mino, he said, and both the figure and the tomb itself too small in scale.

And Mr. Parsons, to whom Dossena confessed making the sculpture, carefully prepared a fourteen-point indictment. The decorative carving he declared too flabby and lifeless, the body too long for the coffin, the figure itself copied from the well-known Beata Tomb by Rossellino, the date of the doubtful lady's death forty years too early, the duplication of the escutcheons unusual and not to be expected, and the surface false and probably artificially aged by soaking in permanganate of potash. What's more, he found one of the hands to be dubious, and doubted very much if the fingers could have survived the ages without breaking off.

Later Professor Mather blasted his Boston colleagues in the columns of the *Atlantic Monthly*. The Princeton man told how, in those prosperous years before the Wall Street débâcle, American museums vied with one another for costly souvenirs of antiquity. "But for the phantom of the Metropolitan," he wrote, "the staff of the Boston Museum would have found the hour necessary to prove the heraldry of the Mino Tomb preposterously unhistorical. Or, if they lacked the books and the herald, they could at least have written a letter to the accomplished herald of the Metropolitan."

It so happened, however, that the museum had consulted Pierre La-Rose, the great heraldic authority, before committing itself to the purchase of the sculpture, and he had given the coat of arms a clean bill of health.

From the vantage point of Harvard across the Charles River, Dr. George Harold Edgell, professor of Fine Arts and dean of the Harvard School of Architecture, watched with keen interest the shifting destinies of the Mino Tomb. Not being a specialist in Renaissance sculpture, he had at first assumed it to be genuine, in conformity with its museum label. Later he accepted Dossena's confession, and the generally held verdict of the experts who now denounced it. Nevertheless, forgery, or no forgery, the work was, in his opinion, far too beautiful for basement dust.

It was natural, therefore, that when Professor Edgell was called to the directorship of the Boston Museum some years later, one of his first acts was to request permission of the art committee to return the Mino Tomb to public exhibition.

But the art committee was probably still licking the wounds inflicted in the Dossena explosion and very likely had little relish for more taunting headlines. If Professor Edgell wished to exhibit the Tomb he would have to first make up his mind if it was to be as a work of art or as a fake. He could display it as either one, but this time there must be no "ifs" or "maybes" about the matter.

Doctor Edgell decided on the simpler course, the course indicated by nearly every scrap of evidence. If the Mino Tomb were false he would prove it so. Accordingly he directed Mr. William J. Young, the museum's youthful Oxford-trained technician to make a thorough examination regardless of time or expense, and then submit a report substantiated by proof.

It was amid the test-tubes, retorts, cameras, microscopes, and chemicals of his newly fitted laboratory that Mr. Young made his astonishing discovery, giving to this fascinating mystery the most remarkable ending in art history.

X-ray, invaluable in the examination of an oil painting or other penetrable object, is worthless in the study of stone. Its rays will not pierce through. The ultra-violet ray, on the other hand, is a surface-finder. Its ghastly purple light plays directly on the object and its findings are immediately visible in the differing degree of violet light that is reflected back to the eye. Examination under ultra-violet is quick, and at the present stage of the game between experts and forgers, quite reliable for determining comparative age. But its effects can be simulated by chemicals. Not very well as yet, for this branch of science is yet new to all concerned. But it seems reasonable to assume that the forger will eventually find a way round this added obstacle to his craft. Polarized light, however, is different. Its use in art detection, in conjunction with microscopic photography, is brand new, and is the triumph of the baffling Boston case.

A tiny cross section of marble is taken from the suspected sculpture and ground down to the transparent fineness of a drop of water. When this is placed on a glass slide beneath a powerful lens, its crystal structure becomes as apparent as the geological stratification of a newly cut mountain pass. A cross section of marble thus viewed through a beam of polarized light takes on rainbow hues, and by observing and classifying these colors as they illuminate the stone's strata it is possible to determine the quarry of its origin. Herein it seems probable that forgery will never quite catch up with science, for it would necessitate changing the actual crystal structure of the stone.

By polarized light Mr. Young established the origin of every component marble in the Renaissance tomb. Thirteen were quarried at Carrara; the fourteenth section came from ancient Greece.

As a final test, various microscopic cuts were taken at surface level and then projected on a four-foot silver screen in the laboratory's darkroom. Here comparative study was made with specimens taken from authenticated antiques and known forgeries. The answer was found in time's breakdown of the surface crystals, and the depth, intensity, and characteristics of the staining. The difference between the old and newly cut marbles was found to be quite similar to that of the pores of a clean face and those of one long unwashed and exposed to embedding soot. You can, if you wish, for purposes of disguise, acquire a dirty face within a few minutes, but it takes a long time really to clog up the pores.

To the delighted surprise of all save its most ardent die-hard critics, Mr. Young established the fact that the Mino Tomb did indeed date from the Middle Ages, although lately restored in several details, and heavily waxed to hide the reconstruction. One of the companion coats of arms and both pilaster caps were found to be newly cut, as was also the funeral inscription. All else showed the surface change of long exposure. The significant thing to remember here is that the question is not merely one of how long the block of marble itself has been quarried, but how long since its surface has undergone change at the point of a chisel. Thus an old block, newly carved, shows no characteristics of age. This all-important distinction seems to clinch the laboratory's case against faking.

The Boston Museum's contention, therefore, is that a genuine old monument, having fallen into disrepair, has been placed in more saleable condition by reconstruction and by newly given identity of both subject and artist. According to this theory, the name of the Savelli family was conveniently suggested by the happy presence of an anciently carved escutcheon panel in the dealer's workshop—the odd, fourteenth piece of Grecian marble. This slab, continues the museum's thesis, was forthwith inserted in the tomb, and a balancing companion one added, together with a mortuary legend to conform with the heraldic device. The whole was then assigned, for want of better authorship, to Mino da Fiesole.

But science, in giving the lie to Dossena's confession of forgery, has overlooked several pertinent considerations. If, for example, the appearance of the identifying Savelli arms is to be ascribed to opportunism, how then explain the highly significant fact that a decorative flying ribbon with distinctive tassel terminal, which is a prominent and integral feature of the heraldry, also is found in similar placement round the inscription panel of the sarcophagus itself? Could mere accident bring about such a remarkable association of ornamental detail? Examination of the chisel strokes, moreover, seems strongly to indicate them to have been cut by the same hand, which means also at the same time. This fact established, the validity of the inscription can hardly be questioned, for it bears out the armorial design. Obviously, these important features were designed and executed as a unit. But when?

If it is a genuine Savelli monument why haven't its European sponsors welcomed the opportunity to prove its authenticity by revealing its history and true provenience? Its very beauty had led Professor Edgell and others to question if Mino da Fiesole, generally ranked among the second-class masters of the Renaissance, could have carved it. Presumably, then, it was by an even greater sculptor. Then why not tell where it came from in order to establish his identity? Its intrinsic value would be increased and the prestige of the dealers enhanced.

If we accept the theory that, despite the obvious connection between wording, heraldry, and repeating ornament, the tomb is ancient while its legend *"Obiit enim Prefata Maria Catharina de Sabello Anno Christi MCCCCXXX"* is newly added, then we must ask why it was that so beautiful and aristocratic a lady happened to be interred in so magnificent a receptacle without proper identification being added to the blank space provided for that purpose.

The most ready answer of course is that it has happened before. In the history of Italian art can be found a precedent for anything. As for the sandal missing from one foot of the reclining lady, that too could easily happen with a sculptor who forgot to fill in the even more important name plate. Dossena, when asked about the missing foot-gear, replied that he made the tomb as a composite from various photographs of authentic ones, and as the print from which he copied that section failed to show the sole of the foot because of the angle from which the view had been snapped, he too overlooked it. But then of course science has said that Dossena didn't even carve the foot itself.

It is typical of Boston's traditional self-sufficiency that the Museum has not troubled to examine in comparative study any of the acknowledged Dossenas. But an outside observer might think it strange that the Boston tomb should now prove to be the one exception in that master's lengthy and excellent repertoire. One's mind might even go back to the evening of March 9, 1933, when at the Hotel Plaza in New York a group of thirty-nine of the *maestro's* "re-creations" went to the auction block and brought less than $10,000.

Might not some of these prove genuine to the joy and profit of their new owners? Might not Dossena, granting him to be the "restorer" of the Boston Mino, have followed in them the same convenient course of assembling instead of laborious chiseling? Why work in the sweat of his brow when unattached masterpieces apparently could be had for the asking?

To such questions as these, inevitable under the circumstance, Director Edgell smiles indulgently, even enjoying the many puzzlers that science's unexpected answer has produced. But Boston, which remained coolly aloof from Dossena during his lifetime, not even troubling to look him up while other museums were wearing a path to his studio door, accepts that verdict as final, while still freely granting to others the right to disagree.

Albert Franz Cochrane's account appeared in 1938. Recently, I wrote to the Boston Museum of Fine Arts inquiring whether there had been any further developments in the case. In reply I received a copy of Mr. Young's scientific report, published in 1937. Apparently, the origin of the Mino Tomb remains a continuing mystery. A.K.

THE PROFESSOR WHO WAS
TRULY BRILLIANT

by Herbert Brean

It began in Philadelphia where Marvin Hewitt was born 32 years ago, the son of a jovial and hearty police sergeant named Samuel Hewitt. One day when he was 10 Marvin wandered into a public library and chanced on a big red book entitled *Functions of a Complex Variable*. Without understanding it, he dimly sensed the stark beauty of its advanced mathematical concepts. He returned to the library and other books on mathematics. After a while he began to understand them. He also began buying books on mathematics, physics and electronics. In his early teens Marvin built up a sizable library. He had a younger brother and sister, but no one in the family could understand him. His father particularly was rebuffed by the shy, solemn boy who preferred books to baseball. His playmates literally could not speak Marvin's language.

"I did not relate to other children," says Hewitt, who presently turned to reading psychology textbooks in an effort to understand himself and his differences with his father. "I was an isolate." When at 12 he came upon a popularized version of Einstein's theory, Marvin again was overwhelmed by mathematics and physics. "It gave me a synoptic perspective of my universe." One day, when he had to give a talk in school, Marvin discussed relativity. Class and teacher listened, utterly mystified.

Marvin was not much of a student. Schoolwork bored him and at 17 he quit high school without his diploma. A half dozen confused, deeply unhappy years followed. He yearned to go to college and study mathematics and physics. Instead, a husky, brawny boy who had once passed through a phase of body-building and weight-lifting, he obtained a succession of heavy-labor jobs in factories and freight yards. A Philadelphia newspaper held contests offering cash prizes for the best solution to social dilemmas. Marvin entered and won a dozen checks. He explains, "I suddenly grew cognizant that in addition to having mathematical ability I was a high verbal type."

When World War II broke out and the Army rejected him, he got a civilian job with the Signal Corps. "It was boring as aitch," says Hewitt, who does not use profanity, liquor, tobacco or coffee but has a weakness for candy bars. He was working as a warehouseman when one day he scanned the want ads and read of a new military school in need of an eighth-grade teacher. Hewitt today cannot account very intelligently for what happened next; apparently he felt an overwhelming desire to teach. He answered the advertisement, describing himself as Marvin Hewitt, Temple Univeristy undergraduate. He got a job teaching eighth-grade arithmetic, geography and history.

On his first day as teacher, facing the class, he felt nervous and uncertain as to how he could control the mischievous boys. Then he found himself being looked up to, and his personality unfolded like a bud in the spring sun. Nervousness ended. Thus at 23 Hewitt walked through a magic door from a dark world of hopelessness and frustration into the bright sunshine of power and prestige. For the first time in his life Hewitt felt confident and at home.

Camp Hill Military Academy folded at the end of the spring term, but Hewitt was content. He had undergone a rewarding experience; he had become Instructor Marvin Hewitt. And why need he stop there?

Hewitt returned to the library. But this time, in addition to seeking out volumes on quantum mechanics, he studied college catalogs, with their brief biographies of faculty members. He selected a name he liked and boldly used it in applying for a summer job as aerodynamicist at an aircraft factory. Aerodynamics, the study of airflow over an object's surfaces, is almost all complex mathematics, and Hewitt had no trouble getting or holding the job. But he had chosen the name of a man so prominent that after a month he knew he could not escape discovery. He quit and went back to the library.

That summer, devoting himself to study, Hewitt developed theoretically the concept of the tiring of light as well as a new approach to cosmology which derived space out of time (Einstein accepted space and time as separate basic entities). The light-tiring concept has been advanced by other scientists and Hewitt does not claim he arrived at it first or is entitled to any credit for it. But he does claim he arrived at the idea independently, without knowledge of the work done by others.

That same summer he met a girl friend of his brother Edward, a tall, grave, dark-eyed girl named Estelle. Soon it was he and not Edward who was taking Estelle out.

Toward the end of the summer Hewitt called nearby colleges, asking if they needed a physics teacher. When he called the Philadelphia College of Pharmacy and Science, Professor Robert N. Jones, acting head of the physics department, asked, "Who is calling?" "Julius Ashkin of Columbia," replied Hewitt confidently. It was a name he had found in a Columbia University catalog and he liked the sound of it. The real Ashkin was about his age, had had a promising career at Los Alamos and the Argonne National Laboratory and was about to start teaching at the University of Rochester. As Ashkin, Hewitt was hired as a part-time instructor at the same $1,750 a year he had received for teaching grammar school students. "Did they take advantage of me!" he remarks.

The pharmacy college then had less than 300 students and Hewitt taught calculus, college algebra and trigonometry. If his experience at the military school had been a warm encouragement, teaching at the College of Pharmacy was a sharp pleasure. The very college students he once envied now listened to him with envious respect as he demonstrated his flair for mathematics by doing calculus in his head. That wide-eyed admiration was heady wine.

Hewitt realized he ought to know something of Ashkin's past; this led him to the discovery that he could write to a university and for one dollar have a transcript of anyone's academic record mailed to him wherever he asked. Knowing the details of Ashkin's academic life gave Hewitt confidence.

He needed it. Among other things he had to supervise laboratory work in physics, and he had had no laboratory experience at all. He managed to bluff his way through. Teaching itself never caused Hewitt trouble, then or later. "Intellectually, it was like clerking," he says. "They gave me a copy of the textbook to be used and told me how much I was to cover during a semester. I mapped it out by lessons and just tried to cover each lesson in a clear manner." For a man who had spent part of the summer pondering a modification of Einstein's theory, algebra presented no difficulty. When the departmental examinations were given, his classes scored as well as other teachers'.

But he had some close shaves in his masquerade. On the street one day with Estelle's father he met one of his students. "Hello, Doctor Ashkin," the boy called out. Hewitt, terrified, walked past without a glance, but he felt the puzzled eyes of both student and future father-in-law on him. One day he and Estelle were in the public library when he suddenly met another pharmacy school faculty member. Hewitt waited with bated breath for the other man to address him as Ashkin. In five minutes' conversation the man never called him by name. Occasionally students (with whom Hewitt always got along well) came to the house and asked for "Doctor Ashkin." Hewitt herded them inside as quickly as possible so they would not be overheard by neighbors, then got rid of them fast. (Only his mother knew he was working under the name of Ashkin.)

One day toward the end of the school year "Doctor Ashkin" sent word that there had been a death in the family and he would be absent from classes for several days. Later he confided to fellow faculty members that actually he had eloped. That was a lie. There had indeed been a death in the family. His father and another officer had both been shot and killed by a car thief and for several days the home and family of the hero police sergeant were besieged by photographers and reporters. Hewitt lived through a double torment: of sorrow over his father and of fear that his picture might be taken and his second identity disclosed. He evaded the photographers successfully.

By spring Hewitt was eager to get out of Philadelphia where exposure threatened on every street corner. He also wanted the salary to which he felt Julius Ashkin, or a reasonable facsimile, was entitled. He began writing distant colleges. Dr. Charles R. Sattgast, president of Bemidji State Teachers College in Minnesota, replied and Hewitt sent him a copy of Ashkin's transcript (He had had photostats made). Growing in technique, he threw in the "Christie Engineering Company" of Philadelphia as a reference after first getting letterheads printed in that name. Then, as Robert Christie, proprietor of a small engineering concern, he engaged a secretarial service to take care of his mail and messages. In due time the Christie Engineering Company received an inquiry from Dr. Sattgast as to the qualifications of their physicist, Julius Ashkin. Hewitt sent back a glowing testimonial for Ashkin and signed it Robert Christie. He got the job, and at $4,000 a year.

He told Estelle that he had a job in Minnesota but that he had taken some degrees in someone else's name and thus must teach under that name. He also told her that he wanted to marry her. Estelle had just graduated from high school; before the summer was over they married and went to Chicago on a honeymoon from which they continued on up to Bemidji. For Hewitt those daycoach trips were wonderful. A city boy whose past had been bound by the grimy streets of lower-middle-class Philadelphia, they gave him the first sense of the bigness and beauty of the U. S. Beside him was the girl he loved; ahead of him stretched a bright future, even though, technically speaking, it was someone else's.

At Bemidji, a placid little college in the heart of Minnesota's hunting and fishing country Hewitt was the only physicist in the department and felt safe. He taught 16 hours a week in painfully simple subjects, analytical and solid geometry, college algebra and physics. Occasionally he appeared as speaker at town group meetings, talking about atomic energy or the atom bomb. He bought a car and began to enjoy life.

There were minor vexations. Sattgast had attended Columbia, so as a fellow Columbian Hewitt-Ashkin had to bone up on the faculty, campus and surrounding streets on Morningside Heights. Again, Estelle's folks wanted very much to drive up and visit the newlyweds. Hewitt, after nervously pondering the considerable risk in so small a town, had dared to rent a post office box under his own name so Estelle's unsuspecting family could write her as Mrs. Hewitt, but he had to beg his wife to stall off their visit until the academic year would end.

Teaching undergraduates soon began to bore him, and he wanted to get into a university where he could associate with minds he regarded as more equal to his own. In gauging the magnitude of Hewitt's achievement it is important to differentiate between Hewitt, the mere masquerader, and Hewitt, the able, possibly brilliant, theoretical physicist. Hewitt misrepresented himself to get a job teaching because there seemed no other way and, to him, teaching was the fulfillment of his whole existence ("I have a compulsion to teach"). But once he had obtained the job Hewitt performed honorably and well. He could do that because he knew his subject, especially in its most advanced aspects. Nuclear physics and associated fields are not areas in which it is possible for an impostor, even briefly, to parrot something learned by rote (like memorizing a Latin conjugation) or to get by on vague generalities (such as "interpreting" Browning's poetry). Hewitt, as time went on, worked and discussed top-level physics with veterans in the field. He experienced occasional agonies that his hoax might be discovered. But he never doubted his ability to hold his own intellectually with anyone, including Einstein, whom he once sought to meet on a vacation trip to Princeton.

That spring Hewitt got out his Christie letterheads and began writing universities. When he received an encouraging reply from Dr. Alfred H. Weber of the physics department of St. Louis University, Hewitt underwent an ecstasy of terror and hope. Unfortunately the real Ashkin was making a name for himself ("I gather that he is one of the best nuclear physicists in the country," says Hewitt with understandable complacency) and about the time Weber asked Hewitt to come down to St. Louis as Ashkin the real Ashkin published a noteworthy paper in the *Physical Review* which naturally listed him as a member of the faculty of the University of Rochester. Weber asked for a personal interview and Hewitt, alarmed that he might have noticed the Rochester reference, declined on the ground that he could not get away. Finally he was hired by mail, at a pleasant $4,500 a year, plus several hundred dollars more for teaching a summer-school course.

To Hewitt, teaching at St. Louis University was enormously satisfying from what could loosely be described as the professional point of view. "We offered the Ph.D. degree there," says he with pride. He taught only 10 hours a week, mainly graduate courses, and gave courses in nuclear physics, statistical mechanics, thermodynamics and tensor analysis, part of the mathematical basis of the theory of relativity. His students liked him, although a few complained his material did not seem very well organized, and his colleagues respected him, although they occasionally noticed odd gaps in his knowledge of the most basic physics. But these aberrations, as well as his inability to drive his car skillfully and a juvenile enthusiasm for science fiction, were readily excused. Theoretical physicists are a breed apart, more at home in the fourth dimension than on a four-lane highway, and "Ashkin's" occasional vagueness surprised no one.

Of course there were narrow escapes. Another professor at St. Louis went occasionally to the Argonne National Laboratory at Chicago to do research work. Once he returned and told Hewitt that he had run into an old friend of his—a man who had worked with Ashkin at Los Alamos. Hewitt broke into a cold sweat over what might come out next. But nothing damaging did; Ashkin's friend had merely asked about him. Thereafter, every time the other professor journeyed to Argonne, Hewitt quietly died. Other conversations with the friend of Ashkin were reported to him, but never once did they contain a reference to personal appearance, Rochester or anything else that might have given him away.

Washington University, also in St. Louis, was a focal point for informal meetings of local and visiting physicists. Hewitt attended several, sitting anonymously in the audience and listening with interest to addresses and discussions—until he discovered to his horror that those present often included men who knew Julius Ashkin well. He never went back.

In the summer Hewitt, who made it a practice to watch the scientific journals for papers by the unpredictable Ashkin, discovered another one in the *Physical Review,* again listing Ashkin as at the University of Rochester. With all the casualness he could muster, Hewitt went to Weber and remarked that it mentioned Rochester because that was where he had done the work on which it was based, a normal academic courtesy. He had no satisfactory explanation for why he had not observed another academic convention: that of naming, under an asterisk, the institution where the author is currently at work.

Toward the end of the year, fearful of staying longer at St. Louis even though he was about to get an associate professorship, Hewitt once more began writing other universities. Soon he received a cordial invitation from the University of Utah. This was a high-water mark in his career. Utah unrolled its red carpet for brilliant young Julius Ashkin. He was met at the Salt Lake City airport, provided with a room in the city's best hotel, interviewed deferentially by the president of the university, entertained and driven about the city. Utah liked Ashkin and checked his references with a view to hiring him. In the secrecy of his hotel room Hewitt waited trembling for exposure. "They can't miss nailing me now," he quavered. They did, though. They called Los Alamos, Argonne and Columbia, and all agreed that Julius Ashkin was an adornment to any faculty. They did not call Rochester, where a duplicate Ashkin would instantly have been detected.

When they talked about money before he returned to St. Louis, Hewitt demanded a salary commensurate with his dignity. A few days later Utah telegraphed it would pay him $5,800 a year, and, since this was higher than the university's scale for associate professor, a title which Hewitt expected, it would make him a full professor. Hewitt accepted. In a year he had moved from assistant to full professor, a promotion which normally takes 10 years. At Rochester the genuine Ashkin was still a mere assistant professor.

But back at St. Louis, saying his goodbys (and covering his trail by telling everyone he was going to General Electric at $10,000 a year), Hewitt learned one cost of masquerading. He had made some warm friends at St. Louis. Now, shaking hands, he knew that sooner or later they must discover the man they knew and respected was an impostor. He was saying goodby forever, a bitter knowledge that he could not share with anyone.

At Salt Lake City, Hewitt's remarkable luck became fantastic. In checking on him the university was assured by a dean at Columbia that there had actually been two Ashkins there, one of whom was somewhere in the Midwest. If Hewitt needed anything to insure him against discovery by a chance remark, that seemed to be it. He taught a mere six hours a week and graduate students only. But one uneasy thing happened. Hewitt and Professor Leon B. Linford, head of the physics department, went down into a basement office one day to see about an office for the newcomer. "Give Doctor Ashkin a nice office," Linford directed a girl clerk good-humoredly. "Dr. *Ashkin!*" she cried. "Why, don't you remember me?" Hewitt broke out in a cold sweat. He mumbled something and maintained his bearing for he had long since learned the value of playing a bluff out to its very end. "I was a secretary in the optics school at Rochester," the girl went on. "I often talked to you on the telephone." "Oh, yes, of course," he said. But as they left he saw the girl staring at him.

When nothing further happened, he dismissed it from his mind. Then a couple of weeks later he received a letter addressed to "Dr. Julius Ashkin (?)."

The envelope bore the insignia of the University of Rochester. Hewitt almost fainted.

It was a letter from the real Julius Ashkin. He wrote that, weird as it seemed, he had learned that someone was impersonating him at other universities. Besides requesting that the masquerade stop, he wrote, "Let me assume that you are versed in theoretical physics and that you are fundamentally a decent man. I should then be willing to help you to relieve yourself of what must have become an almost unbearable burden. It is on these assumptions that I have decided not to take any immediate steps to notify any university officials."

But despite Ashkin's marvelous gentleness the sky had fallen in on Hewitt. There followed several days of panic. Then he was summoned

189

to the office of University President A. Ray Olpin and there told that the university had information he was an impostor. At first Hewitt denied that with spirit. They showed him a letter of proof; Hewitt was so shaken he does not know to this day who wrote it (It was from a Rochester faculty member). Finally, pale and trembling, he muttered, "Let me have a minute . . . this is important . . . I must think." Then he looked up at Olpin. "My name is really Hewitt," he said. "Marvin Hewitt. I come from Philadelphia." It seemed incredible, even to himself. He really was only Marvin Hewitt. Then he began the long story: "I was a very precocious child . . ." and as he did, he once again became the graceless, misunderstood youngster of Olney High School. Hewitt could have wept.

The affair was kept quiet out of respect and pity for him, rather than of fear of ridicule for the university; the few faculty members who learned of it chuckled at how they had been hoodwinked. Since impersonation of a nuclear physicist could conceivably involve national security, Hewitt was asked to stay in Salt Lake City until he was cleared by the FBI. That took 10 days during which the Utah faculty generously drew up and offered him his choice of two humane plans. Either he could stay on at Utah as a research fellow and legitimately (and probably quickly) earn the degrees he had usurped or, if that embarrassed him, he could transfer to another university and get his degrees there. But Hewitt was in no condition to weigh such things, just as he had no clear idea as to how he had been detected. His luck had simply run out; in the space of a month a number of people both at Utah and Rochester had suddenly noticed and questioned discrepancies in letters and conversations about the work and whereabouts of Julius Ashkin. Even Weber back at St. Louis had started a belated investigation into who it was that had taught physics there.

But all Hewitt knew was that the magic door had suddenly slammed on him with an iron clang, leaving him outside. Once the FBI had okayed him, Hewitt could not get out of town fast enough. He slunk back to Philadelphia and his mother's, a beaten man.

One of the friends Hewitt had made at Utah was Richard Thomas, a young astrophysicist. Thomas subsequently wrote Harlow Shapley, the world-famous Harvard astronomer, about Hewitt. Shapley became interested in Hewitt's curious attainments, met him at the Century Club in New York, explored his intellect and then began arranging a meeting between him and J. Robert Oppenheimer, Director of the Institute of Advanced Study at Princeton. That had been Hewitt's

190

mecca for years. But Hewitt, haunted by the thought of public exposure and unaware of the direction of Shapley's efforts in his behalf, presently begged Shapley not to proceed in the matter and settled down to a life of private ignominy in Philadelphia, supported by his and Estelle's families.

It took Hewitt months to recuperate. But by the spring of 1950 he was sufficiently recovered to contemplate teaching and to consider what other subjects besides physics he might enter. There was psychology—"But where was the challenge?" asks Hewitt. "Virtually all psychology is intuitively evident." He finally settled on electrical engineering, a subject in which he already had some knowledge and knew he could master—enough to teach undergraduates at least—in a month's reading. He wrote a teacher's placement agency in the South that George Hewitt, D.Sc., Johns Hopkins graduate and formerly research director for the Radio Corporation of America, was available. Hewitt himself is as awed as anyone at his boldness. "Oh boy, I can't believe it," he giggles. "It's incredible." As a reference Hewitt gave the name of a nonexistent vice president of RCA and also supplied an address for him in Camden, N. J., where some RCA offices are indeed located. The address was that of a secretarial service where, as before, Hewitt had arranged for mail handling under the name of the RCA official. A few weeks later he was hired by mail and telephone to teach electrical engineering at the University of Arkansas College of Engineering. Dean George F. Branigan said that all they could pay was $4,500, but Hewitt, already neck-deep in the role of successful corporation executive, assured him it was the stimulation of academic life he wanted and not mere money. Soon after, accompanied by the philosophic Estelle, he set out for Fayetteville. The magic door again stood open.

In some respects it was more inviting than ever. Of course, there were the usual alarms. On his arrival he discovered that one of his students had attended St. Louis University. But the boy had not been there when "Ashkin" was. It was also the custom in Fayetteville for all new faculty members to be introduced to the town's Rotary Club at a lunch; as his new name and record were read out Hewitt rose, wondering whether the dining room contained students or faculty members from the previous five schools. It did not.

In Fayetteville he had one really hair-raising experience. Hewitt always lived his parts avidly and had an odd sensitivity to the names he adopted. He had liked Ashkin's; he came to hate "George." One day he was thumbing through magazines in a drugstore waiting for a psychology teacher whom he knew when the psychologist called him by his first name. Hewitt did not notice. The psychologist continued calling— "George! *George!* GEORGE!"—louder and louder as he walked toward Hewitt. It was not until he was shouting in Hewitt's ear that Hewitt recognized his *nom d'école* and responded. But he realized that to a psychologist especially that had been a dangerously revealing slip.

Later on when the psychologist and his wife were visiting the Hewitts, the wife asked if she could see Estelle's wardrobe. Hewitt is not sure whether this was sly detective work or mere feminine curiosity about a former big executive's wife. In any case Estelle had to show the visitor her modest closetful of frocks.

Their double life was difficult for Estelle. "There was always tension," she says now, even though she was well liked in the small, often jealous worlds of faculty society. Occasionally she urged her husband to figure a way out of his nightmarish dilemma. For the rest, she respected the strange mixture of his personality and devoted herself to music and to their home.

Life in Fayetteville offered Hewitt one golden attraction. He was using a name which, if not quite his own, had not been borrowed from anyone else and under which he could therefore publish scientific papers. Hewitt leaped into a frenzy of scholarly activity. For a regional engineering society he prepared and read a paper, "The Orthogonality Property in Microwave Transmission," although he felt no more than three of the members understood it. He presented another on "The Theory of the Electron" at a meeting of the Arkansas Academy of Science, although too weary that day to read a second he had prepared, "Measure Preserving Transformations in the Spinor and Tensor Calculus." He worked on two research projects, learned by midyear that he was going to become a father, and concluded that he could become a national figure in electrical engineering in three years.

Then in spring an RCA talent scout, seeking likely young electrical engineers, visited Arkansas and talked to Dean Branigan. "RCA, eh?" said Branigan. "Oh, yes. We have your former research director here, you know. George Hewitt." "Who," asked the RCA man, "is George Hewitt?"

Hewitt was drummed out of the faculty and also became the father of twins within a few weeks. Once again he made the painful retreat to Philadelphia. But with two small sons to win bread for, he could not afford to brood. After again considering other fields he reverted to physics and began studying college catalogs and *American Men of Science,* the who's who of U.S. scientific achievement. He picked on Clifford Berry, an Iowa State University Ph.D. now in industry on the West Coast. Armed with a name he liked ("Cliff" especially appealed to him) Hewitt began calling schools in the East. The New York State Maritime College in New York City's Bronx needed someone to teach second- and third-year physics and calculus, and Cliff was quickly hired at $4,000 a year after submitting the usual homemade references. He established Estelle and the twins in a small apartment under his own name in Hempstead, which is on Long Island, a safe distance from the Bronx.

This may be as good a place as any to point out that the ease with which Hewitt obtained these jobs fills him with indignation. The unquestioning acceptance of a transcript and careless checking of references is, in his fairly expert opinion, a universal weakness throughout the U.S. higher educational system. When he considers what might have happened to a great many people had he made medicine or surgery his field, he shudders. He earnestly advises university authorities to check photographs and academic records of job applicants directly with the schools involved.

At the Maritime College history repeated itself with one difference. That was that Hewitt, like the rest of the faculty, wore a species of Navy officer's uniform, with the result that today he is under the vague impression that he served a hitch in the New York State Navy. He taught with fair success, although as elsewhere there were complaints that Hewitt talked over the students' heads. (By now he was completely bored by the ordinary college subject matter.) He also established a reputation for being unusually absent-minded, even for a professor. Hewitt one day appeared at school wearing his lieutenant's navy blue uniform and brown shoes. A shocked friend lent him his own black oxfords before he went into the dean's office. Hewitt gratefully put on the black shoes, saw the dean, then walked out of the building in the borrowed shoes, leaving his friend in stocking feet.

His boredom with undergraduate teaching grew. He made a list of the industrial jobs he felt he could fill. They included jet plane or guided-missile dynamicist, nuclear physicist worker in solid-state physics (valuable in transistor manufacture), optical-instrument designer, specialist in pulse circuits (a radar basic) and specialist in microwave or television antennae design.

The list so impressed Hewitt that he resigned his job at the Maritime College and began a campaign to crash technical industry. He received

193

a stunning surprise. Industry was far tougher than teaching to crash. Most of the fields in which he wanted to work were highly classified and thus required security clearance. This involved birth certificates, fingerprints, photographs and other unreasonable demands. Hewitt knew he could not face that kind of investigation. Besides, the questionnaire carried a warning that misrepresentation would subject the applicant to penalties.

After spending some months trying to find a large legitimate company that might be fooled by a letter from the Christie Engineering Company, Hewitt gave up and became Kenneth P. Yates, an Ohio State University Ph.D. in physics. In January 1953 he obtained a midyear appointment to teach at the University of New Hampshire in Durham at $4,500 a year. Estelle, who stayed behind in Hempstead, had another boy after he went to Durham.

But now Hewitt discovered an alarming difference in himself. During the semester one of the students in the math department revealed that he planned to go to Columbus that summer and do graduate work at Ohio State. He thus could not help learning about the real Yates and his whereabouts. Exposure threatened again for Hewitt. The trouble was, Hewitt didn't care.

He suddenly realized that over the long years he had only been walking up a blind alley. After teaching a summer term at Durham he learned the student who had gone to Columbus would not return to New Hampshire. He was safe, but there was scant joy in it. Sooner or later his luck must run out and, as the fall term advanced, the delicate instincts of the hunted told Hewitt that the time was at hand.

One of the young men in both his theoretical physics and relativity seminars was a student named Wayne Overman. Overman was a graduate of the University of Virginia, where he had majored in physics. To Hewitt, Overman was a less than satisfactory student and he told both Overman and Dr. Frederic A. Scott, head of the physics department, as much. To Overman, Hewitt on the other hand was a less than satisfactory teacher with odd lapses in his knowledge, e.g., he seemed unfamiliar with certain German words, although a knowledge of German is required in advanced physics. As time passed Hewitt felt Overman was watching him suspiciously. In class Overman began asking pointed questions. "A month before the midyear holiday I was sure he was up to something," says Hewitt.

But, with the stubbornness born of lost hope and fatigue, he refused to run. Indeed he decided to bring Estelle and the boys up to Durham at midyear and to live there in what peace he could find until he was

194

again found out. "I realized that I was functioning in a rather rigid manner," says Hewitt, "and that it was reducing my survival chances."

Overman had simply looked up Yates in *American Men of Science*, found that Yates was an Ohio State Ph.D. and recalled that a dictionary knowledge of German is required from doctors of philosophy in physics. The reference book also said he was working near Chicago for an oil company. But for a month he kept this knowledge to himself.

Meanwhile for Hewitt this cold war had also come to a climax. He felt he could not pass Overman in either course, especially after reading his final examination papers, yet he wondered whether giving Overman a passing grade might not buy his silence about whatever he knew (an unfair inference, since the subject never was discussed between them). Hewitt, however, has always taken pride in his profession, even though he did not belong to it. He sturdily flunked Overman and went home to Hempstead to help Estelle pack their belongings for the move to Durham. Shortly after the final examinations Overman went to the faculty with his suspicions.

When Professor Scott's long-distance call summoned him, Hewitt returned to Durham alone, admitted everything as usual ("I always do all I can to straighten things out") and, as usual, quietly resigned. But, not as usual, the story this time leaked out. A month after he left Durham, Hewitt found himself and his career in the newspapers, described spectacularly but incompletely since up to now he has never told any one person the whole story.

Today in retrospect some of the college authorities he fooled like to feel they were suspicious of Hewitt all along. They say his lectures were not well organized (to be expected in a man who had never even heard a college lecture until he started giving them), that he led a rather secretive life, that they wondered why he always dodged being photographed for college annuals. But they also are astounded to learn that he is not a Ph.D., an academic degree for which Hewitt has the warmest contempt. ("American schools are full of men living on their Ph.D.s. They're not scholars any more—they don't continue with research or study. They just collect their salary.")

Actually, wherever he taught Hewitt was accepted as able at least, and in a number of institutions he was regarded as brilliant. "Just about all I know about the atom bomb, I learned from Ashkin," said one college president, referring to Hewitt. Harlow Shapley has said that while he does not regard Hewitt as a genius, a word that occasionally crops up in Hewitt's own discussions of himself, he does feel that he is "erudite in a narrow field."

Hewitt's astounding performance got some excellent notices. "Don't underestimate him," said a former associate at the Maritime College. The Arkansas faculty agreed that he showed ability and sincerity. "A brilliant self-educated man with an unusual penchant for teaching," said an article in the *New Hampshire Alumnus*. Even Ashkin wrote Utah begging compassion for his impersonator and particularly asked that Hewitt be told it was not Ashkin who had caused his exposure.

What he will do next no one knows, not even Hewitt. He talks of industry, of writing a book, even of going to another country. But he also says wistfully, "If they'd only let me be a professor, I'd never want anything else or lie. You know, I lied only to get those jobs. I was a good teacher. I've never really hurt anyone."

No one has ever claimed he did. Hewitt in fact caused himself more trouble and agony than he caused anyone else, even Julius Ashkin. He was recently asked about how he felt about his final unmasking at New Hampshire. "It was a relief," he said. "I felt glad about it. Once the thing broke in the papers I knew that it was finished for keeps." And then Hewitt smiled his solemn, thoughtful smile at his friend he was talking to. "Or," he asked, "don't you think so?"

When last heard of Marvin Hewitt was employed under his own name, by a nationally known missile manufacturer. The position is commensurate with Hewitt's knowledge and intelligence, and the company cares not a whit that he lacks the degrees all of his colleagues boast. His scientific work has interested the Atomic Energy Commission, the British Admiralty, Harvard, California Institute of Technology and other research organizations.

THE HOAX THAT MADE THE COMMUNISTS SCREAM

by Norbert Muhlen and Frederic Sondern, Jr.

The West Berlin radio interrupted its regular program one day in July 1953 to make a startling announcement. Five prominent political prisoners of the Communists had escaped from the supposedly escape-proof East German prisons of Zwickau and Waldheim, and made their way to the safety of Berlin's western sector. As details came in, it became clear that they had not broken out: they had been released by the Communist prison authorities, who had been hoaxed by forged release orders and telephone calls from a spurious State's Attorney.

While West Germany laughed, the enraged State Security Service and People's Police dropped all other business to find the authors of the plot. Sixty officials were discharged. The Communist press and radio screamed that dastardly American agents had been at work.

Actually, the daring skulduggery had been devised by a young German named Hasso Lindemann and two of his friends.

Lindemann, a bookish, 23-year-old law student, had been rocketed to a position of power by circumstances not unusual in East Germany. In 1949 the Communist authorities of Leipzig had discharged most of the experienced judges and prosecutors in the district as "politically unreliable." A milkman, an organ grinder and a 21-year-old girl became Leipzig's People's Prosecutors. They had power of life and death over their fellow citizens, but they needed someone to advise them about legal procedure. Lindemann, who had worked as a clerk in the Ministry of Justice, seemed "politically activistic" and obedient. He was appointed assistant to the State's Attorney.

Lindemann was a shrewd investigator and wrote brilliant briefs in impeccable Communist legal style. His record was soon impressive. Several prominent industrialists whose cases he investigated had their properties expropriated and were sent to prison for long terms. A dozen young anti-Communist agitators went to jail after Lindemann had made the cases against them. Wisely modest and retiring, Lindemann let the People's Prosecutors take credit for these triumphs. As a result he was popular with his chiefs. He was well fed and housed, relatively well paid, and had a promising career ahead of him.

But Hasso Lindemann had a conscience. As the terrible parade of Red injustice and cruelty—the trumped-up charges, faked evidence and brutal sentences against innocent people—crossed his desk he began to rebel.

One afternoon, when most of the personnel of the State's Attorney's staff were at their weekly Party "indoctrination meeting," Lindemann took from his chief's desk a number of form letters used to order the release of prisoners, and fled to West Berlin. "The forms, the clothes on my back and a few marks were all I had," Lindemann recalls. "Everything else—job, future—I left behind. But I felt much, much better."

197

There were five cases that he was determined to rectify at once. Seventy-year-old Karl Mende had committed no crime, even under Communist law—the government had simply wanted his prosperous glass factories. He was convicted of "industrial sabotage" and sentenced to six years at hard labor; his factories were expropriated. Arthur Bergel, a prominent woolen manufacturer, was the victim of a similar conviction: his offense had been to pay his 1700 workers a higher wage than the government allowed. Horst Schnabel, a high school boy of 17, had been sentenced to two years in the penitentiary, to be followed by transportation to the uranium mines, for possessing a book banned by the Communists. Jürgen Poppitz and Ekkehard Schumann, 20-year-old students, had received four-year terms for firing rockets which showered Leipzig with anti-Communist leaflets.

The obstacles in Hasso's way seemed insuperable. As a former employee of the Communist goverment he was suspect to the various refugee organizations in Berlin. Then, after he had finally convinced the principal anti-Communist committees that he was sincere, a new State's Attorney, whose signature Lindemann did not know, was appointed for Leipzig. The new incumbent ruled that no release order was to be obeyed unless the prison director checked its validity by a personal phone call to the State's Attorney or his immediate subordinate.

It took Lindemann three months to obtain from a friend in Leipzig a document signed by Chief State's Attorney Adam, more time to practice a flawless forgery of the signature. Through a complicated system of couriers and deftly worded, seemingly innocent letters, he learned the exact technique and timing of the telephone verification.

Finally the months of painstaking preparation came to an end. One of Lindemann's aides, Hans Schmidt, was put in charge of the first operation. Hasso had wanted to perform it himself, but his face was too well known to People's Police and State Security Service men.

With forged release orders for Mende and Bergel in his brief case, Schmidt set out for Leipzig and for the particular postbox from which the State's Attorney's communications were always mailed.

Twice he almost met disaster. Two police officers suddenly appeared in his train compartment and ordered him to open his brief case for inspection. Such spot checks are routine in East Germany. Hans obeyed, his heart in his mouth. The policemen saw the envelopes stamped "Chief State's Attorney's Office." "You are a courier of the *Herr Oberstaatsanwalt?*" one of them barked. "Of course," Hans barked back. "We are sorry to have disturbed you, sir." Heels clicked, salutes were exchanged and, without asking for his papers, the officers departed.

198

At the postbox in Leipzig Hans had his other bad moment. Two People's Police were watching the box, on guard against the mailing of clandestine leaflets. But again the official envelope commanded immediate obeisance, and one of the *Volkspolizei* even politely held up the box flap as Hans dropped the letters in.

That night neither Schmidt in Leipzig nor Lindemann in Berlin slept a wink. The release orders should reach the warden of Zwickau Penitentiary in the morning. If the warden telephoned the State's Attorney's Office before the plotters could act, the game would be up.

At the earliest feasible moment, Schmidt braced himself and telephoned Zwickau. "This is *Oberstaatsanwalt* Adam," he bellowed. "Give me the Director at once." Since the German bureaucratic caste system under the Communists is as strict as it ever was, Hans calculated that the voice of an exalted Chief State's Attorney would not be too familiar to a warden. He was right. The director answered with great deference.

"Have you received the release orders for Mende and Bergel?" snapped Hans.

"No, *Herr Oberstaatsanwalt*. But I will attend to them personally the moment they arrive."

"See that you do," Hans growled. "No return call to my office is necessary to verify these orders. Is that clear?"

"Of course, *Herr Oberstaatsanwalt*. I will not disturb you. I have been deeply honored by your personal call."

When Hans hung up he was sweating from every pore. But the most dangerous part of the operation still lay ahead. Mende and Bergel, thinking their release was legal, would doubtless go home, and soon be rearrested. They had to be warned to flee at once to West Berlin. Hans went to Zwickau to wait for them.

Watching Zwickau Penitentiary is a hazardous task. Anyone loitering nearby is immediately reported by the guards to the People's Police. But Hans found a café from which he could watch the institution's main gate. He sat and drank beer—and more beer. He explained at great length to the café-keeper that he was trying to drown his domestic troubles. A People's Policeman examined his papers, fortunately rather carelessly.

Finally Hans decided that the forgeries had been detected. Dejectedly he returned to Berlin.

Actually, the release orders had merely been slow in reaching the penitentiary. When they arrived, Mende and Bergel were promptly led into the presence of the warden and the prison's dreaded Political Commissar.

"The highest authorities in our state have decided to forgive your crimes," the Commissar announced cordially, even offering them cigarettes to put them at ease. "We are releasing you." Presently the two men, provided with civilian clothes, money, and a ration of food for the journey home, stumbled out through the prison gate in a daze.

Their freedom might not have lasted long except for Lindemann's thorough planning. Fearing that Schmidt might be picked up by the police, Lindemann had dispatched another friend—Kurt Braun—to guide Mende and Bergel to Berlin. Braun waited in the neighborhood of the prison for almost 48 hours—without sleep and with three apples for food. He didn't dare go into a restaurant for fear of a police checkup.

Almost collapsing from fatigue and hunger, Braun also finally gave up and boarded a streetcar for the railroad station. As the trolley rumbled away, he took one more look at the prison. Two gaunt men whose clothes hung loosely from their shoulders were coming out the gate! Risking his neck, he jumped from the car. For several blocks he walked behind the two men to make sure they were the right ones (Zwickau changes people's appearances). Finally, he sidled up and pressed a slip of paper into Herr Mende's hand. "Follow these directions," he said quietly. "Get to West Berlin. Your families are there."

Fear and suspicion were plain on the men's faces. This might be a police trap. "Please, *please*," Kurt urged desperately, "do as I say." With that, he vanished around the corner.

The next morning Herr Mende and Herr Bergel were safely in West Berlin. Still hardly able to believe their luck, they had found their families and had come to thank Lindemann. "It was a strange interview—the former convicts and their former prosecutor," Lindemann reminisces happily. "But it was a very satisfactory one, particularly for me."

There were still three more prisoners to free—one in Zwickau, the others in Waldheim.

Schmidt was ready to start again for Leipzig when catastrophe struck. News of the two men's "escape" had leaked somehow, and a West German radio station blared it out. Lindemann was beside himself with disappointment, when suddenly he realized that the trick might work if they acted immediately. All Communist police and judicial chiefs habitually leave the city on Saturday for their country retreats, and cannot be reached until their return around 11 o'clock Monday morning. Lindemann was sure that his plan had more than an even chance.

And he was right. The release orders arrived at Zwickau and Waldheim without delay. Schmidt repeated his first memorable telephone
call to the two wardens. On Monday three bewildered boys found themselves on their way to West Berlin in the care of Schmidt and Braun.

But it had been a close shave. Five minutes after the Zwickau gates
had closed, a big car roared up to the prison. *Herr Oberstaatsanwalt*
Adam himself, flanked by ranking police officers, stormed into the institution.

The escape of Mende and Bergel had been discovered late Saturday
by agents monitoring West German radio broadcasts. Gerhart Eisler,
then Propaganda Minister, happened to be at his desk early Monday
morning and was informed first. Roaring with rage, he tried to contact
his colleagues. But no responsible police official was reached until Monday noon. Then the entire State Security Service and People's Police
were unleashed in an unprecedented manhunt: trains were searched,
automobiles stopped, innocent pedestrians dragged off to police stations
throughout East Germany. They were too late.

In a comfortable restaurant in West Berlin Lindemann, his helpers
and his ex-victims were celebrating. The spare, usually shy young man
raised his glass. "We shall have to use other methods in the future," he
said. "But I think we can do it again."

DAWSON'S DAWN MAN

by *Alden P. Armagnac*

For more than 40 years Piltdown Man was a member in more or less
good standing of the society of "earliest humans," rubbing mandibles
with such distinguished, if lowbrow, company as Peking Man, Heidelberg Man and Neanderthal Man. The startling discovery that he was an
out-and-out humbug abruptly terminated his membership, in December
1953. Principally responsible for unmasking it is Dr. J. S. Weiner, Oxford
University anthropologist.

It was back in 1912 that an amateur fossil hunter, Charles Dawson,
brought the first of the Piltdown finds to the British Museum. He said
he'd found them in a gravel pit near Piltdown Common, Sussex, in

southern England. Dr. Arthur Smith Woodward, eminent paleontologist of the British Museum, took part in later diggings at the site. All told, the finds consisted of more than 20 remarkable brown fragments of bones, teeth and flint.

Outstanding among these was a truly amazing piece of jaw, plainly the jaw of an ape in all but one sensational respect—the surfaces of the two intact molar teeth were flat. Only a human jaw, with its free-swinging motion, could have worn them down to that flat-top shape. Thus the owner of the jaw appeared to be a "missing link" in human evolution. Fragments of the brain case of a prehistoric human skull, found nearby, seemingly identified him.

Remains of prehistoric animals found in the same gravel pit placed Piltdown Man in the early Ice Age, half a million years ago. This made him the earliest known human. In honor of the amateur discoverer, Woodward gave Piltdown the scientific name *Eoanthropus dawsoni*—Dawson's Dawn Man.

For decades the reconstructed Piltdown skull, with its incongruously high forehead and simian jaw, was a storm center of scientific controversy. But Piltdown began really to hit the skids in 1950 when Dr. Kenneth Oakley, a British Museum geologist, applied a chemical dating test. The longer bones lie buried, the more fluorine they absorb from ground water. Dr. Oakley's measurement of the flourine content convinced him that the remains were only 50,000 years old instead of a half million. (His estimate for the age of the cranial fragments was correct, but he was wrong in innocently assuming the jaw to be equally old.)

Oakley's discovery made Piltdown Man more of a riddle than ever. A half-million-year-old missing link had been conceivable. But a missing link as recent as 50,000 years ago was an utterly incredible throwback.

So went the table talk one summer evening in 1953, when Dr. Weiner dined with Oakley in London. Home in Oxford that night, Weiner revolved in his mind everything that made Piltdown such an impossible misfit. Above all, those "human" teeth in an apelike jaw, worn as flat as by a file. . . . A thought struck him like a blow: *Could* they have been deliberately filed flat? He recalled Sherlock Holmes' words: "When you have eliminated the impossible, whatever remains, however improbable, must be the truth."

With a colleague, Professor Wilfred Le Gros Clark, Weiner secured a chimpanzee's molar tooth, filed and stained it, and had a good likeness of a Piltdown molar. Next stop was the British Museum, where Weiner and Clark enlisted Oakley's aid. Out of a locked, fireproof steel safe came the hallowed Piltdown fragments for the most searching anatomical, chemical and physical examination they had ever received. Instruments as modern as X-ray spectrograph and Geiger counter came into play. An improved chemical dating test measured the bones' loss of nitrogen against the passing of time.

Weiner was right. The jaw had come from a modern ape, probably an orangutan. Cunningly the faker had "fossilized" it by staining it a mahogany color with an iron salt and bichromate. An oil paint, probably red sienna, had stained the chewing surfaces of the teeth. Meanwhile, telltale scratches on the molars showed beyond doubt that the teeth had been artificially filed. And they were unnaturally sharp-edged, just as a file would leave them. In plaster casts of the Piltdown jaw studied the world over these details were lost, but they were only too clear in the original specimens.

In 1953 the three investigators announced that the jaw and teeth were bogus. At this time they still assumed that some prankster had planted them in the diggings, near genuine relics, to confuse the excavators. But when the three later came to testing the other Piltdown trophies, every important piece proved a forgery. Piltdown Man was a fraud from start to finish!

The hoax must have been an inside job—by someone, says Weiner, who "can hardly fail to be among those whose names we know." Weiner set out to reconstruct every possible detail. He traveled around the countryside to talk with living eye-witnesses, and with relatives and friends of others no longer living. He pored through yellowed journals of the time and read all the scientific reports of the discoveries.

To Weiner, the resulting mass of evidence clearly exonerates every figure in the Piltdown case but one: Charles Dawson, the original "discoverer." And while Weiner will not, for lack of "positive and final proof," flatly accuse him, all the circumstantial evidence points to Dawson as the author of the hoax.

A successful lawyer, married, living in the little "county town" of Lewes in a part of England rich in fossils, Charles Dawson had pursued his hobby of hunting them with notable success. He had sent Woodward many unusual specimens, including fossils of a dinosaur and a prehistoric mammal of a species new to science, which Woodward named after him.

By Dawson's own account, he was walking along a country road near Piltdown Common when he noticed that the road had been mended with brown flints unusual to the district. He found that they came from a small pit nearby, where gravel was dug for road repairs. Finding two men at work there, he asked them to keep a lookout for bones or other fossils. On another visit one of the men handed Dawson a thick fragment of human skull. Later, Dawson claimed, he found a larger piece himself. He journeyed to London then, and showed Woodward what he'd "found": skull fragments, fossil animal teeth, prehistoric flint tools.

Woodward's eyes popped. He didn't know, of course, that all the principal items were faked, or that the animal remains, whose extreme antiquity supported a similar date for the human ones, had come from elsewhere. Actually, as investigations now reveal, a fossil rhino tooth came not from Piltdown, but from East Anglia. A fossil elephant tooth must have traveled all the way from Tunisia. Any established fossil collector like Dawson would have had little difficulty in assembling these specimens, by trading or in shops catering to collectors. As for the cranial fragments, human skulls 50,000 years old aren't exactly common, but Dawson is known to have possessed some unusual skulls.

The unsuspecting Woodward joined Dawson in excavating at the gravel pit—with a success, if he'd only known it, too good to be true. One summer evening a pick struck the ground, and the faked jaw flew out. First public announcement of the "discoveries" followed, in December 1912.

Miraculous luck continued to favor the diggers. The last spectacular discovery was a "second" Piltdown Man, found, according to Dawson, in a field two miles from the first site, in 1915. Like Piltdown I, Piltdown II was later found to have been artificially stained with iron and bichromate.

During this period no one publicly questioned Dawson's honesty. But some of his fellow amateurs in his home town expressed the opinion among themselves that he was "salting the mine." And a visitor who entered Dawson's office without knocking found him in the midst of some experiment, with bones immersed in crucibles of colored and pungent liquids. Dawson explained with apparent embarrassment that he was staining fossils to find out how natural staining occurred.

The Piltdown "discoveries" ended with Dawson's death in 1916, at the age of 52 and at the height of his fame. Always hopeful, Woodward kept on digging at Piltdown for many years, but never found anything more. Nevertheless a "new" Piltdown find did turn up. It was located by Weiner himself, and may furnish the most direct evidence of the hoaxer's identity.

Harry Morris, a bank clerk and flint collector of Lewes, had somehow obtained from Dawson a "Piltdown" flint tool that never reached the

British Museum—and had discovered for himself that it was spurious. Morris had died and left his flint collection, including the "Piltdown" flint and notes about it, to A. P. Pollard, a Lewes surveyor, who told Weiner about it.

Where was the flint now? Pollard had traded the cabinetful of flints to Frederick Wood of Ditchling for a collection of birds' eggs. Wood had died, but Mrs. Wood might still have the missing cabinet. Weiner hastened to Ditchling and found the cabinet, holding 12 drawers of neatly labeled specimens. The 12th and last drawer yielded the Piltdown flint. It bore an inscription in Morris' handwriting:

"Stained by C. Dawson with intent to defraud (all).—H. M."

An accompanying note of Morris' repeated the accusation, indignantly adding: ". . . and exchanged by D. for my most valued specimen!" A second note declared that hydrochloric acid would remove the brown color, leaving one of the relatively common white flints found on the Chalk Downs of Lewes. Morris was right about that, Weiner found. The "Morris flint," inscription and all, now reposes in the British Museum.

The fantastic Piltdown case seems closed, except for the puzzle of the hoaxer's motive. He gained nothing in money; the specimens were presented to the British Museum. Was fame his object? Was the deception an intended joke that went too far? Whatever prompted the impostor lies beyond reach of chemical and physical tests—and perhaps must remain always a mystery.

THE GREAT BANK BILKER

by Charles Lanius

The New England morning was bright and fine and in the late fall of 1953 the Third National Bank of Boston, along with the rest of the nation, was humming happily in the midst of the biggest financial boom in history. A woman teller was counting her cash when a tall, thin, well-dressed man with a professional air and oozing affability, stepped confidently up to her cage and smiled engagingly.

The distinguished stranger casually slipped a check with a note attached under the grill and waited while she read the note. It was handwritten and signed E. F. Bunyon (Bunyon was the bank's assistant cashier, who sat at his desk less than thirty feet away), and read "Okay —my Uncle Ralph. Thanks." The check was made out to cash for a whopping $2,950 and signed Dr. Ralph Bunyon.

The transaction, to that point, had been handled strictly according to the Third National's check-cashing procedure. The woman teller glanced toward Cashier Bunyon who was busily talking to another customer and decided not to interrupt him. She suddenly remembered that she didn't have large banknotes in her cash drawer and handed the check and note to the man in the next cage.

"Mac," she said, "take care of this for Dr. Bunyon. He's Eddie's brother."

Mac, assuming that she meant uncle instead of brother, asked the poised stranger in what denominations he'd like the money.

"Oh, don't trouble yourself," the man replied easily. "I'll take anything you have handy."

Mac counted out twenty-nine one-hundred-dollar bills, two twenties, a five, and five ones and passed them over the counter. The slender, genial "doctor" thanked him, stuffed the money into a breast wallet and sauntered leisurely out of the bank. By the time the bank discovered the check was bogus and the note a forgery, "Eddie's brother" was well on his way to the sunshine and race tracks of Florida.

The victims screamed for the William J. Burns International Detective Agency, the official check-fraud and forgery investigators for the American Bankers Association. It didn't take H. A. Crowe, manager of Burns' criminal division, long to discover that the Third National had been taken by William Hamilton Harkins, "the greatest lone-wolf bank bilker the world ever produced."

"Harkins is absolute tops in the business," Crowe, who has spent the best part of thirty years on the forger's trail and has been mainly responsible for sixteen of his seventeen arrests, told the Bostonians. "He is a consummate actor, intelligent and polished, with an amiable, persuasive manner, candid blue eyes and a low, cultivated voice. Add an uncannily steady and accurate hand, a crook's heart and ice-cold nerves, and you have the perfect bank swindler."

Harkins specializes exclusively in skinning banks for large sums. A former bank clerk, he is a whizz at figures and a wizard with a pen. Even many of the country's best-qualified handwriting experts failed to pinpoint definitely his work and were forced to return "non-conclusive" reports. His memory is phenomenal.

206

"I never forget a signature," he boasted to police not long ago. "After I get one good look it is photographed in my brain."

His brilliant mind plus early legal training make him a hard man to convict, and throughout his career he has never taken the witness stand. On two occasions he glibly beat lie-detector and truth-serum tests and several times has avoided prison sentences by feigning insanity.

It is almost as difficult to keep him locked up after he is convicted. A bold and accomplished break-out artist, he has escaped six times. Once astonished police discovered he had disappeared from his cell in mid-afternoon minus his clothes, an exploit considered an escape classic.

Often, when arrested, Harkins makes a great show of repenting his past misdeeds, protesting that if given another chance he will stick to the straight and narrow path. The pious pitch occasionally works. His contrite, sanctimonious attitude so impressed a tough Miami cop that he almost choked with sentiment.

"Such a pity," he sighed. "I guess Harkins is the nicest guy I ever had to jug."

On the loose, Harkins is a free-wheeling spender. He likes the high life and mingles easily. A witty and companionable fellow, he spends his money on horses and women as fast as he steals it. Women seem to find him irresistible. Once he charmed a nurse in an insane asylum into helping him bilk several banks, and they fled the institution together.

Although one of the world's most gifted crooks, he is a poor judge of horse flesh. He lost $12,000 at Florida's Tropical Park race track the week-end preceding his last arrest. Once when police nailed him at the New Orleans track he pleaded to be allowed to stay for the fourth race so he could bet $100 on a "sure thing" named Rustem. Rustem lost, but Harkins tried to give the two police detectives an $1,800 diamond ring and a $1,200 diamond stickpin.

"You fellows treated me like a gentleman," he explained, "and I want to show my appreciation."

Some of his most daring strokes came after banks inaugurated the "foolproof" system of refusing to cash checks unless okayed by bank officers. The new procedure stymied many less imaginative crooks, but was only another challenge to Harkins. He soon had it working to his own advantage.

Harkins simply began manufacturing his own okays. He secured specimen signatures and initials of bank officers by buying small legitimate cashier's checks. Then he wrote large bogus checks, forging the bank officer's signature or initials on them, and cashed them with un-suspecting tellers.

Once he purchased a $12.75 order at the Hotel New Yorker branch of the Manufacturers Trust Company. He took it to Charles Caman, a bank officer.

"I just bought this," he explained, turning on the charm, "and then remembered that I won't need it. I'd like to get my money back."

Caman initialed the check and instructed Harkins to collect at the teller's window. Instead, Harkins walked out of the bank, prepared two identical checks drawn on a Boston bank for $1,401, both signed James R. Farley. He copied the bank official's initials on only one. A couple of days later he returned and presented the uninitialed $1,401 check to the teller.

"I'm sorry, sir," the teller said, "you'll have to have this initialed before I can cash it."

"Yes, of course," Harkins replied, and smiled. "I should know that."

A moment later the teller saw him hand Caman a check and turned away to wait on another customer. He had no way of knowing that Harkins had handed Caman the small $12.75 check he had purchased two days earlier, which the officer had already initialed.

"You okayed this the other day," he told Caman, "but I was in a hurry and didn't cash it. I assume it's still good."

Caman politely assured him the check could be cashed any time, and Harkins stepped back toward the teller's window. During the short walk he managed to substitute the phony $1,401 check on which he had forged Caman's initials for the uninitialed one he had shown the teller. The teller cashed it along with the $12.75 order, giving Harkins a total score of $1,413.75.

The con man walked leisurely to the street, hopped a taxi to the horse races and the nearest parimutuel counter. He bet $1,000 on a horse named Sugar Ration to win. The horse came in and he collected $7,800 and left the track. The same week he clipped banks in the New York area for an aggregate of $50,000.

No one knows how much Harkins has taken from banks, except possibly Harkins himself. Many of his forgeries have never been reported to the Bankers Association and others cannot be definitely pinned to his record. Questioned recently about his total take he laughed and said: "Some claim a million dollars, but the more conservative say five million."

William Hamilton Harkins, born at Hamilton, Washington, in 1890, started out in life with better than average opportunities. His substantial middle-class Scotch-Irish parents were deeply religious and raised their son as a church-going Protestant. His younger brother, Hershel, now a Presbyterian preacher in California, adored his big brother Bill.

Young Bill was as smart as a whip and almost everyone predicted a bright future. When he was nineteen a friend got him a job in a Hagerstown bank. He was ambitious, too, and studied law at night school. When the United States entered World War I, he was commissioned a Second Lieutenant in the U.S. Air Corps. Although eager to go to France as a pilot, he was detailed to a dull desk job in the States and never got overseas.

While he was in the service he met and married an attractive young woman from a respectable Southern family. But near the end of the war a small Maryland bank in which they had their entire savings, a total of eighty-seven dollars, failed and they lost their money. Harkins was inconsolable. He irrationally reasoned that the bank had swindled them.

He decided to live by his wits, with the bankers as his victims and get his money back with interest. He nursed the grudge until it became the driving force of his life. His wife, aware that he was burning with a thirst for revenge, tried to dissuade him from his fixed idea. Finally, convinced that it was a simple case of marrying a dishonest man with a twisted outlook, she left him.

Harkins' first recorded arrest came in 1919 on a forgery charge in Chicago. He jumped bond, but in 1920 a rubber check-cashing spree in California netted him one to fifteen years in San Quentin prison. Released eighteen months later, he promptly went on another paperhanging binge and was picked up as a parole violator.

The Reverend Hershel Harkins, claiming that his erring brother wasn't responsible for his actions, succeeded in having him sent to the Agnew Insane Asylum instead of San Quentin. He spent more time outside than inside the walls. Nurse Mary Wilkes fell in love with him and often drove him in a Stutz Bearcat on bank-swindling trips to neighboring towns. When he built up a sizable stake they skipped out of the asylum together.

About this time he perfected the "bereaved-relation" act which involved posing as a grief-stricken son choosing a headstone for his mother's grave. During negotiations he would fake a collapse and ask to rest in the tombstone maker's office, where he contrived to steal a supply of blank and cancelled checks.

He transferred the signatures from the cancelled checks to the stolen blanks and cleaned up thousands of dollars at local banks before the hoax was discovered. Burns detectives surmised that the missing patient was responsible for the flood of bad checks. They ran him down with Nurse Wilkes in New Orleans and he cheerfully informed his captors that he had netted better than $60,000. New Orleans police shipped him back to the Agnew Asylum.

Near Colton, California, Harkins eluded his guard and leaped from the speeding train. He landed on his feet, stole a car and made for Los Angeles. In a couple of days he clipped banks there for $6,000, hopped to Portland where he picked up $7,200, went on to Vancouver, Canada, added another $5,800 to his bankroll, and then forged his way to the Southwest.

The law caught up with him in Pecos, Texas. He was tried in Fort Worth, sentenced to two years in the penitentiary, and, pending transfer, confined on the fifth floor of the county jail. Mary Wilkes showed up at the jail and slipped him a set of saw blades. Two days later he led five other prisoners to freedom in a spectacular break.

Stonecutters' checks were soon bouncing again in banks from Spokane to Charlestown, West Virginia. Five months later Burns detectives picked him up with Mary Wilkes at a Miami race track and he went back to Fort Worth in handcuffs.

He served his time but Utah claimed him for other tombstone check forgeries and he was sentenced to an indeterminate term in the state prison. Three years later, in 1929, he got the biggest break of his life when the warden arranged a parole which ironically prevented the service of detainer warrants from other states.

Harkins managed to stay out of jail until a Bridgeport banker discovered that a large check he had just cashed was worthless and yelled for the police. The ace forger, fleeing south in a new Cadillac, was halted at a road block and slapped into the Fairfield County jail.

He didn't stay long. Mary Wilkes visited him again and when she departed, he had saw blades. At breakfast two mornings later he overpowered a keeper and, aided by another prisoner, sawed out of a third-story window, slid down a rope of blankets and escaped in broad daylight.

Harkins dumped faithful Mary Wilkes and began sparking a New York show girl. Burns Detective Crowe, figuring he would try to contact his new flame, put a stake-out on her New York hotel and, sure enough, a call came through from Pittsburgh on the second day of the vigil. Police picked up their man in the steel city the same night.

He was returned to Bridgeport, tried and sentenced to nine to thirty years. He was pardoned after six, but California parole-board authorities were waiting at the prison gates with an old warrant and he went back to escape-proof San Quentin. In 1940 he was paroled in the custody of his minister brother.

Within a week he was forging checks in Texas and Oklahoma. He was nabbed in Bartlesville. This time he convinced a judge that he was cracked and was committed to an Oklahoma insane asylum. His brother managed to have him transferred back to Agnew and three months later he was declared sane and released.

Like a circuit rider, he cut a swath across the country to New York and back, collecting more than $50,000 from banks along the way. Disaster overtook him in the Anglo-California National Bank in San Francisco where a teller, in the act of handing over $1,900, suddenly recognized him from a police circular. He was speedily sentenced to one to fourteen years in San Quentin and placed in the county jail pending appeal.

Two weeks before Christmas, in 1944, jail inmates elected him to train their Yuletide chorus. But on the afternoon of December 20th, Harkins wasn't singing carols. He had accomplished a Houdini-like feat, vanishing through a barred window, leaving all his clothes behind. How he did it is a mystery to this day.

Police departments across the nation were alerted. On a tipoff police raided the home of Mary Crosswhite, his latest girl friend in New York City, and found him hiding in an upstairs bathroom. He went back to San Quentin for another five years. In 1950 he was again paroled to his minister brother.

He was now sixty years old and a four-time loser—plus. A forger's skill is usually impaired by long years of confinement and inaction, but Harkins was far from through.

In 1953, he was nabbed in Tacoma, Washington, for $3,205 worth of forgeries, but he had executed them so perfectly that a conviction wasn't possible.

Police used every trick to pin the forgeries on Harkins. In Seattle, strapped to a lie detector and openly amused, he talked volubly but the operator was "unable to determine guilt or innocence."

In Tacoma a Pentathol truth-serum test became so confusing that a bewildered prosecuting attorney remarked, "This is the man, all right, but he's such a magnificent liar that I'm beginning to believe he's telling the truth."

211

Washington authorities gave up and waived their priority. Harkins was extradited to Tucson, Arizona, where he was accused of dropping a $2,750 bouncer in the Bank of Douglas.

At the trial, the Reverend Hershel Harkins testified that on the date of the crime his brother was in California and had dined with the rest of the family. Harkins, holding to a lifetime rule, avoided the witness stand, preventing the prosecutor from presenting his record. The jury brought in a verdict of not guilty.

A few mornings later he pulled the Boston bank coup. On his way south he hit several other banks and arrived in Florida with a $12,000 bankroll and headed straight for the race tracks. He dropped his money on slow horses, and a woman teller in a Coral Gables bank brought about his downfall when he tried to recoup his losses by using the successful Boston dodge.

He walked jauntily into the Florida National Bank and Trust Company and gave Mrs. Elizabeth Simon a check for $2,910 signed by Dr. Robert Jackson and initialed by J. B. Jackson, the assistant cashier. He casually mentioned that Cashier Jackson was his brother.

"Great fellow, isn't he?" said Harkins, motioning toward Cashier Jackson.

But Mrs. Simon wouldn't buy that and insisted that she'd have to verify the cashier's initials. Harkins saw the deal had gone sour and made for the door. Mrs. Simon followed, yelling for a policeman, who grabbed the fugitive as he was bolting into a taxi.

Florida waived priority and Harkins was extradicted to Richmond, Virginia, for a $1,704 check swindle and sentenced to a year in the state penitentiary. After that, Baton Rouge wanted him for passing a bogus $1,350 check at the Louisiana State Bank and got the nod.

At his trial Harkins acted as his own counsel and pleaded complete innocence, incurable illness, old age and insanity. But at last the old lone wolf seemed to sense that the jig was up. He surprised everyone by finally resignedly pleading guilty for the first time in his life.

"I guess this is the end of the line," he said slowly, his voice throaty with emotion. "I've never hurt anyone and the only ones who hate me are the bankers." Then he chuckled maliciously and added, "But I've sure given a lot of bankers a hard time."

Detective Crowe is understandably skeptical about the "end-of-the-line" routine. Although he has great respect for the slippery criminal's professional skill, he has none whatever for his promises to reform.

"He always says the same thing," says Crowe, "but don't be fooled.

He'll be forging checks the day after he gets out of prison if he lives through his term. He's likely to do that, too. Besides being one of the cleverest forgers in the world, he's tough as nails."

On October 8, 1954, the master forger was sentenced to ten years in the State penitentiary. He took it with dignity, but at sixty-five he was a forlorn, pathetic figure. Yet his faded but steady old blue eyes gleamed with a defiant warning that his hatred for banks and bankers still smolders, along with a hope that he'll live to fleece them once again.

THE RESPECTED MADAM OF OXFORD

by Jacob Fisher

Bessie Mount's select house catered only to the elite of Oxford. The town itself, comprising twenty thousand souls, is the metropolis of a lush sugar beet and citrus area in Southern California. Its burghers are a lusty lot whose frontier spirit is not entirely dead. While not wide open, Oxford can rightfully be termed a fair example of a free-wheeling town. That is why Bessie Mount could run her establishment with impunity for so many years. After all, she was a woman of discretion who knew when to be tight-lipped. Appointments had to be made in advance for visits to Bessie's place, and the presence of a guest was never betrayed.

No field workers or men from the sugar mill were invited to Bessie Mount's place. Her trade consisted of business and professional men only. Bessie had the knack of making each of her customers feel that he was engaging in his own little intrigue with his very own mistress, instead of regarding himself realistically as a habitué of a public house of prostitution.

All in all, Bessie stepped on the toes of no one, and as time went on she became accepted as an integral function of the community—like the sewage plant, or the water system, or the political organization which ran the town. She participated in all the charity drives, and was never reluctant to sit up with a sick acquaintance. She brought flowers to the hospital, attended church occasionally, and regularly paid dues to both major political organizations.

While the town accepted Bessie Mount, it did so with a sort of Western gallantry because she was a woman. The town appreciated her because it felt that a woman so pretty and personable could have made her way in a much easier line of endeavor. Oxford felt that Bessie was helping the town out of an embarrassing need by supplying such a decorous establishment.

Bessie herself was admired by all who knew her. She had no enemies. Her personal life, outside her business activities, was beyond reproach as far as anyone knew. She never enjoyed the intimacies of the townspeople; this privilege was reserved for her girls. On several occasions, one or two of her especially favored clients tried to develop a liaison with Bessie, but it died a-borning. Bessie had known no sweetheart or love life of her own. This fact did nothing to detract from her popularity, because no rivalries for her affections were created and no wife in town could point to Bessie Mount as her husband's sleeping partner.

Bessie occasionally had parties for her friends. The food, the wines, and the service were superb, and knowledge of this soon seeped into the sewing-circle cliques. As a result, Bessie was occasionally called upon to cater at dinner parties, or to act as the expert adviser at similar affairs in the homes of the wives of her clients. She became as equally famous with the women of Oxford as a "party arranger" as she was with the men. This happy understanding with the good people of Oxford continued for many years, and probably would still be flourishing were it not for the havoc wrought by the war, which enmeshed Bessie in one of its many grasping tentacles.

After Pearl Harbor, there was no holding Bessie down. Where she formerly was a discreetly active figure in local civic efforts, she was now possessed by a frenzy of activity. She was an air raid warden, a blood donor, and she sold War Bonds. It was rumored that she once declared a War Bond Day, when the price of admission to her place was one fifty dollar, face-value bond, to be purchased from Bessie. Bessie and her car were kept busy by the A.W.V.S., and she was active in the Red Cross. She sent overseas gift packages to dozens of Oxford soldiers, some of whom were her former clients.

Into this bustling scene of wartime turmoil, the bolt of romance finally found its target in Bessie Mount, and started the chain of events which made her a war casualty. In her patriotic fervor, Bessie had also become an air raid spotter, and her time of duty at an isolated promontory, a short distance from Oxford, coincided with that of a husky young farmhand named Carlos Perkins.

Carlos was deferred by his draft board because he was a farmhand. That which transpired in the dark solitude of the California night, while a watch was kept for enemy planes, is known but to Bessie and Carlos. How far Bessie's patriotic fervor carried her may be surmised only from ensuing events.

At any rate, one fine day Carlos turned up at the Air Spotter's Headquarters, tendered his resignation, and proudly announced that he had enlisted in the army, declaring that he was through hiding behind a plough.

On the very same day came the breathtaking announcement that shook Oxford to its heels—even relegating the war to page two. Bessie Mount and Carlos Perkins were to be married!

The wedding, which took place on Christmas Day, 1942, is still talked about in Oxford. Caterers came from Los Angeles to handle the reception festivities. The church was packed, and Bessie, a radiant bride, and her handsome, uniformed husband, made a stunning couple.

The groom had insufficient time for a protracted honeymoon, and besides, the bride couldn't leave her business. When Carlos left for his camp, Bessie returned to her many activities, this time as a matron and war wife. If possible, Bessie's position in Oxford became enhanced to a still greater degree. She was one of the many wives whose husbands were away at war. The diehard element that had looked upon her askance unbent somewhat, now that she was a war wife. And Bessie did nothing which would give rise to gossip about her virtue or faithfulness.

The war progressed, and more important events than Bessie's marriage transpired to hold the attention of Oxford's citizenry. The most stirring and significant of these developments was the establishment of a wartime training camp on the outskirts of the town.

Forty thousand men who came from every state in the Union overran the new post. At the end of the rigors of a day's training, the tide receded from camp and flowed into Oxford, clamoring for entertainment. The saloons, the movies, the dancehalls, and other places of entertainment were filled to overflowing nightly. It was natural that eventually the soldiers would learn about Bessie Mount's place.

When the soldiers first called on Bessie, her soul was torn between her patriotism and loyalty to the soldiers in her desire to do what she believed to be the "right thing" for them, and her certain knowledge that she would lose her esteemed position with her "elite" customers if she ran an open house. Bessie's caution won out, and she refused admittance to the soldiers. Her canny business sense, however, told her she was missing the golden opportunity of a lifetime—that she could make a financial killing.

And then Bessie hit upon a plan. She rented several houses some distance removed from the place she had been operating for so many years, procured girls to staff them and threw the doors wide open to the soldiers. The reputation that Bessie had enjoyed for so long helped her to maintain the additional houses without interference from the local authorities.

Bessie's affluence grew by leaps and bounds. Her liberality remained unstinted, and she contributed heavily to the U.S.O. and other organizations catering to the welfare of servicemen. Possibly she fancied herself as running a similar organization.

Bessie visited the east several times to see her husband, and her scattered, involved enterprises did not get the personal and careful supervision that her original Oxford establishment had received. Perhaps Bessie, in her affluence, had become careless. Whatever the reason, the fact is that numerous cases of venereal disease broke out simultaneously in the neighboring camp, and the harassed army medical authorities, together with the military police, initiated an intensive investigation to determine the source of the outbreak. The report of the investigators showed that many of the infected men had recently visited one or another of Bessie Mount's houses.

The same day the reports were submitted, combined squads of medical and military police detachments raided each of Bessie's houses. The official in charge of each detachment was a medical officer who suavely explained that the army was not interested in the violation of the local laws except—and only insofar—as it affected military personnel. The doctors firmly insisted that each girl found in each house must be examined to determine if she was infected. If the girls were found to be free of infection, the military men promised to leave the premises immediately.

The medical officer in charge of the detail which raided Bessie Mount's original place was entirely unfamiliar with the tradition and standing Oxford had bestowed upon the owner of the place. Bessie herself took the raid with much aplomb, even though such a disgrace had never befallen her before. If the army saw fit to examine her girls, she would not object. Bessie was sure her place would come through with flying colors.

When the girls were herded into a room for their tests, Bessie re-

216

mained behind. The young medical officer, however, ordered her into the room with the girls and insisted that she submit to an examination. This was too much even for the patient Bessie. She fumed—she tried to call her lawyer, the commanding officer of the camp, the mayor—all to no avail. The doctor was adamant. Bessie's reputation for inviolability meant nothing to him. She was "one of the girls" as far as he was concerned. Bessie refused to subject herself to the indignity of such a medical examination. She explained that she was the wife of Sergeant Carlos Perkins; she even produced several uncashed family allowance checks to bolster her case. But nothing Bessie did made an impression on the officer.

Finally Bessie had hysterics, but the doctor quieted her with a hypodermic and brusquely ordered two husky military policemen to carry Bessie into the examination room. The reason for Bessie's refusal to undergo an examination soon became apparent.

The grim-faced doctor came out of the examination room. He looked bewildered and unbelieving.

"Bessie Mount is a man," he said.

For twenty years, John Mount, a pimp and procurer, had masqueraded as a woman, taking the name of Bessie Mount, in order to carry on his illicit enterprise in Oxford. He figured shrewdly that the townspeople might tolerate a woman, but not a man, in such a business. The facts, obtained from the confession and other sources, further showed that the marriage with Carlos Perkins was contracted to further enhance and solidify the position Bessie Mount enjoyed in the community.

After the hue and cry died down, no one appeared to want to do anything about prosecution. Oxford may have been ashamed to admit how easily it was deceived. The army camp had closed the houses, and was no longer interested.

The family allowance checks based on Perkins' army service, displayed by "Bessie Mount" in her frantic efforts to avoid examination, however, proved to be her Waterloo. When the checks were brought to the attention of the army's Office of Dependency Benefits, an investigation was immediately started by that organization. It was found that Carlos Perkins had asked that an allowance be sent to his wife, Bessie, whom he married on Christmas Day, 1942. A number of checks had been sent after proof of marriage was submitted.

This was a clear-cut violation, because there could be no wife or marriage, if "Bessie Mount," the "bride," was, in fact, John Mount, a man.

Perkins was guilty of fraud in requesting an allowance for a woman he named as his wife, when he had no wife. John Mount perpetrated a crime when he received and negotiated army checks as a soldier's wife.

Carlos Perkins and John Mount, alias Bessie Mount, were both arrested, indicted, and charged with violating the Servicemen's Dependents Allowance Act. Many interesting questions as to the marriage and trysts between Carlos and "Bessie" remained unanswered, because neither wanted to stand trial. Both pleaded guilty to the offense of defrauding the government in the matter of obtaining a family allowance, and both received penitentiary terms in the United States District Court.

OPERATION U. S. MINT

by William S. Fairfield

The Bureau of Engraving and Printing, an ancient brick building where the Government actually prints its paper currency, is as heavily guarded as Fort Knox itself, so discouraging to the criminal eye that even America's most clever thieves have always looked elsewhere for their plunder. Over a thirty-year span from 1923 to 1953, the Bureau could boast that of all the billions of dollars it had printed, an average of less than a hundred dollars a year was missing, from all causes, including misplacement and clerical errors as well as petty theft.

On December 30, 1953, however, this proud record was placed in dire jeopardy, and a lowly, unassuming Bureau employe named James Landis was solely responsible. His lone-wolf plan was so carefully conceived and so deftly executed that the theft, involving a total of $160,000, was not noticed until January fourth. And except for an accidental discovery made by a fellow worker on that date, the discrepancy might have remained hidden for several months. After such a delay, authorities are frank to admit, it would have been almost impossible to track down the culprit.

Landis, a dark-skinned man with mournful eyes and a scraggly, drooping mustache that lent his face an air of perpetual disappointment, had been employed by the Bureau for ten years. His superiors had never felt any doubts as to his honesty. His record in World War II was excellent; he received the Purple Heart, Bronze Star and Good Conduct medals, rose to the rank of sergeant, and was medically discharged after being twice wounded. His postwar neighbors in suburban Chapel Oaks, Maryland, where Landis lived with his wife and two young sons, considered him a devoted family man.

When he was finally picked up by the Secret Service, Landis, nattily clad in a $150 overcoat of pure cashmere, confessed that the idea for the theft had come to him purely by chance. Several years earlier, according to his story, he had managed a local sandlot baseball team. To advertise the team's games, he had printed a number of small handbills which he distributed to fellow employes and to neighbors. When the team disbanded, he found himself with a large stack of blank white paper cut to handbill size. Belatedly, he noticed that these blank sheets were the same size as dollar bills; and he quickly discovered that, by inserting a sheaf of them between real bills, he could surprise friends with what he called a "flash roll."

In August of 1953, more than four months before the theft at the Bureau of Engraving and Printing, Landis stumbled upon a more profitable if less innocent use for the blank handbills. If they could look genuine when stuffed between dollar bills, he suddenly realized they would look even more genuine when packaged exactly as the Government packaged its currency.

Landis' job with the Bureau was a menial one, but because one of his main duties was to carry currency between the vaults and the packing machines, he had learned just how real currency was handled. The newly minted twenty-dollar bills, he knew, were assembled in stacks of 4,000 with wooden blocks at each end. A machine then placed these so-called "bricks" under great pressure while two steel bands were welded around them lengthwise. From the banding machine, the bricks were taken to another machine where they were wrapped in heavy brown paper. A Treasury seal was glued to one end of the final package, and a label, including the serial numbers of the bills, the date, and the initials of the packer, was glued to the other end. The bricks, each worth $80,000, were then stored in vaults awaiting shipment to a Federal Reserve Bank.

As Landis was aware, Bureau inspectors occasionally broke into these packages to recheck them. And although the bills were promptly returned to the packing machines along with the labels, revised to note

219

the date of the check and the initials of the inspector, it was also true that a wooden end block, an unbroken steel band, or a whole Treasury seal was occasionally overlooked in the rubbish—overlooked, that is, until James Landis saw the value of such odds and ends.

Slowly he began carrying scraps home in his pockets—a wooden block here, a piece of wrapping paper there. By day, he studied the composition of the genuine bricks he was handling. By night, while his wife was busy with the children, he practiced duplicating these bricks. Two months later, in October, he was satisfied with his homework. The label was still missing from one end of each of his packages, but this was merely according to plan: Landis had no way of knowing in advance which bricks would be lying around loose the day of the theft or what serial numbers would be stamped on their labels, and thus he would have to use the real labels if his dummy bricks were to be substituted without inviting immediate detection.

In mid-October, just when everything seemed set, the Bureau suddenly changed the grade of its wrapping paper. Landis waited patiently until he could filch suitable samples of the new paper, and then, on December thirtieth, he was again ready.

The key to the success of Landis' plan would lie in his ability to use the homemade bricks to take the place of the stolen currency. Merely getting a brick or two past the guards was not enough, for the discrepancy would almost certainly be noticed within forty-eight hours, the serial numbers of the missing bills would be broadcast throughout the nation, and the thief would find himself prison-bound almost as soon as he tried to cash the first "hot" bill.

Landis arrived at the Bureau that morning in time to join the peak flow of workers reporting for the 7:30 shift, and under his arm was a paper bag containing the two counterfeit bricks. He knew regulations required that he check this bag at the parcel booth, to be picked up on his way out that evening. But he hoped that the door guards, in the midst of the holiday season, might be somewhat lax. He was not disappointed.

A guard did glance at him as he entered, and Landis obediently walked toward the parcel booth, quite willing to check his bag and try another day if the guard's eyes followed him. When the guard turned to inspect other arriving employees, however, Landis slipped down the hall and took an elevator to the men's room on the third floor.

The waste basket in this room was lined with a burlap bag to ease the job of trash removal, and Landis had selected the bottom of the

220

basket, underneath the burlap, as a temporary haven for his handi-work. The choice was not an idle one, for later in his plan, if all went well, he would have use for still other facilities provided by this men's room, including hot water, a radiator, and a cubicle with a lock on it.

After stowing his dummy bricks in the bottom of the waste basket, Landis returned to the locker room on the first floor, hastily changed into his work clothes, and reported for duty in the packing room next door. He helped clear out the vaults so that others could work inside them, and then was assigned to carry bricks, in serial sequence, from the banding machine to the wrapping machine.

At 7:50 he had loaded the platform leading into the wrapping machine. From long experience, he knew it would be twenty minutes before the reloading.

Bending over, Landis picked up a slightly torn sheet of wrapping paper, as if to throw it in a waste basket. But his path carried him past the wrapping machine to where a stack of recently packaged twenty-dollar bricks rested against the wall. With his back to the room, Landis picked up two of the bricks, with the same motion folding them into the sheet of wrapping paper. A second later he was out the door.

Painstaking exploration of the Bureau had led Landis to decide on a seldom-used storeroom as the safest hiding place for his contraband. This presented certain problems since he was now on the first floor of A-wing, the storeroom was on the fifth floor of D-wing, and the only passage between the two wings was in the basement. But his pace to the basement and then across to D-wing was slow; and his manner in the elevator to the fifth floor of that wing was calm. On several earlier occasions, he had timed a dry run of this step in well under twenty minutes.

In the dusty storeroom, amid broken platforms and dilapidated office furniture, Landis unwrapped the two bricks, first carefully tearing off the package ends bearing the labels and stuffing these in his pockets. He next pulled out a pair of pliers he had borrowed from the packing room, placed each unwrapped brick firmly between his feet so that its contents would not explode when the pressure was released, and twisted the steel bands until they broke. With a sound much like the shuffling of a deck of cards, $160,000 in crisp, new twenty-dollar bills spilled across the floor. Landis brought out two additional paper bags he had carried to work neatly folded in his pocket, stuffed the money into these bags, and pushed the bags out of sight under a low platform.

Then, with no show of haste, he retraced his steps to the first floor of A-wing. He entered the packing room at 8:05, in plenty of time to re-load the wrapping machine.

The next step of Landis's plan required at least fifteen minutes, and he would not have that much free time until his rest period arrived at 10:40. Finally, after two and a half agonizing hours, he was relieved.

Landis quickly returned to the men's room on the third floor. Under hot water, he separated the genuine labels from the brown wrapping paper and placed them between the radiator flanges to dry.

Five minutes later, he retrieved his dummy bricks from the bottom of the waste basket, and stepped quickly into a toilet booth, locking the door. With a small bottle of glue he had taken from the packing room, he fastened the labels to the bricks, at last completing the imitations started at home so many weeks before.

Only one flaw remained: Since the real bricks downstairs were con-stantly being moved about, Landis was not sure he could deposit his counterfeits exactly where the stolen bricks should now be resting, more than three hours after their removal. His only choice was to stamp new dates below the original packaging dates, as if the two bricks had just been checked and rewrapped. When he had done this, using a rotary stamp also borrowed from the packing room, and when he had added a fictitious set of initials, he was one careful step nearer success.

At 10:55, he re-entered the packing room on the first floor, the bricks tucked under his arm in the same paper bag that had carried them to work that morning. Five seconds later, the bag was in the waste basket and the bricks were innocently stacked with their genuine counterparts against the wall.

Landis waded through the rest of the morning, through his lunch hour, and through his afternoon duties, hardly able to conceal his ela-tion; everything had gone perfectly so far. Then, at 3:10, he embarked on the final leg of his voyage.

He left the packing room, changed into street clothes in the locker room next door, and then, with an extra pair of work pants over his arm, went down to the basement, crossed to D-wing, and took the ele-vator to the fifth-floor storeroom.

Landis found the two bags of currency undisturbed beneath the plat-form, but he also discovered that a slight hitch had developed: Neither of the bags was large enough to hold the entire $160,000 and at the same time leave enough room on top for his work pants. He therefore stuffed as much money as he could—$128,000—into the larger bag, placed his work pants on top of this maximum load, and returned the second bag, containing the remaining $32,000, to its hiding place.

For the fourth and last time that day, Landis crossed the long basement corridor of the Bureau. He climbed the stairs to the first floor of A-wing, ducked through the locker room, and headed for the doorway to freedom.

The guards had often been instructed to check closely on employes leaving with packages, and the man now on duty immediately noticed the paper bag under Landis' arm. He questioned its contents with a frown. Landis pulled out one leg of the work pants, but he kept on walking. The guard nodded, turned away, and Landis was out the door. Seconds later, he had lost himself in the swarm of home-bound Government employees.

With his expert imitation packages snugly resting in the Bureau Landis could operate on the well-founded theory that the theft might not be discovered for a long time. According to their labels, as revised by Landis in the men's room, the dummy bricks had already been checked, and there was little chance they would be checked a second time. Instead, they would be stored in the Bureau vaults for as long as two months. They would then be shipped to one of the twelve Federal Reserve Banks, where they would again be placed in storage for a month or two. Finally, they would be shipped to a local bank where, after an additional delay, they would at last be opened.

Only at this point would it be discovered that the bricks contained blank white paper, and perhaps as much as six months would have elapsed in the meantime. Landis could spend every day of these six months busily disposing of the new twenty-dollar bills, the fact that they were "hot" known only to himself.

Discovery of the crime at this late date would place the Secret Service, charged with tracking down the theft of Government currency, in an extremely difficult position, especially if Landis destroyed all the hot money remaining in his possession as soon as the crime hit the newspapers. The Federal agents would be saddled with a cold, six-month-old trail, and even the actual scene of the theft would be a mystery. It might have occurred at the Bureau of Engraving and Printing itself, but then again it could have occurred at the Federal Reserve Bank or at the local bank—or, for that matter, on either of the occasions when the money was in transit.

On the evening of December thirtieth, these thoughts ran happily through the mind of James Landis as he made his way to the home of a

223

friend named Charles Nelson. Landis had previously asked Nelson to get a steel box with a good lock on it, hinting that he had a "big score coming up." But when Landis spilled $128,000 onto his bed that evening, Nelson went out of his mind. "I didn't know what to do," he later told Secret Service agents. "I just jumped up and down, up and down."

Landis himself was more businesslike. Although the theft itself had been a one-man operation, he explained quickly, he would need help disposing of the loot. Even allowing for the greatest possible time lag before the theft was discovered, about thirty-six bills would have to be cashed each day in order to spend the entire $128,000 within six months. Obviously, one or two men could not cash that many new twenties a day without arousing suspicion, so additional recruits were necessary.

Eventually, four others were brought into the scheme, including William Giles, William Johnson, Roger Patterson and Edith Irene Chase, the last two being cousins of Landis'. According to the plan outlined by Landis, the hot twenty-dollar bills would be used to make small purchases, and the "good" money left over would be deposited in a second box, to be split up later. If each of the six conspirators held up to his end of the operation, passing an average of just six bills a day, the $128,000 would be exhausted within the alloted six months. The recruits were only too glad to assure their co-operation, and Landis went to bed that night confident that he had covered every angle.

Less than four days later, however, the entire operation came crashing down about his head. Even to the practiced eye of a Bureau inspector, Landis' imitation bricks were perfect, but they were something short of that to the touch. For although he had packed his home-made bricks as tightly as possible before slipping on the steel bands, Landis could not hope to match the pressure applied by the banding machine at the Bureau. The real bricks weighed eight pounds; the imitations one pound and five ounces less.

On the morning of January 4, 1954, while Landis remained home pleading sickness, a fellow employe at the Bureau of Engraving and Printing was returning a load of packaged twenty-dollar bricks to one of the vaults, picking them up two at a time and placing them in a bin above his head. If this man had selected both of Landis' bricks at the same time, the deficiency might have passed unnoticed. But as fate would have it, one of his hands fell on a genuine brick, the other on one of the counterfeits. He lifted them, frowned at the difference in weight, and reported his discovery to a superior. Within an hour, Secret Service agents were at work, following a trail that was still white-hot.

224

Meanwhile, Landis' accomplices were rapidly demonstrating that their benefactor had one huge blind spot. And this flaw, which could destroy the most clever criminal plan, was a complete lack of ability to judge his fellow human beings. Charles Nelson, who was supervising the spending operation, later told Federal agents that the four other recruits were all holding back a sizable share of the "good" money they had obtained, and when agents asked Nelson what he saw in the deal for himself, he replied, "Why, I'll tell ya, when those thieves got through stealing from each other, I was gonna take it all."

Roger Patterson further rewarded Landis' trust by telephoning him one evening to ask if he could use some of the loot to pay a personal debt. Landis generously suggested that he take "a couple bills." Within an hour Patterson had joined a crap game, slapping at least $6,000 in newly minted twenties on the floor and announcing that no one was going to break him that night.

The very morning the theft was discovered, Patterson, Nelson and Edith Chase were in Prince Georges County, Maryland, embarked on a spending spree that left a score of flabbergasted merchants in its wake. They bought half-pints of whiskey at every liquor store they passed, each time paying with a fresh twenty-dollar bill. And apparently they decided to partake of their merchandise, for two hours later Nelson was seen lighting a cigar with a new twenty.

This was too much. Merchants called the Prince Georges County police; and the police, suspecting that the money was counterfeit, called the Secret Service.

The report of the theft at the Bureau had reached the Secret Service less than five hours earlier, so the agents wasted little time in getting out to Prince Georges County. When they found that both Roger Patterson and Edith Chase were involved in the spending orgy, they quickly focused their suspicions on a Bureau employe and cousin of the pair named James Landis.

Eventually, all six of the culprits were rounded up and all confessed. Landis led authorities to the $32,000 still concealed in the fifth-floor storeroom at the Bureau; and in initial raids on various homes and hiding places, agents confiscated $95,000 of the remaining $128,000 in missing twenties. They also collected almost $6,000 in ones, fives, and tens—obviously the change from bills already passed—and from this figure they were able to estimate that the Landis crew had been cashing a total of almost a hundred bills a day, or three times the necessary quota.

Landis pleaded guilty, and in June of 1954 he received a sentence of

three to nine years in prison. Each of his accomplices received lesser
sentences, ranging down to 180 days.

30 YEARS A FAKE DOCTOR

by Peter Wyden

The patient on the operating table in the Enloe Hospital at Chico,
California, was in precarious condition. His appendix had ruptured
and gangrene had set in.

The time was 1942, and many of today's infection-preventing miracle drugs were not available. Understandably, the head physician
looked grave. However, the new chief assistant, Dr. James H. Phillips,
examined the patient with care—and asserted that he could operate
successfully.

The air was tense as the calm, bespectacled Dr. Phillips made the
initial incision. It was a delicate operation, but his steady hands wielded
the instruments expertly and kept intact his boast of never having lost
a patient in surgery.

The operation was nothing unusual in the astonishing medical career of Dr. James H. Phillips. Just before accepting the appointment in
Chico, he had completed four years as a contract surgeon responsible
for the health of hundreds of boys in Civilian Conservation Corps
camps. Government efficiency reports rated him from "satisfactory" to
"excellent," and when he brought a CCC boy to Dr. E. T. Enloe's hospital in Chico, and operated on him with evident skill, Dr. Enloe invited Dr. Phillips to become a member of his staff.

About that time, coincidentally, a special agent for the California
State Board of Medical Examiners began working on a narcotics case.
Checking a pile of prescriptions, he ran across a couple of hundred
signed "J.H.P., M.D." or "J. H. Phillips, M.D." They had no connection with the case, but it so happens that California law requires doctors to use full first and last names in signing prescriptions.

Though a minute discrepancy, it set the agent to checking into the
background of the man known as Dr. Phillips. It proved fruitful research, for it developed that Phillips had never attended medical school

226

and that his career made up, as the *Journal* of the American Medical Association put it, "one of the most amazing stories of medical imposture" on record.

"The amazing feature is not the man's colossal impudence and foolhardiness," the *Journal* added, "but rather the fact that he was able to conduct himself in an operating room in such a way as to avoid suspicion."

All Phillips had was stupendous nerve and a convincing manner. He fooled not only patients in 11 states, who found the "Doc" satisfactory and never questioned his authenticity, but also the U. S. Government, several county and state health departments, and dozens of reputable physicians, nurses and administrators in various hospitals.

It was all so absurdly simple that the "Doc" could never see why anyone should get upset over his successes. There was no secret to it, the astounding impostor explained. He just never started cutting at anything without first convincing himself that he would be able to sew it up again. Take brain surgery, for instance.

"I've assisted at brain surgery, but I've never done it alone. I know my limitations. . . . I haven't done anything harmful, only good," he insisted, "and I'll stack my skill in medicine against any surgeon, man to man."

Nevertheless, Phillips was given two concurrently running sentences: for practicing medicine without a license, and for illegal possession of firearms (a revolver had been found in his car).

It was a familiar turn of fate for "Doc" Phillips. Rarely has a faker been unmasked more often and less permanently. Certainly, no one has ever gone to so much trouble to remain loyal to his chosen profession.

The "Doc" started soaking up medical lore shortly after he was born Arthur Osborne Phillips on July 18, 1894, in Malone, New York, a county seat south of the Canadian border. He befriended the local doctor's boy and started making the rounds with the doctor.

"He wanted me to study medicine, but we had no money," Phillips recalls. "So I went around with him and absorbed it all. I have a photographic memory and I'm not exactly dumb."

The "Doc" claims to have taken biology and bacteriology courses at the University of Buffalo, but the university has no record of him.

Phillips' baptism as a pill dispenser came in World War I. He was a private in a medical detachment. Investigators report that he served as orderly to Lt. James Herman Phillips, a young doctor from Dora, Alabama, who graduated from the University of Tennessee College of Medicine in 1916. He was no relation, but he turned out to be the key man in the "Doc's" later life.

During the 1918-19 influenza epidemic, the ex-private volunteered for service in a Cumberland, Maryland, emergency hospital. He called himself a laboratory technician, but a supervisor found him poking a finger into a sterile test tube and fired him.

A Cumberland concern needed a chemist and Phillips applied for the job immaculately attired, wearing impressive black-rimmed glasses which were rare at that time. He sold himself as an analyst of metals and had calling cards printed, announcing himself as "Dr. Arthur O. Phillips, B.S., Chemical Engineer."

Phillips wasn't fired from that job. He merely showed up less and less frequently and finally vanished, leaving behind him a trail of worthless checks.

Somehow he got a job with the U. S. Public Health Service, but lasted only three months. Not much later, posing as Dr. Arthur O. Phillips, he was fined $50 and served a week in Tombs Prison, New York City, for impersonating a government officer.

He served time here and there for passing bad checks, defrauding a hotel and false pretense, using these jail sojourns to enhance his medical education. By then, his background was solid enough for Dr. N. B. Steward to entrust him with surgery at Maryland's State House of Correction Hospital, where the "Doc" was quite literally a resident.

"A good worker," remembers Dr. Steward. "Took lots of interest in his work."

At large once more, the "Doc" somehow got word that Dr. James H. Phillips, his former lieutenant in the Medical Corps, had been confined at a mental institution for veterans since 1921. He called on the real Dr. Phillips' family in Alabama, represented himself as a wartime buddy of the physician and asked, for old times' sake, to sleep in his friend's room. On the wall hung a medical license for James Herman Phillips. When the "Doc" left, the license also left.

His next job was making contact with his new alma mater, the University of Tennessee College of Medicine. He needed to know a little bit about the place. He also needed a diploma.

First, the "Doc" wrote the school for old yearbooks and catalogues. Soon, Monroe County Infirmary in Rochester, New York, asked the school if a Dr. James H. Phillips had graduated from there, and was advised that he had.

228

A month before, the University had heard from Phillips. Signing himself as Resident Surgeon, Commission of Public Welfare, Monroe County, he had sent an affidavit stating that he had lost his 1916 graduation diploma during the war. The University supplied a duplicate by mail.

The "Doc," now solidly in business as Dr. James H. Phillips, popped up in Charleston, West Virginia, and was accepted in the state medical association.

One hot day that summer, Wendell Wilcox, for whom Phillips once worked as oiler in an aluminum plant in New York, stopped his car in front of a Charleston hotel. As he stepped out, a man in hospital whites spoke to him. It was Phillips.

Proudly, the "Doc" explained how he had worked his way through medical school after leaving New York and was on the local hospital staff. He insisted that Wilcox look the hospital over and meet some of his associates.

"I went away feeling that this was little enough recognition of a young fellow who had apparently done a fine job," Wilcox says. "It became obvious as I met nurses and other doctors at the hospital that he was popular and highly regarded."

All might have gone well in Charleston if Phillips had not become overly ambitious and submitted a technical paper to the West Virginia Medical *Journal*. This proved a dead giveaway. Discharged from the hospital, he went into private practice.

The next seven years, with only brief vacations in prisons, were a golden era for "Doc" Phillips. He now knew enough medicine to become a trusted doctor in small Southern and Western towns where demand for medical services was great, competition small, and the danger of discovery least likely.

In Cuba, New Mexico, he is remembered as a devoted practitioner who rode his rounds on cow ponies, and also officiated as veterinarian and dentist. He performed orthopedic operations, and did Caesarean sections on kitchen tables.

"You have to do it in 14 minutes," he would explain condescendingly to laymen.

Repeatedly, Phillips worked up a fine practice from which he claimed to make as high as $10,000 a year, the only drawback being that he had to keep moving. Authorities were unable ever to convict him of a single medical misstep, but sooner or later his brash personality and colorful FBI record always caught up with him.

While serving one Federal sentence, he enrolled "by extension" at Pennsylvania State College and became a member of its alumni association. He still carries the membership card in his wallet.

His claim of having earned a graduate degree from Penn State appears overdrawn, however, although he did receive a certificate from the School of Agriculture, quite possibly the only diploma he ever acquired honestly. It certifies that "James H. Phillips, A.M., M.D." completed a correspondence course in stock feeding, butter making and technology of milk.

On June 1, 1949, the genial, pipe-smoking "Doc" with the big, honest brown eyes boarded a west-bound bus in Leavenworth, Kansas, and fell to chatting with a wealthy widow four years his senior. In August they were married. Mrs. Phillips bought the "Doc" a car for a wedding present and the couple settled down in Hutchinson, Kansas, her home town.

The "Doc" was liked in Kansas. As a courtesy, he treated youngsters of his new family's friends with spectacular success and without fee. Everybody who met him thought it was a shame he had no license to practice in Kansas.

The following June, his car collided with a truck and turned over six times. It was a bad accident for Phillips, in more ways than one. He was a patient at the Fowler, Kansas, hospital when an insurance adjustor called on him. The "Doc" had serious neck and arm injuries, but he was cocky and spun a remarkable tale. The adjustor was struck by his story—and by his grimy hands and dirty fingernails—and began checking.

The accident grew into a damage suit. Characteristically, there was no need for the "Doc" to risk a court appearance. He had been sued for $600 over the car crack-up. But he righteously countered with a $40,000 suit of his own, including $35,000 balm for inability to practice medicine.

It looked like routine litigation. Yes, Phillips gravely told opposition counsel, he had practiced for 34 years. Yes, he was also a graduate engineer. Yes, he had lately been an army doctor for the Chinese Nationalists.

Suddenly, after a day's dreary testimony, the attorney turned to him and demanded:

"Your name is what?"

"James H. Phillips."

"Now tell the jury your real name!" the attorney countered.

The "Doc" withered visibly. Asked, finally, if it wasn't true that he was not licensed to practice medicine anywhere, he meekly conceded: "That is right."

Twice tried and convicted of perjury, "Doc" Phillips is now serving three concurrent 15 to 20-year sentences at the Kansas State Penitentiary. He scribbles medical papers in his cell and peruses Penn State alumni bulletins which relatives forward to him, along with medical literature that keeps coming from drug companies, with whom he keeps in touch.

He was furious when prison officials insisted that he stop signing his spurious doctor's title to his correspondence. But everyone still calls him "Doc," which he regards as just recognition for his 30-year "career" in medicine.

THE MANY LIVES AND LOVES
OF HENRI DESIRE LANDRU

by Avery Hale

On a salubrious Sunday afternoon in May 1914, Henri Désiré Landru, a little man of many secrets, was walking along a tree-lined boulevard in Paris when he noticed a well-dressed, middle-aged woman coming toward him. As he drew abreast of the lady, Landru—45, neatly turned-out, and with the sun glinting on his ginger-colored mustache and pointed beard—lifted his derby and twinkled his small brown eyes. In a little while, Landru and Mme. Georges Cuchet, a widow, were sipping apéritifs in a sidewalk cafe.

Landru, his drink finished, crossed his legs, folded his hands on his knee, and began to pump information out of Mme. Cuchet. Madame, who had a 17-year-old son, lived in a little apartment on the Left Bank and worked as a seamstress. Her husband, who had gone under the sod five years before, had left her some rather expensive furnishings and a modest savings account.

Identifying himself as Raymond Diard, an engineer, Landru divulged to Mme. Cuchet, in a rich voice throbbing with emotion, that he had never married because of his devotion to an invalid mother who had recently died. He whipped a handkerchief from his Norfolk jacket, dabbed his eyes, managed a smile, then confessed that he was now interested in matrimony. Mme. Cuchet, completely fascinated by the little man, suggested that he call on her the next night.

When he left Mme. Cuchet that Sunday afternoon, Landru went home to a mean little house in Clichy, a manufacturing suburb, and partook of supper with his wife of 25 years, two grown sons and two small daughters. After the meal, Landru, who was known to his neighbors as François Petit, led the family in evening prayer, helped his daughters with some school problems, listened to some phonograph records, and retired early.

On Monday morning, Landru got into a small car and was off to his place of business—a garage that he ran in Neuilly under the name of Fremyet. Actually, the place was more than a garage; it did a fair-to-middling business as a drop for hot cars.

That night, Henri Désiré Landru, shedding his identities of Petit and Fremyet, reverted to his role of Diard, the engineer, and presented himself at the door of Mme. Cuchet's little flat, his bright little eyes peering at the lady through a huge bouquet of red roses.

Mme. Cuchet's son, André, was a sullen, suspicious youth. Landru tried to get on the right side of the boy but couldn't. After André went off to bed, however, Landru made fast work of getting on the right side of the mother. By the time he left that night he had not only proposed marriage but, telescoping time, consummated it.

In the weeks that followed, Mme. Cuchet, the happy bride-to-be, paid no attention to the protests of André that there was something shady about M. Diard. She paid even less attention to relatives who, meeting the little man, wondered what he was hiding behind all that facial adornment.

Landru turned out to be, among other things, an expert on the stock market, and he soon persuaded Mme. Cuchet to withdraw her savings from the bank and turn the money over to him for investment. And when the first World War broke out, Landru saw his sons off to the front, and then drove Mme. Cuchet's furnishings away in a truck for what he called "safekeeping." Then he took her and André to a villa he had rented in Vermouillet, a rustic settlement on the Seine about an hour by train from Paris.

Busy at his garage and hot-car drop during the week, Landru always got out to Vermouillet to spend Saturdays and Sundays with Mme. Cuchet and André. The villagers, who knew Landru under the alias of

François duPont, found him to be a stand-offish character. Landru, occupied as he was with other projects, didn't get around to marrying Mme. Cuchet. André kept badgering him to make an honest woman of his mother but Landru would just stare at the boy and say nothing.

In January 1915—eight months after Landru had tipped his hat to Mme. Cuchet that day on the boulevard—his neighbors in Vermouillet noticed that he was very busy at night, darting out of the house and setting fires on the grounds in the rear. "Monsieur duPont," observed one neighbor to another, "is the busiest man I have ever seen. He's always either starting fires or attending to them or putting them out."

When, at length, Monsieur duPont extinguished his last fire, the neighbors realized that Mme. Cuchet and her son were no longer to be seen. The winter winds began to blow and the villa was dark and deserted.

Landru was very busy in Paris that wartime winter of 1915—busy at his hot-car drop, busy carving the Sunday roast for the family and saying evening prayers for his wife and two daughters, busy writing letters to his sons at the front, and busy lining up another woman to take to the villa in Vermouillet. He rented a little flat near the Eiffel Tower and started auditioning applicants who were responding to a newspaper ad he was running for a children's nurse.

It wasn't until the spring of 1915, a year after he had first met Mme. Cuchet, that a fine, fat fish went for the bait. The lady this time was a Mme. Laborde-Line, a dark and handsome 45-year-old native of the Argentine who had been widowed for several years. Landru was quick to learn that her late husband, a hotel proprietor, had left her comparatively well off.

Landru was a great one for changing a subject. As he sat there in the little flat near the Eiffel Tower, focusing those dark brown eyes on Mme. Laborde-Line, he began to speak not of a situation as a children's nurse but a situation as a companion to *him*. He had, he confessed, lost his wife and was terribly lonely.

We begin to grasp the Landru technique with women along about here. Mme. Laborde-Line, like Mme. Cuchet and several others, was to divulge the details of their new-found happiness to relatives and friends who were one day to relay the details to Commissioner Jean Belin of the French Sûreté.

The official records of the Sûreté were one day to disclose that between 1914 and 1919, Henri Désiré Landru had relations with no less

233

than 284 women. Landru, says Commissioner Belin in his memoirs, must have been "amazingly virile to meet their sexual requirements." Amazingly virile, indeed! For he ran up that score not as a young man, but as a man in his middle years. It seemed always to be springtime for Henri.

To Mme. Laborde-Line, Landru, alias duPont, was an operative of the French Secret Service. Operative duPont, Mme. Laborde-Line and her friends were secretly informed, had just returned from Occupied France where, while behind the enemy lines, he had lost his identity papers, a little technicality that would hold up the marriage ceremony. And then, one fine Saturday in June, he established her in the villa at Vermouillet.

The villagers of Vermouillet were fascinated by the appearance of Mme. Laborde-Line. The lady, who was fond of flowers, frequently appeared in the garden of the villa, attired in a handsome, bright-blue dressing gown while gathering blooms for the breakfast table.

In July, the neighbors, who had grown accustomed to admiring Mme. Laborde-Line's gorgeous blue dressing gown when she went into the garden of a morning, noticed that she no longer seemed to be in residence at the villa. Then one night Landru started those fires again. By dawn the fires had died out, but the next night they started up again. The following morning the fires were out and the villa seemed to be deserted.

A month later, Landru reappeared with a remarkably homely woman. This third woman appeared in the garden one morning wearing a lovely bright blue dressing gown—the very same dressing gown, the villagers suspected, that the *second* woman had worn.

The last week in August, the fires behind the villa started up again. On the last day of the month, Landru called on the landlord. His term at the villa was up and he had come to return the key.

The landlord, a curious man, asked Landru about the three women and the fires. Landru looked levelly at the man. "I suppose," he said, "I shall have to tell you." He reached into his pocket and flashed the credentials—or what seemed to be the credentials—of the French Secret Police. The three women and the youth? Monsieur duPont's operatives. The fires? To burn secret documents that were never to fall under the gaze of unfriendly eyes. And then Monsieur duPont said he must be off—off on another mission for *la belle France. "Adieu, Monsieur. Adieu!"*

Now we find Landru back in Paris, presenting himself at the Banque de France as Monsieur duPont, a lawyer with a power-of-attorney signed by a Mme. Marie Angélique Guillin. Landru, explaining to an official of the bank that Mme. Guillin had suffered a paralytic stroke, cleaned out the lady's account.

After he returned to Paris from Vermouillet, Landru, possibly feeling a sense of invincibility, decided to make Bluebearding his life's work. He sold his garage at Neuilly, and hired a little office in the heart of Paris. There, under the alias of François duPont, he settled down to business.

We might at this point look into the background of Landru, the better to understand what made the remarkable little man tick. Henri was born in 1869 in a bourgeois section of Paris, the only child of an iron worker and a seamstress. Henri was small and frail and didn't mix with other children. He stayed to himself and proved to be an excellent student in school.

As Henri neared his teens, he became a voracious reader, especially of poetry. He had a special fondness for anything dramatic and colorful. Sometimes he dressed up as a knight and went around the neighborhood plunging a sword into imaginary enemies. At 14, Henri had a remarkably sweet voice. This, coupled with a curiously pious streak in the lad, resulted in his becoming a choir boy in the church of St. Louis-en-l'Ile, not far from Notre Dame.

Landru's father, who seems to have been an intelligent man, was anxious for little Henri to escape a life of smoke and grime such as his own. He encouraged the boy to get a superior education. Thus Henri easily breezed through the stiff entrance examinations at the Ecole des Arts-et-Métiers and began to study for a career as a mechanical engineer.

Henri was only a year into his studies when practically overnight his soprano voice cracked and changed to a deep, rich tone. A girl his own age—Marie Remy, the talkative daughter of a man who ran a prosperous laundry—heard Henri's voice, saw his remarkable eyes, and fell in love with him. Henri reciprocated the girl's feelings.

Within six weeks of their meeting, Marie informed Henri that she had been greeted by an unpleasant lunar surprise, adding that she presumed Henri would do right by her. Henri, who even then seemed hardly to blink his eyes, just stared at the girl, said nothing, and departed. When, a couple of days later, he learned that Marie's father was muttering into his wine, Henri abandoned his studies and found asylum by enlisting in the French Army.

235

After three years of the Army, Henri, 24-years-old and full-grown at 5 feet, 2 inches, wanted out. He communicated with Marie's father and informed him that he would marry his daughter if the old man, who swung a little weight, would get him sprung from the service. Marie's father was only too glad to oblige. His daughter had given birth to Henri's child, a daughter who was now 2 years old, and the marriage of Henri and Marie would serve the twofold purpose of legitimatizing the baby and making an honest woman of Marie.

The new family went to live in a couple of rooms in Clichy and Henri, who had turned out to be a whizz at figures, got a job as a book-keeper in a mercantile house. He looked, talked and acted like the classic conception of a counting-house drudge—pallid, unobtrusive, and dressed in a glazed suit of funereal black, with high stiff collar and dusty derby. To add to his age and dignity, he sprouted a little mustache.

A year after his marriage, Henri's wife gave birth to a son and, a year after that, to a second son. So there was little Henri, at the age of 26, working for a niggardly employer, having to wash diapers at night, and having to wheel the two small kids in a big baby carriage on Sundays while his daughter tagged along. This was hardly the existence Henri had dreamed of before he had been unfortunate enough to impregnate Marie. Marie, who chattered more and more as time passed, was living proof of the Chinese proverb that the tongue of a woman is a sword that never rusts.

The years passed, Henri lost all his hair, and, when he was 30, his employer went bankrupt and Henri was out of a job. Henri started to work on a motor bicycle invention and he borrowed enough money from his father-in-law to set up a small shop. But before the project got under way, the shop and everything in it burned to the ground.

It was the great Exhibition in Paris in 1900 that really vacuum-packed the fate of Henri Désiré Landru and, according to the Sûreté, the fate of at least ten unsuspecting females. Little Henri, wandering around the Exhibition, saw a whole new world opened up to him—the glamorous world of wealth, luxury, and pretty perfumed women. He didn't have much of a struggle convincing himself that fate had dealt him cards off the bottom, so he engineered a deal whereby he tried to swindle a widow out of her marriage settlement. The scheme backfired, and Henri was arrested and tossed into the jug, where he stayed for two years. No sooner was he released than he resumed his swindling attempts. He was a miserable failure. Between 1900 and 1910 he was convicted no less than five times on various swindling charges. Between spells of imprisonment he managed to sire still another daughter, making him the father of four children.

By 1914, the gendarmes had enough complaints on Landru as a confidence man to get him convicted *in absentia* and sentenced to Devil's Island. The little man was in a corner. Legitimate work was hard to come by. He was now 45, and illegitimate work offered him his only opportunity to prepare for a rainy day. So he changed his name to François Petit, encouraged his little mustache and sprouted whiskers and a beard. That's when he knocked off three women and a boy in the villa at Vermouillet.

Upon returning to Paris and deciding to go into the Bluebearding business on a large scale, Landru sat in his little office near the Eiffel Tower reading and writing. What he read were newspaper advertisements from women who sought positions as a governess, a children's nurse, or who were advertising for a husband. What he wrote were replies to the ads. During this phase of his career Landru began to keep a little notebook in which he carefully recorded fiscal data, physical descriptions, and other facts relating to the women with whom he was corresponding.

Late in November 1915, we find Landru journeying to the bucolic hamlet of Gambais, some 35 miles from Paris. Gambais, of all the hamlets within easy reach of the metropolis, seemed singularly suited for what Landru had in mind. Although only an hour from Paris, it was really a century distant. Its ancient, moldy stone houses were without heat, electricity or plumbing, and its residents moved around like sleepwalkers.

Under his duPont alias, Landru rented a four-room stone house on the edge of the hamlet. There was a small, walled garden behind the house and, to one side of the garden, an old cemetery. Not far distant was the dense forest of Rambouillet.

The house at Gambais was musty and forbidding. There was a large stone slab in the cellar which simply fascinated Landru. The first time he saw it Landru walked back and forth, stopping at various points in the cellar to stand stock still, his right hand on his chin, appraising the slab with those little unblinking eyes of his.

Divulging that he was an inventor working on a secret wartime project for the government, Landru told the landlord he would take out the kitchen stove and replace it, at government expense, with a new and larger one. What he replaced the kitchen stove with was not another stove, but a furnace with a huge chimney that rose high in the air above the roof.

In December, shortly before Christmas, M. duPont started the first fire in the furnace in Gambais. He kindled it just as the dusk was deepening on a raw afternoon, and soon clouds of thick, black smoke were issuing from the tall chimney. All that night, and all the next day, and through the next night smoke continued to pour out of the chimney. The wind carried some of it into the hamlet of Gambais. "What is that inventor burning in that place?" one villager, holding his nose, asked a neighbor.

"It smells," was the answer, "like an animal's horn."

The smoke continued, intermittently, all winter long. DuPont, busy little man, darted around the bleak countryside in a small, fast, red car. Often he had a trunk or some other large piece of luggage, strapped to the tonneau. There were stretches of days when the little stone house was silent and dark. M. duPont was probably in the city.

When he returned to Gambais from a trip to Paris, M. duPont was always seen in company of a woman. The nearest railroad station to Gambais was at Houdan, four miles distant, and duPont would always hire the town taxi to drive him to the little stone house.

One night, in the early spring of 1916, some four months after the furnace fires had started, the taxi driver dropped into the inn in Gambais after delivering duPont and a lady to the stone house. "How many women is that you have taken there?" the innkeeper asked him.

The driver said that duPont had arrived in Houdan with a different woman on an average of three times a month for the four months. The innkeeper asked the driver if he thought that the women were mistresses of duPont. *"Mon Dieu!"* replied the driver. "Have you seen any of their *faces?"*

Who, then, *were* the women? "I think they are spies for our country," said the driver. "From what I hear him saying to them I would say they are spies and he is their master." But where, the innkeeper wanted to know, did the women go? What happened to them? M. du-Pont had mentioned to the driver that he drove them to the railroad station at Versailles, some 25 miles from Gambais.

When summer came, and the taxi driver was meeting duPont and a lady every few days, the smoke issuing from the chimney of the stone house became something of a regional problem. The combination of the smoke and the hot weather was nauseating.

But the villagers were loath to complain. Who would complain

238

about a man so dedicated to his country? Even as the dogs of the hamlet lay panting in the shade, duPont was darting around the countryside like something possessed, either delivering a trunk somewhere or carrying a load of coal for that furnace in the kitchen.

As the leaves fluttered from the calendar, Landru continued to arrive every ten days or so with a new woman. The sickeningly-sweet smoke continued to issue from that tall chimney until January 1919—more than three years after the little man had first put in an appearance in Gambais.

But now that the war was over and the armistice was signed, M. duPont's work in Gambais was over. He turned the key of the house over to the landlord. He would not return to Gambais, he feared. There was other work for him to do in Paris, now that his labors in Gambais were completed.

And so we have Henri Désiré Landru, at the age of 49, back in Paris, ready to welcome his sons home from the wars. He was a fairly well-fixed man now. He had, during the three years when he had rented that murder house at Gambais, managed to dispose of a good portion of the furniture and personal belongings of his victims and to channel their stocks and bank accounts to himself. He had, under more than a score of names, safe deposit boxes in Paris banks and large quantities of clothing, furniture and jewelry in storage.

Landru realized, now the war was over, that the risk would be great if he continued Bluebearding; so he wiped his hands of the whole business.

But if he was no longer interested in what he had done, Commissioner Belin of the Sûreté was. The war over, Belin could now devote his attention to other matters. Thus he became increasingly fascinated by quite a few disappearance cases that had piled up on his desk during the international conflict.

The disappearances seemed to fall into a pattern. A small, ginger-bearded man in middle years had materialized from somewhere or other, romanced a well-fixed widow or spinster, and that's the last that had been seen of *that* lady.

Belin went further than alerting the gendarmes to be on the lookout for the bearded one. He enlisted the aid of friends and relatives of the missing women who had met the little man before the women had vanished.

One day in April 1919, a sister of a widow named Marchadier—a widow who had, after a whirlwind romance with a man named duPont, vanished along with her three pet dogs, into thin air—saw Landru making a purchase in a china shop on the Rue de Rivoli and ran to the gendarmes. Belin learned at the china shop that the hairy-faced customer, who called himself M. duPont, lived in a flat on the Rue de Rochechouart.

That night, when duPont was out, Belin gave the flat a toss. He found in a trunk an assortment of false teeth, false hair, and bustles. Under a mattress he found a little black notebook that identified du-Pont as Landru, the fugitive con man, and which contained a diary illuminating the dark recesses of the little man's past. The names of the missing women in Belin's files were the same as some of the names in Landru's diary.

Henri Désiré Landru found Belin waiting for him when he returned to the flat that night. "I believe," said Belin, a blunt man, "you have murdered several women."

Landru just stared unblinkingly at the commissioner. Then he said, "Of course it is your privilege to believe anything you wish to believe. But I must warn you that you need not expect any cooperation from me."

And so Landru was thrown into the bastille on the old confidence-man charge, to which he had been sentenced to Devil's Island, while Belin and a corps of men began to follow the leads in the diary. They went to Vermouillet and dug up the grounds around the villa, looking for evidence of the murder of the three women and the boy they knew had gone there. They found nothing except the stories of the neighbors, which now took on a sinister significance that had not occurred to them when Landru had been in residence in the villa starting those fires.

Belin's men fared a little better, but not much, in Gambais. There, in the grounds back of the little stone house, they found some pieces of bone, but such small pieces that any allegation that they were of human origin would be open to courtroom challenge by a smart defense mouthpiece. They found the remains of three dogs, probably those of the widow Marchadier, with wire looped around the necks. Belin suspected that Landru had strangled his women with wire.

There were bloodstains on that stone slab in the cellar—the slab that had so fascinated Landru when he had rented the place. Belin suspected that Landru had, after killing his women, dissected them on the slab and then thrown the pieces into the furnace and, shaking down the furnace, scattered the ashes through the forest of Rambouillet.

Belin ran some tests on the big furnace in the cottage and the results were interesting. It consumed a sheep's head for Belin in a quarter of an hour, leaving only the teeth. In an hour and fifteen minutes, it utterly consumed a leg of mutton, bones and all.

When Landru went on trial for murder in the ancient court room at Versailles, his counselor was Maitre de Moro-Giafferi, a Corsican who was generally considered the cagiest criminal lawyer in the Republic. The prosecution's case was purely circumstantial. Ten missing women out of a possible hundred or so, were connected to Landru by friends and relatives who got into the witness box and identified Henri as the person with whom the women had last been seen. Then the Republic connected personal articles, found in Landru's possession or sold by the man, with the missing women.

The story about that furnace at Gambais was dwelled on in sinister detail, and fragments of bone found on the grounds were introduced as being part of the remains of the ten women. The villagers in Gambais went into the witness box to describe to the jurors the terrible stench that the winds had carried into the village while Landru was in residence in the stone house.

Landru made a splendid witness for himself. He freely admitted having known the ten women the Republic charged him with murdering. He admitted swindling them, too. But did that prove murder? He gave the spectators a belly laugh when, after admitting affairs with almost three hundred women, he stared at the ceiling, wet his lips, and remarked, *"Mon Dieu!* What will my wife say!"

Yes, Landru made a splendid witness for himself—but not quite splendid enough. Somehow, the jurors got the impression that Landru had experienced no more compunction in killing a woman than a farmer did in slaughtering a hog. And so the jurors found Henri guilty and one dawn in February 1922, in the ancient courtyard at Versailles, he went to the guillotine—almost seven years from that day when he had tipped his hat to Mme. Cuchet on the boulevard.

Years later, when Commissioner Belin wrote his memoirs, he had this to say:

"I remember I had once signed myself by the name of Landru instead of my own in a hotel register some years before when I had gone away for a week end with a girl friend. I have often thought of the complications this trifling incident might have had for me, or, for that matter, for Landru."

PRINCE MIKE

by Alva Johnston

Prince Michael Romanoff, the leading impostor of the twentieth century, has gone to pieces. The most iridescent scapegrace of our time has disintegrated into a successful businessman. This character, who was worthy to associate with the King and the Duke on Huck Finn's raft, today owns and operates Romanoff's Restaurant at 326 North Rodeo Drive, Beverly Hills, California.

Mike was the cousin of the late Czar Nicholas. He was the morganatic son of Czar Alexander III. He was the man who killed Rasputin and the son of the man who killed Rasputin. He was Prince Obolensky, Count Gladstone and Count de Rochemonde; Captain Dmitri, Captain Shaughnessy and Captain Chitterin; Rockwell Kent, William K. Vanderbilt and William Rockefeller. Also Prof. John William Adams, of Yale, Arthur Wellesley, Willoughby de Burke, William A. Wellington, Fleming, Brighton, Ferguson and Gerguson. The entire cast of characters has now boiled down into a restaurateur.

"Restaurateur" used to be the most abusive epithet in the prince's vocabulary. The first Hollywood exposure of the scintillating mountebank was made in 1927 by Gen. Theodor Lodijensky, an aristocratic Russian refugee who ran the Russian Eagle Restaurant in New York City and later in Hollywood. The general presented film executives, who employed the prince as an authority on Russia, with evidence that Mike was neither a prince nor a Russian; that he had been in jail five times in England; that he was described by the French police as a habitual perpetrator of *"escroquerie,"* meaning "picayune fraud"; that he was known to the New York police as Harry Gerguson, of the lower East Side origin—No. 63,967 in the rogues' gallery.

The film executives called in Mike to listen to General Lodijensky's story.

The prince was amused. "I believe you're a restaurateur," he said.

The aristocratic Russian cringed as if Mike had put the brand of Cain on him. The executives squirmed. The prince dismissed them with a careless flip of his hand—a characteristic Romanoff gesture said to have originated in Peter the Great's habit of throwing beef bones over his shoulder at state banquets.

Mike became a scourge of restaurateurs when he was born into the Romanoff family at the age of thirty years. He has probably had more champagne and pheasant on bad checks than any other living man. He has been "in residence," as he calls it, on bad-check charges in Paris, Cannes, Grasse, New York, Cambridge, Kansas City, Salt Lake City, Los Angeles and many other places.

During his palmy days, the prince sold hand-painted old masters for Fifth Avenue dealers. He spent several months in the Tombs after pocketing the proceeds of a sale of art for H. Michaelyan. The dealer said later that nothing had ever hurt him like prosecuting the prince.

"He is one of the most remarkable men alive," said Michaelyan. "I believe his name will go down in history. Maybe mine will go down in history with him."

Michaelyan is a disappointed man. He has little chance of going down the ages with a restaurateur. Others who hoped for an honorable mention in the Romanoff epic have the same complaint.

There are extenuating circumstances. Mike grosses more than $25,000 a month. He has more celebrities in his restaurant than his adopted ancestors ever had in their palaces. Nevertheless, there is a tragic side to it. It is like Casanova's sad end as a respectable librarian or Micawber's finish as a prosperous judge.

A few years ago, when his life was one exposure after another, Mike used to say that he was a social barometer—that only the phonies and upstarts couldn't afford to be seen with him. Today he is a sort of barometer of sycophancy—social climbers feel they have made the grade when they receive a curt nod or a few gruff words from the illustrious publican.

His list of backers is perhaps the most glittering catalogue of big names that ever supported a small enterprise. Most of the backers, however, contributed only fifty dollars apiece—the price of one share of stock. Few of them expected a restaurant to develop out of it. They regarded it as one of Mike's scientific methods of making a touch. Many framed the certificate as a landmark in the art of dignified mooching. The biggest investors were Robert Benchley and John Hay Whitney, $350 each; Charlie Chaplin and Rex St. Cyr, $250 each; James Cagney, $200.

Charlie Chaplin's interest in Mike is obvious. The character that Mike created and the little tramp that Chaplin created are practically identical twins. They have the same physique and psychology, the same resourcefulness, audacity, nonchalance and intrepidity. The little prince has foiled the Federal authorities as frequently as the little tramp has baffled Mack Sennett policemen. The ruling motive of both was to find a place in a social system which ceaselessly threw them out.

Benchley backed Romanoff enterprises for years. For Mike's use on one of his stowaway voyages to France, Benchley wrote a To Whom it May Concern letter, enjoining the officials of all nations not to bother the prince. The letter stated that Mike had not stowed away thoughtlessly, but was engaged in important research work on the stowaway problem.

Mike sold a little more than 6000 dollars' worth of stock and induced a capitalist to build the restaurant. Shortage of funds caused the prince to act as his own interior desecrator. He beautified the place chiefly with portraits of himself. He got most of his tableware from a five-and-ten store, traded the furniture of his apartment for a refrigerator, borrowed a few bottles of liquor, and obtained the use of $250 for one night, so that he could make change.

The first night was big. The high spot of the evening came when a waiter presented the first bank check from a customer to the new restaurateur. The prince, who has been no mean artist in passing bad checks himself, seemed stunned to find himself on the receiving end of suspicious paper. He peered at the check like a connoisseur expertizing a dubious Rembrandt. Pinching a corner of it between his thumb and forefinger, he held it up to the light and peered at it again. His eyes became unfocused and his jaws worked. It was like the fluttering of the eagle that was hit by an arrow tipped with its own feathers. Finally Mike pulled himself together, gave a brisk nod and scribbled "O.K. MR" on the check.

Mike is a perfect restaurateur, except that he has never learned the technique of measuring out his courtesy in exact accord with the customer's importance. The best tables and service go to the prince's oldest followers, whether they are riding high or not. One night a waiter hurried to inform the prince that Jack Benny, Robert Taylor and Barbara Stanwyck were waiting for a table. The waiter, fresh from New York, where many a restaurateur would pay a thousand dollars to get such a party into his place, expected the prince to rush up to them, bowing and scraping and making a tremendous fuss.

244

"The hell with 'em," said Mike.

Mike's neighborhood consisted chiefly of vacant lots when he opened his restaurant. Within a year the street was dotted with little temples of commerce. Jewelers, art dealers and smart haberdashers moved in, so that their shop windows could catch the eye of Mike's rich clientele. He doubled property values in his vicinity.

Even in his own phoniest days, Mike was considered an infallible authority on other phonies. On his first arrival in New York as Prince Michael Romanoff in 1922, he was in the midst of a large migration of Russian noblemen, genuine and otherwise. He conducted a sort of Heralds' College in New York speakeasies, authenticating some of his rival princes, exposing others. At the period when princes were being imported from the Caucasus by matrimonial brokers for the heiress market, Mike was called on to appraise one shipment of them.

"They're perfectly genuine," said Mike. "Genuine Caucasian princes. Everybody in the Caucasus that owns two cows is a prince. It is a valid title, like your title of mister."

When one of his rivals died, Mike reported that the father of the deceased prince had inquired anxiously, "Do I inherit the title?"

Mike's face gives no clue to his origin. Amateur ethnologists have puzzled about it for years. He made a mistake when he stepped into the vacancy in the Romanoff dynasty, as there is no trace of the Slav in him; he would have been more plausible as the Great Mogul or the Akhoond of Swat. His eyes are black, his complexion leathery, his hair tightly crinkled and black, except for a sprinkling of gray, his nose long, straight and somewhat dented by knuckles and monogrammed by seal rings. His voice, a bassoon with an Oxford accent, throws no light on his origin. Neither does his carriage, which is the typical royal slouch, head bent forward, arms hanging well in front of the body, exactly as seen in the old newsreels of George V and Nicholas II.

The most useful key to the Romanoff mystery is held by the residents of Hillsboro, Illinois, a town of five thousand about fifty miles northeast of St. Louis. The prince arrived there in 1904 as one of a batch of New York orphans who were being settled in rural communities. Mike, then known as Harry Gerguson, was taken in charge by Judge Kronck, a St. Louis lawyer who had retired to a farm near Hillsboro. The judge sent him to a rural school. Here Mike adopted his first alias. The name of Gerguson sounded uncouth to Mike's fellow-students and subjected him to ridicule. He changed it to Ferguson.

After a few months, Mike, or Harry, quit the Kronck farm and returned to Hillsboro. Here he ran errands for meals, and slept in the Presbyterian churchyard. The idea of a boy's sleeping out in the open —an unheard-of thing in Hillsboro—excited general sympathy. Family after family informally adopted the boy, but these arrangements soon broke up, both sides complaining of intolerable grievances.

At Hillsboro he attended the seventh grade and is remembered for his devotion to the Frank Carpenter geography books. Continuing these studies in later years, he became an encyclopedia of travel. Experts who attempted to trap Mike in his tales of adventure in strange places found that it was like trying to trap Baedeker's.

Mike had a characteristic dream life at Hillsboro, but he developed no fancy lineage there. The nobility had been queered with the youth of America a few years earlier by the epidemic of little Lord Fauntleroys. The most illustrious creatures on earth in the imagination of boys of fourteen or fifteen were the congressional pages. One day Mike bade farewell to his schoolteachers and friends, saying he was on the way to Washington to accept an appointment as a congressional page. He turned up a few days later at Litchfield, ten miles from Hillsboro, where he remained until he was haled into court for punching the superintendent of schools in the nose. He was then sent back to a New York orphanage.

On March 20, 1923, Harry came back to Hillsboro with a monocle, Malacca stick and Oxford accent, and delivered a platform lecture on the war. He was a British lieutenant and had another man's military papers to prove it. A few days later the St. Louis newspapers announced that St. Louis was entertaining royalty and printed pictures of Prince Michael Romanoff. Hillsboro people recognized the face in the papers as that of little Harry Gerguson, or Ferguson, and the prince was exposed by the St. Louis *Post-Dispatch*.

On October 20, 1936, the little prince stopped at Hillsboro on his way to Hollywood. Running true to form, he was a greater celebrity after exposure than before.

Mike was nineteen years old when he graduated from the New York orphanage. Having observed that the Oxford accent was the heaviest social artillery a man could have, he crossed the Atlantic on a cattle boat in order to acquire it. He spent years in England doggedly polishing himself. In 1915 he tried himself out prematurely on English society under the name of Willoughby de Burke and landed in jail. Ordered out of England in 1921 for impersonating and marauding, Mike became a spot of color at the Ritz bar in Paris, where he was taken up by wealthy Americans. Bad-check trouble in France caused him to migrate to the United States.

On his arrival here, he was detained at Ellis Island. The authorities thought that, although Mike had been in a New York orphan asylum at the age of three, his birthplace was Vilna. He was ordered deported for moral turpitude on his statement that he had spent eight years in a German prison for killing a German baron in a duel at Heidelberg. A little later the prince disappeared from Ellis Island; the Romanoff legend has it that he swam across New York harbor with a silk hat on, but the immigration men said he stowed away on a ferryboat.

A few days after his escape, Mike changed into Prince Obolensky. New York newspapers printed a sympathetic interview with Obolensky on the troubles of an impoverished nobleman seeking employment. Everybody thought it a hilarious joke, he said, when he offered himself as a secretary, a clerk or a laborer. The interview won him some gaudy week ends, but no work. From there he went to St. Paul, where he was feted by railroad and lumber kings. One of his rich friends sent him to the Graduate School of Arts and Sciences at Harvard. He represented the university on a chess team and made a prodigious figure on the campus with his monocle, silk hat and sponge-bag knee pants, until he was expelled for falsely representing himself to have been an Oxford student. A brief period of splendor at Newport ended in exposure at Reginald C. Vanderbilt's *bal masque*. The gilded youth of Dan Moriarity's speakeasy in New York made a comrade of Mike. Paul Mellon, son of Andrew W. Mellon, took the prince on a visit to Pittsburgh. Old families along the Hudson adopted Mike for spells of varying length.

During vacations from the estates of millionaires, the prince lived by the sweat of his fountain pen. He seemed to have an honest conviction that he was the injured party every time he cashed a bad check; that he was doing himself an injustice by parting with his autograph so cheaply. After he had thoroughly papered New York, he went west in 1927 and papered Hollywood. He returned to Hollywood in 1931 and repapered it.

Hotel men honor Mike because he saved them millions of dollars by forcing them to reorganize their protective system against agile fountain pens and itinerant potentates.

Mike outmaneuvered the Federal authorities for the last time in 1932. Claiming to be an American newspaperman assigned to interview Andrew W. Mellon, he stowed away on the *Europa* at Cherbourg and

247

eluded the immigration inspectors in New York harbor. The little prince was unable to live without Royal Yacht pipe tobacco, which costs ten dollars a pound—a habit which he contracted, he said, from David, as he calls the present Duke of Windsor. He went to a Fifth Avenue shop for a tin of it and was arrested.

Federal Judge John C. Knox and Assistant U.S. Attorney William B. Herlands took a sympathetic view of the case. Herlands described Mike as "a product of our public institutions" and said that he had "never had a chance." He predicted that the defendant would go straight if released on a suspended sentence. Judge Knox ordered that no further effort should be made to deport Mike, but sentenced him to three months in jail for perjury. Romanoff, in order to shield friends who had helped to smuggle him in from the *Europa,* had falsely testified before a grand jury that he had entered this country by way of Canada. The judge and the prosecutor personally urged Mike to mend his ways. This humane treatment took effect. Romanoff has never been in any serious trouble since.

After a couple of difficult years in New York, Mike turned farmer. John Walters, a New York broker, bought an estate called Powhatan near Fredericksburg, Virginia, and put the prince in charge of it in 1935. The farmhouse was in ruins. Sheep were living in it when Mike arrived there under the name of John William Adams. The prince, an indefatigable worker when the fit takes hold of him, repaired the house, cleared a field and made a road. His chief companions at Powhatan were a mare named Betty and a cat named Gerguson. Friends from Washington, who visited Mike shortly after Christmas, 1935, found that he had set up two Christmas trees decorated with tinsel, colored globes and artificial snow for the mare and the cat, and had made presents of a package of sugar lumps to Betty and a quart of cream to Gerguson. Word spread, however, that Prof. John William Adams, of Yale, had isolated himself at Powhatan and was writing The Philosophy of History.

Mike quit Powhatan in 1936. Arriving in New York, the prince said he was en route to Hollywood to make a pile of money, so that he could retire to his Virginia estate. Two friends gave Mike sixty dollars one night on his promise to take a bus westward the following day; the following day the two friends discovered Mike in the Canadian minister's box at an international polo game. Other friends gave him fresh money and a broken-down auto, and Mike made his way to Hollywood by slow degrees.

The first man he met there—Leo Morrison—lent him ten dollars and took him to the Clover Club, where the cream of Hollywood welcomed him deliriously. It was Mike's return from Elba. He was such an attraction that the management instructed a croupier to let him win small sums in return for honoring them with his visits. This was Mike's livelihood for months.

Mike gradually established a good credit rating for himself in Hollywood. Frankly admitting that he had been a dangerous risk in the past, he asked Jim Oviatt, a leading clothier, to trust him with the meteoric wardrobe which is considered necessary to a meteoric career in Hollywood. Oviatt turned him into a sparkling bird of paradise, and later told everybody that no other customer had ever been so punctual in his monthly payments. Dave Chasen let Mike eat and drink on the cuff for months at a time, but the prince turned up periodically with a surprisingly good check and settled his account. From time to time Mike confounded old friends by repaying personal loans.

Some students of the prince's career resented his transformation into an honest burgher, but the sordid truth is that the prince always had a bourgeois streak. Every now and then he used to disappear from New York, return with the proceeds of some obscure transaction and celebrate Restitution Day by paying back loans, squaring bad checks and reveling in middle-class integrity. He was a share-the-wealther when he had it.

The finest example of Mike's punctiliousness in money matters took place on the night of the opening of the United Artists picture, *Catherine the Great,* in New York, February 13, 1934. Monroe Greenthal, the U.A. publicity chief, felt that the *première* of the movie about the great Romanoff empress would not be complete without the great Romanoff impostor. Mike agreed to appear if the picture company furnished him with the following inventory—a stunning blonde, $150 for a night's spending money, a Rolls-Royce with a liveried chauffeur and footman, the footman to wear a tan stovepipe hat, tan coat with gold buttons, scarlet vest and knee-high tan boots with buff tops. All the items were furnished. After the *première* the prince took his consort, one of the reigning Powers models, to the Stork Club and El Morocco, where he drank double healths to Great-great-great-aunt Catherine until he had faithfully disbursed all the spending money except thirty dollars, with which he tipped his waiters, chauffeur and footman. Going home, he found that the management had plugged the keyhole to his door for nonpayment of rent. He spent the rest of the night in his old Winter Palace, the subway.

Mike has a lofty contempt for the present generation of frauds and mountebanks. They have never learned their trade, according to Mike; anybody can read them like a book. One day when he was haranguing about the incompetency of the current crop of phonies, the prince was asked what advice he would give to a young phony just starting out.

"I would advise him to stay out of it," said Mike. "There's too much competition."

Mike will probably never quite get over being a Romanoff. His imposture was so thorough that he imposed on himself. When he had a room to live in, it was decorated with photographs of Nicholas II and his family. In one of these the Czar and Czarina were surrounded by relatives; Mike used to point to a small, blurred, unrecognizable figure, saying, "Don't I look ridiculous?"

Once when he was in Jim Moriarity's speakeasy just off Fifth Avenue, immigration officers arrived with a warrant for Mike's arrest. Moriarity told the prince he could escape through the kitchen.

"A Romanoff escape through a kitchen!" exclaimed Mike.

"Your uncle, the Czar, did," said Moriarity.

Honoring this precedent, Mike darted out through the kitchen.

Recently "Prince" Michael Romanoff was granted U.S. citizenship by special act of Congress. "I couldn't prove I was born here," he says, "but they couldn't prove I wasn't. So now I shall become the white sepulchre of respectability, complete with passport."

ESCAPE BY COFFIN

by David Porter

Will Nevison, a seventeenth-century Yorkshire highwayman, was so efficient at his chosen trade of robbery that he achieved what has since become one central facet of the American Dream at the tender age of twenty-one: he made his pile and retired. But, like many a retired businessman, he found the life of leisure a bit boring. Soon he was back on the road. The price of his continued success was steep and dangerous —a high, tempting price put on his head by the Law. In 1676, when Nevison was a graybeard of twenty-seven, one of his associates succumbed to the Judas-lure and Nevison was ambushed, seized and locked in Leicester prison, in a cell he shared with a half-dozen other prisoners.

To make escape impossible, the jailers kept Nevison chained, both to the walls of his cell and to heavy weights; and double-strength guards were on duty twenty-four hours a day. Friends, however, were permitted to visit Nevison during these last days before he would be tried and hanged. What Nevison needed most urgently, he told the first friend who came calling, was a doctor, a sympathetic doctor who could put on an authoritative "show." For his health seemed to have taken a sudden turn for the worse.

A few days later the doctor appeared. He examined Nevison and diagnosed his ailment: the plague. When the prison authorities were informed of this, they immediately had Nevison removed—by the doctor, not the guards—to a cell of his own. But they made the doctor chain his friend Nevison quite as securely as before. And guards were again posted right outside the cell.

The doctor visited his patient-friend several times a day. On one visit he brought along a medical colleague, and the latter made a particularly thorough examination of the sick man. All during the examination the two "physicians" loudly discussed Nevison's symptoms, comparing them with those of other plague patients they had attended and speculating on the chances of an epidemic developing in the prison among guards and inmates. The guards listened fearfully to the physicians' words, their attention distracted from what was actually taking place inside the cell: one of the doctors, using a small brush was painting Nevison's body with blue spots—a well-known fatal symptom which generally made its appearance during the last stages of the plague.

On their way out, the doctors—shaking their heads sadly—told the prison keeper that Nevison was definitely dying of the plague. The keeper asked the official visiting prison physician to take a look at the highwayman. And the latter did just that: took one quick look, caught a glimpse of the blue spots, backed quickly out of the cell without so much as touching the prisoner's cot—and confirmed the diagnosis.

The following day Nevison's faithful doctor-friend came again, administered a long-lasting knock-out potion and, a few minutes later, declared the prisoner dead. He added that the sooner they got the body out of the prison the less chance there would be of a plague epidemic developing.

Within the hour an inquest was being held in the corridor outside the dead man's cell. The official prison doctor testified to having seen the blue spots on Nevison's body which were certain signs of approaching death. That was good enough for the officials; highwayman Nevison, dead by the plague, and good riddance, was their verdict.

251

An hour later the doctor-friend of Nevison's was supervising the removal of the body. Burial at the outer edge of the village graveyard—to which the highwayman's body was relegated on sufferance—took place shortly after nightfall that same day. John Nevison was officially dead.

But John Nevison's "ghost" was destined for an active and merry life, if not a long one. The very next night, in fact, Nevison's "ghost" raked in a fat haul from a group of travellers along a nearby highway.

Some years later, however, in 1685, when he had reached the ripe middle age of forty-five, Nevison made the mistake of trusting a woman once too often. While he was sleeping soundly in her house she turned him in for the reward. This time neither physicians nor artistically painted blue spots could help him. In March of that year in a widely-attended hanging ceremony the "ghost" of John Nevison was finally laid for good.

In life, that is. In ballad and prose it took Nevison just a few short weeks to attain new stature as a "gentleman-highwayman"—tall, handsome, valiant, the finest horseman of the age. And, in due time, legend, accepted as fact by many, termed him "chivalrous" and "wronged," a man who had been pardoned by the King for services rendered, who had reformed and had been hanged illegally (for a crime he had not committed) by someone bent on personal revenge, because Nevison had bested him in rivalry for a titled lady's affections.

Thus, Nevison, who carried out one of the most deceptive escapes in history, continues his deceptions even today, nearly three hundred years after his death.

SULTAN OF THE SKIN TRADE

by Donovan Fitzpatrick

Shortly before 1 p.m. on September 1, 1935, a man in prison clothing crawled out onto a third-floor ledge of the Federal House of Detention on West 11th Street in New York's Greenwich Village. Agile as a mountain goat, in spite of his enormous belly, he teetered on his precarious perch and began to polish a window industriously with a large white cloth. He immediately caught the attention of the half-dozen loungers in front of a saloon across the street, because, despite the narrow ledge, he wore no safety belt.

The 40 or 50 pedestrians who stopped to watch were so concerned with the window-washer's safety that they failed to notice a fantastic aspect of his performance: there was a heavy wire screen between him and the glass, and the ambitious gent was polishing nothing but thin air.

Suddenly he reached under his shirt, and, as his pot belly deflated like a pricked balloon, he pulled out a coil of white rope. The free end, weighted with a ball of tinfoil, snaked down the side of the prison wall to the ground. With the other end apparently anchored to something inside the window, the prisoner slid briskly down the rope. Landing cat-footed on the sidewalk, he whirled, grinned at the opened-mouthed spectators and disappeared around the corner.

Everyone was too stunned by the suddenness of the escape to think of chasing him. Finally one of the bar customers hurried around to the wicket window in the penitentiary door and said to the guard on duty: "Officer, did you know one of your prisoners just ran away?"

The wicket slammed shut. A few minutes later guards appeared at the third-floor window and hauled up the rope. The spectators, somewhat bemused, went their way. Not until they read the papers the next day did they learn they had been privileged to witness a virtuoso performance of Count Victor Lustig, one of the greatest confidence men, escape artists and counterfeiters of this or any other century.

In the 18 years he operated in America—between 1917 and 1935—Count Lustig pulled every confidence game known to the trade and a few he dreamed up himself. And when he turned his considerable talents to counterfeiting, he netted, at a conservative estimate, between four and five million dollars.

Thus, averaging better than $200,000 a year, Count Lustig was enabled to live in a manner befitting his aristocratic title. A handsome, vigorous man, he was of less than medium height, but graceful of movement as a fencer. Long, blondish sideburns gave his pale, serious face a continental touch. He was always faultlessly tailored, and his manners were impeccable, his poise awesome. He lived in the most luxurious hotels and dined in the toniest restaurants—except for those brief periods when he was temporarily installed in the pokey.

A pinch never really bothered Lustig. He was arrested 37 times in this country but, until the last one, he was convicted only once. That, ironically, was a minor rap on a morals charge, when he was caught in an Oklahoma City hotel room with a blonde not his wife. The other 36 times he either talked or bribed his way out of jail, or simply escaped.

253

The Secret Service agents, who had labored mightily or put the finger on the elusive count, were staggered by his unauthorized departure from the "escape-proof" West Street bastille, but they had to admit that Lustig had given them fair warning. When they'd caught him the previous May with $51,000 in counterfeit money, the dapper bunco artist had boasted he'd crash out. "The jail hasn't been built that can hold me, gentlemen," he had said. "I'll leave whenever it pleases me to do so."

He waited until two days before his trial to keep his promise. That noontime, when the rest of the prisoners went up to the roof for their daily exercise, the count pleaded indisposition and stayed in his cell. By a quarter to one, as he'd anticipated, some of the guards were on the roof, the rest were at lunch, and the corridor was empty. Victor Lustig reached under his mattress and took out a rope made of nine bed-sheets, tightly knotted together, which he'd acquired by keeping back one sheet every time the jailer came around to collect the dirty linen and pass out fresh. Tucking the rope under his shirt, he unlocked his cell and trotted down the corridor to the toilet. He cut the wire mesh over the window with pliers, tied one end of the rope to a water pipe and went into his window-washing act. The cops never did figure out where he got the pliers or the key to his cell door, and Lustig never enlightened them.

When the police learned that Lustig had been seen leaping into a black limousine which had been parked on West Street, they decided that he'd made it out of the city before the bridges, tunnels and railroads had been sealed off, and relaxed their search.

But Victor Lustig was, in fact, taking his ease in a rooming house in Greenwich Village, only a couple of blocks from the federal pen. Twenty minutes after he'd hopped into the limousine he had changed into a corduroy coat, paint-smeared trousers and a beret, and had rented a room under the name of Victor Miller, an artist recently arrived from the Midwest. His landlady thought he was charming. Women usually did.

Lustig was plentifully supplied with money, both genuine and phony, and he could have holed up in comfort until the heat abated a bit; but it was not his nature to stay in hiding very long. Like every top-flight con man, the thrill of the game was meat and drink to Lustig. Women, or even the big money itself, were secondary to the excitement of the caper, the intoxication of setting up a sucker and skillfully separating him from his bankroll.

So it was that a few nights later a certain Monsieur Robert Duval, the

254

eminent French banker, dropped in at an exclusive undercover gambling establishment on Park Avenue. Duval was a white-haired old gentleman of perhaps 60, somewhat feeble, but resplendent in elegant evening dress and with a roguish twinkle in his eyes for the ladies around the roulette table. He peeled a few large bills off the top of an enormous roll and bought $10,000 worth of chips.

Duval's luck was abominable, and by midnight he had to slip another 10 grand off the roll. But while his luck stayed bad, his good humor remained intact—he made little jokes with the other players and stood the house's best brandy for all who cared to join him.

By 2 in the morning his second pile of chips had melted. Duval chuckled ruefully and again reached for his bundle. "Zis time," he announced, "I weel make the serious play," and tossed $50,000 to the croupier.

An hour later the old gentleman had dropped another 10 grand. Suddenly he glanced at his watch. *"Mon Dieu!"* he exclaimed, "I must make the important telephone to Paris." He scooped up the $40,000 worth of chips that remained, cashed them in, tipped the croupier handsomely and scurried off.

The next day the management was hit with a bit of bad news. "Duval's $70,000 was such excellent counterfeit," the bank reported, "that it almost slipped by undetected."

In 1890, a boy with the prosaic name of Robert Miller was born to a dirt-poor Austrian family. Little is known about his younger years, but he apparently decided early that honest work was for the birds because the record shows that he was bounced out of high school for petty thievery. He immediately left his dingy home and embarked on a career of crime.

He was spectacularly unsuccessful. Living the life of a guttersnipe, occasionally reduced to panhandling, he was arrested seven times—for petty larceny, burglary, purse-snatching—and convicted seven times. While serving a one-year jolt in an Austrian prison, Robert picked up the delicate art of forgery from an old-timer, and from this point on his fortunes improved. He roamed around Europe producing phony passports for anyone who could afford the exorbitant price and, in the chips for the first time in his life, discovered the delights of gracious living. His natural curiosity led him to explore widely in literature, art and music; he became something of a gourmet, and a connoisseur of wine and women.

255

Eventually, however, Miller's face and fingerprints became uncomfortably well known to the police. *Persona non grata* in no less than five countries, he decided to come to America.

In 1917 Robert Miller stepped off the boat in New York. He was a handsome lad of 27, with a steeltrap mind, a gift of gab in four languages, and a sense that America was loaded with sheep simply bleating to be fleeced. The name on his forged passport was Count Victor Lustig.

This was a time when bona fide royalty was fleeing from an unsettled Europe to the United States by the boatload, most of them impoverished. Lustig was their equal in poise, graciousness and erudition and, moreover, he had money. Looking every bit the wealthy young aristocrat, he checked into the old Waldorf on lower Fifth Avenue.

In no time at all the count was accepted in the drawing rooms of Manhattan's elite. The ladies were fascinated by his pale good looks and almost unearthly elegance; the men liked his way with a story.

After five years of picking up relatively minor scratch by cheating at cards and other such gambits, Lustig was ready for his debut into the big con. America was entering, as Scott Fitzgerald noted, the wildest, gaudiest spree is its history; the smell of big money was in the air, and half the population seemed engaged in trying to make a killing, legitimate or otherwise.

"It's quite true you can't con an honest man," Lustig once observed, "but, fortunately, you don't have to try. There are more than enough of the other kind."

Lustig's favorite grift became the selling of money-duplicating machines, a gadget which supposedly counterfeited U. S. currency. Always pretty much of a loner, the count liked it because it required no confederates, and the mark couldn't raise a hue and cry without incriminating himself. Lustig was a master psychologist in spotting a victim, a consummate actor in setting him up for the kill. From 1923 to 1931 he peddled his machines from Boston to Los Angeles for a total take of $2 million. There was no dearth of suckers, from the Montana poolroom operator who went for $42,000 to the trio of New York gangsters who enriched Lustig by $46,000. No respecter of classes, the count clipped everybody—socialites, hoodlums, law officers and plain citizens.

That a sucker might drop his life savings bothered the count not at all; he had the confidence man's typical contempt for the hypocrite who poses as a lily-white pillar of society but jumps at the chance to profit at someone else's expense. Only once, after having sold a machine, did he ever relent and make a refund. That episode, as might be expected, involved a woman.

One evening in 1925 the count paid his first visit to the fanciest bordello in Pittsburgh, an expensive palace of pleasure run by a lush brunette named Billie Scheible. Entranced by the suave and elegant count, Billie serviced him herself, and before the night was over she confessed her love for him. The count had no such feeling for Billie, but when he learned she was netting close to $1,000 a week he turned on the charm, and they spent the next several days in blissful dalliance.

Lustig showed up one evening with a black metal box, about the size of a portable radio and bristling with intricate-looking knobs and dials. It was a money-making machine, he told Billie, the invention of a brilliant European scientist.

Its operation was simple. You put a bundle of dollar-size blank paper in a compartment in the top, inserted a genuine bill in one end of the machine, turned the crank and waited. Precisely 12 hours later you turned the crank again and out popped two bills—the original and a perfect duplicate.

Billie was doubtful. Counterfeiting got you in trouble with the federal cops.

"Not these," the count assured her. "They're absolutely perfect." He inserted a $100 bill in the machine and turned the crank. "We have 12 hours to wait, my dear. Shall we, ah, enjoy ourselves?"

The next morning he cranked again and two C-notes, one slightly damp, slid out of the machine. Billie inspected them critically. The bills seemed identical, even to the serial numbers. That, of course, was no trick for Lustig, requiring only that he obtain a number of new bills in series and change a 3 to an 8.

"Looks good," Billie admitted, "but would it get by a bank?"

"Suppose we put it to the test," Lustig said, smiling. He bundled Billie into a cab and they drove to the nearest bank. Lustig pushed the bill through the teller's window and said, "Break this into tens, please."

The teller picked up the bill and studied it intently. Billie paled and clutched the count's arm.

"What's the matter, son?" Lustig said impatiently. "Think it's counterfeit?"

The teller laughed. "No sir. We always inspect big bills as a matter of policy. Nothing wrong with this one, sir." He pushed ten tens through the wicket.

Billie was delighted when Lustig said he'd sell her the money machine at cost—$25,000. "I'll make the sacrifice because I love you, my dear," he said. "I usually get double that amount." She handed over the money and immediately shoved a $100 note into the machine.

"The duplicate should be ready at 11 o'clock tonight," the count said, glancing at his watch. "Give me a ring at my hotel when it comes out and we'll celebrate."

Twelve hours later Billie approached the machine, her pretty head spinning with dreams of a life of idle luxury. Two hundred dollars a day, seven days a week—$73,000 a year. She could give up the business, leave Pittsburgh, see the world . . . she turned the crank.

The original hundred appeared, but no duplicate. She cranked again, then again. Slowly, a sickening suspicion grew in her mind. Frenziedly she ripped the black box apart. Inside was a series of rubber rollers, a pile of blank paper, a sponge in a shallow tray of water—and nothing more.

One minute later Billie slammed down the telephone in a fury. The count had checked out of his hotel that afternoon.

Billie Scheible was not the dame to lick her financial wounds in silence. She taxied to the hotel and hunted up a bell captain she knew, who told her that Lustig had made Pullman reservations for Philadelphia. Billie packed a bag and caught the next train.

Knowing that the count always traveled first class, Billie checked the better hotels. She found Lustig registered at the Bellevue-Stratford and stormed into his suite like a tigress. "I want my money," she yelled, "or you'll be sorry as hell!"

The count, who'd never expected to see her again, was momentarily speechless—but only momentarily. Suddenly he began to laugh uproariously. "Relax, my dear, I've been expecting you. In fact, I just put in a long distance call to your place. I'm sorry that my little joke upset you."

"Joke?" Billie said, confused.

"But of course. I wouldn't cheat *you,* my dear," the count said smoothly. He reached in a suitcase, took out a thick packet of bills and handed it to her. "Here's your money, my dear. And I hope you're not in too much of a hurry to get back to Pittsburgh . . ."

The only explanation for Lustig's unusual generosity is that he had apparently become genuinely fond of the pretty madame, and so began a pleasant and profitable association. They toured the country, usually in the count's chauffeur-driven Rolls Royce, while he unloaded his money machines by the dozen. With Billie sometimes posing as his wife when the particular set-up demanded, the count moved with equal

258

ease between high society and the underworld. One week he might be the guest of a distinguished matron at her Long Island estate; the next would find him visiting Al Capone in his Chicago headquarters or Lucky Luciano in his aerie atop the Waldorf-Astoria in New York.

A scream from an outraged mark delivered the count into the hands of the law now and then, but he never stayed long behind bars. If he couldn't sweet-talk his way out of the sneezer, he took the direct approach and sawed his way out.

The count's first attack of really bad luck came in 1929, when the crash not only cut down the supply of ready cash waiting around to be fleeced, but also wiped out Lustig's personal fortune. For the next few years, while he planned new schemes, he was forced to live off Billie.

In 1931 Lustig went to Mexico, having heard of a couple of wealthy ranchers who looked ripe for plucking. The scheme blew up, however, and he had to beat it back across the border. But his luck was running bad. Q. R. Richards, the tough, grizzled sheriff of Maverick County, Texas, had been tipped off by the Mexican police, and before Lustig knew what hit him he was sitting in jail at Eagle Pass on a charge of attempted fraud.

The capture of the notorious gyp artist got quite some publicity in the Texas press, which brought more trouble. An onion grower from Corpus Christi, whom Lustig had tapped for 50 grand in 1929, recognized his picture in the papers and blew the whistle.

While waiting for his trial to begin, Lustig got very chummy with the sheriff, and soon he was spending every evening in Richards' office, regaling him with tales of his adventures in the skin trade while they worked on a bottle of bourbon. The count soon came to realize that Richards was taking more than an academic interest in his stories of the big money. This puzzled him—until, one night, he learned that the sheriff was also the tax collector for Maverick County.

An astute student of human cupidity, Lustig sensed an angle. Skillfully he drew the sheriff out until his suspicions were confirmed— Richards had been dipping greedy fingers into the county till and he was worried sick. His books were due to be audited soon, and he faced public disgrace, probably prison.

Here was a money-hungry mark if the count had ever seen one. "Sheriff, how much are you in for?"

"Thirty thousand," Richards said miserably.

Lustig stared at him in surprise, then sat back in his chair and roared with laughter. "Sheriff, you're a penny-ante piker. You're sweating about a measly thirty grand? I make that much in a month." The count poured them both another drink. "Just for the hell of it, sheriff," he went on thoughtfully, "I'm going to get you off the hook."

"How?" said Richards eagerly, and he was doomed. Lustig went into his spiel about the money-duplicating machine. He'd sell it to his good friend the sheriff for $25,000. Plus, of course, his freedom.

Richards was horrified. "You want me to steal another $25,000 from the county treasury?"

The count shrugged. "What's the difference? You can put it all back in a few weeks."

The next morning Richards announced that the wily confidence man had mysteriously escaped, and that night they met in a hotel room in San Antonio. Lustig demonstrated his machine, including the trip to a bank the next day to verify the excellence of the queer. Richards could hardly wait to hand over the 25 grand and get back to Eagle Pass with the little black box.

The sheriff reacted as had Billie Scheible when she found she'd been conned, only more so. Vowing vengeance, he strapped on his six-gun and went looking for the count. Remembering that during their nightly conversations Lustig had often mentioned Chicago as one of his favorite bases of operations, the sheriff started there, and in less than a week he traced the count to his elegant suite in the Drake Hotel. The Texan burst in on Lustig one afternoon with the six-shooter in his fist. "I'm going to kill you, you sonofabitch!" he roared.

Lustig was in the tightest jam of his life, but he reacted with his characteristic nerveless brilliance. "Put the gun away, sheriff," he said calmly. "If you kill me, you'll never get your money back. And on top of that, you'll face a murder rap."

Richards' eyes took on a glazed look. In his anger, he hadn't thought of anything but catching up with Lustig. The gun wavered.

"I was a fool to try and con you, sheriff," Lustig went on smoothly. "I should have realized that you wouldn't take it lying down. Don't worry, you'll get your money back."

"I'll take it now," Richards said hoarsely, shoving the gun back in his holster. The count relaxed, his mind going into high gear. He realized the sheriff was still a worried, frightened man, and was still ripe for the taking. Adopting a conspiratorial tone, Lustig leaned forward and revealed that he'd just sunk the sheriff's $25,000 into the biggest deal of his career. He'd met an engraver, he said, who turned out

260

the best counterfeit money he'd ever seen, and they were going into business as soon as they raised another $65,000 to buy printing presses and other equipment.

"The hell with all that," Richards said harshly. "I've gotta have my money now. The auditors will be coming in less than six weeks."

Lustig shrugged helplessly, saying that he wouldn't have the 25 grand until he'd sold another money-making machine, and that might take months. Then, apparently coming up with a new thought, he added, "Of course, the twenty-five thousand won't get you out of trouble. You'll still owe the original thirty grand you pinched."

As Richards slumped in his chair, the count lit a cigarette and waited for his man to bite. Finally the sheriff took a deep breath and said, "You say this counterfeit is real good?"

Lustig smiled, reaching in his pocket and tossing the sheriff a couple of $20 bills. "These will pass in any bank in the country." Which was true; the bills were genuine.

Richards sweated it out for several more minutes. "If you had the $65,000," he said slowly, "how long before you could get started?"

"No more than 10 days, I should say. And once we get rolling, we expect to turn out $100,000 worth a week."

Richards' eyes glittered. "All right. I'll get you the money. We'll be partners."

Positively lightheaded with dreams of wealth, Richards hurried back to Eagle Pass, tapped the county till for another $65,000, assured the citizens he was hot on the trail of the fugitive, and scooted back to Chicago.

Meanwhile, Lustig had to dig up some counterfeit in a hurry. He knew of an engraver named William Watts, who forged whisky labels and tax stamps for Al Capone. The count called on Watts, a balding little man with a scraggly moustache, and found that he had, by a lucky coincidence, been fooling around with producing Treasury notes. He showed the count a $100 bill he'd made—almost perfect engraving, but printed on inferior paper. But it was only a hobby, Watts said. He wanted no part of the counterfeiting racket.

It took a couple of days, but Lustig finally persuaded him to run off a batch of C-notes in exchange for half the sheriff's 65 grand. When Richards returned, Lustig wined and dined him in style while waiting for Watts to turn out the queer.

A week later Lustig delivered a package to Richards in his hotel room. The sheriff shook like a schoolgirl on her first date as he inspected the bills. Only the top layer was genuine but, as the count had anticipated, the sheriff was too excited to investigate further.

Assuring the count that he was his friend for life, the sheriff took off for Eagle Pass in a veritable transport of joy. And the very first time he tried to deposit some of the queer in the local bank he was caught, arrested and clapped into his own jail.

Impressed by Watts' skill as an engraver, Lustig decided that counterfeiting offered enormous possibilities. Watts was still afraid of the racket, but eventually he succumbed to the count's spell-binidng oratory and, convinced that he could make a million within a year, the little man began working on plates for 10-, 20-, and 100-dollar bills. The first batch of counterfeit had been only fair, however—a better grade of paper and a method of duplicating the red and blue threads in genuine bills were needed. The latter is a closely-guarded government secret, but Watts hit on a unique solution. Instead of tracing in the threads with ink—the usual method—he tried using actual colored threads, coating them with an adhesive and pressing them into the paper with a specially-designed copper plate. It worked fine.

With Al Capone's help, Lustig set up an organization to get rid of the queer. The pushers bought the output at 40 cents on the dollar, and in the first three weeks of operation they got rid of $200,000 dollars' worth of paper in the Chicago area. When it began drifting into the banks the Treasury men converged on Chicago—whereupon the flood of queer suddenly dried up. Lustig, ever the crafty one, moved East, and West and let the Midwest cool off.

By 1933 the count had no less than 400 pushers laying the paper from coast to coast. Lustig was playing it very cozy. None of the pushers knew him or Watts by name or face, and the money passed through three or four hands before it reached the public. If a pusher was arrested, as frequently happened, he could implicate only his immediate contact.

The Treasury men were going quietly nuts. They had learned that Lustig was masterminding the organization, but they couldn't get proof, and the flow of 10's, 20's and 100's was becoming so great, according to William Moran, the chief of the Secret Service, that it was actually threatening the stability of the United States currency.

So it went until early in 1935 when Robert L. Grady, head of the New York division of the Secret Service, discovered that Lustig was living in his usual high style in a hotel in midtown New York. He assigned 16 men to the count: they tailed him 24 hours a day, monitored his phone calls, searched his rooms—and got exactly nowhere. They could have picked him up at any time, of course—he was wanted in at least 10 states for various frauds—but they wanted to get the evidence that would nail him on the counterfeit rap.

The story of Lustig's arrest is shrouded in contradiction. On the night of May 12, 1935, he was sitting in his Rolls Royce, parked at the corner of Broadway and 74th Street. The government men were tailing him as usual. As they watched, a Postal Telegraph messenger boy came down the street and delivered two suitcases to the confidence man. Convinced that they finally had Lustig with the goods, the agents pounced.

Inside the suitcase were a few items of expensive clothing, nothing else. The agents almost tore the bags to shreds looking for false bottoms or secret compartments.

There are two versions of what happened next. The Federal men say they shook Lustig down and in his wallet discovered a key—which subsequently was found to fit a locker in the BMT subway station in Times Square. And in the locker was $51,000 worth of counterfeit, plus engraving plates for 10-, 20-, and 100-dollar bills.

According to Lustig's lawyer, it didn't happen that way at all. The Secret Service men had received the key in the mail, they said, and Lustig had been framed—perhaps by Billie Scheible, who was reputedly unhappy at the count's attentions to other women.

At any rate, the count seemed solidly hooked, and they sweated him at the Federal House of Detention trying to find the name of the engraver. Lustig wouldn't talk, except to assure the government men, with a great deal of relish, that the queer would continue to appear as usual, since the unknown engraver had recently made new plates. This was a blow: the Secret Service men had been convinced the capture of the plates would end the counterfeiting conspiracy. And when, three months later, Lustig pulled his spectacular rope trick, the government sleuths were right back where they'd started.

They began all over. Since the counterfeit had been showing up mostly in the New York area during the past months, they figured the engraver might be buying his equipment in the city. A battalion of T-men began the dull, slogging job of checking every chemical and ink supply house in Manhattan, searching back records of purchases, looking for someone not connected with a newspaper or a legit photo-engraving firm.

It was a long shot, but it paid off.

During the last week in September an agent dropped in at Eimer and Amend, a chemical firm at Third Avenue and 18th Street. One of the clerks pointed out a skinny, balding man with a whispy moustache who was at the moment buying a large quantity of engraving supplies. "He's not a regular customer," the clerk said. "Name's McMillan."

The agent tailed the little man to a six-story apartment house in Union City, New Jersey, just across the river from Manhattan. McMillan, the superintendent said, lived quietly, had no visitors, no regular hours and no apparent source of income.

That night the government man crept up the fire escape to McMillan's apartment on the sixth floor. The blinds were down, but not quite to the bottom. Kneeling, the agent peered into the apartment. And there in the center of the room, in plain sight, he saw a table loaded with the paraphernalia of the engraver's art—copper plates, jars of chemicals, dies and inks. When, a few hours later, a half-dozen T-men crashed the apartment they also found more than $300,000 of the best non-legit money in existence. The boom had finally been lowered on William Watts.

The engraver was eager to talk. He was sore at Lustig, he said, because the count had been holding out Watts' fair share of the profits.

The capture of Victor Lustig was singularly unspectacular. With perhaps fitting irony, he was betrayed by a gangster he'd once fleeced. On September 28 the FBI office in Pittsburgh got a tip that the count was disporting himself at a certain bordello. They dashed to the bagnio to find that Lustig had left a scant two minutes before. One of the prostitutes said she thought he was heading for a lady friend's apartment, only a couple blocks away.

The FBI men rushed out of the house and headed for the apartment. On the way they spotted the count strolling along the street, immaculate as ever and seemingly without a care in the world. They grabbed him before he had a chance to run, hustled him back to New York and clapped him in jail. His trial was set for December 5.

Lustig was convicted on six counts and Federal Judge Coxe, calling his operation "perhaps the greatest counterfeiting conspiracy in the history of the United States," rapped him with 20 years.

In 1949 a man named Emil Lustig was hauled up before a judge in Camden, New Jersey, on a small-time grift. He was Victor Lustig's brother, he told the court, and said the count had died of a brain tumor in a Missouri prison on March 11, 1947.

Not even the local papers had bothered to write an obit on the man who had once made headlines as the slickest confidence man of them all.

THE ENEMY SPY BRITAIN LOVED DEARLY

by Al Newman

Al Newman, Newsweek's *war correspondent, sent this better-than-fiction story of one reason the Germans failed to invade Britain. This is how it was told to Newman by "a former British undercover agent, an unobtrusive-looking young man with an air so guileless it made you want to kick him for seeming such an idiot."*

In October 1940, Franco's government requested admission to the British Isles for a Falangist who had something to do with the youth movement in Spain. He said he wanted to study the British Boy Scouts during wartime or some such utter rot. Not being such fools as they sometimes seem, the Foreign Office said, "Righto, come ahead." They knew the man of course, and were positive that everything he saw or heard went straight to Berchtesgaden and Berlin.

He was our own pet spy and we loved him dearly. A few others and myself acting as Scout officials met him at an airfield and tucked him carefully into a suite at the Athenaeum Court Hotel. That suite was probably the greatest job of concealed microphones and tapped wires ever accomplished. We furnished him with a great deal of liquor and all the women he ever wanted—ours of course.

That wasn't all we did for him. There were at that time only about three heavy ack-ack batteries in the London area. One of them we moved into Green Park, directly across the street from the hotel. They had orders to fire continuously, as fast as possible all through every raid, whether there was anything within miles or not. Lord, what a bloody row they made. Since there was at least one raid every night, our pet spy spent most of his time down in the air-raid shelter, convinced by the noise that London was thickly studded with ack-ack protection. We let him inspect the battery—a crack 3-incher outfit—and even furnished a few Boy Scouts for the occasion.

Then we took him out toward Windsor to look at more Boy Scouts. By what may have been the sheerest coincidence, but wasn't, just about the only fully equipped regiment in all the islands and all the tanks we possessed, were assembled there. Fine, tough-looking men they were. Guardsmen. We said that they were just a small force which could be spared from the defense of the island and had been detailed as a ceremonial bodyguard for the royal family. We could see how surprised he was, but he swallowed it whole.

Then we took him out to a seaport where every available fleet unit had been mustered. We hinted delicately that secret additions to the Home Fleet enabled us to keep these ships as the defense of one port. His eyes popped a little at that, but there it was before him and he had to believe what he saw. We also showed him more Boy Scouts. He was beginning to get awfully sick of them by this time and so were we, but it was part of the game and both sides had to play it to the finish.

Our greatest triumph of stage management was his trip toward Scotland by plane a fortnight later. You remember how thin our airpower was at this time. A few Hurricanes, fewer Spitfires. Well, all the way up there, we ran into squadron after squadron of Spits. The sky seemed full of them. How could he know that it was the same squadron ducking into and out of the clouds and coming at us from all angles and altitudes?

Then on maneuvers in the Scotland area, we showed him the same regiment of guards and the same tanks that he had seen near Windsor. I was a bit afraid he might recognize a few of the guardsmen, but he didn't. We explained that this was just a small, poorly equipped force, reoutfitting to join others training over a wide area and that the whole maneuver army was merely what could be spared from the main defense forces.

Oh, yes, and there were a few more blasted Boy Scouts about the premises. We ran into more Spitfires—hundreds and hundreds of them—on the way back toward London. If I hadn't known what was going on, I'd have been taken in myself.

Shortly after this he left. Later I saw portions of his report—don't ask me how we got it because that is a secret. The document was just appalling. Britain was an armed camp. Any rumors of her weakness were merely attempts of a crafty foe to inveigle Germany into the inevitably disastrous invasion. All this was eyewitness stuff and apparently great weight was given to it by his masters in Berlin.

I often wonder what happened to him afterward. I suppose he's retired somewhere on half pay now. Pity too, because he was quite a presentable chap. We loved him dearly and cared for him tenderly. But I'll bet ten pounds our pet spy still dreams of Boy Scouts every other night. I know I do.

266

THE PRINCESS CARIBOO

by P. T. Barnum

Bristol was, in 1812, the second commercial city of Great Britain, having in particular an extensive East India trade. Among its inhabitants were merchants, reckoned remarkably shrewd, and many of them very wealthy; and quite a number of aristocratic families, who were looked up to with the abject toad-eating kind of civility that follows "the nobility."

One fine evening in the winter of 1812-13, the White Lion hotel, a leading inn at Bristol, was thrown into a flutter by the announcement that a very beautiful and fabulously wealthy lady, the Princess Cariboo, had just arrived by ship from an oriental port. Her agent, a swarthy and wizzened little Asiatic, who spoke imperfect English, gave this information, and ordered the most sumptuous suite of rooms in the house. Of course, there was great activity in all manner of preparations; and the mysterious character of this lovely but high-born stranger caused a wonderful flutter of excitement, which grew and grew until the fair stranger at length deigned to arrive.

She came at about ten o'clock, in great state, and with two or three coaches packed with servants and luggage—the former of singularly dingy complexion and fantastic vestments, and the latter of the most curious forms and material imaginable. The eager anticipations of hosts and guests alike were not only fully justified but even exceeded by the rare beauty of the unknown, the oriental style and magnificence of her attire and that of her attendants, and the enormous bulk of her baggage —a circumstance that has no less weight at an English inn than any where else. The stranger, too, was most liberal with her fees to the servants, which were always in gold.

It was quickly discovered that her ladyship spoke not one word of English, and even her agent—a dark, wild, queer little fellow—got along with it but indifferently, preferring all his requests in very "broken China" indeed. The landlord thought it a splendid opportunity to create a long bill, and got up rooms and a dinner in flaring style, with wax candles, a mob of waiters, ringing of bells, and immense ceremony. But the lady, like a real princess, while well enough pleased and very gracious, took all this as a matter of course, and preferred her own cook, a flat-faced, pug-nosed, yellow-breeched and almond-eyed oriental, with a pigtail dangling from his scalp, which was shaved clean, excepting at the back of the head. This gentleman ran about in the kitchen-yard with queer little brass utensils, wherein he concocted sundry diabolical preparations—as they seemed to the English servants to be,—of herbs, rice, curry powder, etc., etc., for the repast of his mistress. For the next three or four days, the White Lion was in a state bordering upon frenzy, at the singular deportment of the "Princess" and her numerous attendants. The former arrayed herself in the most astonishing combinations of apparel that had ever been seen by the good gossips of Bristol, and the latter indulged in gymnastic antics and vocal chantings that almost deafened the neighborhood. There was a peculiar nasal ballad in which they were fond of indulging, that commenced about midnight and kept up until well nigh morning, that drove the neighbors almost beside themselves. It sounded like a concert by a committee of infuriated cats, and wound up with protracted whining notes, commencing in a whimper, and then with a sudden jerk, bursting into a loud, monotonous howl. Yet, withal, these attendants, who slept on mats, in the rooms adjacent to that of their mistress, and fed upon the preparations of her own cuisine, were, in the main, very civil and inoffensive, and seemed to look upon the Princess with the utmost awe. The "agent," or "secretary," or "prime-minister," or whatever he might be called, was very mysterious as to the objects, purposes, history, and antecedents of her Highness, and the quidnuncs were in despair until, one morning, the "Bristol Mirror," then a leading paper, came out with a flaring announcement, expressing the pleasure it felt in acquainting the public with the fact, that a very eminent and interesting foreign personage had arrived from her home in the remotest East to proffer His Majesty, George III, the unobstructed commerce and friendship of her realm, which was as remarkable for its untold wealth as for its marvelous beauty. The lady was described as a befitting representative of the loveliness and opulence of this new Golconda and Ophir in one, since her matchless wealth and munificence were approached only by her ravishing personal charms. The other papers took up the topic, and were even more extravagant. "Felix Farley's Journal" gave a long narrative of her wanderings and extraordinary adventures in the uttermost East, as gleaned, of course, from her garrulous agent. The island

268

of her chief residence was described as being of vast extent and fertility, immensely rich and populous, and possessing many rare and beautiful arts unknown to the nations of Europe. The princess had become desperately enamored of a certain young Englishman of high rank, who had been shipwrecked on her coast, but had afterward escaped, and as she learned, safely reached a port in China, and thence departed for Europe. The Princess had hereupon set out upon her journeyings over the world in search of him. In order to facilitate her enterprise, and softened by the deep affection she felt for the son of Albion, she had determined to break through the usages of her country, and form an alliance with that of her beloved.

Such were the statements everywhere put in circulation; and when the Longbows of the place got full hold of it, Gulliver, Peter Wilkins, and Sinbad the Sailor were completely eclipsed. Diamonds as big as hen's eggs, and pearls the size of hazelnuts, were said to be the commonest buttons and ornaments the Princess wore, and her silks and shawls were set beyond all price.

The announcement of this romantic and mysterious history, this boundless wealth, this interesting mission from majesty to majesty in person and the reality which every one could see of so much grace and beauty, supplied all that was wanting to set the upper-tendom of the place in a blaze. It was hardly etiquette for a royal visitor to receive much company before having been presented at Court; but as this princely lady came from a point so far outside of the pale of Christendom, and all its formalities, it was deemed not out of place, to show her befitting attentions; and the ice once broken, there was no arresting the flood. The aristocracy of Bristol vied with each other in seeing who should be first and most extravagant in their demonstrations. The street in front of the "White Lion" was day after day blocked up with elegant equipages, and her reception-rooms thronged with "fair women and brave men." Milliners and mantuamakers pressed upon the lovely and mysterious Princess Cariboo the most exquisite hats, dresses, and laces, just to acquaint her with the fashionable style and solicit her distinguished patronage; dry-goods-men sent her rare patterns of their costliest and richest stuffs, perfumers their most exquisite toilet-cases, filled with odors sweet; jewellers, their most superb sets of gems; and florists and visitors nearly suffocated her with the scarcest and most delicate exotics. Pictures, sketches, and engravings, oil-paintings, and portraits on ivory of her rapturous admirers, poured in from all sides, and her own fine form and features were reproduced by a score of artists. Daily

269

she was fêted, and nightly serenaded, until the Princess Cariboo became the furore of the United Kingdom. Magnificent entertainments were given her in private mansions; and at length, to cap the climax, Mr. Worrall, the Recorder of Bristol, managed, by his influence, to bring about for her a grand municipal reception in the town-hall, and people from far and near thronged to it in thousands.

In the meantime the papers were gravely trying to make out whether the Cariboo country meant some remote portion of Japan, or the Island of Borneo, or some comparatively unfamiliar archipelago in the remotest East, and the "Mirror" was publishing type expressly cut for the purpose of representing the characters of the language in which the Princess spoke and wrote. They were certainly very uncouth, and pretended sages, who knew very well that there was no one to contradict them, who declared that they were "ancient Coptic"!

Upon reading the sequel of the story, one is irresistibly reminded of the ancient Roman inscription discovered by one of Dickens' characters, which some irreverent rogue subsequently declared to be nothing more nor less than "Bil Stumps His Mark."

All this went on for about a fortnight, until the whole town and a good deal of the surrounding country had made complete fools of themselves, and only the "naughty little boys" in the streets held out against the prevailing mania, probably because they were not admitted to the sport. Their salutations took the form of an inharmonious thoroughfare-ballad, the chorus of which terminated with:

> "Boo! hoo! hoo!
> And who's the Princess Cariboo?"

yelled out at the top of their voices.

At length one day, the luggage of her Highness was embarked upon a small vessel to be taken round by water to London, while she announced, through her "agent," her intention to reach the capital by post-coaching.

Of course, the most superb traveling-carriages and teams were placed at her disposal; but, courteously declining all these offers, she set out in the night-time with a hired establishment, attended by her retinue.

Days and weeks rolled on, and yet no announcement came of the arrival of her Highness at London or at any of the intervening cities after the first two or three towns eastward of Bristol. Inquiry began to be made, and, after long and patient but unavailing search, it became apparent to divers and sundry dignitaries in the old town that somebody had been very particularly "sold."

270

The landlord at the "White Lion" who had accepted the agent's order for £1,000 on a Calcutta firm in London; poor Mr. Worrall, who had been Master of Ceremonies at the town hall affair, and had spent large sums of money; and the tradespeople and others who sent their finest goods, all felt that they had "heard something drop." The Princess Cariboo had disappeared as mysteriously as she came.

For years, the people of Bristol were unmercifully ridiculed throughout the entire Kingdom on account of this affair, and burlesque songs and plays immortalized its incidents for successive seasons.

One of these insisted that the Princess was no other than an actress of more notoriety than note, humbly born in the immediate vicinity of the old city, where she practiced this gigantic hoax, and that she had been assisted in it by a set of dissolute young noblemen and actors, who furnished the money she had spent, got up the oriental dresses, published the fibs, and fomented the excitement. At all events, the net profit to her and her confederates in the affair must have been some £10,000.

THE REMARKABLE SIR RICHARD

by Charles Kingston

Throughout the first half of the nineteenth century, Richard Douglas, one of England's most noted professional swindlers, kept a record of every one of his crimes, as well as a profit-and-loss balance-sheet, which he drew up at the end of each year. His diary was an astonishing document.

The impostor was a man of venerable aspect, with kindly blue eyes and a soft, ingratiating manner. He was born with the name of Douglas, but as his father was a small tradesman in a Surrey village Richard thought he had better disown him, and when he had failed many times to earn an honest living he blazoned forth as "Sir Richard Douglas of Orpington House, Kent," and made his two elder sons partners in his criminal enterprises.

When he went to a well-known jeweler in Bond Street to select a "present for my wife, Lady Douglas," he had not the slightest difficulty in persuading the merchant to let him have a five hundred guinea diamond necklace on approval. Most swindlers would have been content to disappear with the necklace and realize its value, but "Sir Richard" was more ambitious. He was back again in the shop the same afternoon, and, greatly to the gratification of the jeweler, announced that "her ladyship" had been fascinated by the necklace, and that he wished to pay for it there and then.

The impostor drew a cheque for six hundred pounds, and, remarking that his own bank would be closed before he could get to it, induced the jeweler to give him a receipt for the necklace and seventy-five pounds in cash. Of course, the cheque came back marked "No account."

While the "baronet" was busy on swindles of this nature his two sons were equally active. They lacked, of course, the suave polish of their father, but they were bright, intelligent youths, and they could pose as army officers anxious to spend the generous allowance their father, "Sir Richard Douglas," made them. The credulous traders willingly cashed cheques for the young Douglases, and were left eventually with bits of paper souvenirs of their simplicity and trustfulness.

A few months' swindling provided Douglas with sufficient capital to rent an expensive house at Ascot, which became his headquarters, and it was to it that he would retire every week-end from the stress and strain of London. Every Monday morning, however, he would be driven in his carriage to the station to catch the train to London, and to start another week's "work." He dressed for each swindle, and played many characters. On one occasion after having entertained some of the leading people at Ascot to dinner he returned to town the following morning, donned the attire of a broken-down clergyman, and cajoled a large sum from the credulous by a story of ill-health and poverty and a starving wife and children. But generally he was the well-dressed man of the world, and boldly swindled tradespeople under the name of "Sir Richard Douglas."

He had, of course, many narrow escapes. Once he absent-mindedly entered a jeweler's shop which he had defrauded only a fortnight earlier. The proprietor pretended not to recognize the self-styled "baronet," and he entered into negotiations with "Sir Richard," who was plainly on the warpath again. Now Douglas had that morning told his elder son, Philip, to hang about in the vicinity of the shop, so that when he emerged from it he might unostentatiously pass on to him the spoils, as the impostor intended to steal a few rings, as well as obtain others by false pretences. The wary jeweler, however, was so unusually alert that "Sir Richard" realized the situation.

He was in a tight corner now, for in addition to the presence of the proprietor of the shop a brawny assistant was keeping guard at the door. The "baronet," however, exhibited no sign of fear or mental distress. He just casually glanced out of the window, and raised his handkerchief to his left cheek and brushed it lightly. It was a signal to his son on the other side of the road.

Philip Douglas was a real chip off the old block, and in a moment he devised a plan to save his venerable parent. Walking briskly into the shop where "Sir Richard" was the only customer, he peremptorily laid his hand on his father's arm.

"It's a bit of luck for you that I was passing and recognized this fellow," he said to the astonished jeweler. "Do you know that he is one of the greatest swindlers in London? I have been looking for him for over a year. Take my advice and see if he has robbed you of anything."

Immediately the door was locked, and the "detective" and the other two men stood round the pale-faced and trembling culprit, who at that very moment held in his hands a diamond tiara which was worth a thousand pounds. But he was so terrified now that he seemed not to know where he was and what he was doing.

The jeweler instantly preferred a charge against "Sir Richard," and, furthermore, at the suggestion of the "detective" added another one, accusing him of trying to obtain the tiara by false pretences. This was just what both the rogues wanted.

"Then you will be good enough to make a parcel of that tiara," said the "detective," with an air of authority. "You will carefully seal it too. I shall have to hand it over to my superior officer to be used as evidence at the trial. Of course I will give you a receipt for it."

Ten minutes later Philip Douglas left the shop and stepped into a four-wheeler with his father and the diamond tiara. The "detective" shouted out the address of a police station, nodded curtly to the jeweler, and drove off. That night at Ascot the family gloated over the acquisition of a prize which would bring them in six hundred pounds at least.

But the biggest *coup* of all was achieved by the "baronet" posing as a messenger. It happened that he was chatting with the manager of a diamond merchant's shop when the latter observed that Lady Chesterfield had given them an order to reset a collection of very valuable stones. They were reputed to be worth twenty thousand pounds, and that afternoon the manager was to call at her ladyship's town house to receive the precious parcel. On hearing this "Sir Richard" murmured that he was due back at his country seat to entertain a Cabinet Minister and, having got outside, rushed to the nearest post office, obtained Lady Chesterfield's address, and drove to it. He was admitted at once, but her ladyship's secretary would not hear of handing over the diamonds until "the manager" established his identity. Had Douglas not been an accomplished swindler he would have bolted, but he held his ground. He had a good memory, and he was able to recall many of the statements the manager had made to him, detailing intimate details of previous transactions with Lady Chesterfield which convinced the secretary that he was what he represented himself to be.

Within a week the whole of the stones were in the possession of a well-known Continental "fence," whose place of business was in Amsterdam, and the Douglas banking account was increased by nine thousand pounds. For weeks the happy family at Ascot enjoyed the newspaper references to the great mystery, and congratulated themselves that the secretary's and the manager's descriptions of the swindler resembled anybody but the bogus "baronet."

Continual success so impressed the impostor that he came to the conclusion that he was under the special protection of Providence. He began a diary, and the entries that followed were both amusing and amazing.

"Jan. 7th. All day ill. Row about stable. Forcible possession taken of it. Row all day with one person or another. Fearful how things will end. Three boys at home idle, all ordering things."

"Jan. 18th. Went to boys' to dinner. Champagne. Very merry. Providence not quite deserted us."

When he raised three hundred pounds in two days by means of worthless cheques he celebrated the "triumph" by writing in his diary:

"My labours ended for the week. Over three hundred to the good. Paid off local tradesmen—genuine cheques. Gave notice to cook. Must get some one who understands serving fish. Looking forward to a quiet week-end. Must read Bible regularly."

He was really fond of reading the Bible, and he spent his leisure at his home in studying it and keeping his diary up to date.

But every Monday morning Douglas would descend upon London, and when the diaries were bulging with records of swindles of all descriptions, and almost every tradesman in the West End was on his guard, he turned for a time to begging-letter writing, at which he proved himself an adept. He was the starving widow with eight chil-

274

dren; the lonely widow of an Indian officer; the one-legged and one-armed hero of half a dozen campaigns; the old woman who had worked for the poor all her life, and was now in poverty herself; and a dozen other characters. These rôles produced enough to pay expenses at Ascot and pass the time until "Sir Richard Douglas" and his greater misdeeds were forgotten by the public if not by his victims.

On one occasion he donned his clerical garb, and went round collecting subscriptions for an aged missionary and his wife. By working ten hours a day for a fortnight he collected several hundred pounds, and he even persuaded two bishops to contribute through their chaplains, although as a rule bishops are very careful to make inquiries before patronizing anything of this sort.

By now the police were on the lookout for the bogus baronet. But Douglas was a quick-change artist, and his keen eyes were ever on the watch. He walked freely about London, and he always spotted the detectives, and decamped before they recognized him.

He was once tracked to a house where he was trying to persuade a rich old lady to buy a tract of land in Scotland. Scenting danger, he ran upstairs into a room, where he found some female clothes, and shortly afterwards he walked through the kitchen—where a policeman was keeping guard—and out of the house by the side door. The policeman explained later that he thought "she was the cook going for her afternoon out."

This escape, however, was so narrow that the "baronet" returned at once to Ascot, and lay low for a month. Meanwhile, his sons had been making the money fly. Thousands of pounds went to the bookmakers at Ascot and other racecourses, and all three of them were engaged to girls with expensive tastes. "Sir Richard" recorded in his diary: "It is sad to think of the extravagance of youth. If we misuse the money Providence has given us we will experience poverty. I have spoken seriously to the boys, but they will not heed me."

He started a matrimonial agency, which was to be stocked with three "baronets," on the lookout for wives. But it was brought to an abrupt termination by the theft of the preliminary prospectus by a servant, who had to be bought off later at a cost of five hundred pounds, an item of expenditure which nearly broke the old man's heart, according to his diary.

Meantime his sons were devoting more time to pleasure than to business, and the knowledge that the authorities were doubling their efforts to catch him was ever-disturbing. But he could not remain inactive, for his brain was always teeming with plans for swindles, and he entered details of several in his diary.

Amongst his acquaintances in London was a widow of fortune. She was in the late fifties, but not averse to marrying again, especially a man with a title, and "Sir Richard's" advances were not repulsed. Mrs. MacCormack had been left ten thousand a year by her husband, and the lady maintained a costly establishment in the neighbourhood of London. Douglas was fascinated by her money.

He therefore proposed to Mrs. MacCormack, who accepted "Sir Richard" with enthusiasm. Douglas insisted upon the engagement being kept a secret, pointing out that it was only for her sake that he did so.

"You will be accused of marrying me for my title, dear," he said in a sympathetic tone, "and that would hurt me terribly."

It was settled that the marriage should take place at St. George's, Hanover Square, and "Sir Richard" told the widow that the Archbishop of Canterbury and the Bishop of London had promised to assist at the ceremony if their engagements permitted. At the last moment it happened that both these prelates were detained elsewhere, and to the rector was given the honour of officiating.

On the morning of the ceremony "Sir Richard" dressed himself with extreme care in the room he had taken at the fashionable West End hotel. He was due at St. George's at twelve. A carriage was to take him there with his best man, who was his eldest son Philip, and the young rogue was posing for the occasion as a friend of the bridegroom-baronet.

Now Philip Douglas had made a few inquiries about Mrs. MacCormack, and learnt that it was really true that she had ten thousand pounds a year, but on the day of the ceremony he discovered by sheer accident that under the provisions of her late husband's will she was to be deprived of every penny if she married again. So at half-past eleven Philip Douglas dashed into the hotel, and confided the sad news to the old sinner. "Sir Richard" gasped, and then when he had regained his composure he and his son drove away to catch the train back to Ascot. Douglas entered all the details of the misadventure in his diary, and he severely censured the widow for not having been "honest" enough to tell him the truth.

For some reason, the "baronet" went to pieces after the abandonment of his wedding. Money suddenly became scarce, and creditors more persistent.

In the midst of the crisis he remembered having heard about a benevolent clergyman of the name of Hamilton, who had a large fortune,

276

which he was in the habit of sharing with the poor. Douglas decided that he would get a slice of it. This time he was supposed to be an elderly priest who had fallen upon evil times, and to play the part properly he took lodgings in a slum house owned by a humble confederate. From there he wrote to Mr. Hamilton asking him to call upon a sick and poverty-stricken fellow-clergyman, who had no friends and no hope left in this world.

Douglas knew that if only Mr. Hamilton called he would be able to work upon his feelings to the extent of two hundred pounds at least. Anxiously he waited for a reply, and his joy was great when the owner of the house informed him that a clergyman was approaching.

The sham priest instantly returned to bed, and assuming a pained look prepared to receive the visitor. Douglas was murmuring a prayer when the clergyman came to his side and looked down at him. Then he opened his eyes.

"You—you are the saintly Mr. Hamilton?" he asked in a quavering voice.

"No," was the startling answer. "I am Inspector Allen, and I hold a warrant for your arrest, Sir Richard."

At the ensuing Sessions he and his sons were sentenced to imprisonment, and after that catastrophe nothing more was heard of the venerable swindler until a newspaper recorded his death in 1858.

NOVARRO THE MAGNIFICENT

by George Herald

An ugly green-eyed little man in well-tailored clothes may at this moment be cheating at cards in Acapulco, rigging a horse race in Casablanca, or swindling a rich widow in Venice with an ingenious variation of one of the oldest confidence games in the world. Because he has beautiful manners and affects a marked stoop, people tend to mistake him for a tired Old World aristocrat. He speaks eight languages fluently and his powers of persuasion are equally great in each one. A Canadian who recently came to borrow a small sum from him, for instance, loaned *him* $3,000 instead.

The list of his dupes includes a New York airline executive, Washington lawyers, movie moguls, a wealthy maharaja—and even bigger game.

This global charlatan has variously posed as Alexander Dannot, Charles Jadeaux Dannut, Della Valle Enrique, Max Frimen, Carlos Ladenis, Max Landeau, Maxim Amadez, Alexander Newborn (after getting out of jail), Count Nevarre Alex, Alfred Roschildt, Prince Alexander Romanoff, and at least 30 other characters. According to his last valid travel document—passport No. 26-148-103 issued by the Spanish consulate in Milan on April 10, 1951—he is a certain Fernandez Antonio Novarro, born in Vigo in 1894.

On a sunny morning in May, 1951, Fernandez Antonio Novarro arrived at the Hotel George V in Paris in a cream-colored Lincoln driven by an impressive chauffeur. Novarro's luggage showed signs of much traveling and his suits, while superior in cut, had a well-worn look.

With his sallow skin, thin mustache and weary gestures, he seemed the perfect example of a decadent Latin in quest of Parisian entertainment. And entertainment he not only got but soon offered on a prodigal scale to astonished French society. Almost every night he gave banquets at which the most exquisite dishes were served to bluebloods and gate crashers alike. And the prettiest girls of Paris began to beat a path to his door.

In two months Novarro squandered some 15,000,000 francs ($43,000). When people wondered where it all came from, he nonchalantly—but vaguely—mentioned iron mines in Peru. Since he always paid cash and tipped well, he became the talk of the places where reputations are made by headwaiters.

In July, the chief barman of the Carlton Hotel in Cannes received a phone call from his opposite number in the George V: "You know, we have got a terrific fellow up here. His name is Fernandez Novarro, and he must be worth billions. He is coming down to you, so please take good care of him."

As a result, Novarro was received in Cannes like a minor potentate and introduced to every society notable at hand.

On the Côte d'Azur, Fernandez played his role of the grand seigneur with the skill of a seasoned performer.

He gave fabulous dances in the casinos. He gambled as if obsessed by an almost demonic passion.

"He was the first to arrive at the tables and the last to leave," a wealthy maharaja recalled. "He never could resist an offer to hold a banco, and he often covered wagers ranging from $20,000 to $30,000."

In August, Novarro opened the second phase of his gambit by start-ing rumors that his present wealth was chicken feed compared to what he would have if he could gain access to certain safe deposits he kept in a number of U. S. banks under various aliases. He couldn't get at them, he intimated, because they contained $60,000,000 he had hoarded dur-ing the Prohibition era while a trusted lieutenant of Al Capone.

"In Chicago gangster circles, they knew me as Kid Tiger," he con-fided. "My job was to arrange the shipment of bootleg booze from Can-ada into the U. S.

"If I now went back to America to fetch my money, the Federal Gov-ernment would arrest me for tax evasion. Of course, I would gladly give a 10 per cent commission to anyone who might help me salvage the money, but who would take the risk?"

Interpol (the International Police) files show that Novarro had ped-dled variations of this theme for 20 years, and had always found gullible ones to advance him sizeable funds at this prospect of becoming a multi-millionaire the easy way. By the time they discovered that there were no safe deposits, Novarro had already decamped to another country.

Unaware of these antecedents, the Riviera nabobs listened to their Spanish friend with a great deal of interest. But before any of them could make him an offer, Novarro happened to dine one night with two showgirls in the San Remo casino. The trio made so much noise that the director came to the table and said, "I am sorry to embarrass you, sir, but His Majesty requests that you quiet down a little."

"His Majesty? Whom are you talking about?"

"The gentleman in the corner over there—Farouk, King of Egypt."

"So what?" snapped Novarro. "I can take on King Farouk any day he wishes. Ask him whether he cares to gamble against me."

Farouk accepted the challenge and the chance association quickly bloomed into a beautiful friendship. The sovereign took an immediate liking to the little confidence man and Novarro at once recognized in the King potential prey of a caliber he had never hoped to meet even in his wildest dreams of conquest.

Farouk and his entourage occupied the entire first floor of the Carlton Hotel and Novarro was soon walking in and out as if he belonged to the family. The protection of royalty gave him great prestige along the coast. He was picked as a member of a beauty contest jury and admitted to a yacht club of the Côte d'Azur, one of the most exclusive clubs on the Continent.

The King and the crook spent long nights together at the baccarat tables, and in order to keep Farouk in good humor, Novarro let him win more often than not. Then, one evening, he mentioned his hidden millions to the monarch.

"What's the hitch?" Farouk asked.

"No hitch, Your Majesty," said Novarro. "The only thing I would ask for is a small advance on the deal, for you know better than anyone does how much I have been losing in the casinos lately. I think a check for $100,000 would do—truly a trifle compared to the sums at stake."

To increase the King's interest in the transaction, Novarro offered to invest part of his regained fortune in the construction of a super casino in the Nile Valley that would be the most luxurious pleasure house of its kind in the Middle East. "It would feature the prettiest show girls money could buy, and Your Majesty would be a partner in the establishment," he said. Farouk listened in rapture and negotiations began. A few days later, his royal duties called him home, but the negotiations continued by correspondence.

Fernandez Antonio Novarro of Vigo, Spain, had come a long way. Actually, Interpol has established, his name was not Novarro and he was not born in Spain but Poland, where he was named Sykowski.

Novarro, or Sykowski, came to America as a small boy. According to Judge Amedeo Lauritano (then assistant U. S. Attorney), who later questioned him, he grew up on New York's Bowery and at 16 joined a vaudeville act as a contortionist. In the world of make-believe he was billed as the "Human Frog" or "The Frog Man."

Novarro came to view the whole world as a stage on which one had to create illusions in order to succeed. He apparently took for the motto of his life the old Roman proverb: "Mankind wants to be fooled."

On June 15, 1912, in Havana, Cuba, the boy came for the first time in conflict with the law when he received a sentence of 40 days in prison for cheating a tourist out of $40. Right after getting out of jail, police caught him at it again, and he got 90 days. That taught him a lesson, but not the one it was supposed to: he learned that small-time crime didn't pay.

As a result, he served two sentences for forgery and slipped back into the country via Mexico posing as U. S. citizen Carlos Nunn. On March 25, 1921, a San Diego court sentenced him to three years in jail for falsification of passports.

After serving two-thirds of that term, Novarro *did* go to work for the Al Capone ring in Los Angeles and Chicago. But he never got into big-league bootlegging, for in November, 1923, he received a long prison sentence for two thefts. When he was released six years later and put on a ship to Germany, he had, with brief interruptions, spent his whole adult life behind prison walls.

As an itinerant con man, Novarro now cheated, cardsharped, smuggled and gun-ran his way to wealth without any major setbacks until 1934, when Madrid police fingerprinted him on suspicion of dope smuggling. Two years later, in Austria, he was caught at a passport swindle, given five months in prison and expelled from the country.

According to Interpol, in July, 1936, he appeared in Switzerland, with a Nicaraguan passport issued in Vienna. As the Swiss police knew that he had been expelled from Austria, they took his prints and, acting on a hunch, sent them to Warsaw for examination. A month later, the Polish Judicial Police definitely identified the man as Abram Sykowski born in Radomsk on July 23, 1892.

Fingerprinting, of course, was not yet in use in Poland when Sykowski was a youngster. The Poles based their findings on an incident in 1930 when he was arrested and fingerprinted as a suspected cardsharp in the casino of Zoppot in the Free City of Danzig. At that time, he had found it convenient to fall under Polish jurisdiction and had revealed certain data about his family in Radomsk which could be checked and obviously was not invented. He later regretted that slip and tried by all means to cover it up. But Interpol possessed enough circumstantial evidence to leave no reasonable doubt about his identity.

A year later, Novarro came to Rome and let word of his "hidden bootleg millions" get around. It came to the ears of a fellow gangster, Benito Mussolini.

"I was introduced to the Duce at the Royal Automobile Club by his girl friend Clara Petacci," Novarro once told police of this episode. "She had heard about my predicament through friends and felt that the dictator might be able to help me. Mussolini saw there a splendid opportunity to acquire much-needed dollars and, at the same time, play a trick on the U. S. Government. He gave me 7,000,000 lira to let him in on the deal."

Novarro decamped and used the lira to buy machine guns for Republican Spain and soon had built up a flourishing arms traffic across the French-Spanish border. But apparently the game entailed some danger. One day in January, 1938, at any rate, he rushed into the offices of the Palm Beach Casino at Cannes and exclaimed: "My name is Carlos Ladenis. I am an old customer of your establishment. At this moment I am being pursued by a gang of Fascists who want to kill me because I have been running guns to Spain. I desperately need a loan of 3,000,000 francs to make a getaway. Will you please oblige?"

Three days later, the French deported him to Spain as an undesirable alien. He set up headquarters in the Ritz Hotel in Barcelona and bragged about the days when he terrorized Chicago's gangland. He was *persona grata* with the Catalonian government—thanks to his arms deliveries—but he became somewhat less grata after cheating the police chief out of $30,000 with his bootleg millions swindle.

He next turned up in the fashionable Mount Royal Hotel in Montreal, Canada, posing as Count Alexander Novarro Fernandez, a cousin of the late King Alfonso XIII of Spain. When doubters looked in vain for his Hapsburg lip and wanted to stick pins into him to see whether he had hemophilia, he drew himself up to his full 5'7" and exclaimed haughtily: "Don't ever touch a person of royal blood."

He did everything possible to make himself appear respectable but, after Canada rejected his application for citizenship on June 28, 1945, he let it be known that he had $340,000,000 hidden in 34 U. S. banks.

A group of men headed by a wealthy attorney and the president of an airline advanced him $125,000 to buy a secret code book showing the locations of the banks. He left the country aboard one of the airline president's own passenger planes.

Police of the Western Hemisphere tracked "the Count" to Venezuela, then to Curaçao, and on September 28, 1946, J. Edgar Hoover of the FBI announced that "Antonio Novarro Fernandez . . . a notorious international confidence man, wanted in connection with a $125,000 swindle," had been arrested when he stepped off a plane in Miami, Florida.

Novarro pleaded not guilty; but when the case came up for trial on February 5, 1947, changed his plea to guilty. Judge Edward A. Conger sentenced the Count to three years in prison.

In 1949, he was deported to Cuba. Two years later, completely unchastened, and as Fernandez Novarro, he appeared in Paris and began his build-up all over again. Within a year he had the biggest fish of all on his hook for, in April, 1952, King Farouk summoned his friend Novarro to Egypt. He arrived at the Hotel Semiramis along with ten European beauties for Farouk's unofficial harem.

Royal secretary Antonio Puli later described this visit in the Cairo newspaper *Akhbar el Yom:*

"Farouk invited the 'delegation' to several conferences in Abdin Palace. In the end, it was agreed that the King would dispatch a special

282

courier to the United States who would be empowered to open the safes in question and take the contents out of the country in a diplomatic pouch.

"In exchange for this service, the ruler would receive a commission of 10 per cent of the total amount salvaged. Moreover, Mr. Novarro pledged to invest no less than 20 per cent and no more than 30 per cent of the funds in question in the Egyptian economy. Specifically, plans were drafted for the installation of a gambling establishment near Cairo designed to attract the tourist trade; 51 per cent of the shares of the new casino to belong to the Egyptian government, 49 per cent to be divided between the King, Mr. Novarro and a number of other prominent personalities.

"But the negotiations reached a major impasse when the King insisted that he be allowed to deduct his entire commission from the contents of the first deposit box. Discussion on that point took so long that no contract had been signed by the time King Farouk was overthrown on July 23, 1952."

This came as a heavy blow to Novarro. He had spent almost a year on "Operation Farouk," had taken large losses at baccarat and gone to considerable other expense, only to see his scheme collapse at the last minute.

Back on the Riviera, the impostor now reverted to a series of small-time swindles. He would, for instance, tell an acquaintance who wanted to exchange say $10,000 into francs on the black market: "Why, that's simple. Just transfer the sum to my account in Switzerland, and I'll give you the counter value in French francs as soon as my bank notifies me."

Once the money was deposited, he refused to pay, or disgorged only half the amount and promised to pay the rest later. He knew that the victims couldn't denounce him without incriminating themselves.

One night he sat down in the Carlton for a game of gin rummy with a professional player that lasted until 4:00 A.M.

"It was a weird spectacle," the barman recalls. "Novarro, pale, hollow-cheeked and nervous, lit one cigarette after the other. Opposite him sat this man with black horn-rimmed glasses, flanked by a horrible canary blonde who kept the score. Novarro first won 1,500,000 francs, then lost them and 2,000,000 more. In the end, he said to his opponent: 'Come to my villa tomorrow morning and I'll pay you.' Next morning at 8:30, the man, contrary to all customs, presented himself at Novarro's villa. It was empty. Novarro had left with his luggage, car and chauffeur."

283

Presumably he fled to Switzerland for on January 13, 1953, a black Packard coming from Geneva stopped at the French-Swiss border post of Moelle-Salaz. In the rear of the car sat Novarro, whom Swiss authorities had asked to leave the country. He jealously clutched a brief case which customs officers discovered to be filled with precious jewelry. In a little van attached to his car, they found a portable pharmacy of drugs against T.B. When he proffered his passport, an official briefly glanced at it and said:

"This passport doesn't show your true identity, sir. No man called Fernandez Novarro was born in Vigo, Spain, in 1894. We suggest that your real name is Abram Sykowski, and that you were born in Radomsk, Poland."

"The Spanish authorities must have misinformed you, gentlemen," Novarro said without apparent emotion. "But I am used to that kind of error, and I am at your full disposition."

Interrogated all night, he admitted there had been some dark chapters in his past, but persistently denied being Sykowski. Pending further investigation, police assigned him to forced residence in Montargis, not far from Paris, as a "métèque" (undesirable alien) and required him to report to the station house three times a day.

At first, this change of status didn't affect Novarro very much. He received many "business" visits from Paris, bet on horses by telephone and showered the personnel in his hotel with lavish tips. A chambermaid who brought a cup of coffee to his bedside and received a $65 pourboire later swore he had taken the money out of a suitcase full of 10,000-franc notes.

But he soon grew restless in his exile and made an abortive attempt to escape over the Italian border with travel papers for San Marino, the famous little gamblers' republic. How he came by these papers, police could not say.

In January, 1957, he did finally manage to disappear—in the general direction of Western Germany. And where he is today only this modern Cagliostro himself knows.

THE ART OF LOVE

Anonymous

There were once two very intimate friends, both of the family of Savelli, in Rome, the name of one of whom was Bucciolo, of the other Pietro Paolo, both of good birth and easy circumstances. Expressing a mutual wish to study for a while together at Bologna, they took leave of their relatives and set out. One of them attached himself to the study of the civil, the other to that of the canon law; and thus they continued to apply themselves for some length of time. But as you are aware that the subject of the Decretals takes a much narrower range than is embraced by the common law, so Bucciolo, who pursued the former, made greater progress than did Pietro Paolo, and having taken a licentiate's degree, he began to think of returning to Rome.

"You see, my dear fellow-student," he observed to his friend Paolo, "I am now a licentiate, and it is time for me to think of moving homewards." "Nay, not so," replied his companion; "I have to entreat you will not think of leaving me here this winter; stay for me till spring, and we can then return together. In the meanwhile you may pursue some other science, so that you need not lose any time;" and to this Bucciolo at length consented, promising to await his relation's own good time.

He then returned to the college, to his former professor, informing him of his determination to bear his friend company a little longer, and entreating to be employed in some pleasant study to beguile the period during which he had to remain. The professor begged him to suggest something he would like, as he should be very happy to assist him in its attainment. "My worthy tutor," replied Bucciolo, "I think I should like to learn the way in which one falls in love, and the best manner to begin."

"Oh, very good," cried the tutor, laughing, "you could have hit upon nothing better, for you must know that, if that be your object, I am a complete adept in the art. To lose no time, in the first place, go next Sunday morning to the Church of the Frati Minori, where all the ladies

285

will be clustered together, and pay proper attention during service, in order to discover if any one of them in particular happen to please you. When you have done this, keep your eye upon her after service, to see the way she takes to her residence, and then come back to me. And let this be the first lesson, first part, of that in which it is my intention to instruct you."

Bucciolo went accordingly, and taking his station the next Sunday in the church as he had been directed, his eyes wandering in every direction except the proper one, were fixed upon all the pretty women in the place, and upon one in particular who pleased him above all the rest. She was far the most attractive and beautiful lady he could find; and on leaving the church Bucciolo took care to obey his master, and follow her until he had made himself acquainted with her residence. Nor was it long before the young lady began to perceive that the student was smitten with her; upon which, Bucciolo, returning to his master, acquainted him with what he had done. "I have learned as much as you ordered me, and found somebody I like very well."

"So far good," cried the professor, not a little amused at the sort of science to which his pupil thus seriously devoted himself, "so far good; and now mind what I have next to say to you. Take care to walk two or three times a day very respectfully before her house, casting your eyes about you in such a way that no one catch you staring in her face; but look in a modest and becoming manner, so that she cannot fail to perceive and to be struck with it. And then return to me, and this, sir, will be the second lesson in this gay science."

So the scholar went, and promenaded with great discretion before the lady's door, who certainly observed that he appeared to be passing to and fro out of respect to one of the inhabitants. This attracted her attention, for which Bucciolo very discreetly expressed his gratitude both by looks and bows, which being as often returned, the scholar began to be aware that the lady liked him. Upon this he immediately went and informed the professor of all that had passed, who replied, "Come, you have done very well; I am hitherto quite satisfied. It is now time for you to find some way of speaking to her, which you may easily do by means of one of those gipsies who haunt the streets of Bologna crying ladies' veils, purses, and other rare articles to sell. Send word by her that you are the lady's most faithful, devoted servant, and that there is no one in the world you so much wish to please. In short, let her urge your suit, and take care to bring the answer to me as soon as you have received it; I will then tell you how you are to proceed."

286

Departing in all haste, he soon found a little old pedlar woman, quite perfect in her trade. Bucciolo gave her two florins, saying, "I wish you to go as far as the Via Maccarella for me to-day, where resides a young lady of the name of Giovanna, for whom I have the very highest regard. Pray tell her so, and recommend me to her most affectionately, so as to obtain for me her good graces by every means in your power. I entreat you to have my interest at heart, and to say such pretty things as she cannot refuse to hear."

"Oh," said the little old woman, "leave that to me, sir."

She set off immediately, taking a basket of her trinkets under her arm. On approaching the place, she saw the lady before the door enjoying the open air, and curtseying to her very low, "Do I happen to have anything here you would fancy?" she said, displaying her treasures. "Pray, take something, madam, whatever pleases you best." Veils, stays, purses, and mirrors were now spread in the most tempting way before her eyes, as the old woman took her station at the lady's side. Out of all these, her attention appeared to be most attracted by a beautiful purse, which she observed, if she could afford, she should like to buy. "Nay, madam, do not think anything about the price," exclaimed the little pedlar; "take anything you please, for they are all paid for, I assure you."

Surprised at hearing this, the lady replied, "Do you know what you are saying? what do you mean by that?" The old creature pretending now to be much affected, said, "Well, madam, a young gentleman of the name of Bucciolo sent me hither, one who loves you better than all the world besides. There is nothing he would not do to please you, and indeed he appears so very wretched because he cannot speak to you, and he is so very good, that it is quite a pity. I think it will be the death of him; and then he is such a fine, such an elegant young man; the more is the pity."

On hearing this, the lady, blushing deeply, turned sharply round upon the little old hag, exclaiming, "Oh, you wicked little creature! were it not for the sake of my own reputation, I would give you such a lesson, that you should remember it to the latest day of your life. A pretty story to come before decent people with! Are not you ashamed of yourself to let such words come out of your mouth?" Then seizing an iron bar that lay across the doorway, "Ill betide you, little wretch," she cried, as she brandished it; "if you ever return this way again, you may depend upon it you will never go back alive!"

The trembling old creature, quickly bundling up her pack, ran off;

nor did she once think of stopping till she had reached the place where Signor Bucciolo stood. Eagerly he required the news, and in what way she had prospered.

"Oh, very badly, very badly," answered the little gipsy; "I never was in such a fright in all my life. Why, she will neither see nor listen to you, and if I had not run away, I should have felt the weight of her hand upon my shoulders. For my own part, I shall go there no more," chinking the two florins; "and I would advise you to look to yourself how you proceed in such affairs in future."

Poor Bucciolo now became quite disconsolate, and returned in all haste to acquaint the professor with this unlucky result. But the tutor, not a whit cast down, consoled him, saying, "Do not despair, Bucciolo; a tree is not levelled at a single stroke, you know. I think you must have a repetition of your lesson to-night. So go and walk before her door as usual; notice how she eyes you, and whether she appears angry or not; and then come back again to me."

He proceeded without delay to the lady's house, who, the moment she perceived him, called her maid, giving her directions as follows: "Quick, quick! hasten after that young man—that is he; and tell him from me that he must come and speak to me this evening without fail; yes, without fail." The girl soon came up with Bucciolo: "My lady, sir, my lady Giovanna would be glad of the pleasure of your company this evening; she would be very glad to speak to you."

Greatly surprised at this, Bucciolo replied, "Tell your lady I shall be most happy to wait upon her;" and turning round, he set off once more to the professor, and reported the progress of the case. But this time his master looked a little more serious, for, from some trivial circumstances now put together, he began to entertain suspicions that the lady might be his own wife. So he rather anxiously inquired of Bucciolo whether he intended to accept the invitation. "To be sure I do," replied his pupil. "Then promise," rejoined the professor, "that you will come here before you set off." "Certainly," said Bucciolo, "I will;" and he took his leave.

Now, our hero was far from suspecting that the lady boasted so near a relationship to his beloved tutor, although the latter began to feel rather uneasy as to the result, feeling certain twinges of jealousy by no means pleasant. For he passed most of his winter evenings at the college, where he gave lectures, and not unfrequently remained there for the night.

In the evening his pupil called again, saying, "Worthy sir, I am now ready to go." "Well, go," replied the professor; "but be wise, Signor Buc-

288

ciolo, be wise; think more than once what you are about." "Trust me for that," replied the scholar, a little piqued; "I shall go well provided, and not walk like a fool into the mouth of danger unarmed."

And away he went, furnished with a good cuirass, a rapier, and a stiletto in his belt. He was no sooner on his way than the professor slipped out quietly after him, following him close at his heels, and truly he saw him stop at his own door, which, on a pretty smart tap being given, was opened in a moment, and the pupil was admitted by the lady herself. When the professor saw that it was indeed his own wife, he was quite overwhelmed, saying in a faint voice to himself, "Alas! I fear this young fellow has learned more than he confesses at my expense;" and making a cruel vow to revenge himself, he ran back to the college, where, arming himself with a sword, he hastened back in a terrible passion, with the intention of wreaking his vengeance on poor Bucciolo without delay.

Arriving at his own door, he gave a pretty smart knock, which the lady, sitting before the fire with Bucciolo, instantly recognized for her husband's. So taking hold of Bucciolo, she concealed him in all haste under a heap of damp clothes lying on a table near the window ready for ironing; and this done, she ran to the door, and inquired who was there. "Open, quick," returned the professor; "you vile woman, you shall soon know who I am." On opening the door, she beheld him with a drawn sword, and exclaimed, "Oh, my dearest life! what means this?" "You know very well," said he, "what it means; the villain is now in the house." "What is it you say?" cried his wife; "are you gone out of your wits? Come and search the house, and if you find anybody, I will give you leave to kill me on the spot. What! do you think I should now begin to misconduct myself as I never before did, as none of my family ever did before? Beware lest the evil one should be tempting you, and suddenly depriving you of your senses, drive you to perdition."

But the professor calling out for candles, began to search the house, from the cellars upwards, among the tubs and casks, in every place but the right one, running his sword through the beds and under the beds, and into every inch of the bedding, leaving no corner or crevice of the whole house untouched. The lady accompanied him with a candle in her hand, frequently interrupting him with, "Say your beads, say your beads, good sir; it is certain that the evil one is dealing with you; for were I half so bad as you esteem me, I would kill myself with my own hands. But I entreat you not to give way to his evil suggestions; oppose the adversary while you can."

289

Hearing these virtuous asseverations of his wife, and not being able to meet with anyone after the strictest search, the professor began to think that he must indeed be possessed, and in a short time, extinguishing the lights, returned to the college. The lady, shutting the door upon him, called out to Bucciolo to come from his hiding-place, and stirring the fire, began to prepare a fine capon for supper, with some delicious wines and fruits. And thus they regaled themselves, highly entertained with each other.

Proceeding the next morning to college, Bucciolo, without the least suspicion of the truth, informed his master that he had something for his ear which he was sure would make him laugh.

"How, how so!" exclaimed the professor.

"Why," returned his pupil, "you must know that last night, just at the very time I was in the lady's house, who should come in but her husband, and in such a rage! He searched the whole house from top to bottom without being able to find me. I lay under a heap of newly-washed clothes, which were not half dry. In short, the lady played her part so well, that the poor gentleman forthwith took his leave. It was really one of the pleasantest evenings I ever spent in my life. But I think I will go and take a nap, for I promised to return again this afternoon about the same hour."

"Then be sure before you go," said the professor, trembling with suppressed rage, "be sure to tell me when you set off." "Oh, certainly," replied Bucciolo, and away he went.

Such was now the unhappy tutor's condition as to render him incapable of delivering a single lecture during the whole day. At the appointed hour came Bucciolo with the utmost innocence, saying, "My dear tutor, I am going now." "Yes, go," replied the professor, "and come back again to-morrow morning, if you can, to tell me how you have fared." "I intend to do so," said Bucciolo, and departed at a brisk pace for the house of the lady.

Armed cap-à-pie, the professor ran out after him, keeping pretty close at his heels, with the intention of catching him just as he entered. But the lady being on the watch, opened the door so quickly for the pupil, that she shut it in the master's face, who began to knock and to call out with a furious noise. Extinguishing the candle in a moment, the lady placed Bucciolo behind the door, and throwing her arms round her husband's neck as he entered, motioned to her lover, while she thus held his enemy, to make his escape; and he, upon the husband rushing forwards, stepped out from behind the door unperceived.

She then began to scream as loud as she could, "Help, help! the professor is run mad! Will nobody help me?" for he was in an ungovernable rage, and she clung faster to him than before. The neighbours running to her assistance, and seeing the peaceable professor thus armed with all these deadly weapons, and his wife crying out, "Help, for the love of Heaven; too much study hath driven him mad!" they really believed such to be the fact.

"Come, good master," they said, "what is all this? Try to compose yourself; nay, do not struggle so hard, but let us help you to your couch."

"How can I rest, think you," he replied, "while this wicked woman harbours paramours in my house? I saw him come in with my own eyes."

"Wretch that I am," cried his wife, "inquire of all my friends and neighbours whether any one of them ever saw anything the least unbecoming in my conduct." The whole party, with one voice, entreated the master to lay such thoughts aside, for that there was not a better lady breathing, nor one who set a higher value upon her reputation. "But how can that be," said the tutor, "when I saw him enter the house with my own eyes? and he is in it now."

In the meanwhile the lady's two brothers arrived, when she began to weep bitterly, exclaiming, "Oh, my dear brothers! my poor husband is gone mad, quite mad; and he even says there is a man in the house! I believe he would kill me if he could; but you know me too well to listen a moment to such a story;" and she continued to weep.

The brothers forthwith accosted the professor in no very gentle terms. "We are surprised, we are shocked, sir, to find that you dare bestow such epithets on our sister; what can have led you, after living so amicably together, to bring these charges against her now?"

"I can only tell you," replied the enraged professor, "that there is a man in the house; I saw him."

"Then come and let us find him: show him to us, for we will sift this matter to the bottom," retorted the incensed brothers. "Show us the man, and we will then punish her in such a way as will satisfy you!"

One of them taking his sister aside, said, "First tell me, have you really got anyone hidden in the house? Tell the truth."

"Heavens!" cried his sister; "I tell you I would rather suffer death. Should I be the first to bring a scandal on our house? I wonder you are not ashamed to mention such a thing." Rejoiced to hear this, the brothers, directed by the professor, immediately commenced a search. Half frantic, he led them directly to the great bundle of linen, which he pierced through and through with his sword, firmly believing he was killing Bucciolo all the while, taunting him at the same time at every blow. "There! I told you," cried his wife, "he was quite mad; to think of destroying his own property thus!"

Having now sought everywhere in vain, one of the brothers observed, "He is indeed mad;" to which the other agreed. Vexed enough before, the professor upon this flew into a violent passion, and brandished his naked sword in such a way that the others were obliged to use their sticks, which they did so very effectually, that after breaking them over his back, they chained him down like a madman upon the floor, declaring he had lost his wits by excessive study; and taking possession of his house, they remained with their sister the whole night. The next morning they sent for a physician, who ordered a couch to be placed as near as possible to the fire; that no one should be allowed to speak or reply to the patient; and that he should be strictly dieted until he recovered his wits.

A report immediately spread throughout Bologna that the good professor had become insane, which caused very general regret. In this situation numbers of his scholars went to see him, and among the rest Bucciolo, knowing nothing of what had passed, agreed to accompany them to the professor's house. He was almost panic-struck on approaching the place, beginning to comprehend the whole affair. Yet in order that no one might be led to suspect the real truth, he walked into the house along with the rest, and on reaching a certain apartment which he knew, he beheld his poor tutor, almost beaten to a mummy, and chained down upon his bed close to the fire. His pupils were standing round condoling with him and lamenting his piteous case.

At length it came to Bucciolo's turn to say something to him, which he did as follows: "My dear master, I am as truly concerned for you as if you were my own father; and if there is anything in which I can be of use to you, command me as your own son."

To this the poor professor only replied, "No, Bucciolo; depart in peace, my pupil, depart, for you have learned much, very much, at my expense."

Here his wife interrupted him: "You see how he wanders; heed not what he says; pay no attention to him, Signor."

Bucciolo, however, prepared to depart, and taking a hasty leave of the professor, he ran to the lodgings of his relation, Pietro Paolo, saying, "Fare you well! God bless you, my friend! I must away to Rome; for I have lately learned so much at other people's expense that I am going home;" and he hurried away, and fortunately arrived safely at Rome.

ONE THOUSAND AND ONE

by Jacob Fisher

At the time the events in this tale took place, Fort Eustis had about ten thousand men. Located on a peninsula in tidewater Virginia, cradled in the very heart of English colonization in America, the historical countryside echoed once more to epoch-making events. Possibly, with the passing of years, the soldiers assigned to the post would regard their stay there as adventurous. At the moment, the isolation and the grueling training were extremely trying.

It was therefore not at all surprising that Fort Eustis—in the throes of the new latrine rumor—had been buzzing with excitement for days. It was too good to be true, it was unbelievable, yet definitely was based on the highest authority—the Old Man's own personal orderly. The WACS were coming! Slews of them.

The rumor was true; only it had been badly garbled in the telling. It was a disappointing shock when just ten tired women in ill-fitting army uniforms reported for duty one morning at Post Headquarters. Just ten WACS had been sent to Fort Eustis, but the soldiers decided they were better than none at all. There was a noticeable slicking up in the appearance of the enlisted personnel assigned to the Headquarters vicinity. This was something to look forward to—a mark to shoot at— women who spoke your language, who didn't outrank you, who lived practically next door, and who were definitely not like the other women on the post, the few nurses at the base hospital—officers all—who lived in their own rarified atmosphere, unpolluted by the presence of enlisted men.

In ordinary circumstances, under normal conditions, the ten women who comprised the WAC contingent at Fort Eustis would have merited no more than a passing glance. They ranged in age from twenty-one to thirty-nine; in occupation, from waitress to school teacher, in appearance, from fairly attractive to just plain homely; and in education, from the grammar school graduate, to one with a college degree.

Each of the ten WACS came from a different state, and Pennsylvania's

293

contribution was thirty-three-year-old Olga Simanski, of Old Forge. Until she entered her middle teens, Olga's world consisted of the grime, sweat, and ugliness of a bleak Pennsylvania mining town.

Olga's parents were second-generation Poles who wanted something better for their daughter than the life of a coal miner's wife. She was the only daughter in the family, and the four boys, who were all in the mines, helped swell the household income sufficiently to send their sister to a business school in Scranton.

When Olga finished her business school training, she went to work in the office of a coal mining firm in Scranton. This automatically made her a "lady" in the eyes of her proud family.

The years fled by as Olga commuted to work by bus from Old Forge to Scranton. The transition that made her a "lady" seemed to bar her from the possibility of becoming a miner's wife, and when she was in her late twenties, everyone was reconciled to the fact that Olga had become an old maid. Her mother, to whom an old maid in the family was a keen disgrace, was pointed in her remarks. Often she wished she had not insisted that her daughter become a "lady," feeling she would have been better off as the wife of a miner. But it was too late to rectify that error. Olga herself had long since given up hope of being asked for dates, and except for a few dinner invitations from office personnel, she had no social life outside her family.

Shortly after Pearl Harbor Olga enlisted in the WAC. She had no hopes or illusions about what would confront her in her new existence. That did not matter as much as getting away from the slow stagnation of Old Forge.

After an uneventful short period of basic training in Iowa, where Olga discovered that the outlook and problems of many of her companions were similar to her own, she was assigned to the Machine Records Unit at Fort Eustis, Virginia.

Ten thousand men, and ten women. Immediately a vista was opened to the ten WACS which is denied to most women in life. Each was a queen bee, surrounded by a horde of clamoring admirers. To companionship-starved, women-hungry men, the plainest of the WACS shone with an aura of wonderful feminine beauty.

Olga finally came into her own. All her frustrated, lean years were wiped out. Her bleak, old maidish inhibitions vanished.

To Olga, Fort Eustis was a heaven, laden with manna in the form of men. She gorged, but never could seem to satisfy the craving that the long, empty years had created.

Olga found out a great many things she had not known before. One was that men are inclined to talk, to kiss and tell. Many of the soldiers who sought her favors were turned away because Olga could not possibly accept all the invitations she received for dates. There were too many. Olga discovered that some disappointed soldiers resented and disliked her. It took some time to discover that they would not have resented being turned down for dates if she had tied up with a "steady" boy friend. Obviously, she was playing the field, and, inevitably, those not allowed to enter the race became disgruntled.

Intoxicated as she was by the exhilaration of her new life, Olga did not care too much about the toes of those she thus stepped upon until she received a summons one day to appear in the Captain's office. The fatherly Captain seemed somewhat embarrassed. He told Olga that many reports had come to him about her conduct. She was creating discord among the enlisted men and it was felt by some officers that she was discrediting the Army by her reported unsavory promiscuity. In a kindly, but firm, manner, the Captain told Olga that she would have to remedy her actions immediately, otherwise proceedings might be brought against her toward effecting a dishonorable discharge.

Panicked by this warning—which threatened to remove her from her new, wonderful world—Olga immediately became, "Private Simanski, the Untouchable." She was definitely willing to modulate the tempo of her reckless existence in order to remain part of this seething, changing world, which was still so much better than Old Forge.

Personnel changes in Fort Eustis, as in camps all over the country, were rapid, because of the constant shipment of manpower overseas. A couple of months after the incident with the Captain, practically the entire personnel of the camp had been shipped out. With the exception of a few hundred men in the regular station complement, the entire camp was peopled by new faces. Olga's reputation as a respectable woman had now been firmly established, and she did nothing to risk losing it. She had had her fling, and if she might have had any thoughts about entering on another, she was deterred by the Captain's warning. The fact that this officer was part of the station complement and was still assigned to the post, might have had something to do with her strait-laced conduct.

It was inevitable that of the thousands of men in Fort Eustis, someone should propose marriage. Stolid, ample Sergeant Alvin Kellman did. Regularly assigned to Fort Eustis as a cook, Sergeant Kellman had been a chef in a Seattle hotel. Crowding forty, Kellman was at the stage where he wanted companionship, and possibly a partner in the new restaurant he intended to open in Seattle when he left the Army.

Olga reasoned it might not be a bad idea. Her adventurous wings clipped by the admonition to behave, Kellman would supply the need of an escort, a man to take her out to the parties she craved, but without the onus of criticism. Besides, there was a little element of pride. She wanted to show the folks back in Old Forge she had a husband. Whatever happened subsequent to the marriage didn't matter so much. She would never again have to listen to the sympathetic cluckings of the stout matrons who used to be her schoolmates. Once she had acquired the prefix of "Mrs." to her name, they could never take it away from her.

After their marriage, her husband sought to find a furnished room or a small apartment in the vicinity of the camp, but Olga discouraged this. She preferred the excitement and changing panorama of army post life. They arranged to have their leave days together and on those day went to modest hotels in Norfolk to assume their connubial state.

The routine established by Alvin and Olga was eminently satisfactory to both until the arrival of orders transferring Private Olga Simanski to Camp Young, California. If Olga was secretly a little elated at the impending change of scenery, she did not show it. Stolid Alvin was philosophical. "The war won't last forever," he said. "It won't be too long before we can go to Seattle."

Conscious of the delay in mail delivery attendant upon a transfer, Olga rented a Post Office box in the town of Indio, California, after arriving at her new duty station. She then notified her husband, her folks, and a few friends of her new address. She also notified the Office of Dependency Benefits at Newark, and she requested that her family allowance check, based on Sergeant Alvin Kellman's military service, be sent to her box in Indio. The Servicemen's Dependents Allowance Act, which provided for family allowances for lawful wives of soldiers, included the WAC in the same category.

Camp Young was another Fort Eustis, only more so. A training camp for desert warfare, its tanks and armored equipment maneuvered endlessly over the furnacelike terrain. To the young soldiers at this post, isolated by the vast expanse of burning sands, the few WACS assigned to the camp were also visions of beauty, to be cherished and sought after.

It didn't take long for the memory of Alvin Kellman, on the other side of the continent, to become dim in Olga's mind. Carefully and selectively she started going out on a few chaste dates. She wanted to do nothing to jeopardize her position in the army. And then, something happened that was unplanned. Private Olga Simanski fell truly in love.

The young giant who captured Olga's heart was a corporal who owned a small truck farm in California's Imperial Valley. Corporal Sebastian Alvarez would sit silently for hours while his buddies harangued endlessly. Long hours of solitude spent in caring for his plants had not promoted any penchant for small talk.

Sebastian liked Olga. Before he ever kissed her, he proposed marriage. Olga knew he was not a man to enter into any clandestine love affair. Her rapidly garnered knowledge of men told her that. But Olga was in the dilemma of being married to Alvin while she wanted to marry Sebastian. She was sure that if she told her new sweetheart that she was married, she would lose him. Besides, Alvin was far away, and Sebastian need never know about him, Olga decided. The technicalities of divorce could be worked out later on—at leisure. Olga and Sebastian were married, and she did not write to Alvin about it, fearing that she would invite complications if she did so.

After a short honeymoon at Sebastian's farm, they returned to Indio, where they rented a small apartment above a restaurant. Olga's desire to participate in the hurly-burly camp life was gone. Her only desire was to be with Sebastian. Whenever they were able, she and her new husband stayed at their little apartment. Several weeks after the marriage, Olga was surprised to receive a family allowance check at their new home, addressed to Mrs. Sebastian Alvarez. She had not entered into her second marriage with any thought of defrauding the government of any family allowance funds. Olga was now the recipient of two family allowance checks, and if she returned one, she would have to disclose the fact that she had committed bigamy.

The post office box proved fortunate, because the mail from Alvin and her other check from the Office of Dependency Benefits were sent there. The Alvarez check was received at the apartment, and Olga decided to accept both checks, as the lesser of two evils.

Olga and Sebastian continued their happy marital relationship until Sebastian's organization was shipped to North Africa. A short time later, Olga was subjected to the infinite wisdom of the War Department's action, and was transferred again, this time to Camp Shanks, a short distance up the Hudson from New York City.

Bedeviled by the two monthly allowance checks which she knew would shadow her footsteps all over the world, Olga rented two post office boxes in two small towns in Westchester County. One was in the

297

name of Private Olga Kellman, and the other in the name of Mrs. Sebastian Alvarez. She notified each husband of the new address to which he should send mail to her.

"Absence makes the heart grow fonder," did not apply to Olga's feelings for Sebastian. "Out of sight, out of mind," became more appropriate. Challenged by the furor of an embarkation camp, exhilarated by her first experiences with New York, flattered by the attention shown her by sophisticated soldiers from the metropolitan area, Olga was soon absorbed by the great drama being enacted about her—and enacted private dramas of her own.

The extra one hundred dollars flowing monthly into Olga's coffers in the form of the two family allowance checks allowed her certain luxuries and entertainments which she had hitherto denied herself. Lulled into a feeling of security by the passing months, she hardly gave a thought to the matter of her two remittances when she received a third proposal of marriage. This time it was Private Richard Lassman who asked her to marry him. She liked Dick too. She knew he was going overseas very soon.

Olga's third husband, Dick Lassman, spent exactly twelve hours with his bride before he was alerted and shipped from the country. Renting a post office box in Newburgh, New York, under the name of Mrs. Richard Lassman, Olga filed her new application for a family allowance, and sent a copy of her new wedding certificate. Soon, a monthly check from the Office of Dependency Benefits flowed regularly to Mrs. Richard Lassman at Newburgh, New York.

Olga's ability with tabulations made her an invaluable operator in the Machine Records Unit, and won her a second stripe. It also made her subject to transfer frequently—whenever unusual activity took place in a camp necessitating the use of additional machine operators. Shortly after her marriage to Private Lassman Olga was transferred to Fort Dix, New Jersey.

After a reconnaissance of her new territory, Olga quickly rented three post office boxes in the little towns of Browns Mills, Bordentown, and Wrightstown—each in the name of one of her three husbands. She notified each husband of the change of address and also filed changes of address with the Office of Dependency Benefits.

Before really settling down to the new post life of Fort Dix, Olga suddenly met a young sailor from Trenton at a U.S.O. dance in that city. Yeoman 2nd Class Haley Turner commuted to war on the Pennsylvania Railroad. Born and bred in Trenton, Haley had attended business school and become an expert typist and stenographer. He was just what a desk Admiral needed. After his boot training, he was assigned to the huge Naval Headquarters, sometimes called the "U.S.S. Concrete" at 90 Church Street, New York City. That was his one and only duty assignment while in the service of the United States Navy. His home in Trenton being only one hour distant by train and ferry, Haley decided to live at home. His regular office hours allowed him to maintain this schedule with ease. A sailor by virtue of his uniform, he often remarked wryly that he should be wearing a chestful of ribbons because of the thousands of times he safely crossed the Hudson River on the ferry, going to and from 90 Church Street.

The details of how Haley Turner wooed and won the hand of Corporal Olga Simanski in marriage are not material. They lived with his family in Trenton after the marriage, and settled down to a rather uneventful life. It is material though to note that Olga started collecting a fourth family allowance from the government based on Haley Turner's naval service. This check was delivered each month to her new home.

Olga's fraudulent conduct might have gone on indefinitely but for a quirk of fate. The routine of the newly married couple rarely varied. Haley drove to the station each morning with his wife. He parked his car, and Olga waited until the New York train arrived. She then kissed her husband goodbye for the day, returned to the automobile, and drove to Fort Dix. At the end of the day, she drove to Trenton, and awaited her husband's arrival from New York at the station. Olga seemed eminently satisfied with this life. Her pent-up suppressions seemed to have been dissipated in her jaunts about the country. She was also extremely satisfied to collect the two hundred dollars from the government each month.

One morning Haley and Olga were at the Trenton station awaiting the arrival of the 6:38 train. There had been a bad sleet storm during the previous night, and no trains were running on schedule. It was a case of catching the first northbound train that came along. As they waited, a long New York-bound train pulled up to the platform, and discharged several sleepy passengers. One was a stocky, fattish soldier, looking dishevelled from his nightlong ride in a coach. He carried a small furlough bag, and started down the platform to the exit stairs. The soldier glanced casually at the WAC and the sailor who were clasped in an embrace. With the conductor's cry of "All Aboard," Haley disengaged himself from Olga and entered the train, as she gayly waved goodbye.

The conductor thought it somewhat strange that the stocky soldier,

299

who had got on the train at Richmond and had just alighted at Trenton, should suddenly make a dash back to the train. Haley Turner had hardly seated himself when Sergeant Alvin Kellman, a little breathless, sat down beside him.

"Cigarette, sailor?" asked the soldier.

"Don't mind if I do, soldier," replied the sailor.

"Nice looking girl kissing you goodbye at the station," the soldier offered tentatively.

"Yeah, I think she's swell, too. She's my wife," Haley Turner said with pride.

Before the train arrived in Newark, the supposedly unimaginative cook had elicited from Haley his full name and organization address, and details about his wonderful wife, all of which Haley was not loath to discuss, especially his wife.

The sailor thought the soldier, who did not disclose his name, a rather nice chap. At Newark, Sergeant Alvin Kellman got off the train.

The rest was a matter of routine detail. Sergeant Kellman, not having seen his wife for over a year, had thought it was high time he obtained a furlough to visit with Olga. It was fairly easy to accomplish this, because it was only an overnight ride from Fort Eustis to Fort Dix where Olga was stationed. He did not notify his wife of his impending visit.

The efficient Sergeant Kellman wasted no motion. Alighting at Newark, he went directly to the Office of Dependency Benefits, and told his story to an investigative officer. A telephone call to the Navy Bureau of Personnel at Cleveland disclosed that Olga Turner of Trenton, New Jersey, was receiving a family allowance based on the military service of Yeoman 2nd Class Haley Turner. Subsequent examination of the marriage documents in the Turner and Kellman files showed that the same woman had married both men.

Up to this point, the authorities had no knowledge that Olga Simanski had also married Sebastian Alvarez and Richard Lassman. But when Corporal Olga Simanski, an enlisted woman and subject to military law, was arrested by the army authorities to await court martial, she confessed to the four marriages.

Olga was convicted, and in addition to a dishonorable discharge, she received a sentence of one year in the penitentiary. The irony of fate which led to her unmasking by Sergeant Kellman, however, did not dissolve their marriage, because theirs was a first marriage for both, and entirely lawful.

The strange aftermath of this tale may be found in a small restaurant

300

near the Seattle waterfront, operated by Alvin Kellman and his strapping wife, Olga. Shortly before her discharge from prison, Olga was visited by Alvin who, in the meantime, had become a civilian.

What happened between them—what vows were taken, what forgiveness sought, or what recriminations made—are locked within the walls of the little Seattle restaurant.

THE FAKE THAT MADE VIOLENT HISTORY

by Mark Muldavin

Most journalistic hoaxes, no matter how ingenious, have created only temporary excitement. Others, like H. L. Mencken's spoofing article about the origin of the bathtub which, contrary to his intention, became almost universally accepted as fact, changed only *past* history. But in 1899 four reporters in Denver, Colorado, concocted a fake story that, within a relatively short time, made new history, violent history at that. Here's how it happened.

One Saturday night the four reporters—from Denver's four newspapers, the *Times, Post, Republican* and *Rocky Mountain News*—met by chance in the railroad station where they had each come hoping to spot an arriving celebrity around whom they could write a feature. Disgustedly, they confessed to one another that they hadn't picked up a newsworthy item all evening.

"I hate to go back to the city desk without something," one of the reporters, Jack Tournay, said.

"Me, too," agreed Al Stevens. "I don't know what you guys are going to do, but I'm going to fake. It won't hurt anybody, so what the devil."

The other three fell in with the idea and they all walked up Seventeenth Street to the Oxford Hotel, where, over beers, they began to cast about for four plausible fabrications. John Lewis, who was known as "King" because of his tall, dignified bearing, interrupted one of the preliminary gambits for a point of strategy. Why dream up four lukewarm fakes, he asked. Why not concoct a sizzler which they would all use and make stick the better by their solidarity.

The strategy was adopted by unanimous vote, and a reporter named

301

Hal Wilshire came up with the first suggestion: Maybe they could invent some stiff competition for the Colorado Fuel and Iron Company by reporting the arrival of several steel men, backed by an independent Wall Street combine, to buy a large site on which they planned to erect a new steel mill. The steel mill died a quick death; it could be checked too easily and it would be difficult to dispose of later.

Stevens suggested something more dramatic. Several detectives had just arrived from New York on the trail of two desperadoes who had kidnapped a rich heiress. But this was too hot a story; the editors might check the wire services or even the New York police direct.

Thereupon Tournay and Lewis both came up with the obvious answer. What they needed was a story with a foreign angle that would be difficult to verify. Russia? No, none of them knew enough about Russia to make up an acceptable story. Germany was a possibility; or, perhaps, a bull-ring story from Madrid? Tournay didn't think bull-fighting was of sufficient interest to Denverites. How about Holland, one of the reporters offered, something with dikes or windmills in it, maybe a romance of some sort.

By this time the reporters had had several beers. The romance angle seemed attractive. But one of the men thought Japan would be a more intriguing locale for it. Another preferred China; why the country was so antiquated and unprogressive, hiding behind its Great Wall, they'd be doing the Chinese a favor by bringing some news about their country to the outside world.

At this point, Lewis broke in excitedly. "That's it," he cried, "the Great Wall of China! Must be fifty years since that old pile's been in the news. Let's build our story around it. Let's do the Chinese a real favor, let's tear the old pile down!"

Tear down the Great Wall of China! The notion fascinated the four reporters. It would certainly make the front page. One of them objected that there might be repercussions, but the others voted him down. They did, however, decide to temper the story somewhat.

A group of American engineers had stopped over in Denver en route to China, where they were being sent at the request of the ruling powers in China, to make plans for demolishing the Great Wall at minimum cost. The Chinese had decided to raze the ancient boundary as a gesture of international good will. From now on China would welcome foreign trade.

By the time they had agreed on all the details it was after eleven. They rushed over to the Windsor Hotel—then the best in town—and talked the night clerk into co-operating. Then they signed four fictitious names into the hotel register. The clerk agreed to tell anyone who checked that the hotel had played host to four New Yorkers, that they had been interviewed by the reporters, and then had left early the next morning for California. Before heading for their respective city desks, the four reporters had a last beer over which they all swore to stick to their story and not to reveal the true facts so long as any of the others were alive. (Only years later did the last survivor, Hal Wilshire, let out the secret.)

The reporters told their stories with straight faces to their various city editors. Next day all four Denver newspapers featured the story on the front page. Typical of the headlines is this one from the *Times:* GREAT CHINESE WALL DOOMED! PEKING SEEKS WORLD TRADE!

Within a few days Denver had forgotten all about the Great Wall. So far, so good. But other places soon began to hear about it. Two weeks after the story had appeared in Denver, one of its four sponsors, Lewis, was startled to find the coming destruction of the Great Wall spread across the Sunday supplement of a large Eastern newspaper, complete with illustrations, an analysis of the key significance of the Chinese government's historic decision—and quotes from a Chinese mandarin visiting in New York, who confirmed the report.

The story was carried by many other papers, both in America and in Europe. By the time it reached China it had gone through many transformations. The version published there—and the only one that probably made sense in view of the absence of any information on the subject from their own government—was that the Americans were planning to send an expedition to tear down the Chinese national monument, the Great Wall.

Such a report would have infuriated any nation. It led to particularly violent repercussions in China at that time. For the Chinese were then already greatly stirred up about the issue of foreign intervention. Russia had recently obtained permission to run the Siberian railway through Manchuria; in 1898 she had also leased Port Arthur from the Chinese government. A year previously German marines had seized the port town of Kiachow, as indemnity for the murder of a German missionary, and set up a military and naval base, as a first step toward extending the German sphere of influence in China. France followed with a forced lease on Kwangchowan. England, in turn, had sent a fleet maneuvering about the Gulf of Chihli and bullied China into leasing her Weihaiwei, midway between the recent acquisitions of Russia and Germany. Faced with this danger of occidental exploitation, possibly even partition, the Chinese government under Emperor Kwang-Hsu, began to institute radical reforms, to remodel the army along more modern lines, and to send students to foreign universities to obtain vital technical training.

An important segment of Chinese society bitterly resented not only foreign intervention, but all foreign cultural influences, as well as the new governmental reforms. In 1898 Empress Tsu Hsi made herself regent and officially encouraged all possible opposition to western ideas. A secret society we know as the Boxers, but whose full name was "The Order of Literary Patriotic Harmonious Fists," took the lead in decidedly inharmonious verbal attacks on missionaries and western businessmen in China.

Into this charged atmosphere came the news of America's plan to force the demolition of the Great Wall. It proved the spark that is credited with setting off the Boxer Rebellion. A missionary later reported: "The story was published with shouting headlines and violent editorial comment. Denials did no good. The Boxers, already incensed, believed the yarn and now there was no stopping them. It was the last straw and hell broke loose to the horror of the world. All this from a sensational but untrue story."

June, 1900, found the foreign embassies in Peking under siege. Hundreds of missionaries were reported to have been killed. Swift coalition action followed. In August, an international army of twelve thousand French, British, American, Russian, German and Japanese troops invaded China and fought its way to Peking. There, the troops not only brought relief to their imperilled countrymen, but also looted the Emperor's Palace, and slaughtered innumerable Chinese, without inquiring too closely whether they belonged to the "Harmonious Fists" or just happened to be passing by. The invading nations also forced China to pay an indemnity of $320,000,000 and to grant further economic concessions. All this actually spurred the reform movement, which culminated in the Sun Yat-sen revolution in 1911.

Thus did a journalistic hoax *make* history. Of course, the Boxers might have been sparked into violence in some other fashion, or built up to it of their own accord. But can we be sure? The fake story may well have been the final necessary ingredient. A case could even be made out that the subsequent history of China, right up to the present, might have been entirely different if those four reporters had been less inventive that Saturday night in the Hotel Oxford bar.

304

"GOOD OLD ORVE"

by James Phelan

One afternoon as a streamliner pulled north out of Springfield, capital of Illinois, a smiling, curly-haired man wearing a $250 imported silk suit and bench-made English shoes strode into the lounge car and ordered a drink. Across the aisle from him sat a pair of young newlyweds, Chicago-bound on their honeymoon. Within five minutes, the man in the silk suit was calling them by their first names and buying drinks from a long-sized roll of $100 bills. When the train reached Chicago, the newlyweds made the pleasant discovery that, in their new-found friend, they had hit a jackpot roughly comparable to one of the loftier plateaus of the $64,000 Question. Although he had known them less than four hours, he supplied them with a shining Cadillac and installed them in a suite at a swank lake-front hotel. The bridegroom protested that he couldn't afford such a layout. Their curly-haired friend slapped him on the back and told him not to worry about a thing. "Enjoy yourself," he said. "It's all on me."

For a week the couple reveled in luxury, occasionally pinching each other to make sure it all was real. When the week was up, the man in the silk suit appeared, unlimbered the green log and picked up the bill for the entire honeymoon.

"Just remember the name on election day," he told them. "Orville E. Hodge, your Republican auditor."

The couple went home with the name of Orville Hodge permanently engraved in their memories, to spread the story of their curly-haired patron among their parents, uncles, cousins and friends. They had had a honeymoon on Cloud Seven—and Orville Enoch Hodge had about a dozen more votes.

The remarkable career of Orville Hodge abounds with such happy little true-life stories. For almost four years, until the summer of 1956, Hodge lavished favors on Illinois voters like a drunken Texan celebrating the birth of his one-thousandth oil gusher. He picked up thousands of bar tabs, from swank Chicago bistros down to the little roadside juke-joints on the Ohio River levee.

"Another round for the house on Orville E. Hodge," he would call out, and the cry became as familiar across the fertile prairies as the "sooooey" of the farmer summoning the pigs to the trough. "Just remember the name," he would add when the throng nuzzled up to the bar, "Orville E. Hodge." He did not, like many a man's man, neglect the ladies. Women blushed prettily when Orve, who was blessed with the same sort of animal magnetism as the late Huey Long, gazed at them with brown spaniel eyes, cooed compliments, and sent them mountains of flowers to remember him by.

While he scattered money in fistfuls, there was plenty left to immerse himself neck-deep in the creature comforts. He had five Cadillacs, two airplanes, two expensive homes, three farms, and a fancy hotel in Florida. He maintained suites on a year-round basis at two Springfield hotels and at the Drake in Chicago. He had a mania for redecorating, and indulged it like a restless rajah. He commissioned decorators to do over the hotel suites, right down to new monogrammed silk sheets. He cleaned out the drab bureaucratic décor of his State House office and installed sleek modern furniture, indirect lighting, wall-to-wall carpets, and expensive draperies.

Such conspicuous display on the part of a politician ordinarily would arouse envy and suspicion among the voters. This should have been particularly true with Hodge. His salary was only $16,000 a year, somewhat less than he spent on hotel suites alone. And his job was the most sensitive financial position in the entire state government; through his hands passed the entire avalanche of state spending, totaling a billion dollars a year.

But Orve was careful that the unpleasant sentiments of suspicion and envy did not become attached to the public's concept of Orville E. Hodge. He passed the word everywhere that he was a multi-millionaire to whom politics was a hobby, and a state paycheck mere pin-money. "I've got the political bug," he'd laugh. "Hell's fire, it costs me ten or twenty times what I earn, but I love it."

Envy of his high living was simply drowned in the milk of human kindness. He shared the wealth as if he had suckled politically on Karl Marx rather than Herbert Hoover. If you were a friend—and to Hodge a friend was anyone who could crawl to the polls and scratch an "X" —he would put you up free at his hotel suites, pour liquor into you as long as you could hold out your glass, stuff you with hors d'oeuvres, and then give you a free ride in a $75,000 plane or a fast speedboat.

306

By such tactics he built up affection for himself much like that accorded to Santa Claus. "Good Old Orve," the men called him; "That sweet Mr. Hodge," the ladies sighed.

This affection swept over the narrow barriers of party politics, sex, age, race and geography. Democrats liked him because he would as soon put a potent Democrat on his swollen payroll as a fellow Republican. Republicans liked him for the most sense-making reason a politician can conceive; he was the hottest vote-getter the party had seen in years. State legislators liked him because he delivered their $10,000 paychecks —in person with a smile and a handshake—on the first day of the session before they had done a lick of work. In return, they happily jumped through hoops when Orve snapped his fingers. After his first two years as auditor, the legislators gratefully jacked up his office appropriation 43 percent to a record-busting $7,602,099. The money had hardly stopped jangling into Orve's till when he came around and asked for an emergency appropriation of $525,000 more. The legislators whomped it through for Good Old Orve without even calling a committee hearing.

The Shriners, Moose, Eagles and Elks liked Hodge because he was the ideal joiner, gregarious as a lemming and open-handed as a tipsy sailor. The Elks honored him beyond precedent by naming him Exalted Ruler three times in a row. His home folk in downstate Granite City honored him with a testimonial dinner in 1955, and named him "Granite City's Man of the Year." Up at the other end of the state, the giant Chicago *Tribune* liked Orve because he was always willing to bounce over to the legislature and lobby through some pet *Tribune* project. Newsmen in general liked Hodge for the lavish parties at his Lake Springfield home, with cases of liquor, platters of huge shrimp flown in from Louisiana, steaks from Kansas City, and coveys of pretty girls. Other politicians liked him because he was a quick man with a contribution; he had the lovable and unheard-of habit of tossing dough into a candidate's kitty without even being asked.

By the spring of 1956, Orve was rocketing high in the Illinois political stratosphere. "Orve's going to be governor sure as God made little apples," a GOP county chairman said. "And it wouldn't surprise me to see him wind up in the White House." He had come a long way in his 51 years. He was born the son of a steel worker in Granite City, an incredibly grimy mill town across the river from St. Louis. He had married well, to the daughter of a prosperous lumber dealer, and built up his own realty company until it was the top firm in town.

"Orville was always interested in politics," said a Granite City friend. "He was a likeable guy, friendly and personable. He had a lot of gall, but somehow you didn't resent it. He wanted people to like him, and he'd be hurt if they didn't."

He got hurt bad in his first try at politics, when he ran for mayor of Granite City and took a shellacking. Hodge was a long time getting over this setback. He brooded for months, and then plunged back into politics. "I think he made up his mind to show us all," a neighbor said, and show them Orve did. He served for a while on the Madison County Board of Review, the local tax appeal agency. In 1946 he ran for the legislature, won and served six years. In 1952, he stunned everyone by announcing as candidate for Republican nomination as governor of Illinois. His friends and the professional politicians convinced him that he was trying to go too far too fast. He withdrew in favor of William Stratton, and ran for state auditor instead. Both were elected, but Hodge ran far ahead of Stratton and led the whole state ticket.

Again in 1956, he announced for governor, and again stepped aside for young Billy Stratton and agreed to run for re-election as auditor. But to his cronies he passed the word, "I'm going for governor in 1960 and to hell with Billy the Kid."

Meanwhile he kept burning the money to keep the affection of the voters warm. He attended a four-day convention in Chicago and got rid of $6,800, of which $110 went for waiter tips at just one luncheon. A fellow stopped in his office and admired a spanking new electric typewriter. "Take it along," Hodge told him. "I'll get another." He added a pleasant fillip to his fabulous parties out on Lake Springfield. At the end of the revelry the guests drew for prizes, and Orve gave the winners little mementoes like a case of whisky, a new set of luggage, a TV set, or a traveling kit with a $100 bill tucked away in it.

"Orve spent money like it was going to be declared illegal at sundown," said a Chicago newsman.

There was one difference. When the sun rose the next day, Orve always had another bundle, drawn from an apparently inexhaustible supply.

There is no such thing, alas, as a universally beloved person. This is a disheartening fact of life, like the existence of double sixes on a pair of dice, that one must learn to accept and live with. Even when Franklin Roosevelt carried 46 out of 48 states, there were millions of people who detested him. Not everyone likes Ike, and some people can't stand Mickey Mouse. Even jolly old St. Nick had his Ebenezer Scrooge, who snarled "Bah, humbug!" at the season of carols and good cheer.

308

Santa-Baby Hodge had his Scrooge, too.

In April, 1956, a man went to see Executive Editor Basil Walters of the Chicago *Daily News*. He had some unkind things to say about the two-legged Irish Sweepstakes who was state auditor. He told Walters that Hodge's payroll was padded.

Unlike the Hollywood version of a newspaper editor, Walters did not leap from his chair and dash for the newsroom screaming "Tear up page one!" He thanked the tipster and went and quietly discussed the matter with other *News* executives. They didn't get very excited about it either. For a big paper like the *Daily News* gets dozens of such tips, and they usually turn out to be the product of either a crank's imagination or political malice.

The *News* decided to check on Hodge because of the identity of Hodge's Scrooge. He has never been publicly named, but he is a political figure who knows his way around in the Illinois jungle. Once before he had tipped the *News* to a major story, the "horsemeat" scandal in which the *News* revealed that Illinoisans were being fed horseburgers and filly mignon in the guise of beef.

So the *News* pitched the tip to its Springfield correspondent, George Thiem. Thiem dug on the story and found that Hodge's payroll was indeed padded. The *News* printed the story. The voters yawned, and the rest of the press ignored it. Hodge fired 15 people, and if it hadn't been for George Thiem, that might have been the end of it.

George Thiem bears little resemblance to the popular concept of a crusading newspaperman. A short, chunky fellow with graying hair, he joined the *Daily News* in 1940 as farm editor, and still owns a farm of his own. He would rather dig in the black Illinois soil than in the steaming compost of a political scandal. But despite his dislike of scandal, he has a talent for rooting it up. In 1950 he won a Pulitzer Prize for disclosing that Governor Dwight Green had dead-headed a flock of newspapermen on the state payroll. Thiem is thorough, persistent and shrewd, and when he works a story he churns his way through it as relentlessly as a tractor.

Thiem had no illusions about the magnitude of his payroll-padding exposé. But he was puzzled by the way Hodge reacted to his questioning. Hodge seemed flustered all out of proportion to the matter at hand. Good newspapermen have a sort of built-in radar, and Thiem kept getting strange blips on the screen whenever he talked to Hodge. "He was too nervous," Thiem says. "I felt there was something wrong."

Thiem began poking a little deeper. After a few days, Hodge barred him from his office, blustering that the newsman was "interfering with our normal routine." This deepened Thiem's suspicions and he revved up his tractor and started plowing in earnest.

Before Hodge closed the door on him, Thiem latched onto a couple of scraps of information. He learned that Hodge had issued a state check for $5,267.65 to a Springfield hotel where he maintained a year-round suite. And he discovered that Hodge was scraping the bottom of the barrel on six state funds he controlled. The funds originally totaled $1,400,000 and there was only $33,000 left in the kitty. They were supposed to last for two years, and Hodge still had 13 months to go. Thiem got the serial numbers on some of the bigger checks that had been drawn against the funds and tucked the data away in his pocket before Hodge politely and firmly pushed him out.

The check to the hotel gave him a lever in his investigation. If Hodge was using state money for a private hotel suite, he was breaking the law. Again, $5,200 was a mere fribble, and Hodge might have an explanation for it. But why was he so flustered? And where had all the money gone from the six funds?

Thiem quietly dropped around to the office of George Coutrakon, state's attorney for Sangamon County, who had the reputation for being a fearless and honest prosecutor. Coutrakon was on vacation in the East, but he had a young assistant, Waldo Ackerman, who is cut from the same cloth as his boss. Ackerman is a 30-year-old, crew-cut young lawyer who served as a naval intelligence officer in the Korea war. Thiem laid his information out to Ackerman. When he was through, Ackerman picked up the phone and called Coutrakon in Connecticut. The state's attorney didn't hesitate. He told Ackerman to start an investigation immediately and let the chips fall where they would.

The auditor's office is an enormous installation, with 600 employees and great banks of robot-like IBM machines. Its operation is so complex that it would bewilder an Einstein. All state agencies sent their bills to Hodge. His staff drew up vouchers for the bills, and from the vouchers wrote checks. The checks were sent over to the state treasurer, who countersigned them, *and then returned the checks to Hodge to be mailed to the payees.* (Keep your eye on the pea under the shell at this step—it's the secret to everything that happened.)

Hodge mailed out the checks. The payees took them to a bank and cashed them. The canceled checks funneled back to the state treasurer, and he sent them back to Hodge to be filed for storage.

Thus the state auditor had full control over the entire billion dollars that gushed out of the state coffers each year. He controlled the supporting documents that authorized the checks, he wrote the checks, he distributed them, and he got them back when they were canceled. Every working day, his IBM machines turned out more than 15,000 of them—75,000 a week, more than 300,000 a month. And once they had been paid, they vanished into an avalanche of canceled checks that were stacked in cartons—like bales of cotton—in warehouses at the edge of town.

Good Old Orve was all smiles when Ackerman said he wanted to look into the complex operation. "We'll give you full cooperation," Hodge said. "You'll find everything in order."

Ackerman tackled something he could understand—Hodge's own office budget. And right off, he ran into a queer little puzzle.

"In checking the payroll, I noticed Hodge had a full-time employee named Harold De Silva," Ackerman says. "De Silva was drawing a top rating of about $700 a month. I looked through some other records and there was De Silva's name again, for a second check every month. It varied from $500 to $900 and Hodge had it listed as 'contractual services.' "

Ackerman couldn't figure out how a fulltime worker could do all that contract work for the state, so he called in De Silva and questioned him. He found that De Silva was bothered by the double checks, too, and eager to talk.

"Every month," De Silva said, "Mr. Hodge's caretaker—the man who runs his Lake Springfield home—comes in with a big list of bills. Mr. Hodge adds them up and then has a state check drawn in my name. He tells me to get it cashed and give the money to him. Then he gives it to the caretaker."

De Silva had saved all the caretaker's lists and happily turned them over to Ackerman. They listed a fantastic array of items. There were cases of whisky and beer, presents, golf clubs, bushels of shrimp and mountains of steaks, flowers, socks, lotions, card tables. There was a telescope, a $58 ping-pong table, a $240 power lawnmower. The folder of bills totaled $18,628.68, all paid by the state via the troubled but docile De Silva. Hodge was outwitting the high cost of living by simply loading it onto the creaking back of the taxpayer.

De Silva's story gave Ackerman a sinking sensation in the pit of his stomach. It is one thing to pad an expense account, but Hodge was systematically faking bills for payment; there wasn't a way in the world you could call a set of golf clubs, a ping-pong table or $80 worth of steaks "contractual services." What made it worse was that Hodge was independently wealthy, a self-proclaimed multi-millionaire. Why would a millionaire charge his lawnmower to the state treasury?

While Ackerman puzzled over this question, Thiem quietly had pried up another big rock and was studying something that looked a lot worse. The *News* had printed a list of some of the larger checks that Hodge had drawn against the depleted state funds. One was for $9,000, made out to a Chicago lawyer named Thomas Fitzgerald. Fitzgerald was out of town when the story was printed but, on his return, he told the *News* that the story didn't make sense.

"I didn't get any check for $9,000," Fitzgerald said. "I haven't any $9,000 coming to me."

But conscientious George Thiem was not jumping to conclusions. Fitzgerald had once done some legal work for the auditor's office, and maybe the $9,000 check was some sort of a mix-up, a clerical error, an unaccountable electronic burp by the IBM machines. There was one way to find out—to look in Hodge's files for the canceled check. If it had been cashed, it would have Fitzgerald's endorsement.

But Hodge had barred Thiem from his office, and by now Ackerman knew that Hodge was giving him something less than wholehearted cooperation. He'd ask for a document and Hodge would come back and give him an excuse instead. And more and more, Hodge was avoiding the office. So was his right-hand man, a personable young accountant named Edward Epping. The auditor's office was sort of running itself, with no one around to give orders—or to answer questions.

Blocked from examining Hodge's records on the puzzling Fitzgerald check, Thiem came up with a brilliant end run. He remembered that State Treasurer Warren Wright made a microfilm record of canceled checks before he sent them to Hodge for storage.

Thiem and Ackerman hurried to the treasurer's office and asked to see the film on the Fitzgerald check. Wright dug it up, and the three men took it to a viewing machine, which projects a blow-up image of the film. Each roll carries hundreds of tiny photographs of the checks. When projected, they show three checks at a time on the viewer.

They turned the projector crank until they had the Fitzgerald check in the center of the screen. The three men huddled over the viewer and made a puzzling discovery.

The Fitzgerald check had been endorsed, all right. But it had been endorsed by typewriter. Across the back was typed "For deposit and credit to the account of Thomas Fitzgerald."

Fitzgerald had insisted that he hadn't got the check. But there it was, endorsed in such a way that it had to be deposited in his account. The endorsement is what bankers call "restrictive"; it means that the check cannot be cashed but must be credited to the payee's account. The endorsement could have been typed by Fitzgerald's wife or secretary and credited to his account without his knowledge.

It could have been, but it wasn't.

"There's something weird here," Thiem said. "Look at the other two checks on the screen."

The one above the Fitzgerald check was made to "Roy Browning." It was for $15,000. The one below was for $5,168.22, to the "C and E Insurance Co."

Both were endorsed by typewriter, too. The wording was identical, with only the payee's name changed. From the blow-up images, it appeared that the same typewriter had been used on all three checks.

The three men looked at each other silently. One of them let out a low whistle.

Thiem turned back to the viewer. "Look at the face of the checks," he said.

The front of all three checks had only the payees' names but no mailing addresses. Hodge's office distributed checks by mailing them in window envelopes with a transparent rectangle where the name and address showed through from the face of the check.

These three checks, all with oddly similar typewritten endorsements, had never been mailed.

The three men turned back to the viewer in fascination. Wright slowly turned the crank, and another check slid into view. It was made out to another firm, for $27,500. It had the same typewritten endorsement and no mailing address. Wright turned the crank again and brought up another one, for $12,500. "It looks like there's a whole string of them," Ackerman said.

They ran the film backward and then forward. The Fitzgerald check was just one of a series numbered from #68900 through #68914. All were endorsed by the same typewriter, none had a mailing address, and the whole batch had been cashed nine months before, on September 15, 1955.

Out of the millions of legitimate checks that had roared through Hodge's IBM machines, Thiem had nailed one smack in the middle of 15 forgeries. There were more, it proved later, many more, but September 15 had been a red-letter day in the happy-go-lucky life of Good Old

313

Orville Hodge. That was the day he had set a new track record in the secret little game he had been playing with the taxpayers' money. That was the day he had stolen $180,000 from the treasury, all in one lovely bundle.

And thus the Awful Truth came out. The *News* broke out the box-car type and blew high-flying Hodge right off his political rocket. When he hit ground, he shook the whole state.

His pose as an open-handed millionaire was a gigantic hoax; instead of giving the voters a free spin on his merry-go-round, he had simply taken them for a ride on their own money. Good Old Orve had had his hands in the public till right up to his dimpled elbows. Almost from the day he had taken office, he had been rustling the taxpayers' money in sums ranging from a few piddling dollars for a case of beer to awesome bales of the stuff. As a rueful downstate farmer put it, "Orve was a millionaire all right, but it just wasn't his million."

Some days he would tote off just a neat $10,000 with a single forged check, on others he would scoop up a whole fortune, like his record $180,000. He favored the wheelbarrow method. He had stolen $80,000 on May 20, 1955, and $85,000 on October 19, 1955, and he had a whole series of thefts ranging from $25,000 to $40,000. Sometimes he stole round sums, like $20,000 on October 19, 1955, and sometimes intriguingly odd figures like $46,344.45 on April 13, 1956.

No one knows the total. It was something well over a million and might top two million. Hodge effectively foiled any attempt to find out by destroying several big boxes of records when Thiem started breathing down his neck. "I don't think we'll ever know what he stole," says Prosecutor Coutrakon. "I don't think Hodge knows himself."

The way Hodge had stolen was childishly simple. "Any small-town bookkeeper could have seen what was wrong with the state's financial control," said an apoplectic Chicago accountant. "You just don't let the same person originate checks and mail them out, too. If you do, you're begging him to turn thief. All he has to do is write up some phonies and mail them to himself."

Hodge didn't even have to mail them. He would write his fake checks, using the names of people doing business with the state. When they came back signed by the treasurer and ready for mailing, he'd pluck them out of line, forge the endorsement and give them to his right-hand man, Epping. Epping would scurry up to Chicago, cash them at a financial institution called the Southmoor Bank, and stagger home to Hodge under his burden of crisp green $100 bills.

The president of Southmoor Bank was one of Hodge's many friends, a dignified, elderly fellow named Edward Hintz. He was the picture of a respectable pillar of finance, complete to the gold-rimmed glasses. Over a period of years he cashed hundreds of thousands of dollars in faked checks for Hodge, although none of them was made out to either Hodge or Epping. When asked why he had cashed checks for people who weren't the payees, he gave a remarkable explanation. He said he thought the checks were legitimate and that Hodge was cashing them so he could deduct his "kickback."

"I thought Mr. Hodge was giving the rest of the money to the proper payees," said Banker Hintz. "It was my understanding that such practices were common in politics. I thought it was all part of the game."

A forgiving judge gently let him off with one to three years for handing a million or so to a man who didn't have it coming to him. Epping, on the other hand, got four to five for his prank of accepting it, proving once again that the Good Book is right—it is indeed more blessed to give than to receive.

Orve not only scorned moderation in his stealing, but he also scorned the show of remorse that is considered proper when a thief is unmasked.

Incredibly, he tried to go right on being Good Old Orve. When the *Daily News* threw the eggs in the fan, he wiped the yolk off his face, grinned as if what had happened had nothing to do with him, and issued a statement to the press.

"I am shocked," he said of the *News'* disclosure that he was looting the public treasury. "This is the first I've heard of it. If all the facts are true, there is something wrong and I'm going to be the first to find out. I will turn over my findings to the proper authorities."

He went into a conference with Prosecutor Coutrakon and came out and said, "We've cleared up a lot of things." Coutrakon followed on his heels and angrily replied that they had cleared up nothing. Governor Stratton demanded that Hodge resign as candidate and also get off the list of delegates to the Republican convention at San Francisco. Orve indignantly refused. Stratton demanded that Orve double his bond as auditor, and then added insult to injury by telling him he wouldn't approve it even if Orve did get it up.

Only then, grumbling every step of the way, did Hodge give in. He quit as auditor, candidate, and delegate to the Cow Palace, and trudged off to tell all to Coutrakon. Coutrakon grilled him for two days, but all he would admit was what Coutrakon had him nailed on, and he insisted on phrasing his confession in the nicest language possible. He had "received this money," it "was made available to me," or "I received credit for it." He admitted forging 46 checks totalling $638,000 and insisted that "was all." Even as he was talking, investigators were pitchforking up dozens of new suspicious checks. And Coutrakon knew something else—that Hodge had frantically pumped back $528,000 into the looted accounts in an unsuccessful effort to cover up.

Why had he stolen? Hodge winced at the uncouth word and replied that he had "used" the money for political campaigning and for "investments." When Coutrakon pressed him for details, Hodge became Good Old Orve again.

"I was trying to do a good job as auditor," he said primly. "These details are hazy in my mind." The only thing he said that remotely approached remorse was, "I must have been temporarily insane." He distinctly emphasized the "temporarily."

If Illinois was disastrously slow in catching up with Orve, no one could complain about the speed with which he was swept off to a cell. Some cynics, noting the approaching political campaign, complained that he was hustled out of sight with almost indecent haste. A federal grand jury indicted him in Chicago, a county grand jury indicted him in Springfield and for several days they played tug-of-war with Good Old Orve as the rope. The federals got him first. Early in August he drew 10 years for mishandling $816,427. A few weeks later he pleaded guilty to several hundred state counts of forgery, embezzlement and confidence game. He was sentenced in the Sangamon County Courthouse, where Abraham Lincoln had served as legislator a hundred years ago.

Coutrakon demanded that Hodge be sent up for the rest of his life expectancy. A Republican judge gave him, instead, 13 to 15 years, which makes him eligible for parole in seven years, when he will be only 58. The judge pointed out, in sentencing Orve for stealing between one and two million, that the prison term was not the only penalty. As a felon, he told Hodge, "You will not be able ever again to run for office."

When he heard these awful words, Orve's knees buckled.

He was sentenced in mid-afternoon, rushed into a patrol car, and whisked 120 miles to the state prison at Menard. The gates swung shut on him just as the sun was going down.

Although justice was speedy in disposing of Good Old Orve, it did something less than a comprehensive job. It left unanswered many little questions, such as how much he stole, where the money went, who was involved in the scandal, and why Hodge wouldn't talk. No one really believed that he had spent a million or two on free drinks and high-living, not even with buying gas for five cars. And his wife said flatly, after he was jailed, "There are important people walking around free who were involved."

If the state could have spared a little time, there were some interesting facts that it could have learned. This writer found a few in just two days, down in the grimy, graft-ridden land that produced Orville Hodge.

One was that Hodge's masquerade was even more fantastic than it appeared. Hodge wasn't Good Old Orve who went wrong. He had been Wrong Old Orve all along. When he had served on the tax board, he had clouted the manufacturers for kickbacks in return for cutting their taxes. When he got too raw, he had been eased out of the job. Later he served as bag man for a corrupt state's attorney. He would meet the mobsters at road-side spots and collect the graft they paid to keep their gambling joints and brothels running.

In a dim bar that fronts for a bookie joint, a veteran gambler unlimbered over 10 bourbons and talked. It is only one theory, and will probably never be proved, but it makes a peculiar kind of sense.

"I'm going to tell you what started Hodge stealing," he said. "I'll tell you because there isn't a way in the world you can lock it down.

"When Hodge ran for auditor, we'd had four rough years. From '48 to '52 Adlai Stevenson used the state police to raid us. He even closed our biggest spot, the Hyde Park Club, and it hadn't been closed in 20 years. So when 1952 rolled around, we wanted to make sure we wouldn't get four more years of the same.

"We got up a real wad of dough. All we wanted was a promise that the state police would lay off. We can handle the locals.

"Hodge set the thing up for us. We trusted him because we'd dealt with him for years."

Hodge arranged a conference, the gambler said, at the start of the campaign. Present were two top gamblers from East St. Louis, Hodge, and another major political figure.

"We were promised that the state police wouldn't interfere," he went on. "The boys handed the bundle over. The Republicans won, but we got double-crossed. Within a month the state cops were pulling raids again. We'd tossed all that dough down the drain for nothing.

"The boys were really burned. But when you're in this business, you can't blow the whistle on the politicians. If you do, you'll never make another deal with the next bunch. But the boys wanted the dough back. When you pay for something, you ought to get it.

"They went to Hodge and raised hell. Hodge said he had tried to keep the deal, but couldn't swing it. He said he was sore, too, but he couldn't do anything about the money because it was all gone.

"The boys laughed in his face and told him to get it up. They told him to get it up, or else."

The gambler looked in his highball glass and smiled.

"If you were Hodge," he said, "what would *you* have done?"

Down within the stone walls of Menard prison, the unpleasantness behind him, Hodge adjusted rapidly to a new life. They say he is one of the most popular convicts in the place.

"It's a good thing they don't let the convicts vote," said a downstate politician, pulling reflectively on his cigar. "If they did, Orve would wind up warden."

THE GIRL FROM MARS

by Fern Marja

Bridey Murphy is an incarnation-come-lately.

The not-so-blithe spirit hypnotically evoked by Morey Bernstein, who describes this experience with considerable awe in his best-selling book, has innumerable counterparts in the so-called dual and multiple personalities accidentally uncovered by medical therapists in the course of treatment.

The chief difference between Bridey and her confreres in ectoplasm is that Bernstein regards her as proof uncontroversial that his subject has led a previous existence on earth, whereas the psychiatrists view similar phenomena as significant symptoms of emotional disturbance—or even psychosis—cast up by the fantasies of their patients.

Actually Mrs. Virginia Tighe, the real name of the Pueblo housewife who was entranced by Bernstein, conjured up a singularly dull and prosaic shade compared to that of a celebrated forerunner, Helena Smith.

Although 60 years and the Atlantic Ocean separate the psychic activities of the two ladies, the parallels between them are irresistible.

Mlle. Smith, a Swiss career woman of impeccable reputation, was the

318

heroine of "From India to the Planet Mars," a report written by Theodore Flournoy, a stubbornly rational professor of psychology at the University of Geneva, before the turn of the century.

Bridey's exploits in 19th century Ireland were almost distressingly uneventful and she died tamely enough in bed. But Helena, as Simandini, daughter of an Arab shiek and eleventh wife of a prince of India, cavorted about in 15th century Malabar, performed religious rites, played joyously with her pet monkey, chanted plaintive melodies in a minor key, spoke some genuine Arabic and Sanskrit and Hindu, danced with languorous grace and finally was burned alive on her husband's funeral pyre.

However Flournoy, the scientist, confronted with baffling and often inexplicable evidences of supernatural powers, was as vehemently predisposed to reality as the contemporary biographer of Bridey is to unreality.

Where business man Bernstein suggests that his experiments with Mrs. Tighe call for investigation of the possibility of the "survival of consciousness after death," the more sophisticated Flournoy saw in the adventures of Helena Smith merely "a resurrection of latent memories" and faded daydreams.

Of the impressive and erudite personages with whom Helena communed while in the trance state and the "continued stories" she produced over a period of years, the psychologist said sadly:

"No one dares tell her that her great invisible protector is only an illusory apparition, another part of herself, a product of her subconscious imagination; nor that the strange peculiarities of her mediumistic communications—the Sanskrit, the recognizable signatures of deceased persons, the thousand correct revelations of facts unknown to her—are but old forgotten memories of things which she saw or heard in her childhood."

Bridey Murphy is no less celebrated today than Helena Smith was back in the '90s. Daniel B. Vermilye, who undertook the English version of Flournoy's account, noted in a preface in 1900 that he had translated the French edition "in response to the demand created by the widespread and increasing interest which has manifested itself both in Great Britain and the U. S."

Apparently history never tires of repeating itself.

Like "Ruth Simmons," the name by which Bernstein referred to Mrs. Tighe in an effort to conceal her identity, "Helena Smith" was a pseudonym. Like Virginia, Helena "shrinks from the publicity . . . thrust upon her," "dislikes extremely the notoriety given to her mysterious faculties" and "refuses to be interviewed."

Unlike Bernstein, who barely touches on Mrs. Tighe's personal background, Flournoy devoted an entire chapter to Mlle. Smith's childhood and youth in a city "on the shores of Lake Leman." Her father was a Hungarian merchant with a remarkable facility for languages. Her mother was a Genovese with an inclination toward the occult.

Like Mrs. Tighe, Helena received no financial compensation whatsoever for her extracurricular romps. Flournoy describes his subject as 30, tall, beautiful, healthy, vigorous, with no linguistic talents and no knowledge of the Orient. She held an important position in a commercial house.

Both Flournoy and Bernstein make it absolutely clear that there is no question of deliberate fraud involved in the histories of Bridey and Simandini. Helena "believed uncompromisingly" in the mystic content of her trances.

Virginia Tighe and Helena Smith had both sojourned on this globe twice before, the former in Belfast and colonial New York in humble stations, the latter as the Indian princess and later as a queen of France.

It should be noted here that the indefatigable Helena, during the five years in which Flournoy attended her séances, also whisked through outer space to distant Mars and occasionally conversed fluently in Martian. In fact, Flournoy patiently analyzes the alphabet and vocabulary of the inhabitants of the red planet before concluding, with a logic that could conceivably repel Bernstein's readers, that the ingredients date back to Helena's childhood.

He emphasizes however that, in the evolutionary process, she has recombined and moulded the elements of the past in "a strikingly original fashion" until it amounts finally to, among other things, the creation of an unknown language.

Here is a sample of Martian as spoken and written by Helena:
"Dode ne ci haudan te mess Astane ke de me veche."
Or:
"This is the house of the great man Astane, whom thou hast seen."

Helena, the incorrigible tourist, arrives on Mars by floating through a dense, technicolored fog—a sequence not at all uncommon for those undergoing hypnosis. She sees vehicles of transportation that move without horses or wheels and emit sparks as they glide, houses with fountains on the roof, a bridge with transparent sides, a man who carries an instrument that enables him to fly.

320

"All things become wearisome at last," Flournoy confesses, "and the planet Mars is no exception." Although Helena did not tire of her extraterrestrial flights, Flournoy did.

Experimentally, he thereupon informed Helena in her waking state of his doubts about the authenticity of the Martian material, pointing out that the language bore a strong structural resemblance to her native French and that Martians themselves seemed suspiciously earth-like.

It was Flournoy's intention to provoke Helena's unconscious into changing the props in her trance fantasy to "please" her audience, a trait characteristic of those under hypnosis but apparently overlooked by Bernstein.

At first Flournoy's strategy produced no alteration in the Martian adventures. But after a month of what the psychologist termed "incubation," Helena spontaneously evoked "an ultra-Martian language and cycle" that escaped the defects of which Flournoy had complained.

He had called attention to Mars' strikingly Oriental features; life on the red planet then became more grotesque. He had impeached Martian syntax as too familiar; Martian developed a peculiar, new rhythm with a construction wholly different from French. He had accused the Martians of looking too human; there now appeared a species of dwarfs with heads twice as broad as they were high.

Flournoy, watching these developments germinate "under the lash of mediumistic hypnosis," decided that autosuggestibility, set in motion by stimulating influences of the environment, "amply suffices to account for this entire cycle."

With a perception stunning for his time, he sums up Helena's Martian escapades as important only as "a psychological curiosity" and views them as nothing less than a former "less evolved state of her individuality" which has "again come to light . . . and become active in her Martian somnambulisms."

But it is the Hindu romance that provides the exciting detective story.

It was at the end of the 14th century that Helena left the home of her Arab father and embarked on a strange boat for the country where she wed Prince Sivrouka Nayaka. Sivrouka, who reigned over Kanara and built there in 1401 the fortress of Tchandraguiri, had a wild humor and very uncouth manners.

But he was attached to Simandini, his favorite, and he in turn was the object of her passionate affections. Unfortunately, as was the custom with the widows of Malabar, she was forced to participate too actively in the rituals following Sivrouka's demise.

Like Bridey Murphy, Simandini recalled her own end. What's more, she acted it out in harrowing detail, struggling against her enemies who pushed her on her husband's corpse as it was devoured by flames, recoiling in terror, sobbing violently, panting and finally suspending her respiration for what Flournoy found to be "interminable seconds."

Bernstein maintains today that Virginia Tighe must have been Bridey Murphy because of the conviction with which she related what purports to be the Irish colleen's autobiography. Flournoy was beguiled by the "agile suppleness" of Simandini, her Oriental speech, her "swaying and serpentine movements" and marveled "whence comes to this little daughter of Lake Leman, without artistic education or special knowledge of the Orient," a perfection of play which could only be attained by "the best actress . . . on the banks of the Ganges."

But Flournoy was not content to stop there. He felt "obliged still to endeavor to discover whence Helena Smith has derived her ideas in regard to India."

It was Simandini's "precise historical information" and her use of authentic Hindu that puzzled Flournoy and were not, he thought, to be explained away by the reading Helena Smith might have done on this subject and then forgotten.

In this year of grace, 1956, William Barker, a reporter on *The Denver* (Col.) *Post,* solemnly journeyed to Ireland to seek verification there of Bridey's existence. Flournoy checked up on Simandini 60 years ago in Geneva by poring through old documents, maps, geographies and histories, but to no avail. He even corresponded with Orientalists, all of whom deprecated Simandini's tales.

Then, one day, Flournoy came across a six-volume history of ancient India by De Marles. It contained passages on Kanara, with references to a mighty fortress, Tchandraguiri, signifying "Mountain of the Moon," built in 1401 by the rajah Sivrouka Nayaka.

Triumphantly Flournoy forwarded copies to the savants who had been ignorant of Sivrouka's name and had even cast doubt on his substance. The psychologist was somewhat crestfallen to learn that De Marles stood in poor repute with the scholars, who uniformly damned him for inventing his "history" out of whole cloth.

But if this dismissed the possibility that Helena had really frolicked in India with Sivrouka, it offered a clue to the facts with which she was well furnished in her hypnotic state. Somewhere, sometime, Flournoy maintained, De Marles' spurious work had crept into the consciousness of Helena Smith, even though he concedes it was virtually impossible for her to have seen either of the two copies of this history that were available in Geneva.

"The fact that she has no conscious recollection of it proves nothing against such a supposition to anyone who is at all familiar with the play of our faculties," Flournoy said.

So the riddle remains unsolved.

But there might be a valuable lesson for Morey Bernstein in Flournoy's modest conclusion that it was doubtless incompetency on his part that prevented him from persuading Helena in her hypnotic state to disclose her secret and that certainly "someone better qualified than I" could find "the joint in the armor."

The validity of Flournoy's approach is underlined in a book published by The Julian Press, "A Scientific Report on Bridey Murphy," edited by Dr. Milton V. Kline.

In a chapter on science fantasy, Dr. Harold Rosen, assistant professor of psychology at the Johns Hopkins School of Medicine, declares:

"Any psychiatrist who, when it seems indicated, hypnotizes his patient during part of the treatment process, could readily duplicate fantasies like Bridey Murphy much more melodramatically, over and over again, almost routinely if he wished. So could almost any facile, clever hypnotist.

"Fantasies can readily be evoked, and to the naïve and untrained observer, no matter how conscientious he may be, they may seem not fantasy but fact. Nevertheless, when this does occur, the hypnotist is, perhaps unwittingly, somehow indicating to his subject or his patient— not necessarily by words; it can be by tones, by gestures, or in other ways—an impression of how that subject should react in order to please him. This comes through over and over again in the Bridey Murphy material."

Rosen then goes on to cite the case of a patient who, under hypnosis, spoke a language current in Italy three centuries before Christ. He had printed it in block letters at the psychiatrist's request and it was found to be Oscan, a language of which the patient had never heard.

The passage he had inscribed was one of a series of magical curses usually inscribed on lead plates thin enough to be rolled up and thrown in graves as a method of acquiring control over various infernal deities.

But a full investigation disclosed that, on an afternoon years before, the patient in question had been daydreaming in his college library about a girl friend. At the same time, he had idly leafed through a book on Oscan grammar that had been lying open in front of him.

On page 243, in English, was the phrase, "The Curse of Vibia," a name reminiscent of his girl friend's. Unaware that he was doing so, he had photographically imprinted on his memory the Oscan curse printed immediately below the English title. Under hypnosis, this memory had returned.

"Patients not infrequently do this—or something very like this—even though in all honesty on non-hypnotic levels they could take an oath to the effect that they have no knowledge whatsoever of the language or the events in question," Rosen observes.

This power, when observed by amateurs, has frequently led to mystic theories of reincarnation.

So much for the Oscan-speaking patient.

So much for Bridey Murphy.

But this reporter, motivated solely by a spirit of scientific inquiry and keeping in mind the long journey to Ireland made by Barker of *The Denver Post* in behalf of Mrs. Murphy, hereby volunteers to reserve space on the first available flying saucer in order to carry on a like investigation with equal conscientiousness for Helena Smith on Mars.

I WAS A DOUBLE FOR GENERAL
MONTGOMERY

by Major Clifton James

It all began accidentally enough. I never had any idea that a trick of fate, which made me look so much like one of the world's greatest soldiers that I might be his twin, would lead to my playing a part in history. Because if the Germans had really been *sure* where we would strike on D-Day . . . But let me tell my story just as it happened.

I was an actor, but when World War II came, I gave up my career to enlist. One night, as Entertainment Officer, I stepped onto the stage at Leicester to make an announcement. Deafening cheers broke out. Both officers and men had mistaken me for General Montgomery, then the most discussed military figure in Europe. Next day my photograph somehow got into the papers and there was comment on the extraordinary likeness between myself and the famous soldier.

Soon after this, my office phone rang and a voice told me that a Colonel Lester would come to see me, and would I show him any stage photographs I might have.

I did. The Colonel looked them over with care, and asked me to come to London. There he saw me behind closed doors, and said abruptly: 'You are to take the place of General Montgomery just before D-Day to trick the enemy. You will be trained in England for the job and then go abroad.

"You will not be going back to your unit, or to your wife and family—indeed, you may not get to see them for quite a long time. You will be under my orders from now on."

At a conference next day I was given the uniform of a sergeant of Intelligence and transferred to Montgomery's headquarters in the south of England. Nobody but Intelligence, Montgomery, Eisenhower and Churchill knew the real reason for my going.

Wherever Montgomery went, I went, too: to rehearsals for D-Day, to "pep" talks, to parades. And always I was studying him, just as an actor studies a part. I studied not only his voice and his more pronounced gestures, but all those little things an actor knows about but which a layman is apt to miss. I studied his walk, the sudden lifting or turning of his head, the carrying of his shoulders, how frequently he would sit or not sit, the difference—or absence of difference—with which he would address officers of varying ranks, the way he spoke to a woman, the way he spoke to a civilian.

It was while General Montgomery was holidaying in Scotland that I was summoned for my first meeting with him and we talked about the strange mission I had been asked to undertake. He had gone to Scotland for four days' fishing and I, as inseparable now as his shadow, had been instructed to join the party. He agreed that I should spend a quarter-hour with him each evening so that I could get a better close-up of him. My own fear was that I should have nothing at all to say to this alert, austere figure, but I need not have worried. No one could have been more charming.

Having trimmed my mustache to resemble Montgomery's, I was taken to a secret place, given the General's uniform with ribbons, his famous beret, and pronounced ready. My equipment was complete, even to the Bible which Montgomery always carried. Then, at the last moment, two highly important factors cropped up.

325

What did the General eat? I was to proceed by plane to Gibraltar in order to deceive the world into believing that Montgomery was in Spain and North Africa, and important things might well happen there. But going to Gibraltar meant that I must meet all sorts of high-ranking officers and diplomats who knew something of Montgomery's personal habits and dined with him before.

"My God," I remember Lester saying, "what does the man eat?"

In the end we had to get in touch with Montgomery, who said: "Don't worry about it. Don't eat meat, fish or eggs, and have porridge without milk or sugar. That is all James need remember."

The second point we had overlooked was that I had a wounded right hand with a finger blown off. When I pointed this out to Lester, I was whisked to a hospital and there supplied with a plastic finger—an amazing piece of work. So equipped, the moment came for me to open the door, walk down the stairs and boldly emerge into the world as General Montgomery.

There was the General's car, flag flying in front, and in another car behind was a brigadier to act as my aide, and a young captain, both from M.I.5. Swiftly we drove through bomb-scarred London, but not so swiftly that knots of people did not recognize me—and they cheered and waved.

At Northolt aerodrome, I found the Chiefs of Staff lined up for inspection. It gave me my first real warming of the heart to find that not one of them showed the slightest doubt of my identity.

Ten minutes from Gibraltar, one of the pilots came through to the brigadier and said, "I'm sorry, sir, but we have little fuel left. What shall I do—come down in Spain or fly on?"

The brigadier answered: "Fly on. Think of the satisfaction it would afford the Germans to know that General Montgomery was either killed or interned in Spain."

Luckily we made it with just five minutes flying-time left in the tanks. As our plane reached Gibraltar, and I looked out to see the high-ranking officers awaiting my arrival, the immediate impulse was: "get through" them as quickly as possible, then go on to Government House and somehow "get through" whatever awaited me there. I told myself "No." I, as a personality, had ceased to exist. I knew there must not only be perfection in the role I was assuming but what every good actor knows is every bit as important—there must be perfection of timing.

And so I walked with slow, quiet stride, as I had studied Montgomery so often, toward the ranking officers, greeted them quietly, dawdled a little, then appeared to make swiftly for the Embassy car. At Government House I was received in state by Sir Ralph Eastwood, the one person in Gibraltar "in the know" and who had been given his instructions. I was taken into the drawing room and met various notables, before whom Sir Ralph called me "Monty" and I called him "Rusty."

And again I found that I must concern myself not so much about the voice, the way I held my head, where I put my hands, the preference to stand up when talking, which is one of Montgomery's habits. These things had become almost part of me. But I must not, above all things, appear rushed.

And so all the time I stood and walked or shook hands, or joked with "Rusty," the old actor in me kept saying "Tempo, tempo." And when at length I got into the library alone with Sir Ralph, he at once smiled: "Congratulations! You were magnificent."

He then took me out into the garden and said that any minute, two Spanish noblemen would be calling to see Lady Eastwood about a Moroccan carpet. It was essential that I should be in the garden when they came in, and we even rehearsed the conversation that should go on between us when the noblemen arrived. It was agreed that as the visitors were about to enter, Sir Ralph should say to me:

"Do you recognize that frieze, Monty?" and I was to say: "Yes, Rusty, but it's gotten a bit chipped, hasn't it?"

It was just as I was saying this that the two noblemen entered, raised their hats to the Governor and were introduced to me. Three hours later, the news was circulating in Madrid that General Montgomery was in Gibraltar. Berlin had it that night.

There was only one man I was afraid of at Government House—the man who, on the many occasions when the real Montgomery had stayed there during his career, had acted as the General's batman. But he did not show the slightest suspicion. I must confess, however, that I went through the same fears when the time came for me to land at Algiers. Breakfast over, I drove to the plane through the cheers of troops, and with an air force and naval guard awaiting my inspection. And when we landed at Algiers, there were the high-ranking officers again, this time of Sir Henry Maitland Wilson's staff, on hand to greet me.

As the door of the plane opened, it was like the curtain going up again—and I was immediately braced for the ordeal. With the leash on so that I should never seem hurried, I inspected that guard of honor outside Wilson's headquarters and went inside. And that, so far as I was concerned, was the end of it.

Once away from everybody's gaze, I was treated to a whisky and a cigarette, provided with a razor to take off Montgomery's moustache, given the clothes of a lieutenant, and quickly became Clifton James again. My job was done.

But I was not yet free. M.I.5 was determined that there should be no mistake. Quickly they smuggled me off to Cairo; and for three long weeks I was required to lay hidden there—weeks during which came D-Day and the speedy advance that followed.

EMMA EDMONDS: UNION SPY
IN MEN'S BREECHES

by Harlowe R. Hoyt

Eleven times Emma Edmonds penetrated the Confederate lines. She became a colored roustabout as nimbly as an Irish biddy peddling cakes and comfits from her wicker basket. As a gawky country lad, she clerked in a Louisville store and amassed information the while. In an emergency, she donned military trappings and became an aide-de-camp. All of which is the more astounding since Emma Edmonds trained to become a nurse with ambitions of serving as a medical missionary.

Emma Edmonds was a Canadian, born and educated in the Province of New Brunswick. From her dour Presbyterian forebears she inherited a hearty strain of religion that found its source in the Bible and its outlet in doing good for her fellow-men. The family moved to the States and settled in New England. Chance found Emma Edmonds in New York City on April 12, 1861, and chance on that day had it that the aged Edwin Ruffin should fire the first gun of the Civil War, while from Fort Sumter, Abner Doubleday discharged the answering shell. Emma immediately abandoned her homeward journey and dreams of darkest Africa to volunteer as a nurse in the forces of the North.

It was while she was with McClellan's forces in the vicinity of Yorktown that the call came that changed Emma Edmonds from nurse to spy. A detachment of the Thirty-seventh New York regiment returning with prisoners from an expedition brought information that a Federal spy was to be shot in Richmond. The camp chaplain suggested the nurse as a replacement.

They did not give her a course in espionage and shoot her full of serums. Instead a phrenologist read the bumps on her cranium and found her organs of secretiveness, resourcefulness, and combativeness largely developed. So she was given the oath of allegiance—for the third time—and embarked upon her career as a spy.

A slight figure was the possession of Emma Edmonds, almost that of a stripling youth. A steel engraving shows her in the riding habit of the period, with square determined face and nose somewhat spatulate, her long hair in unkempt locks, and her black eyes piercingly brilliant.

In the recital of her preparations, the woman is none too definite as to the details of her disguise. At Fort Monroe, she picked up the clothing of a Negro fieldhand. Her head was shaved by the company barber —it was before the day of clippers—and from Washington she obtained a wig of real Negro wool.

"Head, face, neck, hands and arms were colored black as any African," she notes. She was to go into the enemy's camp as a Negro. She was to live the black man not only as one of his race but of his sex as well. What makeup could be applied to last through days and nights, withstand washing and the inclemencies of wind and rain, and yet not fade to an extent to betray her secret? Perhaps she colored her skin with repeated applications of walnut juice until she assumed the golden brown of a mulatto. And for safety's sake, she must have applied it to more of her virgin anatomy than modesty permitted her to confess.

To make certain her disguise was perfect, she returned to camp and hired out as a handyman to the company physician under whom she had served. Neither he nor the good chaplain who recommended her, nor his good wife, either, recognized their intrepid camp nurse in this colored hireling.

Her destination was Yorktown, her mission to report on troops, conditions, fortifications, and the enemy's plans. With a few hard crackers in her pocket, a revolver, loaded and capped for instant use, Emma Edmonds slipped through the Union lines at half past nine of a dark night and by midnight had passed the Confederate pickets unchallenged. Without blanket or covering, she lay on the ground to find what rest she could.

A squad of contrabands with rations for the outpost guard awakened her at daybreak. She begged a hunk of corn pone and hot coffee from them and when they marched back into Yorktown, she was in their midst. The Negroes returned to their work on the fortifications. Emma found herself confronted by an officer.

"Who do you belong to?" he asked.

"I dusn't belong to nobody, Massa, I's free and allus was; I's gwine to Richmond to work."

"Take that black rascal and set him to work," a civilian overseer interrupted.

Pickaxe, shovel, and a "monstrous" wheelbarrow were given her and all day long she wheeled her loads up a narrow plank to the top of an eight-foot parapet. Her muscles ached, her legs lagged and with night, her hands were a mass of blisters. Painfully she drew a sketch of the outer works and listed all the armament. Then she hid the incriminating document in the inner sole of her workshoe, turned in and slept a sleep honestly earned by hard labor.

It was on the second day that suspicion pointed to her. She had traded places with a waterboy. Lee had come to voice an opinion that Yorktown could not withstand the brunt of McClellan's siege guns. General J. E. Johnston arrived with reinforcements to bring the neighboring forces to 150,000.

All of this Emma absorbed with open eyes and ears, carrying her waterpail to the laboring workmen. One of them eyed her quizzically above the dripping dipper.

"Jim," he said, "I'll be darned if that feller ain't turnin' white."

"Gem'im, I allers 'spected to come white," Emma promptly replied. "My mudder's a white woman."

Amid their laughter she beat a hurried retreat. A small pocket glass proved the truth. Her makeup was slowly fading and in some places was nearly white. She retouched the telltale spots with a weak solution of nitrate of silver, determining to leave at the first opportunity.

That afternoon she spotted a peddler from the Federal camp as a spy bringing the Confederates details of McClellan's outfit. The day passed all too slowly as did the next. In the evening she was detailed to carry food to an outer post. Soon after, she was assigned as a temporary replacement for a picket killed by a sharpshooter. With darkness came the rain and at last she fled toward the Federal lines, hiding in a ditch until daybreak when she returned to make her report.

The Confederate rifle that she brought with her is now in one of the Federal museums in Washington.

It was no small task to bleach her darkened skin and her hands were so tender the slightest contact brought stinging pain. Emma Edmonds removed what makeup she could and returned to her nursing. She watched the evacuation of Yorktown and followed the troops to Williamsburg and Fort Magruder.

With time came orders for her second expedition across the lines. Obviously it were tempting Fate to venture again in the guise of a contraband. A female Irish peddler fitted occasion better. It was not difficult to procure a dress and basket for her purpose. Pies, cakes, and knickknacks could be obtained anywhere. A few days devoted to perfecting the brogue of the "rale ould stock of bog-trotters," and the whilom nurse slipped away, as perfect in her part as a character from a Boucicault melodrama.

The bridges across the Chickahominy were not finished so she packed her disguise with her pies and notions, mounted her faithful Frank, and swam the river on horseback. On the opposite shore, she headed her mount homeward and saw him scramble up the other bank where a soldier awaited him.

She was in the Chickahominy Swamp with all its mysterious night life threatening her on every side. Though she had strapped her basket to her back, it was soaked through. Her foodstuffs were ruined, her notions sadly damaged. A hospital quilt was sopping as was her peddler's costume. And then she came down with an ague. Burning with fever one minute, shaken with chills the next, she changed to her sodden disguise, and lay down in the miasmic glade.

Three days passed before she was able to move. That morning she pushed through the swamp guided by the booming of Confederate cannon and in late afternoon cleared the morass where a small white house glistened in the sunset. She tried the door, found it unlocked and entered a deserted hallway. But for a single occupant, the house was abandoned. On a straw tick in the living room lay a half-starved rebel soldier, near death from typhoid.

Emma Edmonds tended the sick man. She found tea, and salt, and cornmeal, made a hoecake and fed him daintily. The youth—for he was scarcely more—told her that he was Allan Hall. He asked her to deliver his gold watch to Major McKee of Elwell's staff. He died at midnight.

With morning another search disclosed mustard and pepper, a pair of old green spectacles, and a bottle of red ink. Her disguise, she decided, could be improved.

"Of the mustard, I made a strong plaster about the size of a dollar," she wrote later. "I tied it on one side of my face. It blistered thoroughly. I cut off the blister and put on a large patch of black courtplaster. With the ink, I painted red lines about my eyes, and after giving my pale complexion a deep tinge with some ochre which I found in a closet, I put on my green glasses and my Irish hood, which came over my face about six inches and left for the nearest picket line. I felt perfectly safe for the watch was sufficient passport in daylight and a message to Major McKee would assure me civility at least."

As she neared the outpost she gave a final touch to her preparations. Rubbing black pepper in her eyes to turn them red and watery, she signalled the advance picket guard, a square of cotton window curtain serving as a flag of truce. He passed her without hesitation.

By the time she reached McKee's headquarters she was five miles from the white farmhouse and the corpse of Allan Hall. The major was on a scouting expedition, due to return at night fall. She procured a simple ointment for her blistered face, for the sore was becoming inflamed and suppurated, and spent the day peddling her wares throughout the camp. By nightfall, Emma Edmonds knew not only the location of each masked battery, the number of men and their distribution, but the general strategy of the forthcoming battle as well.

Ushered before McKee, she told her story, presenting him with her credentials. The major wept. Captain Allan Hall, she learned, was his dearest friend.

She offered to lead a party to the body if they furnished her a mount. Major McKee sent a detachment with her but darkness fell before they had covered the five miles of rough road. The sergeant in charge stationed pickets at all approaches and told off a corporal and squad to fetch the body. His guide he delegated to reconnoiter down the road and to come scurrying back at any sign of the enemy.

And Emma Edmonds rode away, not to stop until she was safe behind the Union lines. This time she returned with a rebel horse as proof of her adventure.

Emma Edmonds undertook nine other spy trips, sometimes as a female contraband—her first experience at hard labor cured her of posing as a man—but more often as an Irish biddy, though her makeup in this character was never the same. She altered each disguise against any possibility of recognition so skillfully that not once during those eleven commissions was she in real danger of discovery.

When the Union forces occupied Louisville, Emma Edmonds was promoted from a spy to a detective. She continued to carry on in disguise just as she had before, though now she worked within her own lines. The countryside was shot with Southern spies, radicals, and copperheads, and it was her task to run them down. Except that help was near at hand, she was in danger every minute for the underground was vicious, as more than one detective discovered all too late.

Vitriolic and blatant in his denunciation of the Yankee invaders was one of Louisville's leading merchants. Because they feared that his unceasing diatribes might lead to retaliatory measures, his employees were decidedly transient. So when a personable young man approached him for a job, the merchant put him to work.

The new clerk was neatly dressed, quiet, and self-possessed. He said he was a foreigner down south to observe the war at first hand, and that he was in need of ready cash. He was an efficient young chap and proved himself a go-getter for business, as when he suggested peddling notions to the soldiers. He packed an assortment of pocket knives, suspenders, and the like, and returned each night for more. At the end of a fortnight he had not only insured his job but had clues to three spies in the very heart of the Union forces.

Confident that she must strike boldly, Emma Edmonds took another tack. She confided to her employer that she believed the North was all wrong. Defeat to the South meant disaster for the entire nation. So strong was her conviction that she wanted to enlist under the Stars and Bars. After much discussion, it was decided that she should go through the lines with "a thorough Union man who had taken the oath of allegiance" with crossed fingers, and who really was a rebel spy.

The attempt was set for the next night. She needed more time to perfect her plans but it was tomorrow or not at all. She volunteered for a final peddling expedition, loaded herself with wares, and contacted the Provost Marshal. He promised to visit the store for final instructions.

Next day Emma Edmonds was introduced to the man who would guide her to the Confederate ranks. A well-known resident of Louisville, above any suspicion, he mingled not only with the enlisted men but entertained officers as well. Realizing that silence was safest, she assumed the embarrassment of a green country boy in the presence of his betters. The merchant gave a splendid sales talk and the deal was made. The Provost Marshal wandered in during the afternoon to make a small purchase and Emma slipped him a note of particulars.

Nine o'clock came—nine o'clock of a dark night with no moon, a night ideal for running lines. As the two headed southward, the clerk's embarrassment turned to open admiration for his guide; and he, in turn, mellowing in the glow of such ardent adulation, discoursed at length upon his exploits in the secret service. Incidentally he disclosed the identity of the other two suspects. One was a sutler; one a photographer who spent his time posing the Union generals. He was still in the midst of his recital when a detachment of Union cavalry swooped down and took them all prisoners.

Two years of trying service had taken their toll on Emma Edmonds. She had participated in both Battles of Bull Run. She was at Williamsburg, Fair Oaks, the Seven Days in front of Richmond, Antietam, and Fredericksburg. Besides playing nurse and spy, she served betimes as orderly, notably at the battle of Hanover Court House. She was at Vicksburg when it fell, once more in nurse's uniform. There her depleted strength forsook her. She fell ill with fever but struggled on until they carried her to the hospital.

They gave her a certificate of disability. They commended her for her heroic service. They placed her Confederate carbine with other war trophies in Washington. And then they promptly forgot her; except for her own volume and annotations in the war records at Washington, all too little recalls the accomplishments of the greatest woman spy of the Civil War—Emma Edmonds.

THE STORY THAT WAS TOO
GOOD TO BE TRUE

by Douglas Collins

On November 13, 1953 Bennett Cerf, head of Random House, publishers of "The Man Who Wouldn't Talk" by Quentin Reynolds, got a telegram from Douglas Collins of the Calgary, Alta., Herald, which said in effect that the book was a fake and did Cerf want to say anything about it? Publishers get screwy wires from time to time and Cerf thought this was just another crackpot. But you have to check, and Cerf did, with Reynolds first and then with Collins.

Herewith is the story of the reporter who exposed George DuPre, "the gentle spy." The italic passages were inserted in New York by the New York News.   *Nov. 22, 1953*

"I must warn you that you are on very sticky ground. If you know anything about Intelligence you know that not everything can be told. I can only tell you that it will be the end of your career if you try to be funny about things. I'm giving you fair warning."

That was what George DuPre said to me when I faced him with his own lies. It was interesting to sit across from one of the biggest bluffers of the century and try to get him to admit he was a fake. He was so good that I had to remind myself continually that I had the facts, and that there couldn't possibly be anything to his story.

It had appeared in the November issue of *Reader's Digest* and at the time I met DuPre was being put out in book form by Random House, both versions by Quentin Reynolds.

In the DuPre case it was a matter of sticking to it until an admission came. Before I came to Canada a year ago I had never heard of George DuPre, though he had by that time achieved considerable local fame. First time I really heard of him was when Quentin Reynolds came to Calgary last August to get additional material for his writing. I had nothing to do with the story of their meeting and when it appeared in the papers there was nothing suspicious about it.

(The book is an extension of the article. It is a mish-mash of all the other resistance and underground stories, true and fictional, and of a number of movies that have appeared since the war ended. It tells how DuPre was born in Poona, India, son of a British officer, and was educated at Harrow and Cambridge. However, it relates, his roots were in Canada—DuPre is stated to be of Huguenot origin, his family going back a couple of hundred years in Canada. He became interested in the Northwest and—this much is true—spent a number of years in the frozen North, mixing with Eskimos and running river boats.

He tells of joining the RCAF and being posted to England, where he was dragooned into the "secret services," undergoing a nine-month training before being parachuted into France to appear as Pierre Touchette, the long-lost idiot son of a family formerly living in the village at which he was stationed. He meets the standard characters of all such books—the village priest, the militant widow, the cagey farmer, the dauntless youths and girls, the brutal Germans and so on. Operations are standard in sabotage and passing fliers along the Rat Run. The Gestapo finally gets him and questions him, but in his character of idiot he only says "Je ne sais pas" until they get disgusted and throw him out. But not until he has undergone a couple of esoteric tortures, including

335

a gargle of boiling water and an enema of dilute sulphuric acid, both of which are rather damaging to his insides.)

There is considerable mention of God in the book, and afterward Du-Pre said that he felt the story might have been useful in bolstering faith in God. The book also adds to the four years in France in a couple of ways. He is sent to Germany as forced labor—a couple of weeks after the acid enema—and in the course of sweeping up around the drafting rooms of a German dockyard in Hamburg manages to filch the plans for the schnorkel device for submarines. He was, the book says, the first British agent to indicate the existence of the device to British Intelligence.

And to finish it off, just before the end of the war and after being brought back to England for his first hot bath in four years, and for extensive medical attention in all directions, he is sent back to Germany to crash land and be captured and sent to a German prison camp to unmask Nazi bigwigs who are masquerading as Canadians.

(*DuPre's stirring story was a thing that snowballed on him. He is a mild and gentle man, with religious leanings, and an enthusiastic Boy Scout leader. He apparently began telling his stories to Scouts, as an inspirational measure. The yarn would be embroidered and expanded as he went on. In time, he began preaching to church groups and service clubs and ranging further afield. A* Reader's Digest *correspondent in Toronto heard his talk and wrote to the head office in Pleasantville, N. Y. The editorial board, impressed by the correspondent's urging that here was a great story "just waiting to be written," invited DuPre down. He came and told it all over again to the board, with Reynolds present. Reynolds himself went overboard and invited DuPre to spend a week or so at his Bedford Village, N. Y., home for further discussions.*

Then Reynolds went up to Calgary to check on DuPre. Everyone he talked to there said what a fine man DuPre was, how unassuming and how earnest and sincere.

Among those who praised DuPre was Bishop Nathan Tanner, a member of the Alberta provincial government, for whom DuPre had worked as a sort of one-man investigation bureau. DuPre was regional manager of Commericial Chemicals, Ltd., from which he had taken a leave to work for Tanner, and to which he returned when the Tanner job was over.

Reynolds, a fast man with a typewriter, whipped up the condensed version for Reader's Digest *and then told Cerf, who publishes his books, that there was enough for a volume. Cerf, knowing everybody likes spy stories, agreed, and they pushed it through, with a first printing of 7,500, a second of 2,500 and a third of 2,500 which was just rolling when Cerf got the word.*)

When *Reader's Digest* came onto the stands in November, an indignant man came into the Herald office in Calgary and asked how it was possible for DuPre to have been in France in 1942 when he, the indignant one, had joined the RCAF with him in Toronto in that year.

It was a fair question, but it was only one man's word. There was always the possibility that even though DuPre had been in Toronto in 1942, he might still have been associated with Intelligence, might still have been in France for a long while during the war, both before and after his long enlistment, and might take any newspaper which cast doubt upon his history for a very long ride. So Editor Bill Allen told me to find out what I could about the story.

As soon as I read the *Digest* article, I was sure we were dealing with a grandiose faker but I also knew we would have to use a good many tricks to get to the bottom of the thing. Several questions arose immediately.

The article implies that DuPre operated in France from 1940 to 1944. But no British agent involved in the kind of activities described was working there as early as 1940. It was not until 1941 that Special Operations Executive put the first "boys" to work and by December, 1941, there were not more than 20 SOE men in France.

I was quite sure that DuPre was not dropped specifically to organize escape routes for British airmen, as the article stated. It was not until 1943 that escape routes got much attention, and then they were secondary to sabotage and espionage. There was little point in diverting the energies of highly trained and valuable agents to such work. Fliers usually had only to contact the French to be passed from one resistance group to another until they reached the Spanish frontier. Further, it wasn't until 1943 that air operations over France intensified and men were shot down in sufficient numbers to warrant the attention of the underground.

In all probability no one was ever dropped by Intelligence in the guise of an idiot, as the article said, the only survivor of a village family, who had been thought dead. Intelligence seeks the inconspicuous and this would be glaring. The whole village would have been interested, and he would have had to register with the gendarmerie, idiot or no idiot. That meant the Gestapo would have learned of his presence from the start, and he would have been questioned at once.

337

DuPre's tale of interrogation and release by the Gestapo ranks with the idiot disguise as the most unlikely part of the story. He might have been beaten up by the local boys as a taste of things to come, but he never would have been freed. Those suspected of espionage or sabotage were normally not released at all, but shipped off to a concentration camp, proof or no proof. They invariably were removed to larger head-quarters for detailed questioning, for the high brass of the Gestapo never let the lower echelons mess around on their own.

If we are to believe DuPre's story of his drop into France, he landed almost in the washtub of the woman who was to be his first contact. It just didn't read right, having only 100 paces to go before reaching the farmhouse where Mme. Thibault was to sing the "Marseillaise" as a signal. This was pretty hammy.

There were a lot of other things in the article that were at variance with reason.

Take the matter of his recruitment into the "secret services." My God, you simply can't recruit an agent even, or rather particularly, in wartime by parading him in front of an ambiguous "Mr. Jones" and more or less telling him he has to join up. Judging by his account, DuPre was over-whelmed by the "casual" secretiveness of it all. Actually, there can be nothing casual about recruiting an agent. Sooner or later the question has to be popped. And it is always a question, never an order. There was practically nothing in the article that made sense. I was therefore certain in my own mind that DuPre was a fake, but I had to prove it. The original informant, who doesn't want to be known, provided some names and addresses and I looked these people up. Two remembered DuPre well.

I had written to London to a couple of people who might be able to make some sort of check (an official one would have been impossible) but there wasn't time for a reply. I was afraid somebody else would latch on to the story, because there must have been hundreds who would see through it when they read it. So the editor and I agreed that we had best get right at it.

It took a couple of days to get in touch with DuPre. He was out talk-ing of his experiences. In the intervening time, I memorized the *Digest* article. He had been working on his story since 1946 and probably be-lieved it himself by this time. Anyway, he was sure to have some slick answers ready, and I didn't want to have to fumble with notes when I asked my questions. I planned pretty carefully.

I went to his office Thursday a week ago at 10 A.M. I thanked him for the opportunity to talk, remarking that he must be a busy man.

"That's all right, Mr. Collins. Though I must say I don't really warrant all this publicity."

"Will you do me a favor before we start? I don't want you to think me childish, but I'd like an autograph on this copy of *Reader's Digest.*"

"By all means. Why not?" He signed the book.

"You know, Mr. DuPre, I was connected with Intelligence in a small way during the war, and it's just possible we came across each other at some time. But on second thought, perhaps I didn't, because you were in France for four years, weren't you?"

"That's right."

"Well, I must say it's remarkable how well you've survived it all. It must have been a terrific strain on you. Such tension could hardly have been bearable. I can't think of anyone else who was in the field for so long."

"Now that you mention it, I think my stint was just about the longest. And it's surprising how a person can acclimatize himself to strain. There may have been a couple of chaps who were at it as long as I was, but as you say, there weren't many."

"Which section of Special Operations Executive were you with? A, B or C?"

"B section."

"Really? Then you must have known dear old Col. Kitchingham, who was in charge of that lot then?"

"Oh, yes indeed. He was a grand chap. One of the best. I knew him well."

"He certainly was. He was a spy himself in the first war and would never send a fellow on a mission he wouldn't have fancied himself."

"That's right."

"And of course you would have known that silly old fool John Cook who was liaison between SOE and the RAF?"

"Certainly. What a character he was."

"And I suppose you did your paradropping course at Wimborne, Dorset?"

"That's right."

By now I knew I was on firm ground. Though the name of the department concerned was Special Operations Executive, there never were any A, B or C sections. I had never heard of a Col. Kitchingham or a John Cook, and as far as I knew there was never a parachute school at Wimborne.

"I have news for you, George," I said. "You're a phony. You were never in Intelligence and what's more, judging from this article, you haven't the faintest idea how operations were carried out during the war."

"Look here, sir," he said indignantly. "What do you mean by coming into my office and making these fantastic statements I can see no reason to sit here and listen to you. How do I know who you are?"

"That's fair enough. I might be a Russian spy, mightn't I? Or I might be still in British Intelligence. Or I might be your grandfather."

"You might be anyone. Anyway, you can clear off and bother someone else."

"I think you would be wrong to have me thrown out. You see, I can prove that you know nothing about operations."

He was now listening hard. I gave him the fill-in mentioned above, about the operations, and he tripped over himself a couple of times in his explanations of matters in the article. He maintained a firm stand, however.

So I paraded his service record. He enlisted in the RCAF with the rank of pilot officer at Toronto in 1942. (He was then 36 and rather elderly for flying.) In June, he was removed to Victoria, B. C., and to Alliford Bay, B. C. Early in 1943 he had been posted to England for an RAF security course and had sailed in February on the *Bayano*. He took the course and sailed back on the *Empress of Scotland* for Newport News, Va., where he landed July 2. He proceeded to British Columbia where he remained until April, 1945, when he was posted back to England. He stayed there until December and then was sent back to Winnipeg, where he was discharged in 1946.

DuPre was unshaken by my recital of these records. "I'm still telling you you're wrong. Give me a few weeks and I'll write to London and get absolute proof that there was a good reason for my appearances in Canada. In any case, some of your dates are incorrect and you'll find that I wasn't in those places at all."

I had foreseen this. I had written myself a letter ostensibly from London. "I have already done that for you, George. Here's the reply. They disown you completely."

"Of course they disown me. Have you ever known Intelligence to recognize an agent?"

"Well, if they don't, there'd be little point in your writing to them, would there?"

He had to think about that. I figured this was my time. If he had lied to millions I thought some trickery on my part was justified.

"You've taken all sorts of good people in, George. If you promise not

340

to tell your tale any more, perhaps I won't tell mine. We are the only two who know now."

He bit. "All right. I won't talk any more."

"But," I said hastily, "whether we publish or not is up to my editor."

He made no reply, but the door was now open.

"Why did you do it, George? Why did you let things get this far? To tell tall tales to the Lions Club is one thing. To let Quentin Reynolds write a book about you is another. Why did you do it?"

He said he hadn't intended to let things go that far. He started telling his stories back in 1946 to friends, and clubs and associations heard about him and from that point things just grew.

"Why did you get in touch with Reynolds?"

"I didn't. They got in touch with me."

"Why did you bring your wife and children into things?"

"I didn't bring her into it," he said. "She never saw Reynolds while he was here. How he wrote the story was up to him." He indicated that he had thought it was going to be a novel.

"And you freely admit you never were in France as an agent?"

"That's right."

Mrs. DuPre, whom he married in 1946, was stricken by the whole thing. She has gone underground, after complaining in a radio interview that she was being harassed by the press. Before that she said she thought her husband might have been "fascinated by the attention and admiration he got from civilians and ex-servicemen alike." Or perhaps, she said, he wanted to look well in her eyes. If so, she said, it was unnecessary, since she liked him as he was, and "he has always been the best husband and father possible." (They have two sons.) She said she wanted to meet Reynolds when he was in Calgary and would have told him the truth because she was "terribly afraid of the consequences."

The consequences for DuPre have been to make him highly nervous. He presumably never discussed money with Reynolds or the publishers. He said he was giving anything he got to the Boy Scouts. He has not done anything actionable and his employer is keeping him on his job at Commercial Chemicals.

(*Reynolds expressed himself as "shocked and saddened" by the hoax. Bennett Cerf is making the best of it. Friends call him up—as friends will do—to enjoy his discomfiture and when he doesn't seem to be shattered by it, they express surprise at his cheerfulness. "What should I do? Cut my throat?" he says. Just how much DuPre made on the*

341

thing has not been revealed. "How much did he net?" Cerf was asked. "He gave it all to the Boy Scouts," he answered. "Yes, but how much did he make?" "It hasn't hurt the sale of the book," said Cerf. "Yes, but how much will he get?" And Cerf told the latest of the stories for which he is famed.

Random House at first considered withdrawing the book, and offered a refund to anybody who wanted one. Then it was decided that this was a little drastic. New ads appeared last week in which the word "Fact" was crossed out and "Fiction" roughed in beside it. And Cerf got the opportunity to insert a good line—"The Book That Was Too Good to Be True.")

THE BUILT-IN LOVER

by Bruce Dobbs

There were, back in the year of 1903, in the comfortable and robust city of Milwaukee, Wisconsin, three ill-assorted persons—a 40-year-old man, his 36-year-old wife, and a 17-year-old boy. Thrown into unique juxtaposition, they became participants in a plot that not only lent impressive weight to the theory that truth is stranger than fiction but which twisted the long arm of coincidence all out of shape. The goings-on in which these three became involved lasted for nineteen long years and didn't come to light until one of them had shot the other to death. The shooting was the climax of a bizarre series of events without counterpart in the annals of crime.

Fred Oesterreich, one of the three principals in our chronicle, was an arrogant, round-faced German who ran an apron factory in Milwaukee. He loved to bluster through the factory, which employed about fifty men and women, verbally lashing the workers on to greater effort. Had the workers taken a poll to determine who they hoped the factory would fall in on there is little doubt who would have won.

Oesterreich's wife Walburga was a well-stacked woman of medium height who, though mostly of German origin, had just enough Spanish in her to make her interesting. The lady was, as it turned out, a nymphomaniac. Walburga had a low musical voice, smoldering dark eyes and a Mona Lisa smile. She worked in the apron factory as a forelady and was very popular with the workers because, after her husband had blustered through the place bawling out everybody, Mrs. Oesterreich would follow him picking up egos and returning them to their owners.

Fred and Walburga Oesterreich, who had been married for fifteen years and who were childless, were not a very happy couple. Oesterreich had, from his wife's point of view, several failings. Although worth about a quarter of a million dollars in 1903, the man was, like many Germans, a careful custodian of a buck. The couple lived in an ugly mustard-colored frame house big enough to require the services of two maids but Oesterreich would not allow his wife even one servant. Worse yet, the man was a heavy drinker. Worst of all, he had become painfully deficient on the connubial couch.

It was this latter failing that Mrs. Oesterreich, what with that Spanish blood and all, simply couldn't overlook. She used to get into terrible battles with Fred in the watches of the night, taunt him about his unforgivable deficiency, and punctuate her remarks by throwing small articles of furniture at him. She raised enough racket several times for neighbors to call the police. If Fred was a lion in the apron factory, he was a mouse at home; Walburga was by all odds the stronger personality of the two.

One day, when one of the sewing machines in the Oesterreich factory broke down, the third principal in our chronicle entered the scene—a 17-year-old mechanic, Otto Sanhuber. Otto was a wizened little fellow, not quite 5 feet tall, with rumpled brown hair, a receding chin, and watery blue eyes behind silver-rimmed glasses. He was so painfully shy that he blushed when a lady so much as spoke to him.

Just as Otto was completing his repair job, Mrs. Oesterreich spied him. What Walburga saw in little Otto is a tribute to the woman's powers of perception. Here was a nondescript youth, less than half the woman's age, who had never gotten so much as a second glance from the girls down by the Milwaukee beer vats. Yet, Mrs. Oesterreich saw in Otto exactly what she was searching for.

Mrs. Oesterreich, the sly one, saw to it that there was plenty of repair work at the factory for the bashful youth. In a few months Otto had grown to like and trust her.

One day a sewing machine that Mrs. Oesterreich kept in the master bedroom at home broke down, no doubt by design, and she asked her husband what she should do about it. "Why," said Oesterreich, "get that kid to fix it—that kid who's been coming around the factory."

343

It was a raw autumn morning when little Otto called at the Oester-reich home. Mrs. Oesterreich, who answered the door, was rouged to the ears, and was wearing nothing but silk stockings, bedroom slippers and a fancy purple silk dressing gown.

Leading Otto to the bedroom, Mrs. Oesterreich propped herself up on the bed while the boy addressed himself to the machine. As he labored, Otto got an occasional whiff of perfume and, every once in awhile, he would sneak a look at the voluptuous lady on the bed. Every time he looked it seemed that he saw less of the dressing gown and more of Mrs. Oesterreich.

W-e-l-l, as the outrageous facts in the office of the District Attorney of Los Angeles County were one day to disclose, a situation such as that in the Oesterreich bedroom that autumn morning could progress in only one direction. By the time Otto Sanhuber left the house late in the afternoon he and the lady more than twice his age had put an in-trigue in motion.

Otto, as Mrs. Oesterreich had so correctly divined, possessed the bi-ological endowments that were the answer to a nymphomaniac's prayer. He would have been worth a chapter all by himself in the good Doctor Kinsey's *Sexual Behavior in the Human Male*.

Things rocked along very nicely for three years, with Otto, who still kept his job with the sewing-machine company, sneaking into the Oesterreich home when Mrs. Oesterreich made one excuse or another to be absent from her duties at the apron factory. Mrs. Oesterreich couldn't have been happier.

Somehow or other, probably through a neighbor, Fred Oesterreich got wind of the fact that his wife was receiving a visitor on those days when she was not at the factory. The apron magnate questioned his wife and she, looking him straight in the eye, assured him that there was nothing to the story.

Mrs. Oesterreich, fearful of discovery, was nonetheless reluctant to let go of little Otto, now that she had found him. So she hit upon an inspired plan. She decided to have Otto move into the Oesterreich home, without her husband knowing it, as a permanent guest.

There was an unused cubbyhole in the attic, immediately above the master bedroom, which was entered through a trap door in the ceiling. Mrs. Oesterreich fixed the cubbyhole up with a cot, a rug, a small table, a couple of chairs, some candles and other necessities of life and, one day when Fred was at the factory, moved Otto right in. She put a snap lock on Otto's side of the trap door so that if her husband should, for

344

any reason, try to get into the attic cubbyhole he would think the door was stuck.

The arrangement worked just fine. Mrs. Oesterreich, feigning one excuse or another, would remain home from the factory and, as the cold winter winds blew outside, would give her signal to Otto—three taps on the trap door—and he would open it up and descend into the bedroom. Otto came out for exercise around the house only during the day, or when the Oesterreichs went out for the evening.

Because of the demands that Walburga Oesterreich had made on him for almost four years now, Otto had hardly grown at all, still being under 5 feet and weighing only 105 pounds. And what did Otto think of all this? He just loved it. Only a mixed-up character would have gone for such an arrangement but Otto was mixed up from 'way back. An orphan, he had had a hard raising. Because of his small stature and his nondescript face, nobody had ever paid the slightest attention to him—until Mrs. Oesterreich had spied him.

Otto was living in a sort of dream world up there in the attic, not having to face the realities of life with all his wants taken care of. Talk about social security! Mrs. Oesterrich supplied Otto with adventure books and, as Otto read by daylight or by candlelight, he was transported into regions far removed from Milwaukee.

Sanhuber had by now developed a voracious appetite. The fellow could eat enough for three men. Mrs. Oesterreich kept him supplied with whole loaves of German rye bread, bottles of milk, cheeses, liverwursts and bolognas, so that he could have snacks at night when the garment manufacturer was on the premises.

There were just two precautionary measures that Otto had to abide by. One, that he was never to make the slightest sound at night when Oesterreich himself might be just below him there in the bedroom. The other, that he was never under any circumstances to go near a window in the cubbyhole that looked out on the back yard. The window was opaque with dust, and the light of a candle, which Otto kept at that end of the cubbyhole furthest from the window, was not visible after dark.

After a couple of years of reading adventure stories, Otto became not only a connoisseur but a critic of the stuff. An urge to express himself, long bottled up, took the form of a decision to write adventure fiction for the pulp magazines.

So Otto started to turn out adventure stories laid, for the most part,

345

in the South Seas and the Orient. Mrs. Oesterreich bought a typweriter, learned how to peck away at it, and typed Otto's stories and sent them to the pulp magazines. She rented a post-office box under an assumed name and used the box for all correspondence on the literary level.

Otto, who was very prolific, produced stories pretty rapidly. During his first year as a writer, he drew nothing but rejection slips. Then, suddenly, he got the hang of the thing and his stories started selling. Although he used a nom-de-plume in the magazines, the checks were made out in his name. He endorsed them over to Mrs. Oesterreich and she opened a special bank account for him. Thus the little fellow became self-supporting.

Sometimes, while writing late at night, Otto would become so engrossed in his work that he would cough or clear his throat. "Where's that noise coming from?" Oesterreich would ask his wife.

"Oh," Mrs. Oesterreich would answer, "it's probably a dog somewhere."

"It sounds closer than that. It sounds like it's coming from the attic."

"It's probably mice."

When the Oesterreichs went out for an evening to visit friends and drink schnapps, Otto liked to go down to the kitchen and raid the ice box. Oesterreich, coming home with his wife about midnight, was a great one for a snack before going to bed. He would go into the ice box, take out a roast, and look at it in a puzzled sort of way. "What ever happened to all the meat on this thing?" he would ask his wife.

"We ate it at dinner."

"We didn't eat *that* much."

Mrs. Oesterreich would just look at her husband and make him feel foolish.

One Saturday afternoon, Oesterreich was out in the back yard, burning some rubbish. As chance would have it, Otto chose that very afternoon to disobey the injunction of his mistress never to go near that window in the attic. Otto not only went near the window, but he rubbed some of the accumulated grime away, the better to peer out. He was peering out when Oesterreich, down in the back yard, happened to look up. Otto ducked—but not quite in time.

Oesterreich ran into the house, yelling for his wife. "I knew there was something up in that attic!" he yelled. "I just saw something move."

Walburga Oesterreich, who was by now equal to practically any situation, feigned puzzlement. "If it'll make you feel any better, Fred, why don't you go up to the attic and look around."

346

Oesterreich tried the trap door, but it wouldn't give. "The damned thing's stuck," he said.

"Fred," said Mrs. Oesterreich, "I want to sit down and have a serious talk with you."

"What about?"

"I think you should see a doctor."

"What for?"

Now Walburga Oesterreich came up with her master stroke. She tapped her forehead. "I think something's wrong in your head, Fred. You're imagining things. Maybe it's because you drink too much or maybe it's because you work too hard. But something's wrong, Fred. Promise me you'll see a doctor."

Fred, fearing the woman might be speaking the truth, would promise nothing of the kind. But thereafter if he heard mice in the attic coughing and clearing their throats he kept his mouth shut about it.

Oesterreich was a great man for a cigar. There were always several humidors filled with cigars around the house. Now Otto (wouldn't you know it) took up smoking. When Oesterreich began to complain that his cigars were disappearing, his wife put her foot down. He must see a doctor.

The sawbones just sat there in his office, looking at Fred Oesterreich while Mrs. Oesterreich did the talking. She told him that her husband was imagining that somebody was smoking his cigars and raiding his ice box, that he was seeing things, like an imaginary face at the attic window, and that he thought he heard mice up in the attic coughing and clearing their throats.

"Is this true?" the doctor asked the apron magnate. Oesterreich said it was. "Do you drink pretty heavily, Mr. Oesterreich?" asked the doctor. Oesterreich admitted that he did. "And you work very hard at your factory?" Yes.

The doctor wrote out a prescription. But the prescription didn't seem to do any good. Oesterreich began to brood about himself. He brooded so much, in fact, that he began to lose his grip. He was no longer the Simon Legree in his factory, no longer capable of lashing the slaves on to greater effort.

Mrs. Oesterreich, still carrying on nicely with her attic Romeo, took her husband to another doctor. The second one suggested a change of houses.

When the Oesterreichs moved, Otto went right along, being fixed up in the attic again. But Oesterreich continued to hear strange sounds every once in awhile, and his cigars continued to vanish and edibles disappeared from the refrigerator.

In 1913, when Fred Oesterreich was 50, his wife 46, and Otto 27, the Oesterreichs moved into still another house. Of course Otto went right along. The liaison between the little fellow and Walburga Oesterreich was still going strong, to the utter satisfaction of both, but Fred Oesterreich was rapidly running down hill. He was still hearing things and imagining things.

Actually, the woman was leading two complete lives—one with her husband at night and one with Otto during the day. Fred Oesterreich, a methodical man, left the house at the same time in the morning and returned the same time at night. When Fred left in the morning, Otto would come down out of the attic, have breakfast in the kitchen, and then either go back to the attic to write or go to bed with Mrs. Oesterreich.

Otto and the lady hit the sack one morning and were making quite a racket when they heard a noise downstairs. Mrs. Oesterreich jumped out of bed, rushed to the open door of the bedroom, and listened. Sure enough, somebody was downstairs. "Who's there!" the lady cried out.

"It's me," came Fred's voice. "Where are you, upstairs?"

"Yes."

"I'll be right up," called Fred.

"No," answered Walburga, "I'll be right down."

While Otto sneaked off to his attic hideaway, Walburga reached for a dressing gown and started downstairs before her husband, who had come home not feeling good, could get upstairs.

One night, not long afterward, the Oesterreichs, who had gone out to play cards with friends, got into a drunken fight with the friends and returned home early. Fred, oiled to the gills, caught little Otto in the kitchen, worrying a leg of lamb. Thinking Otto was an ordinary intruder, he gave the little fellow a frightful beating and tossed him out of the house, little realizing that he was evicting Otto from the only home he had.

Meeting Mrs. Oesterreich on the street next day, Otto found that she had everything all planned. Afraid that her husband would suspect that Otto had been considerably more than an ordinary intruder, put two and two together and bust into that attic, Walburga told her lover to go to Los Angeles. She would keep in touch with him through a post-office box, and soon join him in the City of the Angels. She withdrew from the bank the money he had made as a writer and away he went.

Arriving in Los Angeles, Otto got a job as a porter in an apartment house. After all those years in the attic, he hated all that California sunshine. Walburga had no trouble talking Fred into selling out and moving to California but it took him two years to find somebody who would give him half a million dollars for his apron factory.

Landing in Los Angeles in 1918, the Oesterreichs put up at a hotel while he looked around for a business opportunity and she looked around for a house. Walburga found just what she wanted on North St. Andrews Place, one of the city's tonier thoroughfares—a handsome big residence that just happened to have a walled-off portion of the attic right above, of all places, the master bedroom. While Oesterreich rushed around town, investigating business opportunities, his wife fixed up the attic quarters for Otto.

Oesterreich purchased controlling interest in a prosperous garment factory specializing in aprons, dresses and lingerie, and moved with his wife into the residence on North St. Andrews Place. Mrs. Oesterreich contacted Otto, met him on a street corner one fine bright southern California day and within the hour the little fellow was ensconced in his new quarters, safely in out of the sunshine.

Things rocked along for four years. Then, on the night of August 22, 1922, neighbors of the couple heard terrifying sounds coming out of the open windows, and then they heard what sounded like—and was—the sound of several shots.

The cops found Fred Oesterreich dead on the living-room floor, bullets through his head and his chest. Then they heard the widow yelling for help from a clothes closet in the master bedroom. The closet had been locked by a large, old-fashioned key, which was lying on the floor just outside of the closet door.

Now entered upon the scene a man named Herman Cline, chief of detectives of the Los Angeles Police Department—a hard-bitten man who, rumor had it, each morning glanced into a mirror and looked with suspicion at his own reflection. Cline looked at Mrs. Osterreich, who was near hysteria, then at the key that had locked the closet door, and then at a space of about a quarter-inch between the bottom of the door and the floor.

Mrs. Oesterreich told Cline that she and her husband had come home and surprised a burglar. After shooting her husband the burglar had locked Mrs. Oesterrich in the closet to prevent her from phoning the police.

"What'd the burglar steal?" Cline asked Mrs. Oesterreich.

Mrs. Oesterreich said she had seen the burglar snatching her husband's watch—a handsome timepiece studded with diamonds. The lady was carrying on at a great rate. She volunteered the information that in a third of a century of marriage she and dear Fred had never had a single quarrel.

The apron manufacturer had been slain by bullets from a .25 caliber weapon. "I think I'll go to Milwaukee and look into this Mrs. Oesterreich," Cline told his superior. "She could have locked herself in that closet and shoved that key back under the door. Not only that, but any woman who stands there with a straight face and says she's never even had a spat with her husband is a liar."

All Cline found out in Milawukee was that Walburga and Fred Oesterreich had frequently quarreled. Yet that was enough to establish that Walburga Oesterreich had lied to him. False in one thing, false in all?

Oesterreich had an estate of about a million dollars, but it was in such a tangled condition that his widow had to engage the services of one of Los Angeles' ablest civil attorneys—Herman Shapiro—to untangle it for her. As Walburga was leaving Shapiro's office the first day they met she presented him with a diamond-studded watch. "Here," she said, "this belonged to my dear husband. I want you to have it."

"Didn't I read something in the papers about that burglar stealing a watch like this one from your husband?" asked Shapiro.

"Yes," said Mrs. Oesterreich, "but apparently he didn't. I found this watch under the cushion of a window seat in the living room."

Mrs. Oesterreich put the house on St. Andrews Place up for sale and bought a smaller house on North Beachwood Drive. There was a nice comfortable attic in this house, too, so Otto Sanhuber went right along.

Somewhere along the way, Mrs. Oesterreich had struck up an acquaintanceship with an actor—a fellow named Bellows—and one day when they met for lunch in a Hollywood restaurant she reached into her handbag and handed him a large envelope. The envelope contained a .25 caliber revolver.

"What's this?" asked Bellows.

"I keep it for self-protection," said Mrs. Oesterreich. "But since dear Fred was also killed by a .25 caliber revolver, it might look suspicious if the police found this in my possession. So do me a favor, will you? Dispose of it somewhere for me."

Bellows nonchalantly tossed the gun into the LaBrea tar pits—a piece of Los Angeles real estate that is known to hold more secrets than a Hollywood casting couch.

One day about a year after the murder, Chief of Detectives Cline, still convinced that Mrs. Oesterreich had guilty knowledge of her husband's death, decided to drop into Shapiro's office. He happened to notice the diamond-studded watch. When Shapiro explained where Mrs. Oesterreich claimed to have found the watch, Cline clapped on his hat and headed for Beachwood Drive to arrest the woman and charge her with murder. A holdup man, Cline knew, would not snatch a watch from a man he was murdering and then hide the watch under the cushion of a window seat.

What Cline was hoping for when he pinched Walburga Oesterreich was a confession. He didn't get it. The lady, held without bail, screamed for Shapiro. "Go up to the big bedroom in my home," Mrs. Oesterreich instructed Shapiro, "and tap three times on the trap door in the closet. There's somebody up there in the attic—a half brother of mine who's a sort of a vagabond. Please tell him I've gone to Milawukee on business and will see him soon."

When Shapiro tapped three times on the trap door, the door opened and there was little Otto Sanhuber. Otto, now nearing his 40th year, was the color of library paste but seemed to be in good health. When Shapiro, standing there in the closet and looking up, introduced himself and gave him Mrs. Oesterreich's message, Otto smiled and thanked him. Then, growing thoughtful, Otto said, "I feel as if I know you, Mr. Shapiro. Mrs. Oesterreich has spoken of you many times. It's too bad that she has been so upset over something that I did."

"That *you* did!"

"Yes, I shot Mr. Oesterreich accidentally."

Shapiro sat down on the floor of the closet, got out a pencil and pad, and began to make notes. It seemed that on the night of the murder, the Oesterreichs had come home, quarreling as usual. Otto, who had been cavorting around the house after raiding the refrigerator, had, instead of going back to the attic, decided to get into the fight. He knew where Mrs. Oesterreich kept a little .25 caliber revolver, so he got it, then went downstairs and confronted Oesterreich. "Unhand this lovely woman!" said Otto, stealing a line of dialog right out of one of his own stories. Oesterreich just glowered at little Otto and made a lunge for him. Otto, in a panic, pulled the trigger several times and the first thing he knew, there was Fred Oesterreich lying on the floor dead.

Now Otto drew upon his talents as an author and concocted something to fool the police. He snatched Oesterreich's diamond-studded watch and gave it to Walburga. Then, he rushed to the second floor with Mrs. Oesterreich, told her to lock herself in the closet and shove the key through the crack between the bottom of the door and the floor, and disappeared into his hideaway.

It occurred to Shapiro that Otto had been pretty stupid. He should never have given that watch to Mrs. Oesterreich and he should have locked Mrs. Oesterreich in the closet himself, and left the key in the keyhole on the outside of the door.

Otto, not having talked to a living soul save Walburga Oesterreich (and, briefly, Fred) for four years, couldn't dam the flow of words. He lay on the floor of the attic and, looking down at the lawyer sitting in the closet, began to go over every phase of his long and unique relationship with Walburga Oesterreich. Shapiro, who by now had a crick in his neck from looking up, interrupted Sanhuber to ask him if he wished him to act as his counsel. Otto blinked, nodded, and went right on talking. With Otto as his client, Shapiro would not be compounding a felony by not going to the authorities with the information that Sanhuber was imparting to him, since a lawyer is not required to betray the confidence of a client.

Shapiro, deciding that Mrs. Oesterreich needed a good criminal lawyer, enlisted the services of Frank Dominquez, one of L. A.'s cagiest mouthpieces. "Go out to that house on Beachwood Drive," Dominquez said to Shapiro, "and get that man to hell out of that attic. In fact, tell him to get out of the country."

Sanhuber went north to Vancouver, British Columbia. Dominquez went to the district attorney and, since Otto was out of the country and the lethal weapon was in the LaBrea tar pits, demanded the release of Mrs. Oesterreich, and got it. Shortly thereafter Mrs. Oesterreich got her husband's inheritance and settled down to a comfortable life in the house on Beachwood Drive.

Seven years passed. Chief of Detectives Cline, now retired, wandered around Los Angeles, muttering into his beard. And then, one day in 1930, all hell broke loose. Shapiro, Mrs. Oesterreich's civil lawyer, went to the district attorney. He and Mrs. Oesterreich had gotten into some fierce fights about money and the lawyer, fearing injury or possible death at the hands of the woman, wished to make public an affidavit about the death of Fred Oesterreich. And so Shapiro spilled the whole story.

Mrs. Oesterreich and Sanhuber were both in Los Angeles, but not seeing each other any more. The lady had found several new lovers, who were being paid well for their services. Otto, on the other hand, had married in Canada but, unable to find steady employment there, had returned to Los Angeles. He was working as a night porter in an apartment house so that he could sleep during the day when the sun was out.

When Mrs. Oesterreich and Sanhuber were pinched, she refused to talk, but Otto went before a grand jury and repeated everything that he had told to Shapiro that day seven years previously. Mrs. Oesterreich and Otto were both indicted for the murder of her husband.

Otto, tried first, had as his counsel Earl Seeley Wakeman, a man who had never lost a murder trial. Otto repudiated his confession so that the state was left with Shapiro's second-hand account of the murder. The jury didn't say yes and it didn't say no. It found Otto Sanhuber guilty of manslaughter.

And maybe *that* didn't stir up a fascinating legal dust storm. The statute of limitations on manslaughter ran out after three years, and here was a man who was guilty of manslaughter committed *eight* years previously. Simple arithmetic was all that was needed to establish the fact that little Otto Sanhuber was five years on the laughing side of the limitations ledger. And so the little man was set free, to trail off into the silences, never to be heard from again.

Walburga got on the stand in her own defense and laid all the blame on little Otto. She had not come forward at the time of her husband's death and told the truth because she hadn't wanted to be embarrassed by public disclosure of her private life. Embarrassed indeed!

The jury couldn't quite make up its mind about Walburga; it disagreed. The murder indictment against the woman hung fire for six years and then, in 1936, the district attorney feeling he could never make the charge against the lady stick, moved to have the indictment nolle prossed.

Mrs. Oesterreich began to plunge into the stock market, with disastrous results. In the early Forties, with only a few thousand dollars to her name, she took up residence over a garage in the Wilshire district of the city. Four years ago, when a reporter for one of the Los Angeles papers sought to interview her, he found that she had, like Otto, trailed off into the silences, leaving no trace.

Both Walburga Oesterreich and Otto Sanhuber can, wherever they are, congratulate themselves on having taken the Goddess of Justice for one hell of a sleigh ride. After all, a man *was* scragged. It does seem that *somebody* should at least have been slapped by a good, stiff fine.

THE ROCKET SMASHERS

by Richard Sharpe

During the night of August 17, 1943, every available bomber in England roared out over the Channel and plastered an obscure German village on the Baltic coast. The Russians, who had been pleading for British planes to help their own offensive, screamed in outrage. Armchair strategists all over the world noted the loss of 41 planes, and muttered about the pointless waste of aircraft and manpower. The men who really knew what had happened said nothing.

This raid marked the turning point in one of the war's most baffling detective stories. The killer was still not identified, but now Allied intelligence had time to search. They were not looking for a man, but a weapon. Dozens of espionage agents from all the free nations had pooled their talents and information in a desperate fight to learn its identity. Now, for the first time, they were beginning to win their fight. If they failed, it would be necessary to evacuate not only London, but all of southern England. It would be almost impossible to continue waging World War II, and it might very well be lost.

The entire story of this great Allied victory has never been told before. Espionage agents are always reluctant to reveal their methods. Yet the facts are all available, and as you fit each seemingly unimportant part of the gigantic jigsaw puzzle into place, the fantastic story emerges clearly. . . .

It all began during the summer of 1938, when a British writer and Foreign Office agent named Bernard Newman was taking a cycling trip through Germany. He was traveling along the half-deserted Baltic coast, on the island of Rugen, when he ran into a closed and deserted area. He broke in and found nothing but some huge chunks of concrete scattered aimlessly about.

This curious area intrigued Newman, and he decided to do a little snooping. He began by asking questions of some of the people living in the region. They told him of strange explosions, followed by flashes

354

in the sky and rumblings overhead like the passing of express trains. They said these strange happenings had continued for some time, and then had suddenly ceased. Ambulances had come into the closed area, and had carted away many killed and injured.

Newman's presence became known to the Gestapo, and he was arrested. But, as Germany and England were still technically at peace, he was released and returned to England. He told his weird story to the British Secret Information Service. This story confirmed the suspicions of some British intelligence agents—the Germans were definitely experimenting with rockets.

But, for the first two years of the war, there was no outward sign that the German experiments were bearing any fruit. Most of their factories were turning out the planes which Goering was using to try and smash England. Early in 1942, however, strange reports began to filter through. Goebbels' propaganda broadcasts were beginning to boast about new, invincible weapons. And large numbers of top German scientists were disappearing from their usual posts, even from the top priority aircraft and synthetic gasoline plants. Metallurgists, chemists, experts on explosives, electronics engineers, aeronautical designers, meteorologists—all were vanishing without a trace.

To Duncan Sandys of the British War Cabinet, this meant only one thing—rockets. He had been interested in the subject for a long time, and before the war had corresponded with members of Ley's Rocket Society. He checked the names of the missing scientists against Ley's membership list, and learned that most of them were members of the Society. Sandys went through intelligence files and learned of Newman's accidental discovery on the Baltic coast. Excited now, he began reading everything he could find on the subject.

The clincher was a remarkable article by Maj. J. H. Randolph in the official American magazine, *Army Ordnance*. Writing in 1939, Randolph had stated that rockets then in existence, if perfected, could be used for bombardments halfway around the world. Randolph had laid out full specifications for a rocket installation—chemical factories turning out the fuel . . . a huge concrete launching platform . . . a stretch of lonely sea for a target range . . . a large area of open countryside.

That fitted Newman's discovery and, furthermore, intelligence had reported that a great number of mysterious factories had been built near the Baltic. That northern region filled all the requirements that Randolph had outlined. Sandys decided to take his information and his theory to the Prime Minister.

Churchill was convinced that it was worth investigating, and ordered intensive photo-reconnaissance flights over northeastern Germany to begin at once. They spread from Stettin north, then east and west along the Bay of Pomerania, and over Rugen Island. To the surprise of the pilots, that remote and thinly settled part of Germany was alive with Luftwaffe and dotted with tremendous anti-aircraft installations. Despite so much resistance, the reconnaissance planes were able to find definite evidence of extensive construction throughout the area where the Peene River angles northward toward the Bay.

Now the scene shifts to Warsaw, Poland, and the clock goes back a year. In 1941 the Germans began bringing hundreds of thousands of "volunteer workers" into Germany from Poland, Czechoslovakia, Austria, Hungary, Belgium, Holland and France. These men were little more than slave laborers, and wanted nothing more than to strike back at the Nazis. They had been sent into almost every factory in Germany, and were shipping out information as fast as they learned it.

Just before leaving Warsaw, one of the Polish "volunteers" held a last-minute meeting with Tomas Arciszewski, a leader in the Polish underground. A former cabinet minister and head of the Polish Socialist Party, Arciszewski lived under an alias, knowing he would be shot if his activities were discovered by the Germans. But he felt his first duty was to Poland. "You will see many things," he told the workman, "that could be of use to our allies."

"Certainly, Tomas," the workman said, "but how can I tell you if I learn something important?"

"Just send me a letter. Don't try and tell me anything. The letter will be postmarked, and that will show me where you are working. If you have learned anything important, just include the phrase: 'I wonder how old Aunt Jadwiga would like this weather?' We'll take it from there."

The worker smiled, shaking hands. "Good health to Aunt Jadwiga."

Thus an imaginary aunt, cranky about the weather, took her part in the game of wits against the Germans. The code words were spread, and soon all Polish patriots in Germany knew about their old aunt. Since the name is common among Polish people, the phrase was never suspected.

The Polish workman who had talked with Arciszewski went to the tiny town of Peenemunde, on the Peene River straight south of Rugen Island. He and his group worked as stokers, laborers and cement mixers on a vast, expanding, and thoroughly mysterious installation.

The place was an armed camp, directly under the iron supervision of the Gestapo. Something was definitely going on, so he wrote back to Warsaw about his Aunt Jadwiga and the weather.

In June 1943 a German officer of the Todt Organization, charged with the behavior of the slave laborers, turned up at Peenemunde. He insisted on going everywhere and seeing everything, questioning the laborers in their own language, presumably to test their cooperativeness and their morale. When he found Polish workers, he rebuked them: "Babies! Pining for your old Aunt Jadwiga!"

Eventually one of the workers made the right answer, "I don't think she'd like this weather." Pokerfaced, the officer spoke to him in rapid-fire Polish: "We need maps. Mark all important buildings, the homes of the commanders and the leading scientists. If we can knock out their key men, we can stop their work before it is finished."

The workman shrugged. "I think they are very close to success already. Within the past few weeks there has been a real feeling of elation in the air."

"Then there is no time to lose. I'll be back in two weeks for the maps." The Todt man then launched into a screaming tirade of denunciation. The security officers came running. Apoplectic with rage, the officer shouted: "This man is a fool! He is not to be trusted even with a pick and shovel!"

"A spy?"

"No, a *dumkopf!* A jackal! Give him the dirtiest job on the place! Collecting garbage, maybe. Scavenging is all he is good for!"

The security officers did precisely as they were told. The Todt officer knew that garbage collectors went everywhere in the camp. They knew what each building was, who was billeted in each house, who was important. The map they made was exact to the smallest detail. The Todt man was, of course, half Polish.

In less than two weeks he was back. He looked up his *dumkopf* and crowed derisively over his lowly state. As the worker was apparently cringing under the merciless attack, the map changed hands. Within a few days it was in England.

Meanwhile, the air reconnaissance had been continuing. All photographs were turned over to Allied Central Photographic Intelligence, and routed to a huge old mansion in Buckinghamshire. This was the headquarters of the First Aircraft Section for Photographic Interpretation, and was commanded by a sharp-eyed WAAF named Constance Babington-Smith.

357

After weeks of discouragement, she finally spotted a tiny T-shaped shadow on one of the vast concrete platforms which surrounded Peenemunde. She had the photo enlarged and discovered that the shadow was a tremendous rocket, with flanged fins at the rear, lying horizontally to the ground. The menace had taken shape at last.

It was then that a remarkable piece of information came from an old medieval mansion in Bern, Switzerland. The sender was an extraordinary man named Allen Welsh Dulles (now head of the super-secret Central Intelligence Agency). He was supposedly the special assistant to the American Minister, but was actually working for Gen. "Wild Bill" Donovan and his cloak-and-dagger unit, the OSS. Dulles had a background of experience in the State Department and practice as an international lawyer, and he had set himself up as one of the real good-time Charlies in Vienna. But all the time he was spreading a very useful word.

The United States, he said repeatedly, had no quarrel with either the German people or the legitimate German Army. Our only quarrel was with Adolf Hitler and the Nazis. If the Germans would only get rid of Hitler, perhaps this terrible destruction could be stopped. He talked airily about his close connections with the inner Roosevelt circle, assuring his listeners that his dope came straight from the top.

Dulles knew one thing—the old-timers in the German Army hated Hitler, and might need only a little official encouragement to take steps against him. Finally, in the spring of 1943, one of his best OSS agents approached him at a party and asked innocently, "Would Your Excellency like to drive to Zurich?"

Dulles looked bland. "Why should I? Is there someone in Zurich I know?"

The agent smiled. "Yes, but you don't really know him. He is Hans Bernd Gisevius, the German Vice Consul. The world knows him as a fierce follower of Hitler, but he is actually a secret agent of the Abwehr, the German High Command's Counter-Intelligence Service. He is in constant contact with the old Hitler-hating Junker generals, men like Von Beck and Witzleben. A talk with him is like a talk with them."

Dulles said, "How soon can you arrange a meeting in Zurich?"

The rest of the story is pure melodrama. Dulles arrived in Zurich during a blackout, and was ushered to the German Consulate itself. After a few moments of verbal sparring, he asked Gisevius if his agent's report had been correct.

Gisevius nodded. "What terms will Roosevelt demand for peace?" he asked.

"They're talking in Washington of the total destruction of Germany for generations to come," Dulles answered.

"No!" Gisevius cried. "Destroy Hitler, not Germany!"

"Easier said than done."

The German paused, then said in a low voice, "We are risking our lives to get rid of him."

Hiding his delight, Dulles put out another feeler. "Would you go farther? Would you help us—your enemy—if we promise to try and help you?"

Gisevius slumped in a chair. "I suppose we must," he muttered.

"We are interested," said the American casually, "in rockets. Giant rockets, on the Baltic."

Gisevius didn't know the technical details of the rocket, but he did know that it was over 40 feet long, was capable of traveling 60 miles into the stratosphere, moved faster than the speed of sound, carried a one-ton warhead, had a range of over 100 miles, a high degree of accuracy, and its final tests were a complete success.

Then came the blockbuster. "The Vengeance Weapon 2 goes into mass production as soon as possible. Next week all of the scientists who worked on it, along with the industrialists and technical experts who will be in charge of producing the V2's, will be in Peenemunde. All the test models and blueprints will be there, along with special fuels and parts developed especially for the V2. After this briefing session, production will begin. But in the meantime, they are all there. . . ."

Dulles smiled, shook the German's hand, and promised to keep in touch. That night he phoned Washington, and the news was flashed to the Supreme Headquarters of the Allied Expeditionary Forces. All information was pooled, and then Duncan Sandys went to Churchill. "The time to strike," he said, "is next week."

And so, on the night of August 17, nearly 600 bombers streamed out of England, rendezvoused at Rugen Island, faked a turn toward Berlin, and then roared straight south and dropped their load on Peenemunde. The Polish maps were, as the briefing officer said, "The most complete I've ever seen. Every building was marked in detail, every factory unit labeled. They made our night's work most satisfactory."

German General Walter Dornberger, the commander of Peenemunde, has written a book describing the disastrous effects of that raid on the German rocket program. Over a thousand men were killed, including General Jeschonek, chief of staff of the Luftwaffe, Chief Engineer Walther, Dr. Walter Thiel, one of the heads of German Army Weapons Research, who had designed the V2 motor, and scores of irreplaceable

359

trained workers. The experimental building was completely destroyed, along with the drafting rooms, the administration buildings, the measurement house, the powerhouse, a chemical factory, and the entire store of completed bombs. Other experts have estimated that half of Germany's top scientists were at Peenemunde that fatal night, and that 70 percent of them were killed. To make matters worse, the Gestapo sent in their SS troops the next dawn, and, in a maniacal effort to root out spies, shot down hundreds without any evidence against them at all.

The Germans were foresighted in one way. One copy of all production blueprints, drawings, and vital files had been deposited elsewhere, and were saved. The V2 program could go on, but it would take months to reproduce what they had lost.

No one in England or America breathed a word in explanation of this gigantic, and apparently meaningless, raid. Supreme HQ wanted secrecy, and they got it. They had smashed the nest where the rockets had hatched, but they still knew next to nothing of the weapon they faced. To take countermeasures against it, they would have to find what metals composed it, so they could attack the sources and forges for those metals. If they knew its electronic controls, they could try to counteract them. If they knew the components of the fuel, they could attack the chemical works which manufactured them.

The work at Peenemunde was transferred with utmost secrecy. Despite the streams of information from the slave-laborers, no one knew what to be on the lookout for. Then the next break came from another locale—western Poland. The underground sent strange tales of weird happenings in the towns of Blizna and Sarnaki—mere specks on a map, but now guarded by the whole might of the German air force and the Gestapo. A complete railway had been built to Blizna from the main Cracow-Lemberg line. Dr. Karl Schuster, head of the German Meteorology Services, Dornberger of Peenemunde, and even Himmler, had been seen there. Nightly, there were flying objects with blazing tails, streaking upward toward the stratosphere.

One odd item almost passed unrecognized. A huge tank truck and trailer skidded off the road to Blizna, and crashed. The tanks had burst, and, though it was a warm autumn day, every tree for hundreds of yards had been coated and festooned with frost and icicles for hours afterward. Word of the unseasonable spectacle spread like wildfire, and despite the Gestapo's threats of instant death for even discussing the occurrence, the news got out.

In London, Sandys read it, and called in W. G. A. Perring, then doing research for the Royal Aircraft Establishment. "What do you make of this frosted forest, Perring?" he asked.

Perring smiled. "The Russian Ziolkovsky, the American Professor Goddard, and the German *Doktor* Oberth all used liquid oxygen, or hydrogen peroxide, in their rocket fuels. Either one would frost trees. None of them found those fuels dependable. Apparently, the Germans have."

The OSS in Washington was informed. Their dingy building back of a brewery, in the old National Health Institute, now contained a great assembly of experts on many subjects, from archeologists to nuclear physicists—but no rocketeers. General Donovan went to Secretary of War Stimson and gave him a brief rundown on the rocket situation. Stimson authorized him to recruit anyone he needed, and at once.

Donovan put his chief of Research and Analysis, Prof. William L. Langer of Harvard, in charge. His line was history, but he had at his fingertips the information on what men were experts in the various branches of learning in the United States. He organized what was secretly known as the Rocket Corps, having selected men from every field related to rocket flight and propulsion, and put it under the direction of a man with the code name of "Dr. Martinson." From then on, "Martinson" and his staff in Washington, and Perring with his experts at Cuxhaven in England, were informed of every new development.

Air reconnaissance over Blizna and Sarnaki proved impossible. OSS and British agents were parachuted into the district and, one after another, were caught and shot. The Germans intended to keep their secret this time.

But a few got through and sent back reports on strange occurrences. At Blizna, several times a week, a siren sounded, ordering everyone to take shelter in cellars. There would be a distant rumbling, then an ungodly flare of light, and then a streak of flame racing toward the zenith. Once, however, a rocket went straight up and then came straight down, demolishing much of the installation, frosting the forest for hundreds of yards, and killing dozens at the rocket station.

Reports from Sarnaki matched perfectly. The successfully fired bombs all came down there, just 150 miles away. This, then, was the range of the V2 rocket! Horrifyingly, this whole area was occupied. Sarnaki was a town of 1,000 people being used as human guinea pigs, forced to occupy their homes during this eerie bombardment in which there was no warning sound of the bombs until *after* they had struck. Life there was appalling. When a bomb fell, the Gestapo descended and

361

gathered up every vestige of the missile, carrying the pieces away for study. A villager found in possession of the smallest part was shot. Yet so intensely patriotic were the Poles that they risked their lives to search for fragments.

Now Perring and Martinson had the range, one element of the fuel, and, by comparing firing and impact time, the approximate speed. This was progress, but they needed a break. They got one from Sweden.

Swedish observers had reported regular flights of meteors from Germany north across the Baltic, following identical routes. In early 1944, one of these "meteors" fell on the Swedish seacoast and was found by fishermen. The visitor from outer space was found to be some sort of gigantic man-made bomb.

Sweden was falling over backward to maintain its neutrality, fearing to go the way of Denmark and Norway. Now, with the suspicion that this might be the opening shot in some dreadful futuristic bombardment, Sweden evacuated the district and put it under martial law. Every fragment of the object was gathered and shipped to Stockholm. Air-force experts tried to solve the riddle of the thing, and failed. The effects of the terrific heat generated by its speed, as it fell from an inconceivable height, had fused and smashed its inner machinery beyond identification.

Then there was a second intruder. In June 1944 a farmer was quietly driving his wagon home at dusk near Kalmar, when a flaming monster screamed over his head, stampeded his horse, roared on, and vanished. Only after it passed did he hear its screeching shock wave, and feel the concussion of its flight. Bumped and bandaged, he reported it to the police, who alerted Stockholm.

Again the area was closed. Experts combed the region with mine detectors, and finally gathered up 10 whole crates of bits and pieces. In the air-force laboratories, an army of technicians worked day and night to put the pieces together. They finally succeeded in assembling something that looked like a wingless flying telegraph pole. The control mechanisms were smashed and the fuel tanks so blasted that it was impossible to tell what they had contained, but it was obviously a rocket.

The Swedes were thoroughly alarmed, realizing that the Nazis could now bombard them at will. They decided to reveal their findings to the British, who promptly asked permission to send in experts to examine the remains. The Swedes refused to allow uniformed men to enter, still fearful of offending the Nazis, but agreed that Dr. Martinson and his civilian aides could be flown in. But Martinson learned little more than the Swedes had reported; they now knew the exact shape and size, but the materials that went into the rocket and the fuel it burned were still a mystery.

As the scientists fought to reconstruct the rocket, more concrete platforms were being discovered all over the continent—Holland, Belgium, France—all within 150 miles of London and the channel ports. As soon as they were reported, the RAF blasted them. Again the Russians complained, wanting all available planes diverted to them.

SHAEF countered with a request that the Russians change the direction of their drive toward the west and capture the whole Blizna-Sarnaki area. The Russians demanded reasons and were told only that the whole possibility of a second front depended on their success. Second front was the magic word, and the Russians obeyed. The campaign had a single aim—to capture intact one of the V2 bombs or its crewmen or the scientists who built it.

The attack was launched, and the Germans evacuated the whole area. Members of the American Rocket Corps went in right with the Russians. They found no bombs, but residents told them of the great tripods which set the enormous rockets in place on the platforms, and described how they had risen from the thrust of their own rocket jets, slowly, majestically, and then had suddenly streaked out of sight in an ungodly screaming streak of flame.

This attempt to capture a bomb station intact almost ruined the best break the Allies got. Shortly before the Russians attacked, a bomb had misfired, and fallen near the Bug River. Underground men had found it but, since it was too big to hide, had shoved it into the river to hide it from the Gestapo. Tomas Arciszewski had been tipped off, and he had stolen into the region with a photographer, a skilled technician, and a draftsman.

When the Gestapo gave up their search, the underground hauled the bomb out of the river. The technician examined it and wrote a report. The draftsman and photographer made exhaustive studies of its mechanisms, many of which were undamaged. The full data—films, drawings, everything—were taken to Stettin. There it was given to a Swedish sailor, who carried it between the rubber and canvas soles of his sea boots from Stettin to Stockholm by ship. From there, it was flown to London.

Everything was turned over to Perring, who realized at once that there was a lot more to be learned from the bomb than what the technically ignorant underground members had reported. Working with

SHAEF, Perring sent out a special broadcast over the Polish wave length. The key message was: "Hitler isn't satisfied with paper promises. He wants the real thing. Well, so do we."

The Poles got the point. Somehow, they carried the whole bomb mechanism, weighing hundreds of pounds, to an abandoned German emergency landing strip in a forest to the south. An RAF Dakota bomber flew from Italy to pick up the mechanism, the technician and Arciszewski himself.

The Russian rout of the Germans in the Blizna area drove them southward. The day the British plane was to arrive, German troops were fleeing down the nearest roadway. A whole squadron of German fighter planes landed on that very airfield, to regroup. As the Poles were making desperate efforts to warn the bomber away, they suddenly found it unnecessary. The German squadron took off as suddenly as it had appeared.

That night a dozen peasants' lamps made a flare-way for the plane to land. The hours dragged on, but no plane. Shortly after midnight, when they had almost given up, it arrived. The Polish technician and the crew feverishly loaded the parts of the V2 into the plane. Arciszewski also went aboard, as Poland had become too hot for him.

Again, the lamps made a faint glow on the runway. The motors roared. The plane moved . . . and then bogged down hopelessly in a patch of muddy ground. An agent ran in to tell them that more German forces were passing on the highway less than a mile away. They dared not even race the motors to try to move the plane. The pilot gave orders: "Can't let the old girl fall into German hands. Soak her with petrol, and we'll burn her up."

The crew had already started to work when Arciszewski spoke up. "Wait. There's still hope." He turned to an underground leader. "Get every able-bodied man in the district. Bring spades, plows, shovels, anything with which a man can dig! Quickly!"

A little army turned up in the dark. With makeshift tools and bare hands they dug out that plane. They spread the runway with gravel and dry earth. At dawn, at the last possible moment, the plane tried again to take off, and succeeded. The engine with all its secrets arrived safely at Brindisi in Italy. There it picked up a huge fighter escort and continued on to London.

The fabulous mechanisms were turned over to Perring's group at Cuxhaven. Working with members of the American Rocket Corps, they set to work to reconstruct a whole German V2 bomb.

Now came the break of breaks. In the hospital at Sarnaki, now in Allied hands, the village drunkard was dying slowly, his viscera almost entirely eaten away. The townsfolk muttered that it served him right, since he had drunk everything and anything alcoholic he could lay hands on, all his life. Allied doctors examined him, and found this was no ordinary case of alcoholic poisoning. He was dying from the effects of large amounts of ethyl alcohol.

They finally wormed the story out of him. Terrified of the Gestapo, he had never told anyone that he had found one of the fuel tanks of a fallen rocket, still half full. It had smelled no worse than most of the stuff he was accustomed to, and it packed a wallop. He had sneaked it home, and drunk it all on one gigantic binge. He had signed his death warrant, but he had also provided the missing element of the V2 fuel.

Through him, Perring and the Rocket Corps were able to approximate the fuel in their own laboratories, and, calculating by the fuel tanks and lines, even the proportions. And it worked. At once, SHAEF ordered intensive bombing of every ethyl alcohol plant, every hydrogen or peroxide plant in all German territories. They even bombed potato warehouses, to the mystification of everybody, including their own pilots. They weren't fools. Potatoes were Germany's major source of alcohol.

There remained but one thing missing—the code name for factories making V2 parts. Again, Allen Dulles went to Zurich to visit Hans Gisevius. He found him in a high state of rage. The man exploded, "Himmler has stolen the V2 from the Army! He thinks it can save Germany, and he wants the credit! He holds the contracts for its manufacture, to line his own pocket! That such a *Schweinehunde* should win the war!"

"Meinherr, it is too late for Germany to win anything," Dulles said. "Get rid of Hitler and his gang, and we will talk!"

Gisevius glowered. "The time is near. Hitler is not immortal. We will prove it, in July this year, when we are ready!" (He was accurate. The bomb plot of the Generals on Hitler's life, which almost succeeded, took place July 20, 1944.)

"Your best hope," Dulles said coldly, "is to help *us* win." He smiled. "Surely these rocket bombs are not invincible!"

Gisevius shrugged. "They are ready for full-scale use. By 1946 they will have a two-stage bomb which can bomb New York." (It actually was on drawing boards, at war's end.) "They cannot be stopped once they are launched. They must be destroyed in the factories!"

"Then help us!"

"They are assembled at an underground factory at Nordhausen, east of Kassel. Parts are made all over Germany by Rheinmetall, Siemens, AEG, Lorenz; small departments in each plant. But no matter what part they are working on, they are known, even to the workers, by the code name EW. It stands for *Elektromechanische Werke*." He sighed deeply. "I can tell you no more."

He didn't need to. The million slave-laborers were asked for information on EW plants. Within weeks, a very complete list of factories, making even the smallest item for V2 bombs, was known to SHAEF. Instantly, air raids began against the most unlikely targets—small foundries, pipe factories, radio tube makers, graphite plants. They made sense only to the handful of people who knew that each place attacked made some portion of the V2 bomb.

D-Day—June 6, 1944—finally came. The invasion took place without a single V2 being fired against the invasion ports. Hilary St. George Saunders, the British military expert, credits this entirely to the vitally important Peenemunde raid and the counteroffensive secret fight against the bomb. It was not until September 8 that the first V2 fell on England, at Chiswick, with a second one 16 seconds later, at Epping. Even then this deadly supersonic weapon created no panic in England. The press had been given full details of the V2s—where they came from, how they flew, even what they looked like. The known is far easier to face than the unknown. (The British had, of course, been under attack from the V1, or "buzz bomb." But these were far slower, gave warning, and could be shot down.)

The Germans had planned to start with 100 V2's a day against London, and raise it as production increased to 1,000, and then to 2,000. London could not have stood it. It would have become a ghost town. But the Germans never came within miles of their goals. After all their years of effort, they eventually succeeded in firing only a total of 4,300 rockets against London, the Channel ports, and Antwerp. In all, 1,230 hit London. Yet it was a very narrow squeak, even at that.

The bomb that fell on Sweden had been a lucky fluke. In Volume VI of Churchill's Memoirs, *Triumph and Tragedy,* he tells the tale. A test rocket was being fired at half-abandoned Peenemunde. The radio-steersman for the bomb was green at his job. The terrifying spectacle of the towering, flaming missile so unnerved him that he flung the control lever clear away from him. Before the scientists could unfreeze him, the bomb had risen and, instead of heading out to sea as usual, had veered left and headed north for Sweden.

Only full knowledge of what they faced saved the Allies. By solving the secret of the weapon in advance, they could bomb every plant making its components and prevent its ever being made in mass production.

THE SPANISH PRISONER, THE BEAUTIFUL SEÑORITA AND *YOU*

by Rufus Jarman

This morning—as on any given day—a thousand or so business or professional people in this country found in their mail a mysterious letter that had arrived by air from Mexico. In twenty-three lines of typescript, it promised a chance to participate in some high adventure and romance, like Anthony Adverse or Scaramouche.

It is surprising how many good, solid Americans have secret ambitions to act like Captain Blood or Sir Lancelot, and rescue fair maidens from dark towers. Not a fortnight goes by but some good citizen, who has received one of these alluring missives from Mexico, will heed the call, load himself down with cash and go questing adventure in an unknown land—generally with ridiculous results.

The letters always promise several exciting prospects: a journey south of the border; adventure in shadowed streets, shuttered cafés and picturesque patios; intrigue revolving around an unfortunate prisoner in a fortresslike stronghold; a fortune in hidden money and the enchanting opportunity to rescue and protect a fair *señorita,* who is always beautiful and always eighteen years old.

There is only one serious weakness in this lovely dream—to wit, the whole proposition is a fake. The prisoner, the fortune and the beautiful *señorita* are all as unreal as the imaginary kingdom of Graustark or the illusive castle in Spain. In fact, the proposition is known as the Spanish-Prisoner Swindle or the Spanish Trunk Racket, or, to the Mexicans themselves, as *El Timo del Baúl.*

This ancient come-on—it has been operating now for about 368 years —is so fantastic, shallow and crude that it should be an obvious mess of malarkey to almost anybody. But, according to the United States Post

Office Inspection Service, the old Spanish-Prisoner Swindle is just as effective today as it was in the time of Philip II of Spain and Sir Francis Drake. Chief Post Office Inspector Clifton C. Garner says it has been estimated that United States citizens lose annually at least $600,000— and probably much more—to the mythical prisoner languishing in romantic Mexico.

The racket appeals mostly to persons unusually gullible or tender-hearted or who are particularly bored by the lack of romance in their lives. Some of them, even while halfway recognizing it as a fraud, try to make themselves believe in it, anyway.

Not long ago, a small-town Midwestern minister brought the post-office inspectors in Omaha some Spanish-prisoner letters he had received. He suspected fraud, and the post-office men assured him that that was exactly what it was, showing him case reports of a dozen people. Through believing in letters exactly like his, they had lost their savings and some had their lives threatened by Mexican picaroons.

The minister thanked the inspectors, gathered up his swindle letters and prepared to depart. The inspectors asked him to leave the letters with them for evidence, in case any of the swindlers were brought to trial.

"No," the preacher replied. "I think I'll take them along with me. There just might be something in it, you know."

The venerable fraud works like this: The letter writer claims to be a Mexican banker recently jailed in connection with a bankruptcy case. Before his capture he had converted all available funds into United States dollars, hidden them in the false bottom of a trunk and checked it through to a customhouse in the United States. The trunk reached its destination, but the banker, accompanied by his "dear daughter," was arrested at the border. The two suitcases he carried were impounded. In secret compartments they contained the check stub necessary to get the trunk, the trunk key, also a certified check, usually in amounts of $25,000 to $35,000, and made payable to bearer.

The police did not discover the secret compartments, so the story goes, but impounded the suitcases. The banker was sentenced to three years in prison and fined. If the fine is not paid within forty-five days of his letter's date, the suitcases will be sold at auction. And so the key to the fortune concealed in the trunk will be lost. The amount of this phantom fortune is usually $450,000 nowadays. Ten years ago it was only about $285,000, but the treasure has kept pace with inflation.

The banker prisoner claims he got the name of the American, who receives his letter, from a friend of the American, who is his fellow prisoner. He can't give his friend's name in fear of "disgracing his family," but the banker prisoner proposes that the American business or professional man—doctors are prime favorites—come to Mexico City and pay his fine and court costs—generally just under $10,000. (It used to be around $4000, but inflation has affected that too.) This payment will not release the prisoner, but it will free his two suitcases with the hidden check stub to the treasure trunk and the $35,000 certified check.

The American is expected to cash the check and keep the $35,000 for his trouble and expenses. He is to retrieve the trunk from the United States customhouse, keep one third of the treasure—about $150,000—and turn the balance over to the prisoner's "dear daughter."

She, of course, is the "beautiful eighteen-year-old *señorita*." Sometimes she is referred to as "my poor daughter," "my orphaned daughter," "my unfortunate daughter," "my darling daughter," "my beautiful daughter," or "my beautiful, eighteen-year-old daughter," but just plain "dear daughter" is the most popular term. Now and then, the prisoner will send along a picture of his "dear daughter," which is always that of a sexy-looking babe, of a type some middle-aged businessmen are said to dream about.

If a photograph is sent, it is usually in a second letter, which gives the victim his travel instructions and details of the treasure. It is dispatched only after a potential victim has risen to the bait by answering the first, shorter letter that gives only general hints. First letters are broadcast by the thousands—10,000 to 15,000 every two or three weeks, post-office inspectors estimate. The swindlers learn through them who and where the suckers are.

Usually, every mailing from Mexico turns up several suckers, from Brooklyn to Podunk. They will send self-righteous but cautious replies stating that their humanitarian instincts have been stirred. The prospect of acquiring a large fortune is usually dismissed as quite secondary. A typical reply is this one from St. Louis:

Dear Sir: In regards to your letter of July 22nd, I would like to state that I will be happy to be of help in any way that I can to yourself and, in particular, to your unfortunate daughter. I will, beyond all doubt, center my energies in this direction, as long as these efforts are legitimate and within the law and are in line with the general promotion of humanitarian causes, in the same way that I have helped many others who were in need.

369

The victim is directed to communicate with no one except the contact man, "because of the delicacy of the matter." He is told to write air mail in care of a "brother-in-law" of a "prison guard who is friendly to the prisoner," telling his time of arrival. The brother-in-law is the contact man with the friendly guard, who will arrange for the suitcase, with its valuable secret, to be released to the American.

The sucker usually flies down. He is met at the airport by the guard's brother-in-law, who escorts him to a hotel. Gradually, a whole cast of mysterious Mexicans, like characters in a Richard Harding Davis story, begin circulating about the American. He becomes more and more mystified, confused and, at last, frightened. There is a lot of lurking about dark street corners, whispered conferences by candlelight in dark cafés and the popping in and out of sundry sinister Mexicans, who act as though they had just contrived to blow up the Texas Rangers' headquarters and kidnap Zane Grey.

The American is spirited out several times to the prison, a grim, stone-walled bastion at the edge of the city. There the friendly guard sneaks out for short conferences now and then. He confides that the plan is proving more difficult than had been anticipated, for the judge is starting to get suspicious. (Of course, he is no real guard, just a member of the gang in a uniform.)

Finally, the guard breaks the frightening news that the judge has discovered the plot and an order is being issued for the American's arrest as a conspirator in springing a prisoner. Fortunately, however, the guard has managed to break the seals on the suitcases and retrieve the claim-check stub and the certified check.

By now the American is horribly frightened. He is generally glad to shove the $10,000 he has brought into the eager hands of the guard's brother-in-law, who, in turn, slips the American a check stub, a key and the certified check. The sucker flees across the border. He learns that the certified check is no good when he tries to cash it. The customhouse reveals that there is no trunk to match the check stub. And, of course, the "beautiful *señorita*" never makes an appearance. The victim goes sadly home. He generally keeps the entire humiliating experience a dark secret, if possible.

For all its crudities, the Spanish-Prisoner Swindle is "astonishingly successful," according to the Post Office Inspection Service. It is so successful, in fact, that from time to time the service distributes circulars to all banks in the country, urging them to bring the swindle to the attention of all persons who make unusually large withdrawals. The service also has printed warnings distributed by customs officials to all travelers headed toward Mexico and the other Latin-American countries.

These warnings are only partially successful. Often the suckers on their way to the Mexico City rendezvous are so excited that they haven't time to look over papers handed them at the border. Recently, a seventy-four-year-old Chicago man on such a mission didn't take time to relax until after he had paid his cash to the swindlers and was on his way home by train. It was then that he read, for the first time, the swindle warning that had been handed him when he entered Mexico.

There was the case early this year of a West Coast doctor, himself of Spanish descent, who fell for the swindle letter, borrowed $10,000 on real-estate holdings and prepared to embark for Mexico. He told his daughter what he intended to do, but paid no attention to her notion that it sounded fishy. The daughter told her fiancé, a young man named Elmer. He had seen the Spanish-prisoner warnings, and recognized the scheme right off, but he and the daughter were then afraid to tell papa. He is an old-Spanish-grandee type, who rules his family with an iron hand. The daughter was afraid to let him know she had told her friend. So the faithful Elmer sneaked off to the post office and told the inspectors. They managed to convince the doctor that the offer was a fraud. He abandoned the trip and canceled the mortgage. But he never was told how the post-office inspectors learned about his plan, and probably won't ever know—unless he happens to read this article.

Starting two or three years ago, the swindlers have been changing their routing instructions by telling victims to come via Havana rather than directly into Mexico. This is in the hope that United States customs officials at debarkation points for Cuba, where the swindle doesn't operate, will not be so diligent in handing out swindle warnings as those along the Mexican border.

An early victim by this new route was a sixty-eight-year-old Pennsylvania physician. "In my reply to the first letter," he later informed post-office men, "I said if it was straight, honest and aboveboard, I was willing to do anything in my power to help. But if it was crooked, I wanted nothing to do with it."

Apparently deciding that everything was aboveboard, the doctor borrowed $10,000 from his bank on some securities, and flew away to Havana, as instructed. From there he wired for further directions from his Mexico City pen pal, one Luis Olvera. The latter replied, in the best secret-agent style: "Documents have arrived here. Come immediately." The doctor boarded the next plane and went.

371

He was given the usual comic-opera, cloak-and-dagger treatment by the cast in Mexico City. This so upset and frightened him that, as he recalled afterward, "From the looks of these men, I knew they would stop at nothing. I did not know what to do. They asked if I had the money; I said yes. They insisted I give it to them, which I did. Besides my $9600, they made me pay an eleven-dollar taxi fare."

The doctor left with all speed for Nuevo Laredo, Mexico, by air. He crossed into Laredo, Texas, by car, happy to escape the Mexican authorities or the banditti, he wasn't exactly sure which. But somehow he still believed in the scheme. He phoned his son, a student in a Midwestern medical college, to meet him in Galveston to cash the certified check. The bank people gave them a look of bored pity.

Still believing, father and son proceeded to New Orleans to get the treasure-laden trunk from the customhouse. There was no trunk either. Whereupon the son went back to college and the father returned to his practice. All he got from his adventure was a bum bank draft for $25,000, which, he told post-office inspectors, he had put away in his safe-deposit box.

The Post Office Inspection Service is convinced that it hears of only a fraction of swindle victims. They are often so embarrassed that they would rather take their losses in silence.

Occasionally, a Spanish-prisoner-letter recipient will invite some friends to share. They will go down to Mexico City as a group and all get swindled together. Not long ago, after receiving a letter, an Alabama doctor borrowed $3000 on some vacant lots, and persuaded a businessman friend to come in for $6000. The pair, accompanied by the doctor's son, then lit out for old Mexico.

As there is a certain strength in numbers, the swindlers didn't try to frighten them. Before paying over their $9850, this trio insisted on proof that the $30,000 bank draft was legitimate, and that the trunk was really being held at Laredo. They sent telegrams, they thought, to the "National City Bank" of Galveston, on which the draft was drawn, and to the Laredo customhouse.

Within a couple of hours they had replies. A telegram purporting to be from the bank stated that the draft was indeed good. Another wire, apparently sent by the customhouse, said the trunk was right there. The trio paid their cash and took off for Galveston, where they learned there was no such bank in Galveston as the National City. There was a City National Bank, of Galveston, which was of no use whatever to the three Alabamans. Of course, they found no trunk at Laredo, either.

The swindlers had merely intercepted their messages before they had reached the telegraph office. The gang had facilities to simulate telegrams, and the replies the three thought they had received were fakes.

This was possible because the Spanish-prisoner swindlers avail themselves of all modern improvements and scientific advances useful to their trade. Several years ago a United States post-office inspector managed to get into a swindle headquarters in Mexico City and found everything modern and efficient. The equipment included a dozen electric typewriters, at which the come-on letters were batted out by a whole stenographic pool.

There were Chamber of Commerce membership lists for most United States towns and cities, trade-association membership lists, city directories, Who's Who and even lists of people who had sent in cereal-box tops for toy rocket guns. Currently, the gang is believed to be an international group of some thirty smart crooks out of several Latin-American countries. They operate from Mexico City, with branch offices in Monterrey, Guadalajara, Tampico and Veracruz, and roving agents in the States to scout for prospects. Besides regular business machines, the headquarters viewed by the post-office inspector contained presses to print fake newspaper stories of the banker's arrest and fake copies of his indictment. These are usually sent in letters to victims to substantiate the prisoner's claims. Other equipment at the swindle headquarters included presses for printing the certified-check forms and for faking telegrams.

The Spanish-prisoner racket is believed to have developed as an aftermath of the Spanish Armada's defeat in 1588, when thousands of Spanish soldiers and sailors, captured in battle or driven ashore by shipwreck, were thrown into English prisons and held until ransomed. It was not long before some smart Spanish confidence men used their plight as a racket. They solicited funds from relatives, supposedly to be used for ransom, but kept the money themselves. Later on they added a yarn about hidden treasure belonging to the prisoners, which the prisoners would split with their redeemers. This was to interest persons not related to these unfortunates.

The racket kept right on after the Armada prisoners were long dead and gone. Fresh crops of sharpers wrote to wealthy persons in other lands, posing as prisoners in the dungeons of Spain—a land noted for dungeons—with vast fortunes they would divide with their benefactors. Some literary authorities, incidentally, think this racket may have inspired Dumas' Count of Monte Cristo.

373

As Americans became wealthy, the Spanish swindlers turned their principal attention to this country. In one two-month period in 1900, Americans turned over to postal authorities 1431 Spanish-swindle letters. In 1907, Americans are known to have lost $30,000—probably much more—to swindlers in one Spanish province alone. They usually operated near the French border, for a convenient escape. They bribed well the poorly paid postal and telegraph employees who tipped them off when dangerous-looking strangers appeared in town.

In 1922 some of the swindlers moved their bases to Latin America, principally Mexico, to be more convenient to their prey. Then the Spanish civil war in the 1930's caused all prisoner-swindle operations to move to this side, as the war had destroyed much of Spain's nostalgic glamour that had helped to make the prisoner credible. Besides, the Spanish Government became stricter.

Until about four years ago, the only known prisoner racket was the Spanish version. But, with as many characters as there are around Broadway looking for a fast buck, it was obviously only a matter of time before somebody invented an American prisoner, and set about to fleece the Latins. That distinction went to one Celedonio Sevilla, an artist of sorts who owned the Dalla Advertising Corporation, which had headquarters in the Empire State Building.

His company operated a large screen, like an outdoor-movie screen, on top of a building in Times Square. Humorous cartoon advertisements were projected upon it each evening to entertain crowds on the Great White Way. Sevilla, however, undertook to augment his advertising revenue with an American-prisoner scheme like the Spanish version, except that his potential victims were in the Spanish-speaking countries. His prisoner was a certain "Nelson Lawrence Watkins," a former millionaire, in jail for defrauding his stockholders. He had a dear daughter by the name of Kathlene, who was only fifteen years old. (The Latins like them younger.) And, of course, he had concealed a trunkful of treasure.

The come-on letters were signed by a certain "Father John Miller," supposedly a prison chaplain, acting as intermediary for the prisoner. Father Miller's letters pointed out that the lucky Latin chosen to shelter the fair Kathlene and her father's fortune would have to give proof of his social acceptability and his financial stability. The letter explained that the prisoner wished a Latin American to have this responsibility because he understood "Latins are frank, loyal and trustworthy." The letters were pounded out by the hundreds in Sevilla's Empire State

374

office and sent to businessmen in practically all the Latin-American countries.

One of Sevilla's associates approached the priest in charge of one of New York's Catholic churches. He explained that he was a friend of Father John Miller, a resident of South America who was then touring the States. He asked permission for Father Miller's mail to be sent in care of that church. The New York priest innocently agreed. Before long, Father Miller's letters were pouring into the church at the rate of forty or fifty a day. They contained answers such as the following:

> With deep surprise I have read your pious message, sent to my humble self. I have resolved, after meditation, to offer my services in a cause so worth while as that of the unfortunate Mr. Watkins. My economic solvency and social position are such that I believe will not impede my participation.
>
> Father Miller, as mediator, I implore you to accept my help in serving Mr. Watkins. I hope you will send me the documents, etc., in order that I may have a better understanding of the task you are undertaking.

When these answers were delivered in New York, through the unsuspecting church, Father Miller wrote back, instructing the writer to come at once to New York, stop in a certain hotel on Lexington Avenue, prepare to put up a substantial cash guarantee and reap a treasure that sounded like Captain Kidd's cache.

Father Miller gave some interesting details about that—to wit:

> You must have care in taking the lining from the trunk, and separate the double walls so as not to deteriorate what is there. Among the contents are: one thousand $100 bills, eight hundred $500 bills, four thousand pounds sterling, railroad and oil shares worth many thousands of dollars. Also in the trunk are the jewels of Kathlene's mother: a pearl necklace valued at $10,000, a diamond diadem, which—that her mother may rest in peace—Kathlene must wear on her wedding day, worth $35,000. There is also the mother's wedding ring, worth $5000, a gold bracelet with the mother's name in rubies and emeralds, and some odd jewelry. There are two checkbooks on the National Bank of Argentina, with two deposits—one amounting to $16,000, the other $36,000. The little girl carries the key to the trunk on a little gold cord hanging about her neck.

In spite of all that bait, nobody got swindled in the American-prisoner racket. Sevilla had arranged with a woman who rented desk and office space in a building on West 42nd Street to accept some of Father Miller's overflow mail. She became suspicious when the person who called for it wasn't in clerical clothing, and told the post-office inspectors.

Sevilla was sentenced to seven years for mail fraud, and the new American-prisoner racket died aborning. But not before several eager businessmen from South America, with adventure in their hearts, had arrived in New York, all set to retrieve the hidden fortune and rescue the dear daughter.

And this gives us the comforting assurance that not all fools are on this side of the border.

THE AMOROUS AMAZON IN GEORGE WASHINGTON'S ARMY

by Richardson Wright

She was born December 17, 1760. . . . On her father's side one ancestor came to Plymouth in 1629, having been a member of the English colony at Leyden. Another was a Mayflower émigré. One of her great-uncles married a granddaughter of Miles Standish, and her father married a descendant of the famous William Bradford. . . . In addition, Deborah Sampson's blood was salted by a dash of Gallic, a grandfather having espoused a French wife.

Of her father we read that he had little or no property and that he was fickle and "perhaps too loose in his morals." Well, that's not uncommon with sailors. This particular salt went down to the sea on his lawful occasions, leaving his wife to scrape along as best she could. Deborah's mother had a difficult time making ends meet. Finally news came that he had perished at sea. Deborah had just turned five. Although his death lifted the burden of uncertainty from the mother, she found it beyond her skill to keep the family together. She farmed the children out among friends and relatives. Up to the time she was ten, Deborah had a peripatetic childhood, being shunted about from house to house. Finally she came to a standstill in the home of one Jeremiah Thomas in Middleborough.

"We now view Miss Sampson," says her biographer, "advancing into the bloom and vigor of youth." In other words, she was old enough to make herself useful around the Thomas place—she milked the cows, fed the pigs, tended the chickens, raked hay, spun and wove and did countless other chores until she was eighteen.. A farmhouse drudge with little or no chance for schooling. "During Spring, Summer and Autumn," continues the same devoted chronicler, "she was peculiarly attached to rural speculation." What she did in winter he does not say. . . .

She is said to have "despised revelry, gossiping, distraction and orgies," which leads us to surmise that such things went on in Middleborough, but, since she was merely a slavey, she wasn't invited to them. Most of us dislike the kind of parties we aren't invited to. For a time, when she neared twenty, she taught school, a rather courageous undertaking, seeing that she had had no schooling herself.

Meantime the war had broken out and history was being made swiftly all around her—battles and raids, advances and retreats. Urged by this excitement a brilliant idea came to her in one of her rural speculations. . . . For it appears that one night she borrowed a man's suit of clothes, went to the local "ordinary," as the tavern was called, and enjoyed its bibulous hospitality with the rest of the yokels. The Thomases were doubtless shocked, and berated her mightily. . . . Her masquerading "and other very loose and un-Christianlike behavior" amazed the elders. They labored with her "without obtaining satisfaction" and concluded it was the church's duty to withdraw fellowship.

With a sentence of excommunication dangling over her head Deborah . . . obtained men's clothes and set out to see the world. . . . For a while she wandered about aimlessly . . . but lack of funds prevented her attaining her vagrant dream. As in these days, so then; if you couldn't afford to travel and see the world you joined the army. At Worcester, in May, 1782, she signed up for the duration of the war. Her "enlistment as a soldier was not the original plan, nor patriotism the original impulse." To the recruiting officer she gave the name of Robert Surtlieff. . . .

From Worcester she was sent with others to West Point, and from there went on several raiding parties. One, during June, headed across the Hudson to Stony Point, went as far south as Harlem and then turned back to White Plains. At Tappan Bay—between Sing Sing and Tarrytown—her company contacted with Tories and in the mêlée she received a sabre slash. She appears to have made a good accounting of herself despite the fact that her "buddies" referred to her as the "blooming boy" and "Molly," because she had no beard.

Her sudden and unexplained departure from the bosom of the Thomas family had caused concern. Her brother, we are told, went on a wild-goose chase to Maine to find her, and a friend came to West Point on another clue. Through his gossip she heard news of her mother, although he did not recognize her. To comfort her anxious parent she wrote a letter saying that she had found agreeable work in "a large but well-regulated family," which was certainly paying an unwarranted compliment to the Continental Army. . . .

Some weeks later another Tory-raiding party included Deborah, this time going down the west shore of the Hudson. At East Chester, shortly after midnight, they ambushed a band of Loyalists. A stiff fight ensued, during which Deborah was shot in the thigh. Lest she reveal herself, she told her buddies she had received a mortal wound and begged them to leave her by the roadside to die. This subterfuge didn't work; they carried her back to a dressing station conducted by the French . . . and only by the greatest fortitude and nimbleness of wit was she able to convince the surgeon that she was perfectly all right. She crawled off by herself and for days suffered untold tortures until the wound began to heal. For this she later paid a heavy price.

In November the army retired into winter quarters, but it was no vacation for Deborah. With a detachment she was sent to the headwaters of the Hudson up to Ticonderoga, thence west—to quiet the Indians who had gone on the warpath. This proved an adventure. We read of Deborah, in one of the fights, about to despatch an Indian only to find he was white. Of course . . . she rescued the unfortunate captive.

Next we see this Amazon appointed orderly to General Patterson. This easy berth took her to Philadelphia where the General was sent to help quell a riot of unpaid drunken troops that threatened Congress, and had driven it to sitting in Trenton. Malignant fever was running through Philadelphia at the time and Deborah fell victim to it. She was carried unconscious to a hospital, and during the examination, her sex was disclosed. She recovered almost as quickly as she had fallen ill. To the doctor she confessed her role and won from him a promise not to reveal her secret. And good reason she had for it—she was enjoying her life in the army and also, at the time, as the story goes, she was intrigued by a little "affair."

A girl had fallen in love with her. An anonymous letter is delivered to Deborah, a letter breathing warm admiration. Later Deborah meets the girl. "Timorous as a young roe, yet pliant as the bending osier, with the queen of love resident in her eyes, she rehearsed her plaint of love with that unreservedness, which evinced the sincerity of her passion and exaltedness of soul." We marvel that Deborah kept a straight face through this meeting. Yet it seems she did. The biographer in his grandest manner further tells us that . . . "had she assumed the attire, the cunning of a harlot, the desperate simplicity of the young wanton; had she begun her subtle eloquence with a kiss; and with the poison of asps under her tongue, had represented her bed of embroidery filled with perfume and finally had urged that the absence of the good man gave them an opportunity to riot in the ecstatic delights of love—while our young fugitive would have needed supernatural means to have answered the demands of venerous appetition, the simple might have found satiety in her seraglio." But . . . Deborah listened to her plaint without cracking a smile and promised that the next time she came that way she'd look her up.

One wonders how Deborah managed to preserve her masquerade. Her stature, we are told, was erect, and a little taller than the average height of females. Her countenance and voice were feminine. In her memoir Deborah says that she found men's clothes more convenient than those worn by women. "Her waist might displease a coquette" but her limbs were regularly proportioned. "Ladies of taste considered them handsome when in masculine garb. Several instances are recorded where they were deeply smitten by her good looks." For her voluminous waist, her biographer accounts as follows: "She wore a bandage about her breasts, during her disguise. . . . It is not improbable that the severe pressure of this bandage served to compress the bosom while the waist had every natural convenience for augmentation." He further states that "she was never found in liquor" and that she "never wrestled nor suffered anyone to twine his arms about her shoulders." . . .

In her role as orderly to General Patterson she is said to have crossed the Alleghenies, had thrilling encounters with Indians in what is now Ohio, and finally returned to Philadelphia, via Baltimore. While in the latter city she once again met the girl who was smitten with her charms. During this rendezvous the maiden gave her, as a token of her admiration, six shirts, a watch and twenty-five Spanish dollars. Deborah apparently accepted them in the spirit in which they were offered. Later we find her writing the girl a letter . . . to the effect that this affair simply mustn't go on any further. She signed it "Your Own Sex."

Finally the doctor who discovered Deborah proved to be a sieve. He wrote about her to General Patterson. When that lusty warrior found that his orderly was a woman, he is said to have exclaimed, "This is truly theatrical!" But he was not devoid of wit. Returning to West Point he allowed Deborah to assume women's garb and in this mufti she walked up and down the ranks of her erstwhile comrades. Never a one recognized her! Finally she was mustered out, receiving her discharge from General Knox with recommendations from General Patterson and others. She returned to New England in November, 1783, having been away one year and a half.

Instead of going to Middleborough, where she had spent her dreary childhood, she went to Stoughton, and in male costume found a job on a farm. She adopted the name of Ephraim Sampson. During that winter for diversion, she flirted with the country girls! On the approach of spring she assumed women's clothes and thereafter, except for veterans' parades and meetings of the contemporary equivalent of the American Legion, she never wore her uniform again. Once to gratify the curiosity of the multitude she visited Boston, and in the theatre, "clad in miilitary attire, she went through at the word of a military officer, the manual exercise." Those who witnessed the performance said that "she would almost make the gun talk" every time it came to the ground from her hand, the sound was so significant. This happened about 1801, when she was past forty.

In April, 1784, she yielded to the manly attractions of one Benjamin Gannet, a young farmer, and shortly thereafterward married him.

At this point old-time books display their modesty by saying, "We will now draw the veil." But from the records we do know something about Deborah's married life. . . .

Theirs was a nice enough place—a two-story house embowered with willows, covered with woodbine and with roses growing up to the chimneytops, a hundred acres or so of mowing and cultivatable land with brooks through it and raspberries in the hedges and along the stone walls. Having literally worn the pants, Deborah had a lot to say about its management. . . .

Then arose an embarrassing fact, one that gave Deborah the whip-hand over her husband all their married life: while she was out fighting, what was he doing? Did he put on the Continental uniform for Freedom? Did he slog-slog through mud and cross-country mile on end to take pot-shots at Tories? Did he help subdue wild Indians? Did he get a sabre slash and a bullet in his hip? Not Benjamin. He stayed at home, did the chores around the farm, and let the militant Georges of the time do the fighting.

Benjamin panned out hard-working but ambitionless. A son came and two daughters. Meantime the wound she received at East Chester kept bothering Deborah. The bullet had never been extracted. She was unable to perform any great labor. Benjamin was under heavy expenses for her care. In 1793 the Commonwealth of Massachusetts granted her an invalid bonus of thirty-four pounds, about one hundred dollars. In 1805 Congress granted her a pension of four dollars a month as an invalid soldier. . . . In 1818 the four-dollar pension was doubled and this was paid her until her death in 1827.